I HATE THE MAN WHO RUNS THIS BAR!

The Survival Guide for *Real* Musicians

by Eugene Chadbourne

Foreword by Mike Lawson

6400 Hollis Street
Emeryville, CA 94608

06 05 04 03 02 01 00 99 98 97   5 4 3 2 1
Library of Congress Catalog Card Number: 97-073715

Book design and layout: Linda Gough
Cover photography: Susana Millman

Production staff
Mike Lawson: publisher, Lisa Duran: editor, Randy Antin: editorial assistant, Sally Engelfried: copy editor,
Don Washington: operations coordinator; Teresa Poss: administrative assistant, Georgia George: production director,
Tom Marzella: production assistant

We would like to thank the Hotel Utah for the use of their bar . . . and their cook, John Lamkin . . .
in our cover photo. Also special thanks to Guy Carson, who runs the Hotel Utah, for his sense of humor.
(We never said we hated *every* man who ran *every* bar!)

6400 Hollis Street
Emeryville, CA 94608
(510) 653-3307

Also from MixBooks:
How to Make Money Scoring Soundtracks and Jingles
The Art of Mixing: A Visual Guide to Recording, Engineering, and Production
500 Songwriting Ideas (For Brave and Passionate People)
Music Publishing: The Real Road to Music Business Success, Rev. and Exp. 4th Ed.
How to Run a Recording Session
The Songwriters Guide to Collaboration, Rev. and Exp. 2nd Ed.
Critical Listening and Auditory Perception
Keyfax Omnibus Edition
The AudioPro Home Recording Course
Live Sound Reinforcement
The Studio Business Book
Modular Digital Multitracks: The Power User's Guide
Concert Sound
Sound for Picture

Also from EMBooks:
Tech Terms
Making the Ultimate Demo
Tech Terms: A Practical Dictionary for Audio and Music Production
Making Music With Your Computer

Also from CBM Music and Entertainment Group:
Recording Industry Sourcebook
Mix Reference Disc, Deluxe Edition
Mix Master Directory
Digital Piano Buyer's Guide

MixBooks is a division of Cardinal Business Media Inc.
Printed in Auburn Hills, Michigan
ISBN 0-918371-19-8

Contents

Foreword

I first met Eugene Chadbourne in 1987. I had heard Chadbourne's song, "Sex With the Sheriff," on the local college radio station just as I finished battling our local immoral "morality Sheriff" over music censorship and arresting record store clerks for selling music with dirty words. We played together for the first time in a small town on the Gulf Coast of Florida in the dead of winter in 1987. Three years later, Eugene and I met up in New Orleans, LA, where we began the 5-state, 12-city "Thousand Points of Light" tour that lasted 14 days.

Besides his clever (often brilliant) lyric writing and ability to parody so many subjects and so many songs, Eugene is an incredible musician. But the thing that has always struck me about Eugene is that he is actually making a living doing what he loves: playing music. He makes records; plays concerts; tours overseas several times a year; has recorded with members of Camper Van Beethoven and the Violent Femmes, among others; and has a wonderful time making his music his life. That's why he's written this book.

The title of this book is taken from a song off of his *Vermin of the Blues* album. For better or for worse, he has encountered just about every circumstance you can imagine, and he shares those experiences and wisdom in this book. This isn't a stodgy work painting blue sky about the music business. It's a bare bones, no-holds-barred look at the realities real musicians face. The truths Eugene spells out in this book are universal for every type of musician from avant-garde to blues, jazz, country, rock, folk, whatever. Club owners are club owners, record labels are record labels, and college towns are the same everywhere you go.

If making music for a living is your goal, this book will provide you with an idea of what you can really expect when you set out on the road. It's not a novel;. it's not the story of Eugene's life. It's the survival guide for folks just like you: real musicians.

Mike Lawson
Publisher, MixBooks

Introduction

GISELA CHADBOURNE

Musical beginning: author as child

Are you looking for advice on becoming a rich and famous star in the music business? Then this isn't the book for you.

Perhaps you've heard the expression "paying your dues" and think that's what you're doing now as you wait a few years to become the rich and famous star you deserve to be. Maybe with a few tips you can shave years off the wait and become a household name even earlier than you'd planned.

Alas, this is also not the book for you.

Maybe you've thought about becoming a musician or you already play an instrument or write songs. You like doing these things, although not all of your friends appreciate your efforts as much as you do. You've been thinking about trying to do music full-time. You haven't been thinking about many of the things written about in this book because you don't even know they exist. You really don't even know how badly you need and want to read this.

But if you're the type who sits in one spot and plays every song you've ever written without rest, if you dream entire concerts and then try to write down all the songs from it when you wake up. If you hear melodies in the sound of a blender that's shredding carrots and celery, or if you hear two records playing at once and can play along with both of them at the same time. If you've been surrounded all your life with figures of authority and non-authority complaining that "all you ever think about is music," if you are able to express your feelings through music more articulately than you can with any other form of communication. If you see a world of comfort and serenity locked away in the house of music and can feel the key nestled safely in your pocket. If playing your music to people of all ages all over the world is your dream, but your lifestyle as a struggling musician seems more like a nightmare . . .

If any of this applies to you, then this is really your book. I have been a musician most of my life, and I am writing this book for all of us—past, present, and future.

This is not a book about stars, unless they are the kind you see spinning around your head when you take a tumble trying to carry three guitar cases down a flight of steps. It is not about the musicians everyone has heard of, the ones that spend $800,000 on Italian marble for their mansions. It does not speculate on how one can achieve such lofty status, and it does not contain advice on how to manipulate the businesspeople that stand in your way.

I am writing this book for the real musicians. We know who we are. The ones who could care less about becoming an Elvis, the ones who pursue their art because they love music passionately and recklessly. The ones who love music even though it has made them poor, insecure, anxious, and in general, frayed around the edges (and frazzled in the center).

You don't have to be a fan of the kind of music I happen to play (whatever that is) to get something from this book. In fact, one of the points of this book is that no matter what genre of music you are playing, the life of a musician in this society is pretty much the same. Genres have always overlapped, and this trend continues today. The different musical situations players find themselves in, the type of work available for each style of music, and the hardships musicians are expected to put up with all become part of a vast canvas.

Think of one of the largest abstract paintings you've ever seen–say, a Jackson Pollock mega-masterwork. In one corner there might be a piano player in a hotel, slowly picking through a book of standards while a few dozen couples flirt and/or spat in the background. While the pianist plays, he thinks about his bills one moment, a chord voicing the next, and then, while the chord is still ringing, something

> *Society does not particularly encourage the musically obsessed. The only thing to consistently motivate such an individual is the obsession itself.*

funny one of his friends told him.

In the center of the canvas there is an orchestra playing Schubert. There are so many players sitting together it is hard to make out their individual faces. But each one has a different life and another job, not all of them dealing with music.

Near the orchestra is a composer who has been teaching music at a university for the last 20 years. Over his shoulder one can see a folk songwriter/performer, running to catch the Greyhound between Detroit and Cleveland for a gig that night.

Of course, there are vans everywhere in the painting because other musicians prefer to drive themselves. Some of the vans are old, some are new, and all of them are getting pulled over on the highway by state troopers. There are punk rock, country and western, gospel, jazz, Christian rock, electronic industrial, new age . . . all bands, all driving back and forth.

There are musicians in the picture from all over the world: a Balinese gamelan orchestra, an accordion player who is always guaranteed a free seat on the bus in Lagos, an Indian mridangam player waiting to be picked up at the Toronto airport, and a Tuva throat singer checking into a hotel.

In the sky there are planes with musicians sitting in them, all of them missing someone they left behind at home. (Note: If you are a musician and you are sitting in the first-class section, maybe this book isn't for you. Just kidding.)

If you look closely at the painting, you see that many of the musicians have nice families, own homes with recording studios, collect musical equipment, and enjoy life. They are going to interesting places,

sometimes traveling first class and checking into triple-star hotels. Their neighbors may not have heard of them, but they still envy the traveling these musicians are doing.

And of course, the painting is full of the faces of frustrated musicians who feel as if they are going nowhere with music—sometimes rightly so. Other sad faces in the painting are carrying instruments not to a gig but to a pawn shop.

The general public, the non-musicians, stroll past the painting casually, in a bit of a hurry. They get impatient at the size of the picture and the fact that they can't recognize any of the faces. "Nobody I've ever heard of," they say, walking on to the next painting.

To carry the analogy further, it is common for the public and art critics alike to comment that an abstract painting such as this looks as if it was done by a bunch of chimps throwing paint at the canvas. The medium is different, of course, but you couldn't come up with a better example of the way the public thinks of musicians.

One of the things I want this book to do is to create an accurate picture of this type of treatment in all its dimensions, so that by reading it you will perhaps understand what lies ahead for you if you choose to become a musician. If you have no interest in a music career, maybe this book will entertain you because you can savor the strangeness without having an anxiety attack about the years ahead!

This is a book about what happens to people who are obsessed with music and what they can make happen for themselves. I believe that all musicians, from the semi-mediocre to the greatest, have to be obsessed just to keep playing. As you will see, society does not particularly encourage the musically obsessed. The only thing to consistently motivate such an individual is the obsession itself. Again, I'm not talking about the obsession for success. That has nothing to do with this book other than as a subject for discussion as a possible psychological handicap.

This book will question the entire concept of success as defined in our society and why tying this concept into music, the same way it is linked to everything in our lives, can be particularly dangerous to the musical state of mind.

HOW TO READ PARTS OF THIS BOOK

Some chapters of this book are prefaced with disclaimers about the characters and events portrayed in order to avoid misunderstanding, I'd like to explain what it is I am trying to do in these sections.

I have been writing stories off and on since I was in grade school. As a professional musician, I discovered that I enjoyed writing accounts of various adventures in the music business when I began writing tour diaries. As the cliché goes, it's a way to make lemonade out of lemons. I learned that a horrifying gig can be worth something if you can turn it into a funny piece of writing, even if all you get from it is the satisfaction of knowing other musicians are getting some yucks out of it. But let me clarify that this book is not about "what really happened." Not all of these situations are related exactly as they occurred, and it was not my intention to write a transcript of what happened with so-and-so in their dealings with so-and-so. This book is about the *kinds* of things that happen.

I've read so many books about the music business that are written by and for "music industry" people who sit in offices talking on the telephone and maybe attend a convention now and then. From the tone of these books, you'd think that actually playing music entails a similar lifestyle and that deciding which phone calls to answer is the focus of a person's life.

I wanted my book to contain a lot of information about real situations. I wanted to give a real picture of what musicians are going to find themselves going through. Sometimes, when people read my stories about things that might have happened to any given musician, they want to know who "he"/"she" *really* is and if "it" *really* happened. Let me answer that question once and for all: "It's *not* what really happened!" The point is that these things *do* happen.

Maybe you see yourself in one of these characters, and maybe one of them is really based on you. Let me take a moment to say that this text was not written out of spite. It is not my attempt to settle a score or get a payback. I tried to strike a balance between letting characters and places retain their anonymity while still providing vivid, real examples.

It is my hope that readers will be able to let go of their interest in trivial gossip and get to the real essence of these stories. No matter what kind of music you play, you will be running into characters such as the ones presented here and opening doors that lead into the types of places I will describe. I'd like to be able to boast that reading this book will totally prepare you for dealing with this kind of stuff, but that is not what is really going to happen. It might help, though.

WHO I AM AND WHY I SHOULD WRITE THIS BOOK

It is obvious that many people who pick up this book won't know anything about me. They may have never heard a note of any of my music. However, I feel I am certainly qualified to write a book about the life of an ordinary or "real" musician, because that is what I am.

Let me tell you a little about myself. And even if you are aware of my music and/or reputation, there are still details in this introduction that you might not know about, so read on.

First, let me repeat that reading about my experiences and what I have learned does not require one to be even remotely interested in the type of music I play (which, by the way, has been labeled as "left-wing jazz," "LSD C&W," "shockabilly," "squeaky-boinky," "a bunch of noise," "free music," "avant-garde country," and many other things).

It is of paramount importance that the reader understands a musician's career experiences have zip to do with what kind of music they play. Whether you play polka or poly-ethnic slam-house, you are going to have the same experiences in the world of professional music. Let's broaden this statement even further to say that you will have the same experiences many people will have in many different careers.

You will see the dark side of the world of music. The guiding force behind so-called "bad things happening" is always the same: corrupt, greedy, power-hungry people. The more of them there are, the more bad things happen.

Let's just forget completely about all these labels and my music in general. The important thing is that I have survived as an independent musician for more than 20 years now. I'm not saying that is the longest career in history or even in the top 10,000. But if someone had told me when I was 17 that I would go out and play music for the next 20 or 25 years, it would have made me very happy. I wouldn't have even asked for a lot of details.

Over this period, many things have happened to me, some of them more important than others. I'd like to point out a selection of events that are landmarks to me, crucial turning points in my life. First of all, though, I'd like to brag about a few things, mostly because I hope they will convince you to read on.

In my entire career I have never had anything to do with any major labels or any branch of the "big-time" music industry. Actually, this is a tiny bit of a lie, but the contacts I've had have been so minuscule, short-lived, unprofitable, unimportant, and just generally "un" that they help prove my point that you don't need that kind of help (as you will see when these various mini-contacts with the big shots come up later in the text).

If you dread a career in music because you are afraid that, no matter what you do or how brilliant you are, the road inevitably leads to either dire failure or the frightening, overwhelming, and just plain boring relationships with lawyers, big label A&R people, hotshot producers, and philosophically challenged promotional staff, I am here to say, "Fear not!" You can have a long and prosperous music career without ever having anything to deal with this crowd.

Read on, it gets better.

I have always played exactly the music I have wanted to, given the technical restraints of the situation (mostly my own). This is important to mention because so many people continue to believe that this is an impossibility and one must somehow toe the line ("sell out," "go commercial," or "be accessible"). These people hope that, if they manage to do this to certain overlords' satisfaction, they will eventually be granted the freedom to "do their own thing"—preferably from the shelter of a Beverly Hills estate.

In the real world of music, it can be just as hard and financially unrewarding to play Top 40 as it can be to be an avant-garde outcast. The public in general is only willing to embrace what is "cool." And the definition of cool changes as quickly as air currents do. The great German avant-garde composer Karlheinz Stockhausen recently commented in the British magazine *Wire* that, despite its popularity, dance music is the most insecure type of career, not decidedly unpopular music such as his own, because, as styles change in dance music, the public abandons favorite artists overnight.

So if you feel like playing music a certain way, do it. Don't listen to anyone who tells you to change for any reason, especially if the reason is anything to do with making more money. People like that are complete idiots and probably won't understand what half the words in this book mean, so don't take their advice—but never turn down the free lunch that sometimes comes with it.

The final thing I want to brag about is that I am a happy person. Even though I don't have massive wealth and fame and nobody has ever heard of me, my music has brought me peace of mind. Maybe it's *because* nobody has ever heard of me!

GREAT MOMENTS IN MY MUSICAL HISTORY

These are instances that really stand out. Of course, everything that happens to you has its importance, and it is almost impossible to know how important something is while it's happening. Some people in the music business aren't even aware that something is going on when it is. I dedicate these memories to them, along with the reader who gets encouragement by recognizing something that they, too, have experienced.

One day, when I was 12 or 13 and had been trying to play guitar for a couple of years, I picked up my little Stella acoustic ($18) and started playing before I remembered that the flatpick was still tucked between the first and second strings. The pick was a shade that blended in with the dark fretboard, so I didn't notice it right away, although I did wonder why the strings

were buzzing so strangely. When I finally realized what was going on, I didn't remove the pick because I liked the distorted sound the strings were making.

When my mother came in the room, criticized the noise, and said, "Why don't you learn to really play?" it was also an important moment. Not only did

> *If you feel like playing music a certain way, do it. Don't listen to anyone who tells you to change for any reason . . . People like that are complete idiots . . . so don't take their advice—but never turn down the free lunch that sometimes comes with it.*

I completely ignore her and continue what I was doing, but I was also provided with a taste of something I would hear over and over from aggressive, impolite music audiences—that is, if they weren't too busy having private conversations over the music. That's my earliest memory of developing my creativity and interest in unusual sounds. But there would be others.

When I was 16, I was rehearsing with a garage rock band that had played one or two parties at that point. We were working on our version of the song "Spoonful" by blues artist Willie Dixon, but we were playing it the way Cream had recently recorded it: a long jam version with guitar noodling up and down the neck.

This band, named Daytop Village or the Moslems at different times, had the good fortune to exist during the height of the psychedelic era. In terms of what the audience at my junior high school wanted, long jams with frettucini were about as commercial as you could get. Both the rock radio stations in our town were playing the full-length version of "Spoonful" a couple of dozen times a day.

The rhythm guitar player in the band (who later became a schizophrenic) thought our band's only chance at success—yes, we really believed we could become a famous rock band like the Byrds or Cream—was to duplicate the sounds on the radio. He put his hand over my fretboard at one point and urged me to go home and practice with the record. He wanted me to learn all the riffs the way Eric Clapton played them.

I refused, and I see this as a personality-forming moment of clarity. "I am going to play my own stuff. That's what I want to do," I told him. There were three of us in the band: two guitars and a drummer (an early inkling that I wouldn't care whether I used a bass player or not!). The drummer didn't care which E.C. licks I played, Eugene Chadbourne's or Eric Clapton's. He was just happy playing. So the rhythm guitarist gave in to my desire.

This experience would be repeated with many of the bands I was to be in: three classic personalities— the adventurer who wants to do his own thing, the trend-conscious one who goes along with it, and the drummer who doesn't care what's going on as long as there's a gig—all heading for a break-up the minute two out of the three get discouraged at a career setback.

Between the ages of 17 and 18, I experienced a music listening revelation of sorts. I discovered an artist whose music seemed overwhelmingly challenging to me: the late John Coltrane. This man, whom no one would deny a place in the pantheon of jazz giants, is acknowledged by many to be one of the greatest musicians ever.

I went from hearing nothing but cacophony in his music to feeling a sense of relief and internal peace that I had never experienced before from anything in my life. Once I came to grips with this, I could feel it in every note Coltrane played and then began getting the same feeling from other music I listened to. I dove into a much deeper musical lagoon than I had yet experienced, in which the infinite possibilities of musical expression had not only been revealed but were swimming all around me. I suppose it was then that I decided to make a life of music, because I knew nothing else would make me happy.

In my early 20s, I had an encounter with a musician of international stature that provided another key moment. This was Anthony Braxton, the multi-instrumentalist and composer whose career contains all the elements typical of a creative musician: versatility, prolific output, wide-ranging collaboration, profound philosophy, and intense poverty. Though Braxton himself would be the one most likely to add, "Not necessarily in that order."

I had organized a solo concert for Braxton in Calgary, Canada. He was in Toronto just before that, and the concert organizer there played Braxton a tape of a recent solo concert I had done in Toronto. When Braxton got off the plane in Calgary, he was puffing his pipe and raving about my great playing.

He praised me more in the next 48 hours than everybody else combined had done in my entire life. He did this in the presence of friends and local musicians who until then had either politely tolerated me or thought I was a charlatan.

The way they changed their points of view to match the opinions of this "big star" was a bittersweet experience for me. Of course, I liked the fact that everyone in town treated me with more respect because of what Braxton had said, but I knew that it had nothing to do with my music. Braxton had listened to it, found things he enjoyed, and decided to encourage me because, as we will discuss in this book, that is the kind of thing a good musician does. The public, on the other hand, including close circles of friends and musicians on the local scene, seems to have a natural instinct to discourage unknown players. Their opinions, however, can easily be reversed on someone else's say-so.

This experience was an early example of how mean-spirited the public can be. Unless issued contrary marching orders by someone "higher up," they will automatically put down newcomers.

Another important understanding also came to me through Mr. Braxton. About six months later, I relocated to New York City in order to pursue contacts. As part of his eloquent praise, Braxton had encouraged me to make the move by hinting about various forms of musical employment attainable if I was "on the scene." He mentioned a place in his quartet, creative orchestras, duets, or recording sessions as possibilities. "You must learn to read music!" he had warned me. This became the incentive this long-term "by ear" player needed to get that part of his act together.

Unfortunately, I went through a period of disappointment in New York before I realized he had not been making concrete job offers. He had just been describing different opportunities that were possible—if not with him, then with someone else. It was his way of motivating me, making sure I would make the move and commit myself to music.

I saw other players descend into a cloud of discouraged sulking when the hoped-for call didn't come from a Braxton or some other established player, but I learned that I had to make things happen for myself. I couldn't depend on someone higher up. But it's a foul form of smoke indeed if it leads one to resent a mentor because "they didn't hire me like they said they would."

I realized that I was the "leader" type and, although I might have experiences down the line working for others, I had to eradicate any notion of depending on anyone else or it would result in resentment about what didn't happen. This kind of energy is simply negative! And what really happened was so positive: Braxton kicked my ass! He'd gotten me to relocate, jump into a much more intense music scene (where I was sure to be both appreciated and neglected 100 times over what I had already been through), and provide the final impetus for me to learn to read music. Way to go, Anthony B.! Salut!

> *[The public] unless issued contrary marching orders by someone "higher up" . . . will automatically put down newcomers.*

Another one of my musical teachers was Wadada Leo Smith, currently holding the Dizzy Gillespie chair at the California Institute of the Arts. In the late '70s, Smith explained why he had chosen to overdub a trumpet part on an album without listening to the other tracks: "I can't play and listen at the same time."

This silly comment sat tucked away in my brain for years until it dawned on me that much of the frustration musicians experience comes from excessive self-criticism, which is often merely the result of trying to play and listen at the same time. Even listening later in order to pass judgment can cause problems. Maybe music is too complicated and wide-ranging a form of expression to be judged in simple "good/bad" terms—especially one's own work.

I acquired a more relaxed attitude toward my work through this revelation. I had always been reluctant to form opinions about other people's music, but now I stopped passing judgment about my own music.

One of the reasons I did music the way I did was because I wanted to hear music played a certain way and nobody else was doing it. I did it myself so I could enjoy it, and because I was, and still am, obsessed with hearing music like this, not because I thought I could get rich from it. My enjoyment was enhanced because of my less judgmental attitude. Music writers have described this as an "anti-masterpiece mentality." More on this later.

For stimulating my thoughts and increasing my enjoyment, I thank Wadada Leo Smith. There will be other quotations and ideas from this musical Buddha as we go along, as there will be comments from many other musicians, from many generations. There will be stories, songs, philosophizing, paranoid theories of mind control, and more.

If you feel like you are looking through the door at the largest school cafeteria in the world, where everyone is chattering away at once and thinks they're right, and nobody is paying attention to you, then you are ready to read this book.

Hopefully you have already been taking what you have read and applying it to your own musical world. Perhaps a comment will set you on the road to personal satisfaction the way "I can't play and listen at the same time" did for me. I hope so.

Anyway, the door is open. Come on in.

CHAPTER 1

I Hate the Man Who Runs This Bar!

If I can make it till the end of this song
Before they kill the P.A.
It's 'cuz the bossman, he's upstairs
Rippin' off my pay
It's the man the mob calls for a little dirty crime
He pulled a gun on some boys in a traveling band
I bet he's mad he let me get this far
I hate the man who runs this bar

Oh yeah, he's upstairs
Skimmin' a ten for every ten that comes in
Hark, hark, I hear a loan shark
Rippin' off a crooked narc
They do lines all night in a fancy sports car
While you and I sleep on a floor
He ain't worth the grime on the neck of this guitar
I hate the man who runs this bar

And then he tells you about his sex life
The one he picked up at the Nautilus
And the under-age one he got in trouble
And how he had to terrorize her
Then when he's got nothing more to say
He'll tell you how she took the kids,
Walked out on Christmas day
I bet he's mad he let me get this far . . .

1

Well, I'll start out with the same thing I told the guy in Kansas City. The guy was running at me with a chair held over his head, about to smash my head in. He was a friend of the bar owner, and I was singing "I Hate the Man Who Runs This Bar."

"It's just a joke! It's a song! I'm a friend of Roger's!" No, I don't hate every bar owner. And that's not the only inaccuracy in the song. Not every bar is owned by a man. Often it is a group of individuals, a collective of some sort. Sometimes it is the government. Sometimes no one runs it at all.

As the following "Alphabet of Club Owners" will show, a club can be run by anybody or anything, for any reason. And just about anything can happen in one. Whom you might have to deal with and what they might be involved in can be shocking, enlightening, amusing, or terrifying, sometimes all at once.

The Alphabet is written in non-fiction style, but as real as they may seem, the following people and places are not real. For example, one could not go

> "It's okay for a town to have one club owner and one junkie, but do they have to be the same guy?"
> —player passing through town

and find a club called I in Washington, D.C., with an owner who also calls himself I. Nothing to do with what I refer to as "I" ever existed.

However, everything that takes place in these stories actually *did* happen. Like a collection of *Aesop's Fables* with musicians and club owners instead of animals, the Alphabet is meant to be a guide for the international nightclub gigging experience. Many musicians starting out, as well as the people giving them advice, think that playing in clubs is largely a matter of unpacking and then packing equipment, which is actually the last thing you are going to be thinking about.

Perhaps you are involved in music not normally presented in clubs. No matter how wholesome your use of a club (compared to the normal depraved weekend scene), you will still be in contact with the club owner or owners, booking agent, and so forth. Clubs are full of exciting events such as drunks puking and telling the same stories over and over, pool games, and sometimes a shooting or knifing. But it is these club owners and "artistic directors" that provide the real thrills in your day-to-day life as a working musician.

One point of the Alphabet is to show that no matter how bizarre or anarchistic the nature of the club, no matter how extreme the circumstances and "unprofessional" in nature, there is always the opportunity to make money, thus nurturing your musical livelihood. Another goal of the Alphabet is to help strip away the false sense of security "professionalism" attaches to itself. In reality, there is no security in this business under any circumstances, and no type of club owner is more reliable than another.

Who are these people? Why do they exist? Why are they doing this? How do I get their phone numbers? Here is proof that:

1. There are no easy answers to these questions.
2. You have to be ready for anything.
3. You will hopefully survive these experiences and come out wiser. You will be tired, anyway.

ALFONSO ran one of the only nightclubs in an exotic Western town, a couple of hours from Mexico. Wolf vs. Sheep's organ player was doing their booking but had to pretend he was a William Morris agent in order to get booked because Alfonso said, "I only book professional outfits."

He then encouraged the band to drive all night from their previous show and arrive early in the morning at his place. "We'll have beds waiting. We got a whole sleeping setup! You guys will be really comfortable."

When the band arrived, they found Alfonso and his brother Alfred had been up all night "having an old-time jam." The brothers pointed out a couple of sleeping bags heaped on a wooden stage with still buzzing amplifiers towering over them.

"Y'all can crash!"

Alfonso's eyeballs were the size of kiwi fruit.

Some people in this situation would try to sleep. Others would stay up with Alfonso, who would stage a day full of incidents that create maximum tension because, no matter what the deal is, whoever is in charge of business affairs will immediately begin creating anxiety about the arrangements.

"Will this maniac actually pay our guarantee?" the bandmembers whispered to each other the moment there is privacy.

Meanwhile, Alfonso put in a final day of promotion for the show. He began by chatting it up with cement pourers from a nearby pool job, strongly suggesting they'd be able to find something they'd been looking for if they came by. "We'll be there," one of them promised, waving his bag lunch in the air.

Then it's on to the radio. A blonde from a Top 40 station came by, and he bribed her into several free record spins with an offer of cocaine.

Next he took the band out for lunch at a Mexican place. It was a long belly-buster with many rounds of beer. When Alfonso went to the bathroom, the table discussion went like this:

"Is this lunatic gonna pay for lunch?"

"Is he going to pay our guarantee?"

"Are we supposed to stay with him?"

"Maybe we should drive all night again."

Alfonso was good for the tab, although he put the waiter through a surrealistic ordeal, showing him every single card from his wallet, then asking if he could get a discount in the restaurant based on any of these items, which included an out-of-date New York City YMCA membership and some photographs. "Here is a photo of me on my motorcycle, taken 17 years ago. Here is another photo of me on my motorcycle, taken just last week. See? Same cycle. Same street! Is there a discount for this kind of picture?"

The waiter was always polite. "No, sir . . . I don't believe so."

The paying of the tab set the business anxiety somewhat at ease. As it turned out, Alfonso was good for the guarantee, and he laughed when he realized he had been duped by a musician pretending to be a William Morris agent.

He earned the respect of the band by standing up for them in a ruckus with the local Van Club, who happened to have their Tuesday night meetings in the bar the night of the gig. When several of these jokers complained about the music and demanded their cover charge back, the door girl was instructed to tell them to get lost.

"We'll put you out of business," they threatened.

Alfonso said, "I sincerely hope they do. I hate the bar business."

Overall impression: The Alfonso type turns out to be mostly a good thing, although a little nerve-wracking. He is on the side of the musicians, although he puts them at risk with his reckless goofing. And he's like a little kid going to extremes trying to show off and impress people. He sees the musician as someone he wants to impress, however.

He is hampered by his chaotic, unfocused nature. "The outdoor concert facility" he is building for the club never gets beyond a pile of scavenged

Commands from various bar owners:
This explains my hatred of napkins.

rubble and boards. But the club owner doesn't have what it takes to do more routine, time-consuming promotion for events.

Eventual outcome: The Alfonso type eventually loses his business grip and the club goes under, or if they're lucky, gets sold first. Usually these types drop out of the system altogether, no longer taking on anything more ambitious than day-to-day survival but sometimes accomplishing miracles. In Alfonso's case, he kept that same motorcycle running another 17 years.

BEPE was located by an agent trying to fill a weekend for a bluegrass group touring around Southern Europe. A dead weekend looks pretty bad, so the agent had been casting about, getting desperate. Then a tip from Giovanni: "The Communist Party in Udine, they have a little club."

"With music?"

"Well, uh, no. They don't really like to have music there, but sometimes the owner, that is Bepe, sometimes he will have a special concert."

A virus: A club owner that doesn't like to have concerts but can sometimes be talked into it and inevitably says, "I told you I didn't like concerts," if the event is not a success. Then again, sometimes he is surprised and decides "to have live music after all, on a trial basis." Then he usually gives it up, telling people, "We stopped having live music. It didn't work."

Bepe was still in the convince-me stage. He was a bigwig in the communist party and ran the bar mostly as a social outlet. On this particular weekend, a concert seemed like it might be a nice distraction. The deal was attractive: The group would play Friday and Saturday night for food, they'd sleep at the club owner's, and get 100 percent of the door minus basic expenses, which it was explained, was just the flyer printing.

It turns out that the club was a side room of a bookstore full of anarchist, socialist, communist, humanist, feminist, and so forth publications. The only lighting was overhead, illuminating the whole room at once. A couple of microphones were rigged into a home stereo that had been turned into the club P.A.

Friday night's business was mild, and it was hoped that Saturday would be an improvement. But the Saturday night event was taken over by a lunatic, an old woman who lived in the streets. She came in, demanded the microphone, and did a set-long version of "Somewhere Over the Rainbow" in English and Italian. No one from the club ran her off, nor did they allow anyone else to. "She has her rights," Bepe explained.

Tension was high between Bepe and the musicians. He was having an extramarital affair with one of the barmaids. Each night after the gig, with the musicians waiting in the back seat, he drove this barmaid to her house and made love with her in the bushes. No one was crazy about waiting through this, and what's worse, Bepe's sleeping accommodations had the guys sleeping in bed with each other, a no-no in the homophobic bluegrass crowd. But it got worse: Bepe insisted on settling up Saturday night after both shows had taken place, so they were already exasperated waiting to be paid.

"I think having to wait for my money is even worse than having to sleep with the likes of you," the bassist told the guitarist.

Bepe did the business at a late-night feast. The group businessman tried to collect from Bepe before the first of 20 courses went round, but was put off. "Please, we eat and drink, then we do the business. After the cappuccino!" This was really bad news, because the cappuccino is absolutely the last thing in the Italian meal and doesn't arrive until every single opportunity for additional eating and drinking has been exhausted. This meant the business was transacted at 3 a.m. The payoff was in the tens of thousands of lira—i.e., about five bucks.

"It is the poster that bankrupted us," Bepe explained. His receipts indicated five posters were made for every man, woman, and child in Udine. Nonetheless, no one who had explored the town had been able to find a single poster anywhere. The bill was for nearly half a million lira and gobbled most of the door take.

An ugly fight developed. A mandolin player heaved a box of strings at Bepe, hitting him in the gut. It was an ugly, anxious moment and it produced not even a couple of extra thousand lira in pay, although it did lead to tip-off guy Giovanni being unable to get the villa he wanted from the state-controlled housing system five years later.

Overall impression: The Bepe type exploits and rips off the musicians while he indulges in his own self-gratification. He is willing to go to a lot of trouble to pull off a small rip-off (the forged printing bill), and he has no respect for either the musicians or the audience, as demonstrated by his allowing an inter-loper to interrupt and take over an event people have paid to see.

Eventual outcome: If one can manage to stay on Bepe's good side, he can be an ally for important things in his town: getting a mortgage on a villa and job opportunities. People like this tend to rise to positions of prominence.

CANTALOUPE COOKIE had owned the Cantaloupe Club in an Eastern industrial town for decades. The bar business was up and down, but more importantly, Cookie had tie-ins with the local mob. This place was a front of some sort, although nobody had ever really figured out how it worked.

The rumor was that Cookie was a small-time wiseguy who got called when some unsavory job needed doing, though never for anything really important. He would never kill anybody, he would rarely be the one asked to dispose of the corpse (nobody trusted him to know the location), but he would be first choice if a stinky, disgusting car trunk needed cleaning out or a lookout was needed while a small-time bad loanee was being shaken down.

Cookie never cared for musicians and never went looking for them, they sought him out. It was a hard-drinking town, and most clubs were more than happy just to pour liquor; there was no need to even bother with music. But for some reason, the musicians, especially the young rock crowd, accepted a "no" at other spots but kept pestering Cookie.

One day Cookie picked up the local paper and his club was on the entertainment pages. "Hey Connie!" he shouted in his raspy voice. "It says here our club is the focal point of the local new wave scene."

Cookie got so into it that he took over the doorman's spot so he could watch the good-looking girls come in and, better yet, have first dive at skimming the door take. "Which is getting pretty good," he bragged to Connie the night after they upped the door charge an extra buck, bringing it up to three.

"If we started havin' four bands, we could charge four bucks." Cookie figured it out. He would still have the band divide up the same chunk of the door, say about 35 percent after he was done skimming. But now another extra buck per customer would enter his pocket. That extra buck would be instant skim.

He didn't know out-of-town bands from local ones, but some of the guys pulling up in big vans, pacing around and acting organized and big-time, were getting in his face about the door take. One band had a giant skinhead guy with a little head-count clicker. Cookie didn't even bother skimming the door that night, he knew they were on to him. "Can't outsmart a smartie," he said later. But he was disappointed.

So he made a new rule. "The rule of trust. No clickers." Most bands couldn't afford a full-time door checker anyway, and all one of them had to do was take his eyes off the door for five minutes and Cookie could skim a half dozen admissions. "It's all doolah," Cookie would say.

One night, a serious fight broke out when he tried to garnish a few hundred bucks out of the door, removing the entire profit margin from a band that had been scuffling around the entire country and was in a lousy mood. Tensions got so bad that Cookie decided to go get the pistol that he kept in the office desk. He waved the gun around a little and the band, the Brains of Blood, decided to go off into the night with $167 after all.

Cookie and his club stayed on top of the new wave pile for years, just because nobody else who came along saw the potential to make money off the college music crowd. The bands on his patch of highway had nowhere else to go and all wanted the stop-off point. And what you got after Cookie was done pilfering was still better than nothing.

Standing there by the door, Cookie probably heard more new wave and punk rock than many fans. He couldn't tell any of it apart, but the act that set up film projectors and began playing porno loops seriously pissed him off.

The paper ran another flashy article about the Cantaloupe scene. "In was coming lots of guys with their dates, nice college kids. So this band puts on these porno loops. I blew a gasket!" Cookie said. He punched several bandmembers and smashed the rented projector.

He didn't realize that the bandleader was one of those types who loved playing pranks. So the next day when this joker calls him up, whining about the projector, it really bugged him. And when the guy said, "Oh, and by the way, we never got the door take. Can I come by and get it? It should be pretty good," Cookie flipped his top. Cookie shouted and screamed and heaped abuse on the guy over the phone for nearly an hour, threatening to beat him so badly "your own mother won't recognize you."

The bandleader had been taping the conversation, however. He began circulating the recording through the underground network that thrives on such strange things. That was the bandleader's only compensation because, since Cookie had threatened to maim him, Cookie ended up with the whole door take.

Overall opinion: Because of the shady business deals that kept his place afloat, Cookie was obviously not the way to get a good door take. But for bands wanting a chance to perform, fill in a night, and practice material in front of an audience, he did provide a regular opportunity and a guaranteed, if desperate,

audience. A basic collection lesson is provided by the gun story: If someone is trying to cheat you and you decide to get the loot by getting tough, how tough can you get? It's a losing battle because there are people like Cookie out there. Unfortunately, playing music is a quick way to get to know them.

Eventual outcome: Cookie found out about the tape. He had stated his position on pornography. He didn't smash the projector because it bothered him, he was worried about "all those nice fresh young faces at the Cantaloupe for the first time. As for porno, I don't care. I used to arrange wild stag parties for the FBI. You wouldn't believe what those were like—com-

> *[An] old woman who lived in the streets . . . came in, demanded the microphone, and did a set-long version of "Somewhere Over the Rainbow" . . . No one from the club ran her off, nor did they allow anyone else to.*

pared to them, those porno loops were Walt Disney."

He'd gone into detail about those parties. This got him thinking he should call one of his old contacts at the local FBI office.

"So, some kid made a tape of you. Who cares?" was the response.

"Nah, you don't get it," Cookie said. "They got me talking about the old parties we used to do."

Next thing you know, the FBI came around the bandleader's house. That led to him moving out to Los Angeles and changing his name. But that's another story.

Long-range prognosis: Miracle of miracles, someone finally did come along and open a more student-friendly club near the campus. Several of them, in fact. As soon as these places started booking bands, it whipped Cookie's business. Although between the local drunks and the mob, he never had to close down.

DOUGLAS BROTHER lived in a one-bedroom apartment with a narrow kitchen/bathroom in what must have once been a hallway. A cleverly designed curtain hid his small loft bed from view when he opened up his living room to the community. "I call this 'A Comfortable Spot,' " was how he greeted each person that entered.

It was possibly the only comfortable spot open to the public in this neighborhood with a two dollar cover charge. Aside from a few restaurants and a grocery store, there was nowhere to go and nothing to do around here. It was the East Village, New York City, in the mid-'70s. Stepping outside Douglas Brother's door, one was likely to find junkies, dope dealers, petty crooks looking in car windows for something to steal, walk-outs from various local mental facilities, and homeless people.

"That's why I developed my philosophy," Douglas liked to explain. "I call it Up and Over! Because every morning I am literally stepping over something that shouldn't be there so I can get out and create what I am creating. Sometimes it's a dead body, you dig?"

His creation was a neighborhood center where things could happen and people could get together and do something positive. The trouble was that people in the neighborhood thought his spot was corny, not comfortable and refused to have anything to do with it.

But his reputation spread among musicians. No, it wasn't a really great gig, you wouldn't make any money, nobody would come, the room was too small, you had to bring in your sound equipment, and the owner took half the money, but it was a place to play in the East Village that you didn't have to actually rent. (The going price at that time was $50 to rent a loft for a performance, and you had to pay whether anybody came or not. This is known as the "pay to play" philosophy.) It was a high-finance music business decision perfectly suited to the creative artists of the era: You could risk losing $17 playing somewhere considered "in," or try to go for a $3 profit in A Comfortable Spot.

Douglas had begun the club in a mixed black

Making friends with the bouncer usually pays off: Cookie's bouncer poses with itinerant musician (1983).

and Hispanic neighborhood, trying to provide an outlet for the local people. Now his club was being used more and more by outsiders, mostly white, who were coming to the neighborhood for the cheap rent. He could feel their positive energy. "You're musicians, after all. Making music is always positive, and you radiate that." All that the neighbors knew was that kooky Douglas was turning his pad into a drop-in for kooky whites who played kooky music.

One night, an aspiring pianist in the Duke Ellington style was holding forth on an upright piano that had been jammed into A Comfortable Spot via many a strained muscle. An audience of five showed up, which meant five bucks each for the player and

MIKE SCHAFER

Douglas. But a special exhibit of Ellington band photographs was up, and there was a good feeling in the room.

Right near the end of the show, an elderly black couple came in. After listening to the music, they spent a long time looking at the photos. It turned out they were relatives of the Duke. Getting to meet them was a thrill for the pianist and made the entire gig special. He winded up playing a few extra encore numbers just for them. That night he thought about the joy of being heard by two people that you really want listening to you as opposed to being heard by the so-called "mass audience."

Overall impression: The activities of people such as Douglas would never make it into a book about music business success stories. Places like this are never able to shake a basic unpopularity. Bands that play in the room are considered unpopular just because they are in that room. If you tell someone you have a gig there, they make a face. While these events take place, the people involved in them are often overwhelmed with a feeling of frustration, that nothing is going their way and little is being accomplished. This goes not only for Douglas, but for the struggling musicians, quartets dividing up a five dollar bill after playing two sets for a handful of friends, and the grinning club owner who cheers them off into the night with a hearty, "Up and over!"

But you can learn essential life lessons from these individuals and feel the positive energy they put out, regardless of how little they might get back. They provide an environment where communication takes place completely free of the dictates of the commercial marketplace or so-called "popular thinking."

Eventual outcome: Gentrification claimed Douglas' neighborhood and he moved on, never to be heard from again.

EVAN FREEB says he got the idea for the Fishing Hole while he was fishing. He thought if you went to a big city where the clubs were all a drag, and then you opened a place that was like the relaxed, comfortable clubs you remember from college days in towns such as Austin, Louisville, Dayton, Tallahassee, and Madison, it might go over really well.

There are only a handful of really important music-empire-building cities in the world. They're where the competition is fiercest. Whole scenes are sewn up for generations, with no openings for greenhorn outsiders. Freeb ventured into such a metropolis and wasn't surprised to find the inbred culture-snob network had shut out most of the new trends he and his buddies had been enjoying since their high school years.

You had to be an advertising executive to afford the cover charge and drink minimum at jazz clubs, so forget the jazz scene. Some good rock bands were working at the smaller clubs, but the glut of prefabricated commercial schlock bands in search of investment dollars made it hard for bands with several releases and a half-dozen tours under their belts to get a drumstick in the door.

Just booking everybody that was being shut out by the trend-conscious clubs ensured a full calendar. But would anybody come? By keeping the door charge and drink prices reasonable, Freeb made the Fishing Hole a hangout for the same crowd of musicians who were onstage. As long as they kept coming to hear each other's bands and bought a few beers each, his tiny room stayed open.

This was a music metropolis, though, and that meant that the players gathered at the bar were sometimes the best in the world. Their music gained popularity, and crowds of music tourists began showing up and buying imported beers. Freeb and his partner had enough saved up to get rid of their grouchy neighbor, knock down the wall, and expand the room capacity significantly. The club had taken off and was now flooded with requests for bookings. Other clubs imitated the policies and tried to get similar acts, meaning more work for everyone. As the place got trendier, it was easy to bump the admission price up.

As for the players, the crowd who had gotten in on the ground floor were getting good door percentages and swimming out of the Fishing Hole with hefty chunks of money. New acts begged to work there and said they didn't care about the financial deal, hoping that this might give them an edge over the ones that did. Freeb realized that by paying musicians less, he could make more. As a musician, you must remember that wherever you go, there is someone thinking this.

Freeb's profits now allowed him to hire helpers to do everything he'd been taking care of, and he began to have more free time to contemplate his business. He thought of ways to expand his club into an empire: a Fishing Hole booking agency, a Fishing Hole record label, a series of international Fishing Hole clubs, a Fishing Hole Web site, a *Fishing Hole* radio show, Fishing Hole Coffee, a Fishing Hole Travel Agency to organize group jaunts to Fishing Hole clubs (particularly when a Fishing Hole Festival was taking place).

Slowly and surely, these things came to pass. Artists came to be known as "Fishing Hole artists." Many of them lusting for this distinction because it seemed like it would be better than being unknown.

Some of Freeb's ideas were greater successes than others, but every venture provided work for musicians, although some of them griped about their pay cuts or overdue royalties. One called the Fishing

Hole "the plantation" and refused to work there for several months. By this time, the pay policy had degenerated into a take-it-or-leave-it cut of the door that was distributed among three or four acts. It had more polish than Cookie's hand in the jar at the Cantaloupe, but the outcome felt the same in your wallet.

The problem was that the music metropolis had worked its spell. The old outpost of the rejected had become the new stronghold of the in-crowd. Once you've been accepted, who wants to go back to being rejected? You make even less money!

Overall impression. The Freeb story illustrates the ability of non-musician promoters to create enterprises that make a greater profit than the music itself. By the time the club owner has created an international franchise and fielded the world-wide distribution of hundreds of CDs on his own imprint, he has no doubt purchased several nice pieces of real estate and is living in a somewhat better style than many of the musicians he employs. Meanwhile, the musicians' real income actually goes down over the years of involvement with the Fishing Hole.

It must be stressed that this is a complex issue where there is more than just a bad and a good side. Many of these promoters become involved out of a love of music. They energetically promote certain artists they admire, often snazzing up their careers or bringing about comebacks. Once again, they provide a forum and opportunity for many musicians to rehearse and polish their creations.

Because they are businessmen and not artists, it is only logical that they will benefit more from the business. After all, they don't have the fun of playing the music, only that of counting the money. On an individual basis, their actions may seem greedy. Yet often the profits of one night with a popular band will allow them to pick up the tab for an adventurous program on another night.

A tasteful, ambitious, and clever promoter can and does create an incredible amount of activity, often building up personal wealth and power in the process. They go from being fans to almost controlling the people they once admired.

Eventual outcome: Freeb is here to stay, and he might be more dedicated to the music business than some musicians. Maybe because it's so much fun counting the money!

FERNANDO graduated in Huntsville—or practically graduated anyway. He had nothing to do but knew that lots of kids liked music and would probably go somewhere to drink beer. If he could figure out a way to set it up for all ages, it would be really good because there was a young crowd into some of the bands. If the bands wanted to make money from

the door, they needed to draw this audience. The club owner would only take, say, 10 percent toward the P.A. they were going to buy. That seemed fair, and by touring band standards it was a good deal.

If enough of the older crowd came by and drank, the bar could make money; and there were always the happy hour alcoholic locals who could be depended on. Maybe that would pay the light bill.

Thus began a trip into the unknown for Fernando, a mild-mannered but fun-loving kid whose military father despised anything to do with punks and rock and roll. The whole crowd Fernando had fallen in with was into nothing but punk. His friends knew about dozens of bands that were touring. By chatting it

> *In reality, there is no security in this business under any circumstances . . .*

up with them, Fernando was able to pick out the good ones from the phone calls he was getting.

Every now and then a band would want a guarantee, but most of these shows, Fernando found to his delight, ended up making a profit. He and a series of partners started working their way through all the eligible buildings and landlords in town. Luckily, in the last election they'd voted in a sheriff with an "off the streets" mentality who favored anything the kids did that would keep them from wandering the streets. They're in a club? Good. Shut the doors. We don't want to hear about it. They promised not to come into the club as long as there were no complaints from the neighbors about anything.

Unfortunately, however, complaints from the neighbors were something you could rely on. Fernando and his friends had gone through three buildings downtown and now had their eye on a rundown bar on Grant Street. For years, the place had been attracting only about five people during weekends. The vice squad would tell you that's a sure sign of something going on, but the neighbors didn't make a stink until the punks started showing up and slam dancing. The neighborless locations downtown had been better, but landlords kept coming around with sudden demands to triple the monthly tariff.

Fernando, living on the premises in order to save money, began to develop some sleazy habits. "I don't get it, I was always neat in my dorm," he shrugged to visiting bands, who would proceed to make the usual dressing room mess in Fernando's bedroom.

Heroin was really the main bad habit; it got in the way of everything. The beer delivery guy would be pounding on the door and he'd be nodding off in the dressing room/bedroom.

The sound system guy would come by every night and pick up his 10 percent of the proceedings. Sometimes it was $7, sometimes $100. Eventually, though, he smelled something—or, rather, didn't want to sniff something—so he simply removed his gear one day. Fernando had a bank loan the next morning to replace the stuff.

He hadn't turned into a total loser. It was a strange, schizophrenic thing. One moment he'd be doing smack, and the next he'd be Mr. Effective, talking the campus into letting him organize an entire concert series and bringing in nice checks for some of his cool musician friends.

The neighbors were meeting at the community library to discuss the threat of the club. Musicians urged Fernando to go to the meeting to explain the importance of music to the community, the difficulty of maintaining an environment for presenting original music, and the need to encourage creativity. But, although Fernando believed in all these things and was the only one making it happen in this particular town, he made a bad impression at the meeting because he was dingy, smelly, and had been sleeping in his clothes in a room smeared with a million stains of road funk.

This got back to the landlord, who, wanting to let him down easy, told Fernando he had an offer from a dry cleaner who wanted to lease the building. It was still hard on Fernando, but the landlord didn't know he had made the weird little punk club owner homeless.

Overall impression. All it takes is one person to get something going in a town and create opportunities for lots of players. For that we have to be thankful. Unfortunately, because some of these characters are screw-ups, it's easy to count them out completely, but that would be a mistake.

Eventual outcome: Two years later, the club building remains unoccupied. It is a spot for dumping garbage and a hangout for bored sleazeballs. But the neighborhood prefers things this way.

Fernando keeps battling his heroin problem and trying to improve himself. He talks about a new club, but assistant at a local disco one night a week is as far as he has gotten right now. It's discouraging that only one person in five years has been willing to do what Fernando did here. But, as a player passing through town put it, "It's okay for a town to have one club owner and one junkie, but do they have to be the same guy?"

GUT did not open Gut's Club out of love for the community. In fact, it was just the opposite. It came to him in a dream one night. A place for people who hate going to clubs. This would be the ultimate because it would be the most hated club in the nation.

The staff was made up of the rudest people he could find. People had to wait outside to get in. If it was raining, they had to wait longer. Mean-looking doormen ruled out various groups of people from entering and finally selected only a dozen out of perhaps 200 potential clients. The rest were sent off into the night—rejects.

"Go somewhere else!"

"Sorry, no blondes from New Jersey tonight."

"No, I'm afraid no Japanese tonight."

These standards were completely arbitrary from night to night.

Once inside, clients were treated to the latest disco hits via the sound system that the army used as a weapon against Panamanian strongman Manuel Noriega. The bass speakers made your heart thump. Sometimes someone would lose control of their bowels.

The bartender was always talking on the phone, and the only way to get a drink was to shout and be abusive. Ditto for getting attention from the waitresses. Gut even sent them to a special Art of Ignoring Seminar held at the famed Edisto Island resort, Aloof.

Of course, the place was popular and many musicians in town wanted it for live gigs. Gut said sure, rent the place from me. A typical night's rent was $750, plus $75 each for a doorman and a soundman. Then you could keep the door.

It was a big nut, but bands usually did great, making a grand plus profit. You couldn't keep people out of the place. The more people they kicked out each night, the more came begging to be let in the next night. It didn't matter who the band was. The only thing that mattered to Gut was the rental contract for the gig.

But then it started to bother him that the bar did slightly better with the disco than with the live shows. He added up the difference over a year and realized it was the price of a Porsche. He had another dream: He'd thrown the band offstage after half their set, had his massive security guard strong-arm them out the door, and kept their full rental. Then he reopened the disco to big doolah at the bar.

He put this policy into action the following night at the Gut Club. When the band wanted to pay $75 less because their encore had been cut off, he had them talk to a 300-pound ex-wrestler whom he'd instructed to "break any of their arms you want." The wrestler didn't have to. The band was smart enough to pay and get out.

The guitarist was into witchcraft, though, and put a spell on Gut. Never underestimate the power of this stuff. Some people put out so little positive energy that even amateur-hour witchcraft can cause them trouble.

Take Gut. He was visited by the city electrical inspector just one week later. The guy found one problem after another and seemed eager to be bribed. So Gut offered him an envelope and the guy turned bright red. "You are going to be charged with bribing a city official."

Sure enough, they convened the grand jury. This interested the tax department who started going through Gut's records, finding all these $750 cash payments from bands with no tax paid on any of them. And that was just one of his hustles.

Overall impression. It's a tragedy that places like this get popular. Why do people flock to them? It sure is fun, though, when you can get in on the receiving end of the door money, despite the fact that, once again, some businessman is making out better than the musicians and ripping off the government in the process.

Eventual outcome: Jail.

HANNAH bought into Hoop's as one of three partners, all of them college graduates with lots of good memories about the bar, most of them having to do with love and music.

Hoop's was the only bar in town that wasn't of the ultra-conservative-jock-football style. As long as anyone could remember, it had been the hangout for the alternative sort—black, brown, gay, hippie, redneck, redneck hippies, then punks, guys with dreadlocks and pierced noses, and so forth. All met there and mingled, and there was never a problem.

Hoop's old-timers could be lured out for special events, when a really well-known band, or one that had been playing in the area for many years, set up a gig. Then the door would do really well, and it was usually Hannah's partner Ronnie out there scooping up the $3, $4, and $5 cover charges.

The band would get all the money. No cut for the bar. There was never any question about that. This was a drinking bar, and everyone came in there to drink. Usually by happy hour half-time, the bar had already done quite a bit of business just on shots. But more importantly, all the partners were musicians of one sort or another and knew that for most touring musicians, that door money was all you were going to get. So that was that: The musicians got 100 percent of the door.

It is not always true that dealing with musician/club owners is easier, but in this case it was. In every aspect of the booking rigmarole, Hannah was a

pleasure to work with. She was pleasant with any musician who called, no matter how pathetic or inexperienced their proposal. If audition material was sent in, she tried to deal with it quickly and have a firm response ready.

She had the ability, rare in club owners, to be outright negative about a submission if she thought it would help. Once an eager-beaver promo guy representing some kind of Swiss disco act came through on a scouting swing. A European record conglomerate was picking up the entire cross-country spree for this joker in the hope the group in question would take off like other trendy acts such as Bananarama, Fogbreath, and Metallic Flight.

This style of music had not taken off at all in this part of the USA, and if it did, Hoop's would be the last place anybody that liked it would wander into. "This isn't really what we have down here. People like blues, psychedelic rock, the new punk bands," Hannah was telling the guy, as the members of the Eddie Kirkland Blues Band loaded in through the front door.

The Swiss promo guy was of the ilk who will keep pushing, calling, following through, sending new promos, and checking you out. This kind becomes that

> *Never underestimate the power of [witchcraft]. Some people put out so little positive energy that even amateur-hour witchcraft can cause them trouble.*

way because most club owners or bookers, no matter how arrogant they seem, get nervous about coming right out and saying, "No!" They seem to like the attention they get from stringing people along and the endlessly ringing phone that they can either choose to answer or ignore.

So the Swiss guy kept it up with Hannah about how big the group was going to be. He could send her the new set of reviews; and the new CD would be out in six months, but he could get her an advance copy if she could pencil in a date . . .

"No! There's no point," she said in a tone that took the breath out of the guy. "People really never come in here looking for that kind of music. It isn't popular at all here. It would be a waste of everyone's time."

"The record company might be willing to rent the room outright, they have done this before . . . "

"No," Hannah persisted. "No. That's a waste of their time."

Finally the guy was out the door.

The Kirkland bassist had put in years as the guy who made the gig phone calls for whatever band he was in. He told her he wished everybody he called would come right out and say no if that was really the answer. "It might hurt their feelings," Hannah agreed, "but it's good for them in the end. They don't waste time and money on calls."

After a few years, Hannah became the sole owner. She bought out her two partners because they had been overdoing the drinking. Neither was clearheaded enough to run the bar. That was Hannah's trick. She kept a clear head and did the same routine week after week: put up flyers, contact papers about the show, hit the campus radio when there was something to give them, make sure the posters were still up, and so on. And it always worked to some extent. At least no touring band had ever accused her of not promoting the show. Everyone did pretty well.

Hannah then married a widower with two small children. He built them all a beautiful cabin out in the woods, and for a while things were going well with this family, their palace, and their happy musical empire. Until Hannah started having trouble keeping things clear. It was okay out in the woods, but once she got to the bar, things started getting fuzzy for her. And the way the business was going, with so many little details, it was always three or four in the morning before she got out of there.

If she had too many drinks, she'd take a snort of speed from an inhaler. She was getting the stuff from one of the bikers who came in sometimes and hung around after closing. One thing led to another, and by the time her husband packed up the kids and left her—on Christmas day, which is where the line in that song comes from—he could pick his reason: Hannah was hooked on speed, she was a drunk, she was having an affair, and she was almost always down at the bar. When she wasn't, she was off indulging in her new habit of driving the family pickup truck around at 110 mph.

Left alone in the woods, Hannah decided she would never set foot in the bar again. Hoop's passed into several hands, until it was resurrected by a name we will find further down the alphabet.

Overall impression: Hannah was a great club owner when she had things together, but she was victimized by the tavern environment just the same way many musicians are. This was clearly the case of a good person with clear goals who was completely corrupted by the setting she had to work in and the peo-ple who came there. The most depressing thing about this is that Hoop's represented the best the town had to offer in terms of a bar environment: Many of the patrons were thoughtful, successful, creative people.

Eventual outcome: Hannah got out of the bar business and resurrected herself as a counselor for teens. She stays away from Hoop's, even though she still likes the music they have there.

Her story is one the working musician will come across regularly: The people who are really easy to work with and do a better than average job wind up ditching the music business, usually because it is wrecking their life!

I is the name of the manager at the top nightclub in Washington, D.C. The club is also called I, although many of the musicians scrambling for gigs are too uncool to know the guy's real name and try to reach someone named Eyeball.

The I club is "it": the most expensive, the most profitable, the most crowded. It's the top of the club scene; and at the top there is always money, chaos, corruption, and scandal.

People who have had prolonged exposure to either I the man or I the club have never come forth with any details. The musician who gets a peek at the place with an opening slot, triple bill, or what have you can usually count on seeing something they will never forget, including bizarre examples of petty thievery committed by millionaires.

The Radio Combo driving down from New York encountered a freak rainstorm and called ahead to say they would be late. The drummer had been forced to make the call from a windswept, rain-splattered, unprotected pay phone on a highway pull-off. He wanted to leave a short message so they could drive on, but the club manager insisted on hooking up a conference call with I who was at some swank restaurant. I gets on, hemming and hawing, and then has the conference call hooked up to yet another booking assistant, who is at a reception in some hotel suite. What are they discussing? How much to dock the band for showing up late!

"But this is a sudden storm. You should see it," the drummer pleaded.

"It's unprofessional, that's what it is," someone said. I came up with the figure of $75. That was how much less they would be paid, bringing this band's total guarantee down to $125.

The Kick Babes were supposed to open for Violent Femmes with a $300 guarantee. The afternoon of the show, I's assistant Hill calls the band and says, "We've changed our mind. We only want to pay $200. Take it or leave it."

Another manager who was a favorite of I's worked up a contract where headliners were required to play an afternoon all-ages show. Usually for no extra money. The band usually agreed to this because a good price had been worked up for the evening show. The trick was that when the band pulled up for the all-ages thing, they would find a sign in the window: "Band didn't show. Canceled." So it's pound, pound, pound on the door, followed by hysterics when they get let in by some jokers who have, of course, been sitting upstairs laughing, waiting a calculated ten minutes before they go down to open up.

Of course, there was a clause in the contract stat-

> The I club is "it" . . . It's the top of the club scene; and at the top there is always money, chaos, corruption, and scandal.

ing that the management had the right to cancel if the band didn't get there on time for any of the events. This would all be based on some cock-up about the start time of the all-ages show. No matter how early the band thinks the show is going to be, the club can always say it was going to be earlier because none of these late night party band types would show up in the morning.

Then the band would stand there in the office and beg, afraid of having no show at all that night and losing out on the big money they were counting on. In other words, the club would be able to renegotiate the contract from a position of strength that could best be described as "foot on gonads."

The big crowd would come for the evening show, and the club would end up with a bigger cut. Nobody ever complained about the canceled all-ages shows because they were never actually advertised by the club.

All the doolah was divvied up in a hidden office upstairs by one guy every musician got to know: the accountant. He would track them down on the bandstand after it was over and say, "Come with me."

No one in any band that ever played there would be able to find the way up to the office without an escort. A series of winding corridors, an elevator ride down, more hallways, an elevator way up to the top, a whole hidden hallway accessed with a combination code, a staircase down, then a door with five key locks and a combination.

That was where all the club money was handled. It was like being in the accountant's office at a mob casino. The accountant led you into his tiny cubicle where he would take a small metal box out of a safe, count out the band fee, and hand you the money. Then, always the same dialogue. The moment you touched the money, he would ask, "Have fun?" Then he would lean across the table and glare at you, his look implying many things: music was a fun way to make money, the club is the ultimate in fun, being a musician is more fun than being an accountant (or vice versa). Who knows what he meant, but he almost always asked the question, then shooed you out of his office. Except in a few cases.

If the show went really well, the bands were sometimes invited back to the accountant's pad. The accountant would take the band over there, get everyone settled in, then announce he had to get back to finish up some work. This was usually about 5 a.m. Then he would disappear and not return for several hours. The bands thought it was a gesture of hospitality, but the accountant did it so he could put hotel rooms for six on the books, forge a receipt for tax purposes, and then skim the difference.

The final job of the day, as he explained it, was taking all the cash the club had taken in and converting it into huge bags of cocaine. At least, that was the policy under some house managers. Whether this was the way I always did business and what it had to do with I's personal fortunes are matters for speculation.

The I club was so corrupt that when one of the booking agents was caught asking a band manager for a $2000 bribe to get his band booked at I, no disciplinary action was taken other than some tepid grousing.

"Where's he get off, selling bookings like that?"

"And the dumbest thing was that the band already has a booking at I!"

"I'm not saying anything to I. I want to keep my job."

Overall impression: I goes on and on, a festering pool of corruption, once again happily paid for by the public. Every night of the week they are lined up around the block; and on the weekend, special police need to be brought in to cordon off the traffic.

Eventual outcome: I keeps riding high; and if you're a musician that is not popular enough for the place, you should feel blessed.

JUANITA King was hired to run the spacious bar connected to a big, money-making Mexican restaurant in the Ozarks. Having a restaurant to back up a club venture with live music usually means you'll stay in business longer, and this was the case with Triple Jays, as they called the new venture. It was also a great room with the sort of stage and sound system musicians dream about.

The town was on route for anyone touring so Juanita was able to keep an incredible variety of bands coming through. Cutting edge punk, zydeco, big name blues, a Mexican Elvis impersonator, well-known singer/songwriters on solo tours, surf music, gospel, jazz, chamber quartets, mariachi; it all went down five nights a week to good crowds. Sometimes the place would be completely packed from Wednesday through the weekend.

Juanita had a knack for handling the place and its responsibilities. She would sleep late in her little trailer with five puppies cuddled around her. Then after a nice lunch, she would take care of the one or two nightclub responsibilities that might touch the daytime world. She made sure all the regular details were taken care of, not once neglecting the promotion and advertising for upcoming acts.

She made sure she had the energy to show her face at the club for at least a couple of hours of the show. If she happened to like the act, and she tried to book acts she felt excited about, she would stick around to pay the musicians personally. This way, she got the feel of the club on a good night. She also got to see a lot of the regulars, tell them about upcoming shows, and see how her hunches were working.

After about seven years, Juanita decided to go back to graduate school and take up her interest in anthropology. She spent a long time picking a successor because she wanted Triple Jays to be in good hands; she eventually settled on a kid, Luto.

He showed every sign of being a good choice. He was fanatically into the club and her taste in music. He'd been hanging around there ever since she had opened, and he liked getting to know the bands. He couldn't wait to get started and told everyone that putting the first month's calendar together was the thrill of his life.

But during the second month, the thrill appeared to be over; he started losing interest in Triple Jays. He refused to enter the place and now had a kind of a religious conviction against returning phone calls. "The bar makes me tired," was his explanation for never attending the shows he'd booked. "I can do the booking at home."

Promotions were also falling apart. There were double bookings and mixed-up dates. These kinds of mistakes could be expected from just about any club, but this had never happened at Triple Jays under Juanita's leadership.

Still, the crowds kept coming to the place. If Luto spaced out on listing the name of the special blues guest on the Blue Wednesday series, the regulars would come by anyway to check it out. Mariachi Sundays would have been packed even if the club had been wrapped in barbed wire. Things kept working at Triple Jays. Until the new security guards were hired.

What proved to be the club's undoing was a simple accident. Luto was asked by one of the restaurant managers to suggest a replacement for the old bouncer who was "retiring." He gave the manager what he thought was the phone number of one of his cousins, but he ended up writing down the wrong number. Before he could correct this mistake, the guy who answered at the wrong number had been hired on as the new security guard. It just so happened that he used to be a bouncer—or that's what he said, anyway.

The new bouncer also managed to get jobs for a few of his cronies because the owner of the place thought that they could use a few more guards at some of the better-attended shows. Especially the punk ones that brought big crowds of rowdy kids who were always jumping around.

The next thing you know, the old mellow, fun Triple Jays had become a hell-hole where kids were jumped and beaten up by beefy, sadistic bouncers. After a half dozen incidents, including one broken

Here's the only way you can get to the gigs:
An official visa to visit the DDR as a performer.

neck, two broken arms, and three dozen minor lacerations, word got out: No matter who is playing there—even if it's the Jimi Hendrix/Sid Vicious Duo—don't go. It is not worth the beating.

Triple Jays' show posters, once Juanita's pride and joy, were now being defaced. Under the line that read: "Cover Charge Still Only Five Bucks," people were scribbling "Plus Hospital Bill."

The shows were bombing, the door take was in the "near gas money" category, and the guarantees to the big name acts were making the restaurant owner fume. All his taco profit was going out in loss payments to "a bunch of musicians." Eventually it made him so ill he was hospitalized.

Luto was given two weeks to show some improvement. In desperation, he dropped by the club. There, a waitress explained to him that the bouncers had been beating people up. Luto immediately fired the thug team and got his cousin in there. The new bouncer policy could not have been more different, the place was now a love-in. But the question was: Would the word get out among the old audience fast enough to save the club?

Overall impression: One mistake can destroy everything a club has built up. Sometimes these things happen without anyone even trying to sabotage the place. Someone else can step into a completely solid enterprise and screw everything up just by writing a number down wrong or by assuming things will just run themselves. If you are on tour and plan to visit a place you have been to "a million times," have your guard up anyway because you never know what "minor" change may have had a major impact.

Eventual outcome: The importance of that talented person who has what it takes to get a music scene going in a town is once again proven beyond a shadow of the doubt.

Budding club owners should take note of the subtle things that drive audiences away from a place. For example: They don't like getting beaten up.

KUNSTLER Agentur or "artist's agency" were the people you dealt with if you were working as a musician in East Germany, the Deutsche Democratische Republik (DDR). Since all the clubs were owned and operated by the state, a state agency set up the disbursement of funds for club programs around the country.

These clubs actually felt more like social clubs, churches, or youth clubs than American nightclubs. (Of course, describing anything from East Germany in terms of something American is hopeless.) Each of the East German clubs were run by small committees officially allowed to carry on these activities, and all incidental expenses were paid by the state. Unlike the American bars where liquor is the big money item and music is the bleeding ulcer, in East Germany, the main concern for these club owners was the state review board for professional musicians and clubs that would decide whether the music they were playing should be sanctioned by the state.

East Germany had jazz, rock, folk, reggae, classical, and probably other types of music clubs. They were held in old fallout shelters, wine cellars, high school classrooms, restaurants, or wherever a group of people could get a charter for a club. Once chartered, the club would be given an annual budget. The financial highlights for the clubs were the years that represented significant anniversaries for the DDR. Then the clubs would be given special budgets for DDR birthday celebrations.

"All year, we are waiting without much money for programation," a club owner in Halle explained. "But when we receive the birthday money, it is clear we will make no birthday celebration at all. Only to keep the money and the whole next year is funded. It is that much money; enough for 12 concerts."

Whatever the funding was, when ex-East German musicians became part of the bigger combined Germany and its domination by the western music scene, they missed it. East Germany did its best to keep out western pop music, even banning it for many years. By the time it was allowed, the state had punk rock and its radical political connections to worry about. It seemed ironic that music considered radically left-wing and anti-capitalist in the West was also considered a threat by the Communists. However, the punks managed to retaliate by starting the street protests that eventually overthrew the entire regime.

Meanwhile, foreign performers were included on the Kunstler Agentur roster. These foreigners got to play the merry game of DDR Monopoly Money. They would be paid about 1000 East marks a day, none of which were allowed out of the country. They could spend the money there or use one of the agents or a friend there as a "banker," who would open an account and take care of their money. Some artists made so much money there that they eventually bought castles. Others spent their days pushing through Communist supermarkets, such as the Karl Marx Stadt Konsumer-Mart, buying East German, Yugoslavian, and Russian goods.

The state also owned and ran all the enterprises that created these goods. The DDR was a unique experience for the foreign artist, to be sure. The country singer Hank Gonzalez clothed himself completely in DDR and Yugoslavian duds for four years, and the various styles passed muster even in Opryland.

A foreigner might also be asked to include a discussion session as part of the gig. This was an opportunity for the East Germans to pick the brains of the visitors and get some uncensored information and, of course, likewise for the foreigner if they were interested in what life was really like behind the Iron Curtain.

There were basic similarities in the lives of professional musicians in the Iron Curtain countries and the opportunities available to them. Eastern musicians, like their Western counterparts, were subservient to various power-cliques organized and run by non-musicians who made judgments about quality

having the Kunstler Agentur picking up the tab, was a much more relaxed working environment than a West German and certainly an American nightclub. Occupational hazards such as doormen skimming dough, a disappointing door take, or musicians not getting paid a guarantee are things that would never happen there.

East German chartered clubs were part of the East German policy of insuring that musical events were taking place, providing culture for the populace. A very different motivation than someone who

Papers please! This one shows where the money is. Government salary accounted down to the last pfennig—but inaccurate.

and importance, usually with very little thought put into them. The Eastern method is just a variation on the same theme. They have a centralized booking agency and review board for professionals and only one state-owned record company. In both the East and the West, the musician must fight society's urge to maintain control and have some kind of dominant influence in terms of content and artistic trends.

The East German club scene, just by nature of

opens a nightclub to make a profit. This kind of government policy is something you wouldn't find too many musicians complaining about.

Overall impression: Although "DDR Theme Parks" are springing up around Germany, and they may attempt authentic reproductions of everything once created by a state "V.E.B. Factories of the People," this is going to be harder for an amusement park to recreate than a train ambush.

Music as it was presented in the DDR was a good experience. The audience was always hungry for more live music and showed its appreciation heartily. And you got paid for your work. If you were an invited foreigner, it was also a chance to be a musical diplomat and widen your own experience with international politics.

Eventual outcome: The old Cottbuss jazz club is now a Porno-Mart. The luxury hotel where playing groups were housed has been shut down, too. The music club that met in the high school in Salzwedel is no longer funded by the new city government, and they haven't replaced it with anything. There are just no more gigs. In Dresden, the new city government managed to shut down everything connected with the arts over a one-year period. And so on.

There was nothing inept or inefficient about East German musicians and their club and concert scene. Currently, an appraisal of the state-subsidized art scene of the DDR period is happening in the West. And the results are leaning toward the favorable. This system is gone now, and the Western side seems to be drawing a blank on creating anything to fill the gap.

LOUIS and his brother came over from France for the American adventure they'd always dreamed of, calling it their "easy rider." While knocking around Mississippi, they were surprised at how different it was than the movies they'd seen. Instead of being accosted by shotgun-wielding hippie killers, they were offered jobs.

Louis' brother wrangled a temporary job with the state archeological team. At first he was just loading pickup trucks with pottery shards and clay lumps, then they had him sifting through boxes of stuff similar to that found at one of their major museum sites. There was plenty of work stacking said boxes in various storerooms and then eventually sorting them.

Meanwhile, Louis had found a local club he liked, Toss It. It was what he thought America was about: good beer, funky music, college girls doing the boogie, and fat hippies rolling their own. "Man, I love this place," he would tell everyone.

Still the locals would say the club was on the skids. "Ah, you shoulda seen it in the old days."

"Hampton Grease Band useta play here."

"Man, that was the '60s!" Louis said.

"Even in the '70s this was a better place. That moron Tomlin let it all go to hell."

Tomlin was a local no-account whose rich dad was constantly setting him up in different businesses. When the last owner of Toss It got tossed in the local sanitarium, the bankruptcy court made a sweet deal with Tomlin Sr. Then, to everyone's distaste, Tomlin Jr. was suddenly running their favorite bar.

His booking policy was fascinating. Tomlin knew nothing about music and thought musicians were "queers." However, while he hung around the office helping himself to shots from the bar's most expensive bottles, the phone kept ringing. It was always musicians or an agent talking about music.

He didn't want to appear a complete fool, so he figured out a way to do the booking. Music had always done all right at Toss It, more or less, so he figured it was safe to book anybody whose name he recognized from the posters that were tacked up around the office.

As for the stuff these acts would ask him to do, like put up posters and arrange a P.A. system and soundman, he just spaced on it. There had been

> "*I used to arrange wild stag parties for the FBI . . . compared to them, those porno loops were Walt Disney.*"
> —Cookie Cantaloupe

money in the old books every month for a soundman, but by not hiring one, Tomlin figured he'd make that much more himself.

When bands showed up and got pissed off, he didn't care. He wouldn't have cared if the Russian navy had pulled up in the harbor. If it ever did irritate him, time for another shot! His dad asked him if he'd rather ditch the bar. "No, you know, I like having my own place to go play pool," he said.

He booked Cliff Dixon, the famous soul singer, and when the bus pulled up, the road manager tried to corner Tomlin about the lack of a sound system. Tomlin kept moving around the pool table taking shots, saying he'd make a phone call. He went into the bathroom and urinated, came out, and shrugged at the roadies. "Couldn't find nobody."

The band didn't play. They had the humiliating experience of checking into a local motel on their own dime. They discovered what the locals already knew: "You could knock the crap out of him, but you'd wind up with another pile the same size. Be no point in it." Now the bar was for sale again and the French brothers realized that, with the dollar currently down low against the franc, they had an advantage and could swing it!

One of Louis' first acts as the new manager was

to write a long letter to Cliff Dixon, apologizing for what had happened to him. "Now there is a place again for you at Toss It as there always used to be. We please invite you to come play your music for us, and we will pay you well."

It was encouraging for Dixon. "Just when you think a club is finally down for the count, it springs back!"

"Yeah, and with a French guy behind it," the road manager said.

Their return gig to the club was a dream date. They enjoyed the personality of the new owner, drew a big crowd, made great money, and had some fine meals. They spread the word to others who did the same. This, combined with Louis' own fine taste in music, eventually turned the bookings around and suddenly the club was at its peak.

Overall impression: Two French brothers recognized something Americans take for granted in their own culture, in this case the good-time ambience of a local music bar, which, left to the locals, would have ended up a boarded-up ruin before long. *Vive la France*!

Eventual outcome: Toss It continued to be prosperous. Louis, though, wanting to find something new to do, farmed out his responsibilities as soon as he could afford to while still spending his time hanging out at the bar. Figuring he could do that at any bar he owned, his new plan is to open a place he likes even more. "Smaller, with more blues and jazz music and less rock." As for Toss It, "Let someone else buy it."

MOONMAN and his band, the Moonmen and Moonwomen, did what so many bands fantasize about: They opened their own club called Moons.

"What a fantasy life," Moonman said the other day. "I've never worked so hard in my life. It's turned my hair gray and taught me the meaning of the word stress like nothing ever before." "Taught" is really the key word, because just the process of keeping a place open for business becomes a series of lessons in the fine art of business.

They founded the entire operation on the premise that a profitable restaurant can support a more experimental club, not realizing that running the restaurant itself was more experimental than anything anyone planned to do in the club. A club could not supply full-time incomes for the five or six band-members, but a restaurant would be able to do this, they thought.

But their venture failed to bring in the kind of money they'd hoped for. The Moons realized that, since there was no profit and they owned the business, they were working for nothing. They decided to

cut back on the restaurant operation, and some of them took on outside day jobs.

The club is now breaking even. Because it's run by musicians (and sensitive, caring musicians at that), it has become a place a cut above the normal club experience. The music is presented in a pristine setting, the layout is designed to afford the best view of the stage, and the crowd is encouraged to enjoy the performances politely.

The Moonies try to avoid the kind of power plays, condescension, and exploitation that characterizes most "big business" bars. When figuring out what percentage to take from the door, the club makes sure that the musicians involved feel the transaction is fair.

There is no liquor license, so they avoid the massive expense of dealing with the city alcohol bureaucracy. Discrete drinking by well-behaved patrons who make a small contribution to the cashbox through a corkage fee is allowed.

The attractive cabaret-style setup is also used for theater events and workshops, dance classes, poetry readings, and films.

Overall impression: If you are a musician and serious about what you are doing, you will seek out places such as this, support them with your energy, and contribute to their well-being by bringing your audience there. These kinds of clubs prove that the right combination of business sense and artistic integrity can produce environments much more pleasant for the musician to work in. This could be the future . . . and wouldn't it be loverly?

Eventual outcome: The Moons hang in there, live shows Wednesday through Sunday, and a few items are still offered from the old menu.

NAKAYOTO was the main man on the Hokkaido jazz scene. He did everything for the concerts there while also holding down a full-time job at his mother's fruit and vegetable stand.

The club held one concert each month. The year's program was usually decided at the beginning of each year, with several organizers in Tokyo suggesting possible groups or soloists to book.

A soloist from a country outside Japan would usually choose one or two Japanese sidemen to appear with them. Who these sidemen would be and who got to pick them were hot topics for musicians and organizers alike. If a musician was also an organizer, as was the case with some of the Tokyo guys, then he would pick himself or one of his buddies to play with the international artist. A non-musician would also pick a friend, no doubt, so concert organizers such as a Nakayoto realized that the artistic purity of each year's selections was constantly under attack from social deal-makers.

The Hokkaido organization was Nakayoto, who did all the work, and several friends, who helped out by coming along to the after-show banquet and eating huge piles of barbecued meat.

The latest topic of conversation was Hinko, a Tokyo drummer and ex-sushi chef, who made them all mad. They would discuss this among themselves while slathering on the tasty ginger, soy, and horse-radish sauce. Nobody thought Hinko was much of a

A virus: A club owner that doesn't like to have concerts but can sometimes be talked into it and inevitably says, "I told you I didn't like concerts," if the event is not a success.

player. Okay, so maybe he could play once a year, but showing up at sometimes half the shows, either backing up the visiting artist or with his own projects? It was too much. It even affected attendance. The last show had slipped below 20 people, down from 25. That was serious.

"No one likes to see Hinko playing every concert. We are not making the concert to study the music of Hinko," Nakayoto explained to a visiting artist who had made it to Hokkaido Hinko-less. ("This is to eat, not to look at," Nakayoto reminded this musician, because he was staring into his soup so intensely it would be impossible to concentrate on the Hinko complaints. It was a soup of live baby fish. They looked like little worms, swimming around in a soy sauce broth. "Suck them down quickly, then they swim in the stomach!" Nakayoto suggested.)

Affairs with the Tokyo promoters were also at a stomach-turning level. Nakayoto had a talk with Hinko and frankly criticized his playing and told him his activities were hurting the music scene. This was heavy stuff for Hinko, who went into seclusion. For three weeks, the only person he had talked to was the old man who strolled through the neighborhood at suppertime singing about the fresh tofu cakes he had for sale.

Nakayoto said, "I spend my days preparing fruit and vegetables for the neighbors and thinking about music. I do not have time to get musicians together to make their friends happy." He was very serious about the music scene maintaining the highest possible standards. According to Nakayoto, it was practically a sin against mankind for the audience to lazily follow their old favorites when newcomers were making what he thought was better music and getting little recognition.

Each concert was staged in a tea shop over a combination art supply store and printmaking studio. This was a serene environment. Old friends came together to catch up on talk, then sit back and give their total concentration to the music event.

A foreign performer would be asked to pose for a picture with the entire audience. A copy of this would arrive promptly two weeks later in the musician's mailbox, followed by a scrapbook detailing their whole day in town, from their arrival at the train station to the Korean barbecue after the show.

Before Hinko completely split with Nakayoto, he arranged for the Dutch drummer Vondar Brundik to come through for several solo concerts. The schedule got messed up and Brundik wound up stranded in Hokkaido for nearly a week.

Nakayoto was a wonderful host, splitting Vondar's stay between the town and a nearby family farm where they could really unwind, go swimming, and take long walks. He showed Vondar, whose music had been a profound influence on him as he was growing up, a place he called Hanging Spot.

A childhood friend had committed suicide there, hanging himself from a small tree. Nakayoto had been the one to find him. The event had haunted his adolescence. But by tempering this with music like Vondar's, he finally felt at peace.

Overall impression: What can you say about a person like Nakayoto? His love of music is deep and rich. He really thinks about very little else. He is not blind to the frailties of musicians, but he has no patience for artists such as Hinko who don't understand how to measure themselves out to the available opportunities and organizers.

The Hinko problem emerges whenever musicians are organizing bookings and have to decide how often to include themselves.

Nakayoto turns all the events surrounding the actual concert into art. The posters, the thoughtfulness and humor of the audience photo shot, the scrapbook, and the actual concert environment all show how artistic promotion can be. He can be depended on completely when a crisis, such as the stranded musician, arises. When a touring stop becomes practically a spiritual experience, it is usually because someone like Nakayoto is around.

Eventual outcome: Nakayoto became so critical of

what he thought were flaws in the music scene that he felt the concerts no longer deserved the attention he was devoting to them. However, he continued preparing fruits and vegetables and thinking about music.

OH GOD, as he called himself, must have liked seeing the bar called O's Place in the film *Lone Star* because he used to have an O's Place of his own in San Antonio. He also used to call the bar Metal Shack, Boneyard, X Factor, Thrillorama, Skulls Galore, Skull Shack, X Bones, and finally, Burrito Factory.

Oh God was a seven-foot-tall drag queen. His establishments were wild. Anything went. Police would never come around. Or if they did, they would say, "What do you expect? You're practically in Mexico," sometimes even before anybody would tell them why they'd been called.

He got the bouncers from a release program at the prison, and they liked O's Place because it was one of the few establishments that hired ex-cons and actually preferred guys with violent records. "I know how to control them," Oh God would assure a visiting band when they started sizing up the situation. "I just feed them acid, it works." Sometimes one of these bouncers would go running off after somebody and never come back.

An out-of-town band would enter this club, meet the management, and then huddle in the back alley for a discussion.

"What's going on here?"

"Do you think this weirdo is going to pay the guarantee?"

Local musicians would come by with the following words of wisdom:

"They've never paid a guarantee."

"They've ripped off every band."

"We just play here because people come in to look at the weirdoes. I've never gotten paid to play. Imagine that, making some money and sending it home. Wow!"

O's Place on a typical night would be so dimly lit that you could barely see the people coming in.

Bands would come onstage and find the audience quite interested in hearing what they were doing, particularly if it was original music. Expecting an orgy or a riot to break out, the musicians would always be a bit stunned to see the crowd behave more like they were at a string quartet recital.

Sometimes the second set was canceled so the audience could strip an abandoned car in the parking lot. "What do you expect, this is almost Mexico," a shocked bystander was told by a guy pillaging a suitcase in the back seat.

Does Oh God pay the guarantee? The answer is yes. But only after about an hour of distracted delays, finally asking the band, "Can I have a complimentary record?"

To which the bandleader inevitably replies: "Can we get our guarantee?"

Overall impression: The road serves up another total freak, but he turns out to be good for his word. Meanwhile, the atmosphere he presides over couldn't be more intense for someone on tour, and the town itself is splashed with a disturbing chaos not found in every American city. You never know what you are headed for each day, so don't even try to imagine what the worst possible scenario might be. Don't listen to local scare stories, except to remember them for use later as potential humorous anecdotes.

Eventual outcome: A place as strange as this, in a town that's almost Mexico, can be counted on to vanish without a trace. The people who run it are not going to be around to help you out a few years down the road. If you ever see them again, just hope you'll be surprised enough to say, "Oh God!"

PHONG was a well-known name in Columbia, South Carolina. When school was in session, the Phong Kong House near campus did a great lunch business—and had since the '60s. Things slowed down sometimes, but that just gave the big Phong family a chance to hit the beach.

The non-family working sector of the Phong enterprise was made up of various young college-town types. Dishwashers, assistant cooks, and the guy that cleaned out the garbage cans were all either musicians or at least into music.

One day a waitress asked Mrs. Phong about the unused basement room. "What about starting a club down there for live music? You know, the bands around here have nowhere to play, and the students don't like going to the redneck bars."

Mrs. Phong gave the go-ahead, and the place opened two weeks later, with a one dollar cover charge.

A seminal local swamp psychedelic, Southern boogie band whose name has been lost in the annals of local legends wound up playing a 378-night stand at Phong Downunder. Later, booking schedules were made up of whoever happened to call first. This was not a "send a tape" operation. Nobody involved had the time or interest to audit tapes.

"It works like this," Mrs. Phong told a music student who dropped by to see about booking his jazz combo, the Funky Beaters. "You have some music or a group that wants to play. We have a stage in the basement. Actually, it's a platform we built to keep anything we're storing from getting wet when it floods." This being South Carolina, the flooded basement syndrome was pretty much a quarterly occurrence. "You provide the doorman and the sound system. Mr. Phong works the bar. You keep the door money. That's your business. You pay the doorman."

This was not only a 100-percent-of-the-door gig, but it was also a place where the management didn't even look to see what had come in. There were no judgments made about who was drawing more or what crowd drank the most beer. The restaurant was making money, so the club didn't have to. It just had to prove its legitimacy by attracting both musicians that wanted to play and some kind of audience that would listen to them.

As a result of this leniency, the music there could be just about anything. Naturally all the most experimental and original music bands played there, but the atmosphere was also good for old-time boogie and dance bands. They knew they could pack the place and keep all the money.

The place existed for years, through many different trends in music. Children whose parents brought them in would wind up onstage with their own garage bands years later.

The death of the place turned out to be water leaks. Leaks that, to be properly patched up, would cost tens of thousands of dollars. Mrs. Phong never considered this kind of renovation for the place.

A benefit for a new creative music society held on the night of a typhoon surprisingly attracted a record-breaking crowd. Water was leaking in from everywhere. There was a five-foot patch on the stage that was safe to play in, and the audience squatted here and there, some of them holding coats over their heads to avoid being wetted by the splish-splash.

The gate that night was more than $700, but it was the last show ever held there. "When I saw all the water, I knew it was the end," Mrs. Phong said, announcing that the basement would become something else the community needed, a meeting place. It could be open less frequently and shut down while it was flooding without causing the cancelation of any big events. As quickly as it was opened, the Phong Downunder was closed.

Overall impression: If local music scenes could have saints, it would be people like Mrs. Phong, so for the purpose of this summation, let's call her St. Phong. Some simple but important principles are at play here. First, St. Phong takes something she has a surplus of, namely space, and turns it over to an intangible but obviously thriving part of the community, who proceeds to make use of it over several generations. Not everything that happened was wonderful. Still, the use of the space and the few hours of management required for the endeavor were not so great a sacrifice that it threatened the existence of the club.

Another important factor was that St. Phong opened the doors of the club and allowed it to run, but after that she kept her nose out unless something ridiculous happened. Example: the time the night manager helped himself to multiple six-packs and then wallowed all night on the floor surrounded by empty bottles.

There was no reign of terror with a manager standing over the bookers and musicians, constantly threatening to throw them all out unless some miracle of business occurred.

Compare St. Phong to Cookie Cantaloupe, one of the few in the Alphabet with a similarly long-running operation. While he tried to steal as much money as possible and even turned himself into a violent and destructive one-man censorship squad, St. Phong was no doubt curled up in bed with a good book the night the leader of the Fantastic Revolution of the Senses Orchestra decided to crucify a teddy bear onstage at the Phong Kong Downunder.

Examples like this are good to know about, because there is a tendency to think the only hope for music scenes are the rare individuals who possess some kind of fanatical commitment to music. It doesn't require such specialization, however, to provide musicians with an opportunity. St. Phong just specialized in being kind and generous, and that's all that is necessary.

Eventual outcome: You already know the place closed, and you can probably guess that nothing came along to replace it. How many thriving businesspeople have an extra room that no one is using who would consider using it as a music club? And then donating the proceeds to the musicians? A more typical attitude would be restaurant entrepreneur "Fats" Goldstein: "We could have music, but I'll tell ya' something, I'd want to take most of the door for myself just for putting up with all the noise."

As of this writing, some people in the community are starting to drop hints to St. Phong about maybe re-opening the club: "Kids are more into music than ever!"

Q-BALL was the nickname everyone in Barre Hunt had for strange Johnny Jopley, the only kid in the Jopley family. Johnny owned the old Barre Hunt Hotel, which was turned into the Barre Hunt Club when all the floors above ground level were condemned.

When young Johnny took over the club, he was ordered to make no changes. It was open Friday and Saturday nights to a different country and western dance band each night. The groups would get $200 flat. No cover was ever charged, but a good dance band made people drink enough to cover a couple hundred bucks. He was allowed to change the name of the club, however. In its new incarnation, it was Q-Ball. "That's what they call me, that's what they call my club," was his rationale for the name change.

Everyone thought that the locals wouldn't know where or what Q-Ball was, that they would need a lit-

> *Roberto Jimeniz . . . [had] recently been to a booking seminar [but] the subject of how to deal with club owners who hack up the bar without prior cancelation of the Friday night $200 gig never came up.*

tle background. So all the posters and newspaper and radio ads said, "Q-Ball, formerly the Barre Hunt Club, formerly the Barre Hunt Hotel, in Barre Hunt."

This was what was written on Alvin Davis' datebook for the fateful night of March 11, 1974. The Davis Brothers were on their way to one of these Friday night $200 deals. Playing in a C&W band on the East Coast involved many of these gigs, none of them pleasant, impressive, or successful.

A snowstorm was making it slow going, and Barre Hunt was accessible only on the smaller roads, the old Barre Hunt Hotel being in something of a ditch that led away from the end of town. One light was burning in the window when the Davis' rocked up the driveway. It was 8 p.m.

"It's late," the bassist said.

"Not much going on here," Alvin said.

He squinted ahead at the building, which was an enormous mansion that looked like a haunted house. As they got closer, they could see two elderly people rocking on an enclosed porch. "You must be the band," the old man laughed. They were what New Englanders call "codgers."

The old woman was laughing now, the odd wheeze working its way in. "Same thing happened last week. Band showed up. Had to send 'em on their way."

"Gotta few months booked, Johnny did, guess it's gonna be this way for a while now," the old man said, stamping his feet.

"Yep, bands gonna be showin' up."

Meanwhile, the bandmembers were all interrupting with demands for an explanation. The old people just kept laughing and remarking how silly it was to have these bands showing up who were so put out and so, so disappointed. Finally, the band was led downstairs to what used to be Q-Ball's, formerly the Barre Hunt Club.

Young Johnny had gone crazy and hacked the place to pieces with an axe.

"Just went daffy one night, that's all. Nothing special happened," the old man said. "He was cleaning up at the end of the night, then, next thing you know, he was smashing the place all up."

He pointed at one corner where strange pieces of chrome and glass and piles of old 45 rpm records were massed in heaps. "Started in on the jukebox over there. Still some good records he didn't wreck. We been taking 'em to the flea market."

There's one guy in every band who is a little slow and takes a while to see the big picture. Right about now he says, "So there's no show?"

"What about our guarantee?" the business manager pipes in. The best they could come up with was Johnny's phone number on a wrinkled post-it note. He was hanging around town because, after all, "They can't lock you up for smashing up your own nightclub. It ain't agin' the law."

The Davis Brothers band had just begun working with Roberto Jimeniz, a booking agent trying too hard to make an impression on the local scene. He'd recently been to a booking seminar in Boston held by a so-called "expert agent" who charged amateurs $100 a pop to listen to his theories on how to book gigs. The subject of how to deal with club owners who hack up the bar without prior cancelation of the Friday night $200 gig never came up in the seminar. Jimeniz was clutching the phone number, though, and he knew his duty as an agent: Get a number and dial it. And in this case, act pissed off.

The hapless band had gone back to the Jimeniz estate, a two-bedroom shack with winter winds whistling through the walls, to call Mr. Q-ball. First Jimeniz left several messages: "This is the Davis Brothers Band's representative, Roberto Jimeniz. It is about the Friday night engagement and the $200 guarantee. We are expecting full payment because of the cancelation." Several messages later, Jimeniz hinted he would take 50 bucks for the trouble. "But no less! This is a professional outfit!"

He repeated the threat to the club owner when he finally picked up the phone one day. By then the tour was old news and Jimeniz was working on new things, never again to consider an engagement at the former Barre Hunt anything for any of his acts.

"Gee, but I'm sorry to, uh, inconvenience you," Q-ball said. "But as my folks showed you, I wracked up the bar a lil'. No problem about the 50. You'll get a money order." The money order never came. Jimeniz, however, learned a life lesson the night that they were supposed to have played the Q-Ball. This lesson was worth more than a $200 guarantee . . . although perhaps not as much as a $500 guarantee.

The plumbing in Jimeniz' old place had screwed up that night, and while the Davis band sat around, grousing, drinking beer, and feeling miserable, a stream of water and several large lumps of excrement had floated slowly from the bathroom to the bassist's feet. He was a little drunk so he didn't move right away, but just sat and watched a small pool of fresh dung form around his feet.

The pedal steel player had been mid-speech through one of those diatribes about how "we aren't gettin' anywhere . . . all that rehearsin' . . . we sound

> Tomlin kept . . . saying he'd make a phone call. He went into the bathroom and urinated, came out, and shrugged at the roadies. "Couldn't find nobody."

pretty good . . . all them tapes sent out . . . look what we got . . . nothin'."

Jimeniz had something, though: a supreme urge to laugh. So he began cracking up hysterically, and several members of the band joined in. All that work, the long drive through the snow, the apprehension, only to find the bar hacked to bits. Top it off with a plumbing problem, and he couldn't stop laughing.

Through misty eyes he looked at the faces of the bandmembers, and knew the ones that could laugh about this misadventure the very night it happened were the ones that would survive the music business. This wasn't something he learned at that $100 seminar, either.

Overall impression: Every night's performance is a lesson of some kind, and you could say this one was Numero Uno. The Barre Hunt Club had been served up as a warning to develop a sense of humor or get lost.

Eventual outcome: Despite his great sense of

humor, Jimeniz finally decided he'd had enough yucks as an agent. A real sucker for hilarity, he changed careers and began performing his own music.

The old Barre Hunt complex got hit by lightning and burned to the ground. The old people survived. Johnny Jr., dropping the nickname of Q-Ball, actually got himself elected to the Barre Hunt city council.

RIEDMAR had walked with a limp ever since the evening one of the Right Hell bar clientele stabbed him in the back.

Right Hell was the first place you saw when the train pulled into the Swiss town of Bern. In olden times, the Right Hell building had been a stable belonging to the king. His coaches, all the horsemen, and maybe even all the king's men had been housed there; there was certainly room for them and quite a few others. In fact, when the long-abandoned ruin was re-opened by a series of ambitious squatters, just such a come-one come-all situation developed.

The concept of a squatted or occupied building is pretty impossible in the USA, where property owners are more powerful than the old Swiss king had ever been. In some European countries, though, Switzerland among them, it is the duty of the landlords of these unoccupied buildings to explain to the city why he let his property go abandoned. Meanwhile, whoever has moved in is given a year or two to stay. Sometimes they end up with the building, sometimes they have to move on to another one.

The old stable was such an eyesore that the fairly progressive city council agreed to give it a go with the young Right Hell squatters, and in a way, the project succeeded. Over the years, the city made it official and even donated money for repairs.

Housed in this building was a thriving restaurant, a film theater with progressive programming, mice (who only become progressive when the lights were suddenly switched on), two different concert venues, an office, a community library, and a complete printing setup for publicity, including a Right Hell monthly newsletter. This was the stuff run by the "good" side of the Right Hell squat.

There was also a section occupied by a kind of drug mafia who sold hash and probably heroin from behind spike-and-barbed-wire covered metal doors. Their presence was always felt but never seen, and they lurked in their barricaded headquarters thumbing through the yearly take of an estimated one and a half million francs (more than a million bucks). In the front of the building is a small plaza, the Veerplatz.

Quickly after the stable was first squatted, caravans of alcoholic gypsy punks began arriving—outcasts from various countries where they were wanted on various charges. These dignified visitors opened their own bar in the Veerplatz. The atmosphere: tattoo-covered, pierced-everywhere types covered with grime getting steadily drunker and drunker the darker it gets outside, pouring drinks for small groups of customers who also scowl around, paw through garbage, and kick aside debris. The Swiss German dialect has an odd cadence anyway, but in the Veerplatz you could hear a mixture of different languages, drunken exclamations, bottles breaking, and quite often, the sounds of someone getting hurt.

Riedmar and his friends were dedicated to staying out of the Right Hell experience, which they described quite accurately as "a social experiment." Here was an attempt to let people live together on their own in a kind of a reality that was removed from the way things normally happened in Bern. It was depressing to think that it could turn out to be an even worse lifestyle than the one the straights had concocted. Somebody had to fight the evil influence.

The good side of Right Hell met in the library to do something about the bad influence. They armed themselves with sabots, and marched on the Veerplatz, where they were met with chains, knives, and broken bottles. This action resulted in a draw. Word spread about these violent happenings, resulting in the audience dropping off drastically.

Now, the musicians who roll into town and see Right Hell looming up, quickly recognize the charged atmosphere. Riedmar is constantly locking and unlocking doors so that the good can keep the bad out. "Life here is keys," Riedmar philosophizes. "It is all a battle of locks and keys. Last month they superglued the locks again. They do this every now and then."

A Right Hell gig is a long evening of fiddling with keys and always watching over your shoulder. Menaces appear to be constantly lurking, but sometimes it turns out to be just one of the musicians in the opening act. With concert audiences wary of the place, money is often lost on guarantees. One trick of the promoters is to get the restaurant to go in on some of the fees, which results in tension when the profitable food business has to shell out dough to cover low audience turnouts.

Ironically, a typical squaresville music situation is developing right in the middle of the ultra-radical squat: a restaurant bitching about losing money on live music.

Overall opinion: The squats and the good they accomplish for the occupants and the city far outweigh the trouble they cause. Although being part of the ongoing battle is as nerve-wracking an experience as anything a tour can toss at you. A professional musician of this day and age has to be able to go into these situations, be comfortable, and deal with the people and the things that happen.

In the wee, wee hours when the last lowlifes have crumbled onto benches, the Right Hell becomes a haunting monument drenched with strange shadows, stranger graffiti, and the ever-lingering presence of intense human energy, expressing itself in both creativity and violence.

Eventual outcome: Riedmar, looking worse and worse, keeps threatening to give up on the place. The city of Bern promises the Veerplatz mob their own little space to set up a squatted bar, just to take some pressure off the situation. Some people are relieved; others are frustrated that they need the city to resolve their business.

SPOOKCHASER began life as Sadowsky and was a bar owner first and a "poltergeistologist" second—in chronological order, not intensity.

The pub Drinks ran itself. Tucked away in a Smoky Mountain town, it had two things going for it: the local populace, old-timers as well as college kids, all had the live music habit; and the money kept rolling in, courtesy of the neighborhood drunks and the simple but tasty pizza oven.

The little downtown building contained a lot of history. As a music spot, it had resisted disco, jukeboxes, cover bands, and "not doing live music anymore" and had been going strong for decades with live original music seven nights a week, local as well as national and international touring acts, every style of music.

One day, a cab driver came in for pizza. It was only two or three weeks after Sadowsky had bought the bar. "Man, you got a nice place here," the cabbie kept saying, looking into the back. "I used to play poker here, back in the 1930s!" Sadowsky loved nostalgia and kept talking to the guy.

When the cabbie felt Sadowsky was comfortable with him, he solemnly asked if anybody had ever noticed anything in the place along the lines of sudden cold drafts, strange noises ("some of the bands," somebody cracked), unexplained movements of furniture, and so forth. Everyone waited for him to go on.

"Guy got shot in a poker game here in 1937. I wasn't down here when it happened, but everybody heard about it. "You see, they caught the guy cheating. These was serious players, there was no way they would let that go, and they all had guns back then. I mean, back then this was a really wild place.

"Guy that got shot was a blues fan. They used to have blues in the front room, gambling in the back. Well, he never got to go home from the card game, and he feels bad that he cheated. They say now he haunts this room. He's stuck down here in this club and can't get out. Only time people see him is when there's a blues concert, because like I say, he likes his blues. If there's a blues show, somebody will see him, or feel him, or notice something that can't be explained.

"One night, the soundman took off in the middle of a show." He looked at Sadowsky. "This was when you was still a kid. This soundman was an addict, and he went out to get some stuff at break. But he was in a spot, owin' money to the dealer, so they took him to someone's house to talk to him a little, scare him. He never made it back that night. He didn't get hurt, he just wasn't back to mix the last set. But you know what? People that night say they saw them buttons movin' on the mixing system over there, but there was nobody movin' them!"

"After hearing this stuff," Sadowsky swears, "I believe it. I checked it out. There was a gambling den there, and a guy did get shot, just like the cabbie said. Since then I have dedicated my life to keeping the club open and making life comfortable for the ghost. I started calling myself the Spookchaser so maybe he would come out and visit me more."

Late at night after shows, some of the traveling guests bring up their own club-related ghost stories. Jughead, the house manager of the old Starlight Lounge in Covington, Kentucky, had the following tale to tell.

The puritan clean town of Cincinnati made it so rough on vice-lovers that they had no choice but to drive across the state line to this little sin den, really just a few rows of bars with card games and strip shows.

Supposedly, one night at the Starlight, there was a wild poker game with mob bigwigs and movie stars, most notably Marilyn Monroe, who got so turned on by the action that she jumped up on the table and did a sexy dance, partially stripping.

Jughead thinks maybe it was the most exciting night of Marilyn's life because he claims her ghost would materialize in the dressing room sometimes when Marilyn's departed spirit felt like reliving the good old days. "Must be hard on her, comin' back here and findin' this dump with this pathetic music!"

This story also had an effect on song selection, and bands played cover versions of tunes such as "Diamonds Are a Girl's Best Friend" to try and entice Marilyn's ghost.

"The only ghost story that tops Marilyn's is the one from Mobile," Spookchaser says. "That one is outright creepy."

The way this story goes, there used to be this live music club in Mobile that would make guarantees, even though nobody ever came in. "Don't know where they get the money, nobody ever comes in. Must be a front or something," musicians would say.

Mark Lincoln, a singer/songwriter, pulled into town, traveling alone, which always sort of creeped him out as he got further from familiar turf. He knew no one in Mobile, and no one came to the show. The bartender didn't have much to say. He looked around the place, walked around back to front, didn't see much of anyone or anything. The place had a kitchen, but it was empty.

Finally, a guy showed up at the break. Lincoln knew he hadn't been there for the first half because this was only the second time in his 25-year career that he had performed for absolutely nobody. Except the bartender, of course. Anyway, the guy came in and approached Mark as if he were interested in the music.

"Have you ever heard, 'Think I'm Psycho, Don't You, Mama?'" the stranger asked. Lincoln kind of knew the song. It was actually pretty sick (nowadays it shows up on compilations of the most demented country songs). It tells the story of a man who admits to his mother that he killed a puppy and a little kid, and at the end, he kills his mother, still singing to her.

Lincoln found the guy amusing, so he didn't think twice about following the guy out to his car to listen to a tape of the song. It wasn't the kind of thing someone asked you to do every day, but Lincoln didn't have any other offers to do anything, and he was bored half to death by his tour.

Halfway through the song, Lincoln got an anxiety attack and thought, "Who the hell is this guy and why am I in his car listening to this awful song?" It was dark outside, and there were no other cars in the parking lot. He started getting frightened, thinking maybe the stranger would do him some harm. It would be so easy for something to happen on tour, meeting all these strange people, nobody really keeping track of you or watching out for you.

Well, nothing happened. They heard the song, and Lincoln rushed back inside. He expected the guy to be there for the second half, so he went up to the bartender and joked, "At least I got one in the audience for the second half," trying to figure out what kind of percentage increase this was so he could joke about that, too.

"What are you talking about?" the bartender asked.

Lincoln looked around. The stranger was nowhere to be found. "Well, he's probably outside still. He'll come back in. You saw him before, right?"

"Who?"

"The guy that came up and talked to me."

"I didn't see nobody. But I wasn't really looking." Wipe, wipe on the bar top.

Lincoln kept up the chat. "He's pretty weird,

that guy. He wanted me to go out to his car to listen to the song, 'Think I'm Psycho, Don't You, Mama?'"

The bartender froze in his tracks, eyebrows raised. "Man, that's weird." He then told Lincoln a story.

About 20 years before, the manager discovered some stolen goods the bartender had stashed behind the bar. So the manager decided to blackmail the bartender for a share of the loot. The bartender put up with this for a while, then he decided to kill the manager and burgle his house on the way out of town.

> *While knocking around Mississippi, [Louis and his brother] were surprised [that] instead of being accosted by shotgun-wielding hippie killers, they were offered jobs.*

"He got caught, though. They gave that bartender the chair," the current bartender said. "They fried him! And you know what?" He glared at Lincoln. "Do you know what his favorite song was, the one he used to play all the time in the bar? It was a hit back then! It was 'Think I'm Psycho, Don't You, Mama?'"

Lincoln couldn't sleep for weeks. Only much later, did the story become one of the high points of his collection of road adventures, the tall tale of his life. One night he was telling it to one of Jimmy Buffett's sidemen, who lived in Mobile, and the guy's face kept twisting up funny while he listened to it. Finally, he told Lincoln to stop.

"Man, you got it all wrong. First of all, that murder you are talking about, that didn't happen 20 years ago when 'Think I'm Psycho, Don't You, Mama?' was a hit! It happened just a few years ago. It must have been only a week or two after you played the bar. The manager actually found some stuff that had been stolen from his house in the bartender's locker.

"See, he'd known all along about the burglaries. The bar was a front for a ring of burglars. They would meet their fences down there and everything. But when the bartender stole stuff from the manager's house, that really caused a problem.

"The guy that killed the manager was that bartender you talked to. And he got caught because he'd been talking about the murder thing with various customers for months. He'd say stuff like, 'Oh didya hear there was a death threat on the manager?' He never got no electric chair, though! He's still sitting in the state prison. They haven't sent him up to the federal place yet.

"He claimed the manager tried to rip him off, beat all his goods out of him, even tried to kill him. He tried to say the murder was self-defense. The jury didn't believe him. Anyway, they wanted him locked up 'cuz he'd broken into half the best homes in town. The guy that played you that tape had nothing to do with it. Neither did that song.

"But that bartender! The one you talked to the night of your gig. He was a murderer!"

Overall impression: Most people go on the road to make money, but sometimes you get paid in ghost stories.

Eventual outcome: Spookchaser is still hoping to meet his house ghost, whose existence is yet another good reason to become a full-time blues player.

Lincoln wrote a country song, "The Killer Who Poured Me a Shot of Jack Daniels." He had hopes that the liquor company would pick it up for advertising, but it was never much of a hit, and most readers have probably never heard of it.

Note: Six out of seven Marilyn Monroe biographers deny she ever went to a wild orgy/card game in Kentucky.

TWICE-THE-GIG TWINS was what they called the concert promotion team of Orin Duncan and Thompson Keithless. So, it was really two club owners, although between the two of them they couldn't get the scratch together to open a regular club. The best they could do was rent the local Veterans of Foreign Wars hall.

Their partnership was formed through something musicians like to call a "supreme foul-up [censored version] in booking." This is when two events are booked for the same date, the same club, the same city, two out of the three, or all three.

Twice-the-Gig was so named because, on one phone, Orin Duncan booked Rhode Island psychedelic band Undead Mike, while on another phone Thompson Keithless was pinning down a date and deal for James Wager and the Illiad, a kind of dance band in tight clothes. Both shows were supposed to happen at the VFW because they hadn't found more than one room in the entire city where anyone was willing to let bands play. The VFW folks let it happen but sniffed around like bloodhounds each morning after, counting the silverware in the kitchen and checking the drapes for fingerprints.

It was a commonly shared opinion that even if, by some miracle, another concert space was found, "the scene" in St. Louis could never support the two shows on one night; one of them would bomb. Or the audience would be split and both would barely break even. Or people might become overwhelmed and decide to stay home.

Because neither promoter wanted to give up the great band and the great gig they had lined up, they decided to just combine the two shows as a double bill, then co-promote it.

This was an unlikely union. Keithless was straightforward in his business dealings; everything was organized and by the book, and a gig for him was almost dull in its precision and complete lack of anything chaotic or problematic.

Duncan, on the other hand, was a substance abuser and a swinger, which is what had brought him into contact with clubs and bands in the first place. He was the groovy hipster on the scene who knew how to find anything that didn't have its own listing in the yellow pages.

When Keithless put on a gig, it was like dealing with Carnegie Hall. Contracts were delivered, signed, and returned, and they were specific about everything. Press dealings were handled efficiently, and unused material was returned (a freakish thing when the norm is to leave publicity material unopened under piles of other publicity material and old donut boxes). Keithless would sit down after a show and list where every dollar that had come in had gone. Every expense was documented on a neat, handwritten ledger. He even did follow-up cards: "We enjoyed having you. Please let us know when you are in the area again."

With Duncan there would be no contract, and there were differences in the numbers every time they came up. Phone calls would never be returned whether anything was wrong or not. Publicity material sent by bands suffered a fate worse than the under-the-pile death because somehow the more important the delivery, the less chance it would show up. This meant Duncan would demand a last-minute extra submission of material, which would also get lost. Sometimes there was a poster for a Duncan date if a fanatic fan happened to come by willing to stick them up. Otherwise, there were very few posters, and those would be covered up by a Keithless flyer.

Combining the two had the look of genius. Duncan never cared about promotion because he could count on all his nightlife cronies to show up. Keithless brought crowds in with his promo efforts. He had to because he was too tired from working and never went out at night except to his own shows.

When the first collaboration went down, Keithless spent two weeks trying to sit down with Duncan about the business arrangements but could never get him on the phone. Or if they set a date for a meeting, Duncan wouldn't show up. They tried to hash it out on the night of the gig. Each had made the same guarantee to the bands. The ticket price had remained the same. The audience would probably be the same, maybe 100 people. So, two bands had to be paid out of one door gate.

Should you steal from a club to right a wrong? . . . If you have to do it, watch the last minute scramble for extra sausages—it could be dangerous.

"Let's alternate!" Duncan said with excitement. "Like, you take a ticket, then me. We'll just alternate splitting the gate." Keithless pointed out that this was stupid. They could just divide at the end and save the you/me stuff.

"Good point! Now let's figure out a percentage to work out sharing the loss if there is one. Or maybe we'll make some money," Duncan hoped out loud.

"Well, we could discount the bands. I didn't want to bring it up on the phone, but since we had to double up on the shows, both bands would probably take less. We could say that otherwise we would have had to cancel," Keithless said.

"Wow, that's a great idea!" says Duncan, proving himself a true promoter. "But how can we say we were going to cancel. We're here now taking tickets. Obviously we're not going to cancel."

"At the end of the night, we'll just say we don't have enough money. No matter what the take is!" Keithless explained.

The lackluster St. Louis turnout prevented this duo from having to actually discount the bands. Instead, they were short $100 or so, and they went to their respective acts hat in hands.

Keithless had no luck. Being such a straightforward promoter, he really couldn't argue that a guarantee was not a guarantee. He didn't want to appear unprofessional enough to be balking, so the only avenue he could explore was appealing to the band to cut him a break, which they did—for ten bucks.

Duncan had an easier time performing a dissection on the guarantee promised to Undead Mike. They were a confused, unorganized outfit whose business manager's approach was to go along with anything anyone offered (or didn't offer) and then have a mood swing about it later.

On this night, in an attempt to recoup lost gig money, the group raided the VFW banquet larder. Unfortunately, when the plump organist dashed back in to rip off another couple dozen frozen Polish sausages, this put the value of stolen goods over the grand larceny limit. And the VFW filed charges.

Twice-the-Gig Twins then had to search anew for a venue, eventually landing one in the side room of a strip joint.

Overall opinion: Twice the promoters? Twice the problems and half the money. On the other pair of hands, it is instructive to compare the two promoting philosophies, each with its own strong points.

Should you steal from a club to right a wrong? It is a pretty easy way to get arrested because they are going to know who did it. If you have to do it, watch the last minute scramble for extra sausages—it could be dangerous.

Eventual outcome: Undead Mike's leader plea-bargained down to community service time.

As for the promoters, guess which guy is still booking shows at clubs and is now on salary with an owner? And guess which guy got run out of town by a drug dealer? Tune in next week for the answer.

UJAZZ was born out of the Alberta jazz societies in tribute to the University Heights neighborhood where so many jazz fans lived. It was right next to the University where many a closet bebopper resided. The only distinctive thing about this recently constructed suburb was that the street names all began with U.

Professor Hutt McCloud would tuck his jazz sides under his arm, leave his house on Uganda Drive and stroll over to his pal Verkaff's place on Underwriter Lane. There he would spend an evening of sides, wine, smoke, and complaints about how nobody ever came there to play live.

These guys and others got involved in the proposed club to bring in some actual live jazz players. Eddie from over on Uteski Place worked at the newspaper and found out that the last documented jazz concert in Alberta had been the Louis Armstrong Band in the 1940s!

Victoria, a disc jockey from Edmonton really got things going by founding the Edmonton Jazz Society. She thought she was into much hipper jazz than most of the Calgary contingent and found these people a little distasteful, a little too into the freaky, far-out modern-style jazz. "We need all these people's energies to get this stuff going," she would tell people at the initial meetings, and she meant it. Even Johnny Picklejar, the really square-looking, gray-haired cat who would show up in a leisure suit, gold chain around his neck, snapping his fingers, and saying stuff like, "Wouldn't it be a groove to get Sonny? What about Dizzy, with a quintet?"

Sometimes on her radio show, Victoria would sermonize about how the factions in jazz ought to get together.

Just like a sinning Southern congregation, the jazz society would react by turning the organizational meetings into violent clashes over the worthiness of various jazz eras.

"The free thing is jive!"

"Bird was a faker!"

"Keith Jarrett is just easy listening!"

"The Blue Note thing was the ultimate!"

"Ornette is just like Dixieland! Learn your traditions!"

The fighting really hampered the bookings, because each time Victoria got a call from Hammis, the West Coast booking agent handling jazz acts, she had to run the proposed name by all these jazz society factions. Reactions would run the gamut from "Beautiful! He's the greatest," to "No way! Too modern!" Nobody ever agreed about anything. Welcome to jazz central.

The concept was that if both Calgary and Edmonton bankrolled a show, expenses would be cut in half, making the previously too-expensive concerts accessible to the fans. Backing up the concept would be a jury of moneybags who would each put a little into the shows (that's where the guarantees would come from), but not enough to bankrupt them if there was a loss. Every time she got the money from the various backers, Victoria got to hear all their little sob songs:

"This guy is getting too much for a modern guy!"

"We pay the modern guys crap, but you bring in an old drunken bebop character and he gets big money."

And always from Picklejar: "What about bringing in Dizzy with his quintet?" Victoria told Pickle just to forget his blessed Dizzy. "Dizzy has to work with his own band and the transportation is too expensive. It's out of sight, man. We have to start on a small scale with soloists who can work with a local rhythm section. We have already proven that this works, Johnny."

This developed into a tussle over who the local rhythm section would be. Would it be a Calgary or an Edmonton section? These two provinces competed over everything: sports, first-run movies, touring rock bands, vacation spots, convention attendance, and the Calgary Stampede vs. the Edmonton Klondike Days. Another possibility was two different groups, one for each city.

Victoria didn't like the latter idea because it threatened the groove. "Two different groups makes it hard to get a groove going," she argued convincingly. "Plus, the Edmonton players are hipper!"

Of course, this provoked another battle overridden by a separate dispute about how it was unfair to the city that got the group on the first night because they would have not developed a groove yet (or at least wouldn't hit it till halfway through the show).

> *Sometimes the second set was canceled so the audience could strip an abandoned car in the parking lot.*

"I don't want the show without the groove," Verkaff said. He added that since he was a backer paying ten times more than anyone else in the audience, he should get to hear the best quality groove.

"I'd be into paying less for the show without the groove," somebody's cash register chimed in.

"What if the groove happens in the middle of the first night?"

"Or what if they have a groove on the first night and burn out and have no groove on the second night?" The debate continued.

So they experimented with the local rhythm section concept and brought in a star horn player who was famous for having earned $10,000 to play one note on a Santana record. It was finally agreed that the Mack Feta Trio from Calgary would back the soloist.

The gig with Feta and the star soloist was held in the public library and consisted of a series of temper tantrums. The tenor player would blow several notes of a lovely ballad, then turn to Feta and shout, "Modulate to E flat, you idiot!" Or he would point the sax at Feta or the bassist and blast low notes at them until they made eye contact, then he would put his horn down and yell the names of chords at them.

"This proves Edmonton rhythm sections are hipper," Victoria said at the end of the night.

Victoria finally had to override the Calgary society completely when it came to the great Rahsaan Roland Kirk. He was willing to do three shows for $600 a show, and Victoria succeeded in bargaining

him down a little on the condition that two of the shows were in the same locale: Edmonton. The third night was to be in Calgary, but the conservatives, dominated by Picklejar, shouted it down and, late at night, phoned Victoria to say there would be no Calgary gig.

Victoria decided to promote the show herself. A massive snowstorm hit on the night of the show but it didn't matter. The line for Kirk went down the stairs and out into the mall in front of the student union. He got five encores out of the audience.

The successful promotions really helped launch Victoria's Edmonton society and, what was more, gave her great confidence. She was a good promoter and organizer and knew when to move on something to get results. She spent more time expanding on these activities and had a dream to have both a winter and a summer festival that could be subsidized by government grants and some big businesses.

With enough backing, bands could be booked that would fill the cities with music and keep all the factions happy. Edmonton and Calgary would become jazz cities.

Calgary became more of an ally when Picklejar and his buddies dropped their interest in jazz. Hatcherphone, a famous vibraphonist had come to town with his band, and since Picklejar thought this guy was fantastic, he had tried to horn in on all the social arrangements.

Victoria tried to discourage Pickle because she knew most jazzers would find him "a drag," but there was nothing she could do because the guy was too jazzed about knocking heads with "Hatch."

He went to the musician's motel prior to the gig where he found the whole gang shooting up. It was all legal methadone treatment, but it still made Pickle go out and puke behind his car. "I will never listen to jazz again," was what he told everyone. "It's just dotted eighth notes anyway."

With Pickle out of the jazz jar, Hutt and his friends took over, and Calgary began to push for more and more avant-garde music. It was a little annoying, but at least Victoria knew where they stood and what they would go for. She also liked the new name for the society: Ujazz.

With her people skills, Victoria kept attracting volunteer labor and expertise in all the right areas. She diplomatically smoothed over tiffs between the different styles of jazz, patiently explaining the new thing to fusion-loving paperboys and then phoning the CBC jazz critic to argue his recent mild pan of a Dexter Gordon concert. Ten years later, she was put on salary to run the society all year long, planning both of the festivals that had once been just a daydream.

Overall impression: Victoria and jazz gave each

other life. She brought jazz to life in an area with no history of live jazz, and jazz turned what was at first a volunteer hobby into a well-paid profession. It was a positive turn of events that hopefully can serve as an inspiration to budding promoters.

Eventual outcome: Like a business running a nightclub, members of music society boards such as these like to throw their weight (and opinions) around.

Victoria, however, never reached a point of no tolerance with these people as she did with the various Canadian tobacco and liquor companies that began putting money into her festivals in return for heavy advertising in programs and print media. The name "Ujazz" was in much smaller print than the various musicians, and these in turn were dwarfed by the names of tobacco and booze brands.

These businesses, the only ones she had found that were remotely interested in sponsoring jazz, began sending PR reps to convince her that it would be much better to hold a really commercial jazz festival with big names, such as Chuck Mangione, Kenny G, the Gap Band, and Yamo Neeme. That was the year that Victoria told them to shove it, she wouldn't hold a festival with this kind of pressure.

The next year they asked her to do the festivals, anything she wanted to do. Just don't skip another year, they begged.

VARNA and the gang from the Vienna Kulturehall had to go down to the West Bahnhof to pick up the Chirpo Electronic Ensemble who were going to Budapest tomorrow. The Ensemble needed to get a visa to cross the Hungarian border (which, at that time, was still outfitted with barbed wire and guard towers). They had 50 minutes between the time the train arrived and closing time at the Hungarian Embassy some distance away.

Varna had two assistants scouting the station for foreigners pushing luggage carts. One was Suzy, a British teenager who had worked in Johnny's Bar in the Kulturehall since it opened last year. And the other was Michelle, who was tired of being teased about that stupid Beatles song.

The three of them finally located Chirpo and dashed over to the embassy. Luckily, there was no traffic. They got their visas and were happy . . . for a while.

At the Kulturehall, the Nazis had marched up from the southern Vienna train station, the Sudbahnhof. For the Nazis, it was business as usual: They shouted racial epithets and threatened to beat people up. At the head of a key intersection, the police had set up a barricade.

When the American band showed up, they got out of their taxis and gaped until they noticed some of the neighborhood louts were more interested in the Chirpo equipment than the standoff with the riot police. So they stored their equipment in the backstage facility and nervously began thumbing through their address books for somebody in Vienna to flee to until showtime.

When they returned, the near-riot had dissolved and the Kulturehall proved to have a high-energy club scene going strong. Four different bars each had their own ambience. It turned out to be one of the highlights of the tour, although everyone expected it to be the death of them.

Months later, the cops busted the Kulturehall "criminals" for "breaking into" the building that the city had forgotten about. After serving six months in jail, the gals got involved with a more legit club, M.O.Z. Some of the business interest in the place was coming from Russia, so the club naturally got involved in bringing in musicians from Russia and Eastern bloc countries. The M.O.Z. basement club room started making money and was able to attract some support from the city.

In the eleventh year of the program, Tharg, one of the main managers and money backers started acting hostile toward everyone else involved. Some viewed it as a power play by the Russians, others just the rise of an ego. In any event, it led to a mass defection from M.O.Z. by Varna and her friends and just about anybody else with positive energy.

As the weeks went on, Tharg blamed the rainy Vienna weather for the rotten turnouts and was forced to shell out guarantees to bands that the club had committed to before the defection. He really began to hate musicians. They drank the cheapest beer and would follow him around with their hands out late at night when he wanted to go to sleep.

He decided to start welching on the guarantees the same morning that Chirpo, with the same membership after 15 years, boarded a Vienna-bound train for a gig at M.O.Z.

When they arrived at the "under new management" club fourteen hours later, they were in shock.

"God, what happened?"

"Where is everybody? Nobody I know in Vienna is here."

"I heard there was a boycott of the club."

"I heard they ripped off the opening act!"

"I wonder if we'll get the guarantee."

"He's getting it out of the bank tomorrow," they were informed by the bandmember that did the business.

"We need it at 9 a.m. We've got to change it and catch the train."

"I told him I wanted it at 9 a.m.," Mr. Business said, knowing full well that at 9 a.m. tomorrow when everyone else was snoozola, he would be up pounding on the manager's apartment door.

Sure enough, Tharg's nightgowned wife answered the door. "He is sick. He has the influenza."

"We have to get our money."

Her face was sympathetic, yet practiced. "Come in please for a coffee." She made the coffee and strolled over and opened their bedroom door, waving her hand at a heap under some blankets. "Must we wake him?" she asked. While Business sipped coffee and mulled this over, she remembered an errand and rushed out, leaving him in the apartment.

Business started making long distance phone calls, something he did whenever he suspected a rip-off. Just as he dialed someone in Bolivia, the manager came rushing into the apartment, not sick in bed after all. "I thought you were sick."

"I am."

"I thought you were in bed, but you are up."

"Yes, I had business." But it obviously wasn't the band's business because when Business asked for the dough, Tharg still didn't have it. "I have it for you this afternoon," he said.

"I have to change some and buy train tickets."

"How much do you need for this?" he asked, jamming his hand in his pocket. Business ended up with his hands on about a tenth of the shillings that were due him for the gig.

He broke the news to the others when they finally got out of the rack. Over rolls and coffee, they planned to take a later train to be sure they got the money from the man they had now begun to hate.

"This place sure went downhill," was all they could say.

Overall opinion: You can never really count on getting paid. Even angry Nazis cannot stop a show or keep a guarantee out of a hot, sweaty musician's hands. And once again, we are reminded that you can't take for granted that a place will be the same every time you visit it.

Eventual outcome: By mid-afternoon, the notorious Tharg had settled into his office routine, announcing to the pacing paymaster that a M.O.Z. assistant was rounding up the money at the bank.

Tharg intentionally killed time until 3 p.m., knowing that the Americans wouldn't be aware that the banks closed then. At 3:10, he said to Business, "All right. What is it that I owe you?" Tharg had been holding the money in his pocket the entire time.

Arguing over the exact amount of the exchange, Tharg came up with 15 percent less than what the band had decided was the right figure, based on their own experiences changing money that week in Austria. There was no way to convince the Austrian, so Business took the money and rushed in the rain over to the local bank, which was closed. After finding several other banks closed, he realized what Tharg had done.

The band had no option but to make their way to the train station. Tharg figured that the Ensemble probably would not come looking for him, and if they did, there were a million and one little holes to vanish into in Vienna. There would be no way they'd ever find him . . . not them or any of those other lousy bands.

WESSE was proud of Spit. He called all his musician friends up and down the East Coast to brag about it and get them in on it. "It's not exactly a club. I just rented this rehearsal space. It's really big, though. You can set up a band at one end and then there's room for about 100 people to come in.

"Of course, I never expected that many people to come, and we don't always get that. But because there's so few good bars around here, all my friends and the friends of all the bands that practice here like to come over and listen to the music. The place is cool to hang out in, everyone brings some booze, it's just mellow."

Running a concert series was no problem. Taking up the door was resulting in some halfway decent pay for various touring groups, and since the town was right in the middle of two bigger towns that bands always played in, they could add an off-night at Spit with a transportation expense risk of only about $10.

Wesse played drums, so he was particularly thrilled Spit was going to host a solo recital by the fine Indian mridangam player, Trichy Ralpujni. The concert got off to a great start. They were over capacity with about 150 people, and Trichy was shaking, rattling, and rolling. Everyone was really into it until a crude, slimy version of "Whole Lotta Love" by Led Zeppelin came blasting through the walls from an adjacent studio.

The cut-rate sound system Wesse had assembled was promptly overwhelmed by this intrusion. Trichy stopped dead in his tracks, hands shaking. He had been performing for 25 years and been in many strange situations, including being in a field surrounded by Brahma bulls, but this was a first.

Unfortunately, Wesse had problems with confrontation. The realization that he was going to have to deal with the heavy metal band down the hall or lose his credibility as a concert organizer made him shake from head to toe. And the heavy metal guy's attitude (and the fact that he was quite a bit bigger than Wesse) was no help. He sort of pushed Wesse back down the hall so he could see for himself the huge audience that had been assembled.

"To see a guy from India, huh?" he sneered.

"Well, I got news for you. This is not a night we can lay off. We invited this chick singer, she came all the way down from Long Island. We gotta get ready for a battle of the bands."

The heavy metal guy went back at it while the audience moaned. Trichy made a short attempt to play over the band, but this was a hard combination to sell to the world music listener back then.

> [T]he bar did slightly better with the disco than with the live shows. He added up the difference over a year and realized it was the price of a Porsche.

Then, with a flash like a lightning bolt, the power went out. A fuse somewhere was blasted to smithereens by the excess machismo of the rock lead guitarist. A few seconds later, after a few giggles from the audience, Trichy was on his way again. In the dark now, but all rivals vanquished.

Overall opinion: Sound problems can definitely be the end of a club.

Eventual outcome: Wesse decided that because he lacked backbone, he would become part of a cooperative group to put on shows. He fell into a building where people were operating all kinds of enterprises including a soup kitchen, a drug counseling center, a tattoo parlor, and a weekend nightclub that had no closing time and brought in hundreds of people at $5 each.

The bands got a nice chunk of the cash, although, to be honest, the clientele was paying mostly to get a look at the strippers who hung around at the club after the places where they worked shut down.

One night, one of these paying customers turned out to be the tough guy from the heavy metal band Wesse had dealt with previously. "This your place?" he asked. Wesse nodded. The guy came back a little later, once he'd confirmed the place was as wild as he'd heard—in other words, once he'd seen a couple of strippers. "Sorry about what happened that one time," he said to Wesse. "I didn't think you were into anything besides that weird Indian music."

XANTHIPUR was a freewheeling, slightly pretentious hippie who lived in Boulder, Colorado, in the '60s. He and about a dozen of his musician pals shared an old house on Bluff Street, and some of the smart-asses in the neighborhood nicknamed it Woodstock.

One of the guys in the house, Otis, was deep into old-time blues and played harmonica and guitar and sang. He spent a lot of time in the summer set up on the front lawn, playing through the songs he knew.

A 13-year-old neighborhood kid began listening to his blues. Because he was frightened of the Woodstock house, the kid most often sat in the big drainage ditch at the side of the unpaved road, so he could hear what Otis was playing without having to be seen.

Xanthipur noticed the tyke one day and told Otis, "There's an audience for your music. Over there. In the ditch." Otis couldn't see anything and went back to "Mama Got Mad at Papa, He Wouldn't Bring No Coffee Home."

"Don't you get it? If you can attract a crowd into a ditch, just think what you could do in a place with chairs."

Around the corner from the Boulder Courthouse in the basement of some kind of insurance building, they found the place with chairs, which came to be known as the Xanthipurian Realm of the Mystic.

The neighborhood blues fan noticed the psychedelic sign painted on the glass door that led down to the Realm, but he tried the door for several weeks and it was always locked. Then one night he noticed a sign tacked to a telephone pole, advertising the Otis Taylor Blues Experience live at the Xanthipurian.

The show didn't start till midnight, so the kid killed time with Dr. Igor and *Creature Features*. Lon Chaney Jr. was on that night, which was a good omen for the evening.

He arrived at the Realm at a quarter to 12. It was still locked. He waited around. Nobody else showed up. Someone finally came up the stairs, unlocked the door, and pulled back a metal gate. The guy introduced himself, with no handshake. "I am Xanthipur."

The kid sat down at a table. There were maybe 20 seats. Three guys were set up to play. It was Otis plus another guitar and a bass. The other two guys might have lived at the Woodstock house, but the kid had never gotten close enough to the place to see the hippies' faces.

It was $2 to get in and 50 cents for a cup of weak tea. Nothing else was available. The kid listened until 4 a.m. He liked it, although it wasn't as good as when the guy played on the front lawn. The backup was weak.

Xanthipur didn't do much to put anybody at ease, but rather prowled around like one of the characters in the Lon Chaney Jr. movie. In fact, he looked a little bit like Chaney as Son of Dracula. Only six or so other people had come in. None of them talked to the kid.

Over the next few months, the kid went almost every weekend. Otis converted to a one-man band, then that broke up. The kid almost got up the nerve to sit in by playing along with Otis on a selection of tea cups with chopsticks. Xanthipur had even encouraged him. "Do it, man! He really needs you! He's not strong enough solo." But fear kept the kid from becoming the star blues teacup player he could have been.

The next act to come in for a long booking was a much more talented musician named Jimmy Towne. He said he was from somewhere in Texas and

> Players who lack hope and see only the endless obstacles, failures, setbacks, cancelations, and disappointments of music, take heed! Even war cannot damage the spirit and energy of a country's music scene.

played in two styles. One set was blues, along the lines of Lightnin' Hopkins or John Lee Hooker. Then he would break and come back with some condescending comments about how the blues were really too simple and now he was going to play something "much more complex." These were long instrumental raga things done with the guitar in various chordal tunings. The kid loved these pieces and became transfixed listening to different motifs Towne would refer to from concert to concert. But the guitarist's penchant for boastful comments at the end wrecked the mood. "Oh, that was really complex," was a typical example. "Now I'll do another of these complex pieces."

After Towne took off with a beautiful, complex blonde, the club booked a sitar player and a pianist, creating a kind of fusion of Indian and American improvised styles, although they spent most of the time playing cards, waiting for someone to come in.

The club had peaked in attendance figures during the Towne run. Now nobody was coming in anymore. The kid tried to get his junior high friends interested in this Xanthipurian realm, but they'd been so rowdy on the first visit that the manager had told the kid his friends weren't allowed anymore.

Eventually, the Woodstock house was sold to a family, and the kid sort of forgot about Xanthipur until he ran into him in the parking lot of a hamburger stand. By then, the kid was in high school.

"Hey, do you still have the club?" he asked.

Xanthipur looked at the ground. "Of course we do, but you don't come in anymore. I haven't seen you in a long time."

Immediately the kid felt guilty. He had just been blabbing to one of his friends about how there was nowhere to go hear music. As if reading his thoughts, Xanthipur started grousing.

"The reason there's no place to hear good music here is because nobody supports it. A good artist like Otis Taylor, and nobody comes to hear him. Can't even keep a band together. Do you know I had Otis back down there at the Mystic Realm for a three-week run, and we got four people total?"

"No," the kid admitted.

"He told me I should have had the club in the ditch, that would have made more sense. Ah, I'm going to close it," Xanthipur said. "There's no use. I can't stay in business." And with a "see ya," he got in his car and vamoosed.

Overall opinion: Xanthipur's rates highly because it is the first club of any kind I can remember going to, except for daytime all-ages rock band shows at Boulder campus bars such as the Sink. Readers can speculate whether the kid in the story is the author or perhaps someone else—such as hotshot Boulder guitarist Tommy Bolin.

Eventual outcome: The still active Otis Taylor says for a while Xanthipur would pop up in different parts of the country, each time with a new little club. Finally, though, Otis lost touch with him.

"He never made money," Otis said. "But the place in Boulder, that had to be the worst of all the businesses. I don't know how he kept that place open. They served that tea that was expensive to make. They watered it down a little, but still they barely broke even charging 50 cents for it. They gave the whole door to me. I think my record money-making night there was $48. I remember that because I lived on it for a month."

YELLOWSNOW adopted his nom-de-promoter because right away it established his top priority: Zappa, particularly late period Zappa. The earlier stuff was impossible to get in Romania because it had been released during the period when stuff like that had been heavily censored.

Like many of his friends, Yellowsnow had been educated as an engineer and worked now in an engineering firm. There was a hope that one day, great things would be built in Romania. For now, all they hoped for was to get the garbage cleaned up, especially psychological debris left over from the rule of the dictator Ceaucescu. "After the great earthquake in Bucharest, Ceaucescu was jealous," the story goes. "He wanted to show he could wreck buildings better than God could."

Yellowsnow's best guest to date was Clifton, an ex-Zappa sideman traveling to Bucharest to promote one of his new releases with the student radio. It wasn't quite Zappa, but there is a Romanian expression that sums up the sideman's status: I have met the man who has met the bear. Why the guy wanted to promote in Romania was a mystery, but Yellowsnow and his friends were thrilled that he was there.

In actuality, one of the guys in Clifton's band had borrowed so much money against his salary that there was no money left to travel on. They had to crap out in the middle of the tour, send everyone home, and leave the rented bus by the side of the road somewhere near Stuttgart to avoid facing the unpaid rental company. Since the rental company had pressed charges, the agent thought it might be smart for the guy to be in Romania, not realizing he was in more danger being a tourist there than he might somewhere else being hunted down by the police.

Yellowsnow was following his usual procedure for booking: Do nothing until the person actually shows up at the train station because it is hard to believe anyone will actually come to Romania even when they tell you they are. If they do arrive, you hope they are staying at least one week so there is time to organize something.

Gabriel, Yellowsnow's assistant, jumped out of the shower to the ringing phone.

"It's Clifton," the sideman said. "I've been at the station two hours. I had a hell of a time getting a coin for the phone. I had to ask a soldier to change money . . . "

"You asked a soldier?" Gabriel interrupted. "I don't believe you did this." It was insanity. Changing money was totally illegal, and asking a soldier to do it was like standing in line for the firing squad. It would take an hour to get down there and rescue this guy on the Bucharest subway, but he had to do it. When he got there, he asked Clifton how long he could stay.

"I gotta leave in six days."

"Six? I was hoping you could stay one week. Only then is it possible to organize something. But we try."

They met with Yellowsnow and several others and made a list of possible places, including a small theater, a coffeeshop in the engineering college, the student radio cafe, and the jazz school. It was all quite promising.

At the jazz school, Clifton did loose jam sessions, which he found interesting. The school was near the beautiful city park and accessible to other parts of the old city.

One day, after a meeting at the jazz school, Clifton found a wad of money on the ground.

"How is this possible?" Gabriel asked in amazement. "There is one thing that nobody in Romania loses. And that is money." The foreigner was suddenly Joe Moneybags around Bucharest.

The theater gig seemed like it was a go but it was eventually canceled when they received a phone call that the police had shut it down and surrounded it with "yellow police tape." When Clifton mentioned this to several jazz players at the school, they were incredulous. "This is impossible. There is a mistake. In Romania the police would never do this. We do not have yellow tape in Romania."

Meanwhile, things were coming together for other gigs, but none of them were happening until the last night of the trip. Then it seemed that the club would sponsor two gigs, the first at the radio cafe, then a rush across town to another one on one of the campuses sponsored by the drama club.

Actually it was sponsored by a mildly pornographic newspaper that one of the jazz players worked for. Only recently active because of the breakdown in censorship, the paper had such a hard time buying material to print they had to resort to running excerpts from Henry Miller and James Joyce. "Which is sort of great," the guy bragged. "These people are looking for smut and we trick them with literature."

The week continued with Clifton treating the Romanians to cab rides and Cokes. Nothing he had ever experienced could prepare him for Romania. Ceaucescu was gone, but the people were now in an economic straightjacket, which seemed no less restricting.

Every day new businesses descended on Romania, figuring out the best way to make money from its people. And Clifton engaged in strange conversations about the differences between Romanian cigarettes, which cost about one cent a pack, and "the Marlboro man," which equaled the average days' wages.

The student radio show was in a really odd neighborhood where wheelchair-bound amputees rolled around from one street card game to another. Others gambled on dart and roulette-type games at makeshift stands.

"This is your audience," Yellowsnow joked.

Actually, the audience was mostly American,

some of them from local relief agencies. Nobody bothered to sell tickets, so Clifton had no door take. But Clifton wasn't too upset about it.

They rushed on to the next gig, only to find themselves in an abandoned waiting room in a campus reception center. "Maybe they come in one minute," Gabriel said. There was a poster announcing the gig taped on the door of the building.

After a while, a man showed up with what must have been his class, about a dozen drama students. They took a look at the musician with his electronic keyboard and exchanged glances. "We await an important Italian stage director," Yellowsnow translated for Clifton.

After a quite serious discussion, it was understood that either the newspaper manager had been bluffing about the gig and had never contacted the drama department, or the drama guy was lying his brains out.

In the meantime, a pair of students that had seen the poster came in, interested in the concert. The drama teacher said it was impossible to hold the event there because they were awaiting the Italian director. "A concert is not possible simultaneous to this meeting."

Yellowsnow made a couple of calls and arranged a quick alternate plan. "Quick, we pack up the keyboard and this audience and ride the train to my friend's apartment." He had found a friend who would host the concert, provided the noise wouldn't bother the neighbors.

The new venue was a very small apartment. The woman lived there alone with her teenage daughter. The audience totaled seven. Clifton had 11 for the radio concert. So, he'd traveled all the way to Romania to play for 18 people. It reminded him of the years he had gigged in New York. The whole year dragged by with audiences of one, two, sometimes three. There were few gigs, and by the end of the year he'd played for 14 people total. "I did better in one night in Romania than a whole year in New York," he consoled himself.

He tried to sell a few of his recordings but was told, "Nobody in Romania has any money now, the Marlboro man has taken everything."

Overall opinion: This story is a kind of litmus test by which to judge all other concepts of touring disorganization, chaos, and, yes, outright insanity. If arrangements anywhere are as nutty as they are in Romania, you know you're in trouble.

Eventual outcome: Despite promises that Clifton's initial probe into the Romanian music scene would result in him being hired for "big money" Romanian festivals, there has been no further contact from Yellowsnow and his organization.

ZORAN used to greet foreign bands with "Welcome to Yugoslavia," then it was "Welcome to Slovenia." From his porch you could see the Adriatic coast winding around from Italy and the Gulf of Trieste. "On this side, there was always the border. On the other side, my country. Now, any way you look, there is a border. And a customs man. And soldiers."

In the '60s, Zoran was a familiar face to Yugoslavian rock fans. His band, Borek Jabba (in English this would be something like Frog Pastry, a nice band name), was the most important Yugoslavian rock band of this time. By the '80s, he lived in the town of Koper, which became part of a tiny swath of coast the Croatians were willing to let the Slovenians have. He was getting sick of watching the young people drift around aimlessly and was deeply committed to making a positive change in his own community. "They are learning nothing, eating and drinking everything. When there is nothing left, they will be too stupid to ask what happened."

He got a building to give them a place to go and rehearse a band, do or see a gig, put on film showings, have organizations and meetings, start a record library, anything. Originally, the place had been in ruins. And in Yugoslavia, no ruin is a mere ruin. "Everything is more ruined in Yugoslavia. Even now, we call this the ex-Yugoslavia. 'Ex' because ruined.

"To make a club in Yugoslavia is so ridiculous that every club is always either some kind of secret or something that they create out of nothing. You see the big truck that doesn't really fit into the alley?" Koper's streets were built for Roman times. "This truck is all the clubs of Yugoslavia—well, at least all of the clubs in Slovenia and Croatia. For so many tours, we are following the band around with the truck. When they get to the place they say, 'Where is the club?' I say, 'First we unload the truck.' When they see all the gear lying on the ground, I tell them, 'Take a look, that is the club.'

"In Pula, they must have my truck to have club. This is big summer resort or was before the war. Still, no sound systems, only my truck. Each time I must cross border now, and they go through truck for two hours. Every time, the same soldiers, the same guy driving, me, and the same truck, and the same two hours.

"Maybe worse is the Italian border, where they are going to enter all the parts of ex-Yugoslavia. Everything is scrutiny here, so each time we have a concert with non-Slovenian band, we have to worry that there is no concert. It is a great situation. You have the audience in the club ready for the concert, and a few meters away at the train station you have the band and all their equipment, and the soldiers saying, 'Oh, no. Today you cannot move the equipment into town for the concert.' Many concerts do not happen because the border crossing is not permitted."

One day, Zoran and his wife buzzed up to the Trieste station to meet the Ray Del Rey Blues Band, a backup unit for touring American blues soloists who were based out of Germany.

Ray Del Rey had already paid his dues on the Slovenian club scene. He'd thumbed through stacks of the pale Slovenian "tollars," writing down expenses in the millions of lira, converting it to dollars, changing the tollars into dollars and so on, the number at the bottom of the columns getting smaller and smaller.

A Yugoslavian expression proclaims the merits of "ending on a positive zero." This is a reference to prewar inflation when a container of yogurt would

> *He tried to sell a few of his recordings but was told, "Nobody in Romania has any money now, the Marlboro man has taken everything."*

cost 100,000,000 dinar and people calmly tossed stacks of currency into wishing wells. "I guess this is a positive zero tour," Ray told Zoran on his first trip to Yugoslavia.

Ray had come to play three Yugoslavian gigs, which he thought would be in Ljubjana, Belgrade, and Skopje. He knew he would be riding the trains a lot of the time, and that was fine by him; it was a good way to see the country first time through. When in Slovenia doing pre-gig publicity, though, he found out the other gigs had been canned because of "a lack of cooperation from the Serbians and the Macedonians."

"What about Skopje?" Ray asked.

Monika held up a handful of scribbled notes. "I have left 16 messages. I leave one again. I hoped your concert would be part of the science fiction convention they are having at the university, but the real science fiction is the idea to organize something between a Slovenian and a Macedonian."

A fill-in gig did come up, in the Nova Gorizia bunker described earlier. Nova Gorizia had been part of Italy until the division after World War II—or was it the other way around? Anyway, at some point there

had been just Gorizia, then they ran a border through it and called one side Nova, or "new." Italians and Slovenians who were local residents could wander back and forth without passports, just ID cards.

The strange thing about this gig was that the date it was booked for was ten years to the day since Ray had last played in Gorizia. Back then, Ray remembered, Tito's picture was still up in grocery stores, post offices, and hotel lobbies. He always wore a sky blue suit.

The dinars from that first trip were no longer in use the next time he toured. It took him a while to realize that they'd created a whole new currency since then and had set fire to the old one. People were sympathetic.

"When my grandmother heard they were changing the money, she announced she would never go out and buy anything again. So she just stayed in her room," a bus driver told Ray when he showed up in Split.

Ray snapped back to the current tour as the train pulled into Trieste. The Italian, Slovenian, and Croatian railways hadn't come to an agreement on how to establish a direct route down the Adriatic coast, so Zoran had to drive the band down there. But he was required to bring the truck anyway, or there would be no club.

Financial transactions were negotiated in deutsche marks because nobody seemed too serious about the new Croatian currency, the kuna, meaning weasel.

The next day, the band, Zoran, and the truck had crossed back over to Slovenia, witnessing something strange in the process. While they cooled their heels at the border, a strange guy pulled up, took two giant bottles of Sprite out of his trunk, carried them into the soldiers' offices, briskly came back out, and sped across the border.

"What the heck what that?" the ever-observant Ray asked.

Zoran seemed only slightly interested. "Typical Croatian and Slovenian border transaction."

"What, is Sprite illegal or something? Is he bribing them with Sprite?"

"Maybe something else is in the bottles, not soda."

"Some kind of explosive?"

Zoran nodded. "They say that Bosnia is full of weapons and explosives. There are only a few places where it comes through. This is one of them. If they have the supply it is said they do, it is only possible if the stuff is coming through here all day long, every few minutes. Otherwise the war in Bosnia would run out."

The band had to get to another Slovenian/Croatian border area, this one in the mountains. The train that went there was full of warnings not to stick your head or hands out the window because the terrain was too dangerous.

Zoran wasn't needed because this place had its own sound system. "This Illistrice Bistrice is one of the better organized clubs in the ex-Yugoslavia," he assured the band before sending them on their way.

They did find the club lively, and Ray was fascinated by the war stories associated with Illistrice Bistrice. This was where the armistice had been signed between the Allies and Italy. In fact, the club they were playing had been the old USO club, and the signing had been done in the spot that would have been a dressing room if anyone ever got around to removing all the discarded furniture, boxes, and amplifier shards that were stacked to the ceiling.

This had also been one of the flash points in the infamous seven-day war between Slovenia and Yugoslavia. Slovenians who got off lightly compared to other independence-seeking ex-Yugo states liked wallowing in guilt about the whole war. "I'm afraid we started it," was a typical Slovenian comment. "The entire war is the fault of Slovenia, we were the first to go."

Another local described how his unit of draftees had been sent to defend or, if necessary, destroy the border station in their neighborhood. "We were in the Yugoslavian army unit, but we knew that we were seceding from Yugoslavia so we didn't have to follow the orders. We knew the Slovenians would be taking over the border station, so we did a nice thing and cleaned it for them."

The final night's gig was somewhere in a village in the mountains, again close to the Croatian border, this time at the edge of the mountainous Krajina region. It had been Serbian territory, but the Croatians had just recently taken it back. It is ridiculous terrain, as if some cosmic force had taken a mountain chain and tried to make pretzels out of it. A few farm houses were scattered hither and yon, and the signpost for the town proclaimed a population of 119.

A Dutch band on the bill showed up. They looked the place over. "Where's the club?" they asked. Inside the meeting hall was a stage but nothing else resembling a club. It doubled as a basketball court and some locals were playing.

Everyone watched the sun go down and waited for Zoran to show up with the truck. After a truly awesome sunset, lights started sparkling around the valley. A truck rumbled up the hill and stopped at the church. Zoran tumbled out of the front seat. The Dutch surrounded him, asking, "Where's the club?" Local volunteers were already unloading.

"The club is on the ground," Zoran said. "But we can move it anywhere."

A third band that was made of guys from the village was also scheduled. Thanks to them, there was a guaranteed audience.

"This is an important night," the local promoter said. "Because for one year there has been a ban on these concerts. It is because somebody took paint and turned a directional sign into a satanic crucifix." The guy drew the symbol on the ground with a stick. In the villages they said this showed the music was turning the kids into demons.

"Now, they have forgiven," Zoran said. The neighbors did seem to be going about their business as usual, including shutting out the lights and going to bed.

Some people in the audience were refugees from Bosnia. Del Ray at first thought they were asking for free goods when they approached the merchandise table and told him where they had come from. Instead they just wanted to know if he took deutsche marks.

"It's funny that those war refugees have money to spend on CDs," Ray said. A tall guy with black hair approached the table.

"Do you remember me, Ray?" he asked.

He did look familiar. It turned out that this was a Sarajevo organizer whom Ray had dealt with in his last visit here. Ray remembered spending a day with him and really liking him. "You know since the war started, I tried to write you," he told the Bosnian. "The letters were returned to me. And then someone in Germany told me you were dead. I heard that from somewhere else, too."

For musicians of Ray's generation, the Yugoslavian fighting was the first time war had broken out in one of their touring patches. He was used to wondering whether last year's promoters were dead or alive, but not for these reasons.

When most of the lights in the hills had been turned off and only a few cars were left to illuminate the parking lot, the lone streetlight turned off and the light in front of the church dimmed. Blackness and quiet enveloped everything, even the mountains. Distant booming sounds might have been mortars blasting in the Krajina or just reverberations of gigs past.

Overall opinion: The blues band returned home with only a little bit of money, but in terms of hope it was a big payday. Rick had shaken the hand of a fellow he thought was dead.

Eventual outcome: An expanding network continues to build up the Slovenian and Croatian club scene. Musicians see the standoff between Serbia and the ex-Yugoslavian states as a challenge to keep communication open and exchanges of music going; a determination that has also spread around the European music scene. Bands have gone to great personal risk and trouble to go on tour in these areas, some of them developing intricate routes on small roads that bypass the big checkpoints.

Players who lack hope and see only the endless obstacles, failures, setbacks, cancelations, and disappointments of music, take heed! Even war cannot damage the spirit and energy of a country's music scene.

CHAPTER 2

Welcome to My Worldwide Community of Musicians

Who are these people? Don't tell me you've never heard of any of them! You know, one of the things I like most about my days is wondering who I am going to hear from and where the voice will be coming from.

I have friends, or at least contacts of some kind, in every European country, west and east. Lately, a musician from Chile has been writing to me. Last week a letter came from Taiwan. When the phone rings, I never know whether it is going to be a fax dispatch from Australia or Japan or a local friend.

It literally *is* a worldwide community of musicians. Because of my experiments combining various genres, I hear from friends who play lots of styles. One caller might make me laugh with her amusing accounts of a London concert conducted by the great but aging Yehudi Menuhin. Then a bluegrass banjo player will be on the line, only to be interrupted by some fringe character from a bizarre world of music that hasn't even been labeled yet. I love all these friends and contacts. I got them by being unpopular. Remember that.

For me, it all began when I was taking my first steps toward professionalism in the '70s and reached out to the European avant-garde and free-improvised scene. It wasn't an offhand gesture or impulse; it was a matter of musical desperation that's so common it's become a tradition.

The music I was playing had grown out of, or been heavily influenced by, the world of jazz. Jazz is great American music that is neglected in America. (Sorry, seeing people in suits holding tenor saxophones in liquor and cigarette advertising is not an example of the music finally receiving recognition!) Ever since this music began, players were forced to tour Europe in order to make ends meet and, more importantly, to feel appreciated. Many great jazz players simply moved to Europe and never came back.

With my kind of music, all I could do for promotion or gig-searching was to write letters to all the possible USA contacts. That took a couple of afternoons. After that, there was nothing left to do but figure out how to cross oceans.

Europe. Japan. Players of all styles of music naturally set their sights on international work. In most cases, it is because the music is not "popular" enough at home to keep them there. With any kind of specialized music, the segment of the public that is interested enough to provide support grows and diminishes in numbers as new generations are born. When I was in high school, being interested in real blues as opposed to Led Zeppelin cover versions was considered totally freaky. Nowadays, blues is a popular interest among young and old, and there is more enthusiasm for pure blues artists than for white, long-haired blues cover artists.

Poland

December 1, 1986

Eugene Chadbourne
Covington, GA.

Dear Eugene,

Hi! I really love listen to the Country Music
and read about its Artists. I'll with your assisting know
better Country Music. I have been interesting them almost
10 years, but still my knowing about nicest Music across
the World is really poor. I still never heard your sound.

I would like to ask you if you could send me picture of
yourself, discography + bio, fan button and an magazine about
Country Music. It would be greatly appreciated.

Perhaps you possible to send mealso yourself Album COUNTRY
PROTEST (I think it is most interesting). But please do not
inconvenience yourself for me, I know it might be most expensive.
However, I hope you can help me, because our stores do not offer
Country Music Albums and our radio play it very rare.

Unfortumately, I am unable to purchasing any Albums in the
USA, because I have not any money (US $$$ currency) to do it.
So, I thank you from all my heart in advance for your inter-
national goodwill and trouble in this matter. Many thanks!

Wishing you all the best of health and happiness everyday
and much goldies, platiniums and glory forever. God bless you
and yours always. Have a Merry Christmas and a Happy New Year.

Warmest regards,

A man from Poland reaches out: His closing has brought me good luck for years.

In 1986, the only way avant-garde musicians could make people listen to their music was to tie it to a rock beat and sell it as "new wave" or "punk." In 1996, interest in avant-garde music of all persuasions experienced a resurgence among college listeners. On every campus, there seemed to be bright yet twisted minds searching for neglected geniuses. Also, back then very few new wave or punk fans were interested in country or folk music. Now a lot of them are.

The point is that whether a style of music is "in" or "out" according to the public, musicians are driven to communicate with each other and form bonds. It's the nature of the profession. Again, I must stress that desperation and unpopularity provide the most impetus, but these bonds circle the globe. It is a United Nations minus disagreements about politics, religion, and national boundaries.

It is amusing how many young musicians buy into this frustrating dream of "making it big" and becoming someone that "everyone has heard of." This dream ends up crushing most of them because it is just not going to happen. Yet there is a reality that seems much better than that silly dream, and the reality is that one can become part of a supportive international community simply by sending out a few letters. This isn't just a matter of having a lot of strange stamps to paste into scrapbooks.

If playing music is actually going to be a main part of your life, these friends will become your support network; they will help you in times of trouble. If you are selfish and don't like giving your time and energy, don't go around introducing yourself to musicians who come through town to perform or get stranded. They will very likely turn to you and say, "Do you know where I can get the bridge on this fiddle repaired? Who is good at soldering pickups around here? Do you know how to get there? Do you have a car? Our van is broken down." And so forth.

Once I dragged a bass player around Göteborg, Sweden, all day because he was crazy enough to introduce himself to me. The pickup on my banjo had gone out and needed replacing, I had complicated train reservations to look into, and there were several other problems for which I needed local assistance. "Thank you so much for giving up your entire day to me. I made you run around everywhere," I told this gentle, patient fellow when it was all over. (Well, almost all over. It was time to wolf down a dinner before soundcheck.)

"Oh, it's nothing," he said graciously. "It is part of being a musician. I will come to your town one day and do this to you." I am still waiting for him, but he's right, I am ready to give up my day for him or another of my contacts in trouble. This is part of what it is to be a player.

Another part is to understand when a musician turns down requests for help in similar situations. Sometimes people are just under too much pressure to drop their own responsibilities to help people get around a strange town repairing things and making arrangements. Rest assured, though, that wherever you go, you will find someone to help you if you need it, and the help will be provided, for the most part, because you are a musician.

The better the music you make, the more help you will get, by the way. This is one motivation to make really good music. Some readers may become perplexed at the thought that a musician might need reasons to make really good music. I mean, don't they just want to do it, anyway?

I will attempt to prove that the public's war on good music is so destructively influential that just the opposite motivation prevails in many players' heads. Philosophies such as, "There is no point to making good music," "Good music is wasted on the public," "The worse the music, the more people are there," and of course, Frank Zappa's immortal lines, "The public wouldn't know good music if it bit them on the ass."

The reality is that good players need reasons to keep making their music better and better. Reasons they can think about when the struggle is really getting to them. The chance to communicate and make friends with people all over the world is one of the greatest opportunities that a person can have. Surely many of the problems threatening the world are because most people have no access to other cultures or even a reason to think about them.

While most Americans were happy to have clouds of misinformation floating around in their brains concerning life behind the Iron Curtain, I used to actually go there, talk to people, and see what it was really like. This didn't mean I was able to save the world. It just meant that, personally, I made real connections in a situation where most people were simply isolated. This happened only because I was making music. These kinds of contacts make the world a better place, and in a small way, they help to counterbalance every phony "nuclear weapons proliferation treaty" or "international conference on nerve gas."

International contacts lead to international work and the chance to travel. For many American musicians, it is the chance to play music in a better setting because, for reasons we will look into, the war on music is less successful in some foreign cultures, particularly Europe but other continents as well.

And although not everyone gets to travel to remote parts of Africa and Asia, studying traditional roles of music in these cultures is truly enlightening. Just reading about a place where someone who plays a good drum solo can become the focal point of an entire village's attention, yet is not elevated to the phony and destructive lifestyle of a star, should be enlightening to any player. It is something you can think about the next time some joker leaning over a bottle of beer shouts, "Put the jukebox back on!" during a drum solo.

You should feel good knowing that a drummer somewhere in Burundi is part of the same international community of musicians as you are. As is the old accordion player sloshing through the streets of Reykjavík, Iceland, to see if the compact discs he put on consignment in a local store have sold. (He seems

> **[M]usicians are driven to communicate with each other and form bonds. It's the nature of the profession.**

not to have read my chapter on such enterprises.) As is every punk rocker, every classical music student, every composer of commercial jingles. We are all in this together.

Are you all alone, sighing at the word "together" like it is only a remote possibility? Nobody in the cafeteria will talk to you? Do research. Let's say you are interested in electronic music. You own a couple of cheap synthesizers you happened to see being unloaded at Al's Electronics. These are hopelessly out of date, you are told. But you are a weirdo, and this is the first thing anyone has said to you in a week, so you don't care.

You have been making tapes on your new old machines for a few months, but the two friends you have would be more interested if you were working on an alphabetical list of skin diseases.

Go to a record store, a good one that is not part of some chain, and look for music that is similar to yours, whether it is electronic or Inuit throat singing. There is a good chance that this music is unpopular and the recording you are holding has been sitting in the shop for a year. If you can't buy it, write down the address of the record company. As we will be discussing, the record company may actually be a box under someone's bed. Whoever put this record out might very well answer whatever letter you write. Sometimes they are happy to provide lists of other contacts, or often the musician has put out their own record and will write back to you.

Three weeks after I sent out copies of the first album I ever pressed, I received three flattering letters back from some of the players I admired most in the world. It can do a lot to offset the senseless abuse one will receive at the hands of the public. Do this with ten CDs, and your mailbox becomes stuffed.

Before you know it, you are linking up with people. Certainly you can find some kind of magazine or publication that deals with your music interest. There is someone publishing something about every kind of music in existence, no matter how unpopular or esoteric. In fact, the more unpopular it is, the easier it is to get the participants to communicate with you because they are reaching out in desperation. To many, it's like spreading the gospel. Publications about esoteric music tend to be filled with contacts, people writing in practically begging others to write back. Some of these people can become lifelong friends. They have in my case.

Some of the contacts I made like this years ago were totally unknown when I first met them but, two decades later, are now well-established in the music business with loyal followings of their own. So, communicating with other musicians is obviously of importance to the stardom-struck as well.

You can also volunteer for a radio station shift or become similarly involved. You will have access to a huge amount of incoming published and recorded material of many musical styles. Again, addresses, addresses, addresses. Write to people! They will write back! This kind of correspondence is of paramount importance for every type of work activity in music. A few years ago they started calling it networking, but people have been doing it all along in music and in many other businesses as well. The Yiddish word for it is "schmoozing," although this is more accurately a particular style of networking and communication.

This type of communication provides you with an inner strength that won't be found in other enterprises where "profit" and the "bottom line" are the ultimate motivators.

Sure, I will say time and time again that any musician who wants to keep playing music has to figure out how to make it profitable. Just about anyone you communicate with will have this going through their heads. But because you are in the international community of musicians, you are going to contact people who will be interested in you just because you make music, not because that music is more profitable than someone else's.

Oh, they might answer your letter a little faster if they think you are really doing well. People are people, and people need their dollars, lira, guilders, francs, marks, dinar, or whatever. In the music community, though, you can always get past this and obtain respect and admiration simply for being dedicated to what you are doing and for putting your love and sweat into it regardless of the financial outcome.

Get to know these people, let them into your lives, keep in touch with them as you grow old. You are going to need them, not just to help you find a good repairman in Zagreb, but because they are the only people you are going to come in contact with who, purely and simply, respect creativity.

CHAPTER 3

What's Good About Music?

I do not want to be overly cynical about the possibility of meeting people who are supportive of musicians. Do I really mean that a musician sending off letters to Burundi, Croatia, El Salvador, or Iowa is the only way to meet anyone who is not disrespectful, condescending, over-demanding, and never satisfied in their attitude toward musicians? Yes. The exception might be someone you meet in your own hometown. There might be someone else there who is as much an outcast as you are because of their creative urges. You might even wind up in a band with someone like this. The point is that you are going to have to seek out your peers.

This might be a dark and disturbing way to begin a chapter that asks the question, "What's good about music?" But we are going to examine the public view of music as well as the role music plays in everyone's life. And a lot of this discussion is negative, negative, negative. Some of this energy comes from musicians, but most of it comes from the public and the media that pulls the strings. So it is important to emphasize the "everything good" aspect of music.

Having already established that no one is going to get rich and famous, there's bound to be the question, "What's the point?" Other than starvation, disrespect, and endless reminders of one's anonymity, the answer is that music is a positive activity, something for the good of all of us. Maybe it sounds like an epistle from dippy (thanks, Donovan) that one should feel proud of doing something for the good of mankind, but what else is there? Believe me, when you reach middle age, you are going to want to have something to look back on and feel proud of. Big financial scores diminish as soon as the money is spent. (Often this is six months before the check arrives.) Major artistic accomplishments such as CD releases or special concerts might linger in someone's memory or bring back a glow now and then, but they are, for the most part, not endlessly recyclable as recollections of grandeur.

Let's look at music and all its positive energy. I'll start with my own beginning with music. I can remember hearing music in the house as far back as my memory goes. I remember wanting to play music when I saw the Beatles on TV. Actually, I wasn't thinking about anything other than my game of army being interrupted. My brothers insisted on stopping our game to go in and watch them because they'd heard a buzz about it at school. My decision came the next day at school when I heard girls talking about the Beatles.

All my friends thought they were totally stupid, couldn't believe the haircuts, and had "no comment" on the music. The girls, though, thought the Beatles were cute. Which they really weren't (at least not all of them). But their music made them cute. I realized that, for once, girls were showing an interest in something that guys were doing besides being good at sports or being big and tough. This was a major thing for me because I had been failing in both the sports and the tough department. By having a guitar, girls became interested in me. This might all seem trivial in retrospect unless one looks at the big picture.

The social revolution in the '60s opened up avenues for many people who had been outcasts. Suddenly they were getting attention. This wasn't the beginning of this phenomenon by any means. It was just the first time I had noticed it. It is very important for children to find acceptance and peer admiration through a variety of possibilities.

Now I tell parents that when their children become interested in music, they are entering a field that has the potential to provide them with enriching experiences that will continue for their whole lives. They can make friends around the world (see "Welcome to My Worldwide Community of Musicians" chapter). Above all, they will be on a positive track because music, no matter what it is about, is creative; and creativity is a positive outlet.

Society creates wars between "good" music and "bad." This is an essential part of the War on Music waged by the public, the media, and all other aspects of society. This all-encompassing assault on creativity exists in the relationship between society and all the arts. It is not just musicians who have the right to whine about it. This idea of good and bad should be tossed out the window by anyone interested in being a musician. It is as useful as a race car driver looking only in his rear-view mirror while going 120 miles an hour.

There are no "correct" judgments about good and bad when it comes to music. This is one of my essential philosophies, and I call it "No Correct Judgments." All music is good. We are talking about the general aspect of making music. Whether it is a filthy song that no radio station will play or something so popular that everyone is sick of it but no radio station will stop playing. It is all good because it is music.

Religious fanatics and other social zealots will say that this is wrong. A song about killing police needs to be censored. The record companies releasing this kind of music encourage and often stimulate this kind of negative attention because the media is much more interested in attacks such as this then in the dull, boring, day-to-day creative life of musicians. The act of killing police is bad. But songs, books, films, TV shows, etc. are creative representations. They cannot be considered bad on their own.

The same goes for music commonly labeled as "smut." It is no worse than the score to *The Sound of Music*. The two musical activities are both forms of creativity. They are not even aimed at different audiences. I don't have to go far to find someone who likes both types of music equally. I simply have to walk down the hall to one of my daughter's bedrooms and I will find someone who loves "My Favorite Things" as much as the absolute filth created by recording artists such as Adam Sandler. The point is that both of these musical creations are equal when looked at in a certain way.

In every style of music, there are those artists who are exalted, placed high on pedestals, and praised. To have a really good attitude, however, musicians should be able to accept and appreciate the work of all other musicians, whether it is a master musician with 50 years experience or a newcomer who plans to start studying music seriously after they've released a dozen recordings and made it big so they never have to work again.

The general public seems quite enamored with musicians as individuals. When isolated in a one-on-one conversation, I have the impression that people are more interested in me because I am a musician than they might be if I cleaned gutters. Social reactions to various occupations are quite predictable, of course. If you announce, "I'm a musician," you will next hear these questions:

"What instrument do you play?"

"What kind of music do you play?"

"Where do you play?"

"Have you made any records?" (Despite the so-called victory of the CD in the marketplace, hardly anybody will ask if you've made a compact disc—even kids.)

Some questions also have categories of sub-comments. With "what instrument," you will be told about someone else that plays it. Here is where it is an asset to play one of those instruments few others play, such as sitar, oboe, contrabass clarinet, or valhila. If you answer "guitar," you are going to hear, "You know who I really like? Eric Clapton!" This is only offered up because the task of listing all the family members and/or friends who play guitar is too daunting.

As for style, I have been stuck all my life telling people that I don't know what my style is or that I play lots of styles. I used to like saxophonist and composer Oliver Lake's answer to the "what kind?" question: He would say, "the good kind." However, this is in direct opposition to other philosophies that have been expressed only paragraphs away, so I would never say this is the only good answer.

If you are versatile, you can always answer the question with another question: "What kind of music do you like?" Then, whatever they say, you say you play that kind of music. Hopefully there won't be an instrument handy and you won't be asked to demonstrate.

The "where do you play?" question may get you the most admiration if you travel. I find that telling Americans that you go to Europe regularly produces waves of jealousy and people never treat you the same again. Most people are so frustrated in their attempts to see the world that they become incredibly envious of someone who gets paid to travel, no matter what problems they might have as a result. Don't bother trying to tell anyone about the problems of a traveling lifestyle. They don't want to hear it. One friend tells me he "lives vicariously" through me. Of course, he would never want to live vicariously through six-hour practice days, canceled gigs of great financial importance, or other business and/or artistic frustrations. Names of foreign cities and comments like, "It was great!" are what these people want to hear.

The "have you recorded?" question produces reactions of intense curiosity if answered positively. Once a musician admits to having done anything remotely professional, a great skepticism fills the air because, in most cases, the person "hasn't heard of you" and for some reason considers this important. This is where you get into problems with public perception. It is something to pay attention to, think about, and come to grips with because it is not going to go away unless you actually become so famous that everyone has heard of you. What would it take for most people you have met to have heard of you? Let's examine this.

There is only one musician I have ever worked with whom I could honestly say most everyone has heard of, at least in the USA. That would be the late Tiny Tim, with whom I collaborated on the 1995 CD release, *I Love Me.*

There are many reasons I was thrilled to work with Tiny Tim. He was a brilliant singer, musician, and musical historian, as well as a really eccentric character. The public's identification with him, however, is based on none of these things, nor does it have to do with his fantastically successful career. Yes, Tiny Tim worked right up until the end, but it was the type of work that the big music biz types scoff at: singing songs for obscure baseball teams at half-time and wandering around signing autographs at state fairs and small clubs. Despite his great fame, he was

not paid that well and lived in simple Holiday Inn hotel rooms.

But everyone has heard of him, because of his one attention-getting act: On Johnny Carson's *Tonight Show,* he got married to a girl who wasn't yet

> *Once a musician admits to having done anything remotely professional, a great skepticism fills the air because, in most cases, the person [you're talking to] "hasn't heard of you" and for some reason considers this important.*

out of her teens. Following a logical train of thought, we should realize that the public remembers people mostly for stupid or horrible reasons.

Many of my friends say I am "a prophet without honor" in my hometown. This means nobody has heard of me and no attention is paid to my musical accomplishments. If I wrote a symphony tomorrow and it was a masterpiece, I could not call the newspaper or local TV stations and expect coverage. In fact, they would laugh at me. But if I burned my house down while my children snoozed away, then suddenly my name and photograph would be broadcast throughout the world. I would be a musician that everyone had heard of!

Charles Manson was a songwriter (and let's remember our promise not to make quality judgments). If a big Hollywood producer had not turned him down, he could have become a recording star in the '60s and '70s. This also leads to speculation that perhaps none of the horrible crimes he planned and his minions carried out would have happened had he been able to release his frustrations through music.

I don't have a comment on this, but one thing is certain: If Charles Manson had become a recording artist, even made a few hit records, and never been involved with murdering anybody, most people would not have heard of him today. There would be zilch interest in him. If he had been the greatest classical composer alive, nobody would care. But being a murderer is different. Everyone has heard of you and wants details on every little thing you do.

So the next time someone says, "Why haven't I heard of you?" you can always answer "Because I haven't killed anyone." Like many things in our world, this is sad but true.

Music remains important to people, of course. Many people will tell you they love music. They want it on in the background no matter what they are doing. "Whistle while you work," we are told, it makes life easier. People want music at their weddings and funerals, making at least two (count them) instances when people are willing to pay musicians without a lot of argument.

People remember what song was playing during their first kiss. In fact, most people have dozens of memories attached to music. Memory association, how a bar of music can recreate so many emotions and thoughts so vividly, is fascinating.

Are people capable of watching films or TV, something that occupies who knows how many millions of hours for zillions of people, without a music soundtrack? The people who make these cinematic masterpieces don't seem to think so. Advertisers think a good song can sell a product, and they are right.

"A good tape deck makes a car," I was told by none other than the world's expert on stripping and rebuilding cars, Bobby McDermott. He said this with Hendrix at Woodstock blazing in the background. Here is a guy who spends every waking hour either fiddling with greasy parts or wiping grease off. And in his final analysis, the ability to listen to music on a really good sound system is what makes a car really special.

This year I laughed when I read about how the record industry was in a panic because, for the first time since World War II, their numbers had come to a dead halt. Overall sales for 1996 were just about the same as 1995. I think the number was in the billions, although I can't say for sure because I torched the clipping on my little "Cry Me a River" altar. Do these sobbing CEOs and A&R people realize that, in ancient times, music was classified as part of the quadrivium?

"The who? I haven't heard of them! Send me a demo package!" would be their response.

"Quadrivium. Those were the four essential sciences dealing in measurement."

"Uh, I have a call on the other line!"

As part of the quadrivium (love that word!), music was joined with geometry, astronomy, and mathematics. No one doubted that music was an accurate and reliable science of measurement then. Science and music were once so closely linked that it was impossible to study the history of modern music theory without bumping into scientists.

The greatest classical composer to emerge from Greece in contemporary times, Iannis Xenakis, was also a master mathematician. The second century astronomer Ptolemy, whose concept of the planetary system was accepted for more than 1000 years, was also the author of the primary work on Greek music theory. Ptolemy's book, in turn, was the main source of information for many other books on music theory that followed. There were also the geometry whiz Euclid, the physicist Huygens, and the mathematician Euler, all of whom wrote works on music theory.

> *In ancient Greece, the Spartans, renowned masters of war, liked having certain types of music blasted at them before they attacked because supposedly it made them numb to pain. An early form of heavy metal?*

Then we get to Kepler and the three basic laws of planetary motion, a revelation that kicked off the 17th century in fine style. He had a serious background in music theory, and my research indicates he would never have developed any serious theories without it!

In 1952, the great German composer and writer Paul Hindemith, to whom I am indebted for many of these historical facts, wrote in his book *A Composer's World, Horizons, and Limitations:* "It may well be the last word concerning the interdependence of music and the exact sciences has not been spoken." Of course, by then, music had been watered down (maybe we should say liquored up) from part of an esteemed group of essential sciences to just another sport that the public gets to go ga-ga over.

If, instead of asking you how your work measuring the universe is going, people ask, "Have you made any records? Why haven't I heard of you?" they are confirming this. They are expressing a certain social philosophy, without even realizing it. To society, the only possible point of carrying a creative act such as composing or recording to its completion is a desire to be rich and famous. Those that do these things without achieving this end are failures.

None of this is expressed out of any great concern for the musician, either. It's not like they are saying, "Oh, you seem like a really nice person, and I wish you could be living in a mansion and making 60 million a year." No, it is just selfish. They just want to be able to go somewhere and say, "Hey, guess who I met! That guy that makes records, you know, he's really famous."

Let's forget these shreeves asking questions. What we are really saying is that music, once considered an important science, is now merely a form of entertainment, classified by elite snobs as "cultured" or "uncultured." If it could be packaged in little plastic containers and eaten with a spoon, they would do it. In fact, they are probably working on it right now.

Live musical events have degenerated into fashion shows, whether it is dressing up for the symphony or dressing down to hear Megadeth. "Underground" music achieved its nickname because when you are talking about the audience that goes to seriously listen to music, you are talking about a group of people that will fit into someone's basement.

Hindemith describes how, in the philosopher Boethius' times, musicians would be "classified according to their intellectual and scientific abilities." Nowadays the public makes these types of judgments about musicians:

"He has a nice ass. It looks good in jeans." (From a CNN pre-concert interview with Bruce Springsteen fans in Wales.)

The public makes judgments based on non-musical phenomenon. The concept of the "one hit" artist or musical fads, records that are in everyone's house one day and then headed to the used record pile the next, are indications that thousands of people bought and listened to a certain musical creation for some other reason than actually really liking the music.

If you want to be a serious musician and not become popular because of your looks or allegiance to a certain trend, then you will engage in some form of study, organized or non-organized, so that those that do take music seriously will be able to form a positive opinion of you based on your "artistic" activities. This can keep you busy your whole life, running around trying to be considered artistically essential to universities, critics, music festival organizers, and record companies while trying to keep up practicing scales, sight-reading, ear-training, harmony, orchestration, etc.

The present day musician seems as unconnected to the past as a robin redbreast is to an extinct dinosaur, although scientists will tell you they have a couple of bones in common. (And some of these scientists have cute butts!)

Other roles have been assigned to musicians throughout history, too. When we come to Plato—

"The Plates? Haven't heard of them! Can you send a demo package?"

In Plato's Dialogues—

"Is that his new CD? Can we get a promo copy?"

The way Plato sees it, a musician is here to create neither entertainment, measurements, nor positive energy. If you play an instrument, sing, or compose, your job is to help the government educate the people to be better citizens because Plato felt music had some kind of ethical power.

"Fortunately, Plato's Republic has remained theory," Hindemith wrote, but he lived in the times before Jesse Helms and the attacks on the National Endowment for the Arts.

It is ironic that the more seriously a form of music is taken in our society, the more rigid controls are placed on it. Classical music is considered the highest form of musical culture in our society. The massive publishing administration bureaucracy has only two labels for music: "serious" and "other." Only music that can somehow be described in classical music terms be considered serious.

Of government support for music, the lion's share goes to classical music. This is true on an international level. No other music even comes close. You are supposed to "dress up" and "look nice" for a classical concert. The musicians dress up even nicer. If you don't, it is enough of a publicity gimmick to launch an entire career. (As in violin virtuosi with pierced tongues.)

A star system involving conductors and guest virtuoso soloists also results in the members of the orchestra being viewed as cattle. Or, more accurately, their value as individuals is on a par with whatever slave hauled the 7896th piece of sandstone up to the 12th level of King Tut's pyramid.

When music is taught to children in our school systems, it is usually classical or band marching music. Is it because these forms of music require heavy discipline and involve no personal freedom, or is that just a coincidence?

In high school, the main purpose for learning to play classical music seems to be to turn off as many people as possible to so-called "serious" music by making them all practice and listen to it being played out of tune. There are many forms of music that sound good out of tune, but introduce them to a high school curriculum and you'll wish you were the librarian that put *My Secret Life* on the shelf.

As for marching band music, I happen to like it, but let's face it: Is there a more militaristic, over-organized form of music in existence? I think not. Let's not forget that it wasn't so long ago that marching bands actually accompanied troops into battle. In ancient Greece, the Spartans, renowned masters of war, liked having certain types of music blasted at them before they attacked because supposedly it made them numb to pain. An early form of heavy metal?

Leave school and you will see that everywhere you turn, music has been sucked into some kind of repressive activity, such as the entire lust for fame and stardom making so many people feel like they are failures. Many of them give up music, then. Good, society says! You were no good anyway. I had never heard of you.

> In high school, the main purpose for learning to play classical music seems to be to turn off as many people as possible to so-called "serious" music by making them all practice and listen to it being played out of tune.

The ones that do achieve some kind of success do not become role models to others to be creative or pursue original ideas. No, they become admired for their wardrobes, cars, fancy houses, and touring entourages. More enticement to abandon creativity for commerce. Good, society says! Let's do some business!

Alright, if we have to. Today I'm in the business of selling evidence that no matter how hard society tries to push it away, creativity is here to stay. It's time to put the "closed" sign on the door, but before I do, I have great bargains on two of my favorite quotes. In fact, you can have them for free:

> I hate a song that makes you think that you are not any good. I hate a song that makes you think that you are just born to lose. Bound to lose. No good to nobody. No good for nothing. Because you are too old or too young or too fat or too slim.
>
> Too ugly or too this or too that. Songs that run you down or poke fun at you on account of your bad luck or hard traveling.
>
> I am out to fight these songs to my very last breath of air and my last drop of blood.
>
> I am out to sing songs that prove to you

that this is your world and that if it has hit you pretty hard and knocked you for a dozen loops, no matter what color, what size you are, how you are built, I am out to sing the songs that make you take pride in yourself and in your work. And the songs that I sing are made up for the most part by all sorts of folks just like you.

> I could hire out to the other side, the big money side, and get several dollars every week just to quit singing my own kind of songs and to sing the kind that knock you down still farther and the ones that poke fun at you even more and the ones that make you think you've not got any sense at all. But I decided a long time ago that I'd starve to death before I'd sing any such songs as that. The radio waves and your movies and your jukeboxes and your songbooks are already loaded down and running over with such no good songs as that anyhow.
>
> —Woody Guthrie

Among the multitude of listeners there exist large groups who demand more from music than a permanent lulling accompaniment to their most banal activities. And not all performers are as godforsaken as many of our virtuosi with their limited repertoire of circus tricks.

The durable values of music are not forgotten; they are as alive as they were thousands of years ago, and we as musicians can do nothing better than to accept them as the guiding principles of our work.

> —Paul Hindemith, from *A Composer's World, Horizons, and Limitations*

CHAPTER 4

Take Yourself Too Seriously

The alternate title to this chapter was "Don't Take Yourself Too Seriously." Either bit of advice could be of great help in a music career. Is this a contradiction? Yes. Is that a problem? Only if you fail to understand the basic rule of creativity, which is my "No Consistency Rule," also known as the "No Answer Is Correct" approach. It is the *only* approach because different people can offer contradicting advice for the same situation. Anything can work for anybody. You never know what it will take. This rule gives you the option to completely ignore, or do the opposite of, anything anyone advises you to do.

Creative activity is not like painting a house, fixing a car, assembling a rocket engine, removing an infected spleen, or a myriad of other activities that, if not done a certain way, will cause havoc. Art and music teachers or experts can't tell you what to do or how to do it. No one can. The more expertise someone develops in the field, the more likely they are to overlook something simple that might work for someone else because they have become so entrenched in the philosophical dominion they inhabit. Take me, for example. The best advice I might give would be that you not listen to anything I say (especially this sentence).

When I started out trying to be a professional musician, I already had some experience dealing with other professionals through my volunteer activities as a promoter and organizer for arts centers. As a journalist, I had the opportunity to interview famous musicians, such as Freddie King, Suzi Quatro, Tim Buckley, Richard Heyman, Sam Rivers, Steve Lacy, B.B. King, Liberace, Dr. Hook and the Medicine Show, Rompin' Ronnie Hawkins, Gary Lewis, and many others. From these activities, I developed a mental picture of what it might take to really get somewhere playing music. As both a promoter and a journalist, I liked the friendly, easy-going musicians better. When you heard other promoters ragging about a recent act that had been too temperamental and picky, they would often say something like, "I'll never book that guy again!"

This made me think that if you were nice, you would get ahead in the business. There's a certain amount of truth to this, but of course it gets run over and squashed flat as a badger in the road by the No Consistency Rule. Because I kept meeting musicians who were rude, arrogant, demanding, and satisfied with nothing, and their careers seemed to be doing great!

When I lived in New York City, a keyboardist moved to town and I couldn't believe how little this guy had to say about anything. It wasn't that he was shy, rather he acted as if nothing was worth talking about and anyone who tried to communicate with him was a moron. When he saw you on the street, he would grunt and look away. Any attempt to engage him in dialogue and stir up enthusiasm about anything and the guy would practically punch you. I used to think to myself that "with an attitude like that, the guy will get nowhere." Instead he became an in-demand producer. Big labels were turning over the keys to offices and, at this writing, the guy has total control over seven different custom labels. Is the key to mimic this guy? Not consistently.

Career musicians seem to be on a quest for eternal knowledge, constantly studying one thing or another. The great ones do, that is. They eat, breathe,

4-2-91

Dear Mr. Chadbourne; I am a Camper VAN

Beethoven "AVID LISTENER". When I saw "Camper

Van Chadbourne" I was compelled to buy it simply

because it contained the Campers. Much to my

disappointment when I gave it a listen — I thought —

"This ALBUM TRULY SUCKS!". It has been

collecting dust ever since. I am devoid of

any attraction to your singing. I think the

Campers disgraced themselves by appearing on

your album. Anyway, I just thought I

would let the creator know what I felt of

this disaster on vinyl.

Thank you for
Listening

P.S - Send all Refunds to this edress

Oh, well. You can't be a star every night. Not every piece of fan mail is going to go down smoothly.

and sleep music. But not all the time. One great saxophonist who daringly topped the charts with previously unpopular styles was supposed to have been more interested in his snowmobile than anything having to do with music.

Contradictions flow like wine. And while we're on that subject, is it good advice to tell someone never to get drunk when they are performing? I would say so, after trying to do a gig with a guitarist who was like a rum blotter. On the other hand, I watched Dexter Gordon drink an entire bottle of vodka, then come onstage and play like a saint.

Express your personality through your music and the public will love it. They want truth, you are told. Okay, great. Then explain the popular singer with the friendly, lovable voice and cheery songs who supposedly painted every room in his apartment black and contemplates suicide all the time. Or the grumbling singer who offstage is like a small child with her infectious enthusiasm. There is only one explanation: No Consistency.

Some people carve careers out of low-budget enterprises, saving a nickel here and there until they are millionaires. Others just keep doing it until they run out of nickels and pennies. Others spend a million to establish themselves because cash promotion can have such an impact on the public. I'd say let's not forget the people who do that, but it is too late, they've already been forgotten.

A scandalous incident can destroy a career, so watch your habits. Then again look at all the performers who become more and more popular the more trouble they get into.

Seek professional business help is another bit of advice. Get involved with lawyers, accountants, investors, people that really know how to make money talk. This works for some musicians, and before you know it they are on top of the world. On the other hand, ask Willie Nelson about it, he's in a better mood now that he gets to use his golf course/recording studio again thanks to wealthy friends who bought it back from the Internal Revenue Service. They came after Willie because of what his professional business people were doing.

Go on tour! That's the way to build audiences, many groups are told. Yes it is. And no it isn't. For some bands, it actually insures they will never have an audience because the pressure makes them break up. In other cases, the band is so crummy live nobody will ever want to listen to them again. Don't go on tour, other people advise. It's a waste of time and resources. People are perfectly willing to buy CDs by people who have never showed up in their town and played at the Dew Drop Inn. True. Not.

Concentrate on recording, not touring.

Concentrate on touring, not recording.

Move to a big city, that will get your career going. Oops, it would have been better to stay in the small town where your talents were more noticeable.

Speaking of talent, this is even a contradiction. Do you need talent to make it in the music business? Everyone agrees you will need to work hard, or at least everyone who isn't hip to the No Consistency Rule. But even these schmendricks can't decide whether you need talent or whether talent is actually a drawback. Talent often leads to new ideas and approaches. This is the last thing the public wants, and the business people want it even less. At least that's what it looks like. However, that's not always the case.

Speaking of cases, it is good advice to get the best possible ones for your equipment while traveling to protect the instruments. They are your livelihood. Why get second best? But you didn't hear that from me. My advice would be to get the cheapest possible cases and keep duct-taping them together. Not only will no one try to rip off your equipment, but some baggage handlers will actually treat your stuff better out of sympathy.

Speaking of sympathy, it is a good idea when getting jobs to try to get sympathy from whomever you are talking to. Your band needs the job, your tour needs it, please pretty please. This is good advice even though many bookers are more likely to go after an act that seems completely disinterested in even setting foot in the venue.

In any case, ask for as much money as possible. If they pay you half, they think you are giving them a deal, meanwhile you are getting what you want. Except that in a lot of cases the high figure will scare the people off completely, especially if other phone calls they are getting about the same date are from musicians who are trying for big sympathy, not a big guarantee.

Speaking of guarantees, always get one. Always get a guarantee and then you will watch some club owners making out like bandits over what comes in at the door above the guarantee. Always get a guarantee mixed with a percentage, then you are okay. Except in the case of many club owners who have percentage deals down to a science, a science that I call Nomoreforyouology.

Get an advance man when you go on tour. Unless you think it isn't necessary. You are right, either way. Don't you love it? Be a bandleader, in any case. Then you can make more money and be in control over your destiny. Which might end up being a nervous breakdown while the merry, happy-go-lucky sideman with no responsibility other than to show up and noodle around during the sets keeps cashing in. Or it could be the sideman who has the breakdown because the rich, influential, and well-adjusted band-leader decides to fire him.

Try to stay healthy when you are playing. If you get fired, use the time to get back in shape. Oh, and by the way, the best concert I ever saw in the '60s was Spirit, all of them down with a horrible Asian flu.

Okay, I think you've had enough. I defy anyone to come up with anything to do with music that can't be contradicted in less time than the average Top 40 single takes to play. (The contradiction, of course, being Richard Harris' *MacArthur Park.*)

Now let's get inside your head. What are you going to think about all this? After hearing the work of some musicians, one might come to the conclusion that the verb "think" is not applicable. The reality, though, is that you are going to have plenty of time to think because of many aspects of the music lifestyle. On the road, there is always time to think because there is always time to kill. Same goes for recording studios. Are you on a tough practice schedule? What do you think about when you are sight-reading?

You will also be confronted by people who are not creative. They will want explanations about why you do everything you do, even though they have already decided it is wrong. This will force you to think about what you are doing, to try to cast it in some light that your interrogator can understand. For more advice on how to throttle these folks, turn to the chapter "Understanding the Non-Creative Mind."

So anyway, what do you think? No matter what it is, you will find it riddled with contradictions. Let's say you have played clarinet since age five. You have added some other instruments, and you are just plain brilliant. You can sight-read, transpose, do anything technical, and have already graduated from music school with honors. You are the type who, when a Volkswagen goes by and backfires, mumbles "E flat" to yourself. Nobody could say you aren't an accomplished musician. You could impress anybody. Whip through Bach, Mozart, then wail on a New Orleans number. So how do you think about yourself? Do you think "I'm great," or do you think, "I'm doing nothing important?"

There's no answer. Last chapter's borrowings from Hindemith established that, historically, the development of musical knowledge, theory and virtuoso technique amount to nothing more than a betrayal of higher forms of musical enterprise in order to titillate an ignorant, sensation-happy public.

And if that doesn't get to you, you can always go to a little bar where some joker who knows three chords and can't sight-read a train schedule has people dancing around with big smiles on their faces, something that never happens when you're playing.

Hmm. Sounds like it would be more fun to be inside the head of this tavern rocker than the over-trained genius. So what's he thinking about? Right now, he's watching the girls dance—or maybe the guys. At other times, he hears different styles of music and wishes he could understand them. He tried playing along with a song the other day and after an hour still didn't have one chord of it. He thinks about how limited he is in his musical knowledge and how he'd like to expand it. It seems gloomy and depressing to him, to sit in a room by himself and practice, practice, practice.

We used to have a fifth grade teacher, Mr. House, who perhaps was an ancestor of the inventor of the '90s dance music craze. He used to tell us, "Whatever you decide to do, just do it with everything

> *"Sure, young players are on fire! Usually it's because they've lit their own butt on fire by mistake."*
> *—Tex-Mex combo leader Hank Gonzalez*

you've got. Don't monkey around."

Be serious about your music. Make it really great, no matter what the context. Don't relate the content of the music to how successful it is financially or how many people will buy tickets. You will hear a maxim repeated often, and it is the golden truth: "The better the music, the less people are in the audience." Even if only one person is there, make it the most incredible experience they ever had.

Contradiction time. Don't be too serious about it. Don't be disturbed by opinions that differ from yours. Let anyone say anything they want to about your music because they are free to. Bear in mind they could change their minds overnight and not think twice about it, so why should you?

If you can't make up your mind how to think about yourself, how about thinking about your fellow musicians? How seriously should you take them, or not take them? With no danger of seriously penetrating the barrier of No Consistency, I'd like to suggest that certain attitudes are good just because they can make life easier for all musicians.

I've heard some of my peers criticized for some-

I Hate the Man Who Runs This Bar!

thing they call "sussing" in England. I first noticed this word when the multi-instrumentalist and composer Steve Beresford said he was feeling "sussy" because certain well-known players were in his audience that night. Then I heard someone complaining about an Italian drummer. "When he meets you, he is trying to figure out if you are important and can help him in any way. He's always sussing you out!"

I picked up on this and have tried not to act sussy when meeting new people, although it is dishonest to say that thoughts about so-and-so being a good contact still don't cross my mind. Try not to view other musicians only as stepping stones or contacts. The wife of one contact said, "I like you more than [Blank]'s other friends because they are always trying to get jobs out of him." Of course, I was also trying to get jobs out of [Blank], but it is good to know I did it in such a way that his wife didn't pick up on it. These niceties are important.

The whole subject of thinking a big star is going to help out your career because they like you is worth discussing. Naturally it is flattering to have someone like this take an interest in your music. It is more of a boost than the praise of 100 so-called regular people. Most musicians assume help is on the way in terms of whatever strings these big shots can pull. Musicians in these situations sometimes sit and wait for this help to arrive from the moment they first meet the big shot. Then they become bitter when nothing happens. They sometimes jeopardize the friendship because the "help me!" part is not being fulfilled.

I saw a quote from an R.E.M. bandmember about this predicament. "Everyone thinks I can help them, but right now I couldn't get Bob Dylan a record contract."

Often some famous person just wants to be friends because they like you. They would be happy if you were a big success, too, but is it logical to think they will make it happen for you or help in some big way? What is this based on? It seems like it isn't based on anything that has really happened. On the contrary, the more you read about musician's careers, the more it seems the reverse is true.

To me, the ultimate anecdote about this subject came from the late, great queen of the stage, Ms. Mary Martin. (That's *Peter Pan . . . Annie, Get Your Gun . . . The Sound of Music . . .* you know.)

In the early days she was singing at a little nightclub in Los Angeles. She had a good piano player and together they had worked up a swinging version of the song "Shoeshine Boy." Bing Crosby, about as big a star as you could be then, started coming by the club to hear her. He made it a regular routine. He was there every night, for weeks, and he always requested "Shoeshine Boy." In Ms. Martin's autobiography, *My*

Heart Belongs, she describes the way she used to fret about why Bing Crosby wasn't helping her career, still hoping it wasn't a matter of why but when he would make a few calls and get her out of the little clubs. It never happened. Years later, Mary Martin wound up doing a film with Bing Crosby. They were talking about songs, and when the subject of "Shoeshine Boy" came up, he began reminiscing about a girl singer he had really enjoyed a few years back. Ms. Martin promptly went over to her pianist and went right into the arrangement while Bing's jaw dropped.

Okay. Now, if Bing Crosby didn't try to help out Mary Martin, who is fifty times the singer and dancer of anyone around today, then let's stop expecting anyone to help anyone. Less of these expectations will make the climate easier for musicians.

Players, let's not be so hard on each other! I've noticed certain genres of music stress cooperation while others thrive on athletic feats of prowess and back-biting. In a rock jam, usually someone will call a blues, boogie, or something simple so that everyone can get into it and maybe it will start cooking. At a jazz session, however, there is invariably someone who will try to call a tune that will shut out someone else. A guitarist friend told me about working up the courage to sit in with the great saxophonist Sonny Stitt, only to have him choose a tune in a ridiculous key with an unbelievably fast tempo so he could chuckle over the novice as he floundered around. Even a master musician will quickly put aesthetic considerations aside if there's a chance to best someone.

Soprano saxophonist Steve Lacy was touring Western Canada in the mid-'70s; I helped organize solo concerts for him in Alberta. In Edmonton, the Jazz Society organizers had taken him to a late night jam session at another club after the official gig was over. I asked him how the meeting with local players had gone, and Lacy grimaced. "It was a drag. They were trying to compete."

There was a moment of silence and then he said something I'll never forgot. "They have to understand. There is no competition."

I'm glad I heard this when I was 20 because it saved me a lot of wear and tear. Much of this competitive spirit is encouraged by the audience. Jazz players whine about "high note" festivals, where the only way to get a response from the crowd is to hit a higher note than anyone else. An optimistic point of view about this phenomenon would be that if the music kept getting higher it would disappear from our range of audio understanding, and all the problems we are discussing would fall into the laps of dogs. (Do dogs have laps?)

So bear in mind while you are doing all this thinking that even when the music disappears, the audience will still be there. Mary Martin begins a chapter dedicated "To the audience" with some lyrics from the song "Three to Make Music":

If nobody writes it there's nothing to play
If nobody plays it there's nothing to hear
If nobody hears it it's plainer than day
You just haven't got music, now isn't it clear
It takes three to make music.

People starting out their careers may think the "three" is the total number in the audience (if they're lucky). Mary Martin feels that the live audience adds something essential to the performance and is a dynamic part of the entire creative partnership. And so, musicians must think about the audience as well as themselves and each other.

At first this might consist of wondering where the audience is, anyway. Or there might be no question about what they are thinking because by the end of the night you have had long discussions with all six of them. (Hey, the crowd has doubled since the last time!)

Stick with it, more people will come. Worry about the ones that are there. If half of the dozen jokers who show (hey, you've doubled your crowd again!) talk through the show, forget them. Play for the ones that are listening. Play for the one that might decide to listen because of what you just played.

Ms. Martin describes an audience's love as "the wave of affection, of joy, that sweeps across the stage like a glimpse of heaven with Gabriel blowing a hundred trumpets." Early in her career, a friend told her that the important thing was acting like you loved what you were doing because then the audience would, too. Ms. Martin writes about how audiences differ from land to land and also admits that some audiences are just duds.

She doesn't go quite far enough, though, in attempting to reveal the dark side of the audience "mob" mentality. Sure, love the audience and what you are doing, but don't be a ninny. Bear in mind that the worst possible behavior you can imagine from an audience will be just a bare inkling of what they are truly capable of.

I have always been intolerant of mob behavior. When someone throws a glass of ice, a beer bottle, or anything remotely dangerous at a performer, whoever is onstage should definitely refuse to continue until this person is removed from the venue. Nobody should be allowed to throw things at performers in public, no matter what the performance. Just because these people didn't have a proper upbringing doesn't mean you have to put up with their shenanigans

when you are working. Stand up for your rights.

I learned a sad lesson about audiences the day my radio rabble-rouser friend Charles Rosina played me a bootleg tape he'd made at a live Neil Young show in Boston. Fans had paid about $50 a ticket to see Neil Young solo with his guitar. He doesn't do that very often, and he has lots of fans. The hall was packed.

[The] worst possible behavior you can imagine from an audience will be just a bare inkling of what they are truly capable of.

We got to a part of a tape where Young announced that he was going to play a new song, one he wrote last night. Then he went into it. That's when the audience started blabbing away like there was no tomorrow because they haven't heard the song before!

Most musicians starting out would like to be Neil Young, have his kind of long career, big following, the respect from many different generations, and a ranch that looks pretty darn nice from the photographs I've seen. But he doesn't have an audience willing to listen to his music and I've heard the proof on tape. And if there's anything you should take seriously, that would be it.

Ed Cassidy has published *A Musician's Resource Manual,* packed full of valuable tips and insight into all aspects of the business. Cassidy's career is fascinating in that he has been a part of so many different activities. Being the oldest performing rock drummer on the scene meant that in the '60s, when his band Spirit was having hit singles, he could look at things from a more mature perspective. And believe me, when we are talking about developing a good attitude, maturity cannot be underestimated. ("Sure, young players are on fire!" Tex-Mex combo leader Hank Gonzalez acknowledges. "Usually it's because they've lit their own butt on fire by mistake.")

Now in his seventies, Cassidy is currently coming to grips with the accidental death of his stepson (guitarist, singer, and songwriter, Randy California), certainly a member of Spirit that cannot be replaced. Cassidy will get through this tragedy and continue his

I Hate the Man Who Runs This Bar!

remarkable career if he practices the attitude he espouses in his text: "Be a good example. The universe will appreciate it." One of the main reasons is because, as he puts it, "Musicians are in a unique position as working people in that they always have an opportunity to connect with a sense of meaning in their work. Satisfaction with one's own artistry and craftsmanship can help balance the books." But even Cassidy asks, "Wouldn't it be nice if we could enjoy our music as much as our audience does?" (Does this include Neil Young's audience?)

So, the next time no one seems to be listening, lavish yourself with inner praise. You have hit the top. Just don't take the view from up there too seriously.

CHAPTER 5

Understanding the Non-Creative Mind

Do you remember the movie, *Fiend Without a Face,* where the little brains with tails fly through the air attacking people? Oh, how I wish creative people had survival problems as simple as this. Instead, we find that, though mankind was created with a few thousand stock faces and physical features, the options in terms of minds are much more limited. In fact, there are only two: the mind that sees things creatively and the mind that doesn't.

The creative person's mind is in control of an outer force, something that combines the brightest aspects of religion, UFO paranoia, the work ethic, superstition, and perhaps a touch of witchcraft. If you decide to be an outlet for creative flow, hampered only by your own physical stamina and mental potential, then you will be setting yourself on a collision course with another kind of mobile mind.

The first people you remember "meeting," your own parents, might not have been creative or they might have been the ones who set an example for you with their own creativity. Often there is one parent with creative binges and one who takes care of all the "responsible" chores (this is how a non-creative mind sees it, mind you).

You will not be attracted only to creative people. You may seek a relationship with someone you feel is "like" you, only to realize that this is more trouble than taking on a non-creative partner. Individuals vary, but unless you are a hermit, at one time or another, you are bound to come under the scrutiny of a non-creative mind. And when there is a meeting of these minds, both sides are doing plenty of scrutinizing.

"She is certainly creative! She is always creating something. Once she starts one of her projects, she doesn't stop until it is done. And then she's usually started something else on the side."

"What makes her think she can get away with being totally obsessed with what she is creating?"

"He would never understand, he just isn't creative. He is steady, completely solid. Not a creative bone in his body."

"The way she does things is crazy! I could never think up things like that."

"The problem with you creative people is you are so busy with your creations that you have no time for the people you are supposed to be close to."

"You can go on all day if you want, but eventually you will shut up and want to relax and then, you know what? You will reach for something created by someone creative, who does it only because of dedication, who does it with hard work, and who probably does it while arguing with someone like you telling them it's a waste of time."

Like these kind of arguments? You will hear them eventually. It is an age old conflict of humanity.

One time I wanted to print a poster. I had a black and white photo of myself practicing guitar. It was shot on high speed with blurry fingers, arms, and rhythmic head-bobbing movements. The look I had in mind was very simple: the photo with my name and the date overlaid in red ink. Of course it would look homemade; that's exactly what I wanted. The printing guy was aghast. While making fun of me to his co-workers, he stared at the photo as if trying to will it to come into focus. He thought I was too cheap for typesetting and a real chump, by the way. "Nobody is going to come to a show with a handwritten poster," he informed me. "Too bad you couldn't get a good photographer," he lamented.

"The photographer is in her third year of photography at college," I said.

"I'd like to see her grades," he said, showing the photo around to colleagues who rolled their eyes.

I left the place humiliated and scared to death to pick up the work a few days later, but the job did get done—no thanks to those clowns. All in all, a mild brush with the non-creative squad.

Creativity isn't simply making homemade things with fuzzy photographs, although it can be. It can just as well be about pristine typesetting and clear, sharp photography. It can also be hand drawings, ink blots, or mud rubbed into red ink. It's creativity, after all, so it can be anything.

The non-creative actions in this anecdote are easier to define. They involve arrogance, bossiness, and rude treatment of others. The non-creative joker ensconces himself in the usual-Joe job, taking orders at the printing place, then starts to play Louie the Lord with the customers. The non-creative person can smell the creative one coming with his creative project—all wrong, of course—and begins to bristle. Here is where any sensitive types begin to mistrust the human race. Why is there such a negative reaction? Why does the non-creative clerk act like an animal establishing turf rights? What is going on?

I remember originally attributing encounters such as this in my childhood to macho dominance bully trips, but many of them were probably moments of friction between creative and non-creative types. I seriously believe the neighborhood bullies could sense the potential for creativity in someone, and that was reason enough to beat them up. These same types grow up to be powerful businessmen, politicians, school principals, judges, and lawyers. Their campaign against creativity is relentless, irritating, and depressing, but inevitably a failure.

Someone bitten with the creative bug will carry on no matter what. The non-creative type will be quick to remark, "That's their whole problem!" Whether you see it as a problem, an alternative to a problem, or a solution is irrelevant. It happens and it doesn't stop happening.

If you are a musician, it doesn't automatically mean you are creative. However it is an endeavor that attracts people who are at least interested in creativity. Karlheinz Stockhausen said to Jonathan Cott in the 1974 book *Conversations With the Composer:*

> I'm working all the time to construct things. But I have to recognize and use and transform the forces of destruction. Once, when I was verbally attacked during a discussion in Frankfurt, a man got up and said that I was a *Stehaufmannschen*— a stand-up man, one of those little plastic toy men with lead in his feet; you can throw him anywhere and he always returns standing up. The person who called me that really described my whole life. Whenever I lost the dearest things—things that I had gotten too attached to—then after the shock of losing them, I turned this loss into something positive. I began to see what was essential again. I began to see the whole and to live for the whole.

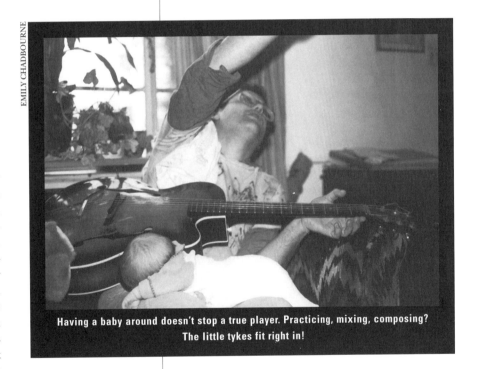

Having a baby around doesn't stop a true player. Practicing, mixing, composing? The little tykes fit right in!

I am fond of this quote. It expresses so much about creativity. Seeing the whole is not always just a form of channel surfing for the positive, however. If you enjoy being creative and want to keep on doing creative things, you are going to have to see the world the way it really is: full of forces intent on halting creativity. We live in a society where, from the youngest social experiences, creativity is encouraged by the same person trying to eliminate it.

The teaching field attracts creative people, who are interested in working with other creative people. Meanwhile, the school system itself seems engineered to burn out as many of these talented individuals as possible. As a teacher begins to give in to the non-creative demands of their superiors, they are transformed from prophets of creativity into minions of oppression. Our society suffers dearly as a result. And this is not a situation that everyone is working hard to find a solution for. On the contrary, this problem is part of the overall plan.

For the most part, the younger the child, the more creativity is allowed. The classic negative view of the high school experience is that it is one of society's last shots at changing young, potential troublemakers into anonymous automatons before they get out into the so-called "real world." A certain sense of freedom is encouraged in the college experience, but only because it's considered a person's last bash, the glorious college days you will look back on nostalgically when you settle into a responsible job such as, say, an assistant to a stock broker.

My schooling experiences were full of incidents when teachers completely lost their patience with me, always over some enterprise that was too creative for them. I recall a circus we tried to build out of clay that got so complicated, with so many different acts happening and animals wandering around, that the teacher came along, wadded the whole thing up, smacked us, and sent us into the hall. We were on the verge of some kind of childish creative orgasm; she knew it, and she didn't like it.

In my early teens, a witch of an art teacher drummed me out of class during the infamous church assignment. She told us to design and build a model of a church: any religion was acceptable. So I studied up on various African tribes and began building a mud temple. At first the teacher seemed to tolerate my direction, but when I rolled in a small wheelbarrow full of fresh mud, she lost her cool. Not only did I get an F, but I was bumped out of the class completely.

Art teachers are famous for being control freaks. I remember seeing one during a news broadcast in Alberta who got in trouble because she wasn't allowing students to use certain colors next to each other. I started making fun of her and immediately got into an argument with several other people watching who agreed with her!

Having non-creative types teach creative subjects must be one of the stock parts of the whole non-creative battle plan, so watch for it. These teachers are intent on making clones of themselves. Their students might think that the teacher wants everyone to be like them

for egotistical reasons, but really the intended outcome is just that everyone be a bit less creative.

Dealing with these kinds of conflicts and resolving them are important parts of the creative process. They build a person's character or at least their supply of patience. None of this is really as problematic as the main relationships in your life: those with your parents, your spouse, and your children. These long-range relationships are where you will really be tested. Large doses of creativity will be needed just to figure out how to continue to be creative when a person is up against a power-hungry, non-creative parent, lover, or partner.

These people in your life will make you want to scream. They will make you feel like smashing your head against a wall. You will cry. You will be pushed to be a "success" based on standards that you have nothing to do with and are usually measured in dollars and cents. You will fail. You might even contemplate suicide. All of this might be nothing compared to what you are doing to them with your obsessions, compulsions, and strange ideas. But this book isn't for them, the non-creative duddyfuds. Let them find someone else to write a book for them.

A person possessing real creative talent who decides to dedicate themselves to the music craft is, by definition, going to irritate a lot of these types of people along the way. Whoever wrote the blues lyric "I don't believe you really love me, you just like the way my music sounds," must have been sipping too much Jack Daniels. The usual case is that someone might love you, but not your music.

Mrs. A boasts proudly that she "doesn't have the time for music anymore! And if I did, living with a musician would have ruined it for me, anyway."

"My wife and children haven't heard a note of my music in five years," says Mr. A, who like everyone quoted in this chapter, is hiding under an alias.

Mr. B, a movie scorer, spoke for everyone creative when he said, "Don't you dare use my name! The person I live with will kill me."

This is because non-creative partners would immediately recognize themselves in these situations. They do not accept the creative mind's interpretation of the scenario in which the non-creative partner plays the villain. Reading about it is not only personally embarrassing, but it is also a further rebuff from the creative side, taking personal hassles and turning them into a mildly enjoyable text.

There they go, taking real life and turning it into art again!

Love is supposed to involve some sort of understanding about the person you are in love with and the way their mind works. This is as good a time as any for a snickers break. And I don't mean the candy bar. Is there a species in existence less understanding and less tolerant of each other than humans in a "love" relationship? Maybe, if you are talking about certain parents and children. Or aardvarks digging for grub worms. The natural desire to control each other is strong in either case. As a creative person, you have to decide that you are not going to let someone else control you.

One day I was walking through the neighborhood with my wife and our daughter. We had moved to town recently and were looking for people in the

> *Is the person who tries to convince you to give up playing music capable of committing murder? Probably. Nothing in my experience indicates otherwise.*

neighborhood with kids. We met the mother of one such family who made a triumphant face when I told her I was a musician. "My husband used to do that," she said. "But I made him give it up."

If I was a violent person I would have beaten her to a pulp. Down the line a decade or two, I remembered this evil creature and really laughed when I saw the film *To Die For.* Based on real events, the film features Nicole Kidman as a woman who has a pair of high school dipsticks knock off her husband. But as a prelude to this, she gets hubbie to give up playing drums.

Is the person who tries to convince you to give up playing music capable of committing murder? Probably. Nothing in my experience indicates otherwise.

A pianist I knew showed great talent, potential, and energy. I was happy when he fell in love and got married because I liked this guy. His wife began getting on his case about music right away. Next thing you know, he's given up playing and is studying computer programming. I visited the couple a few times and always found them depressing. He seemed like a prisoner on work release, always watching over his shoulder to make sure he was pleasing her. She was constantly making insulting references to him, whether he was around or not. I often wished he would pick up his instrument again, if only to drop it on her from a great height. Happy ending? Yes, he got

rid of her and quickly got back into music. "I wasted a few years of my life but at least not the whole thing," is how he describes the experience.

Want to waste your whole life? Listen to someone who wants you to stop being creative. There is no quicker way, although the life you wind up living will feel like an eternity.

Don't give up playing music because someone else wants you to. Neither of you will be happy. And don't forget, you were happy before you gave up music, but whoever talked you into quitting has never been happy. Don't let someone like this be the happiness expert in your life! If someone even raises the subject with you, consider running them out of your life. Why wait until they become pushy about it? Anyone that tries to hamper your creativity simply doesn't have your best interests at heart.

They may say they don't like seeing you go through all the ups and downs, but don't start feeling sorry for them. They don't like the ups and downs because they don't like dealing with them, not because they think it is bad for you.

Are the ups and downs of creativity bad for you? I really don't know. They are a part of the total picture, just like night follows day. There really isn't anything you can do about this. It will take a lot of self control, concentration, and determination to prevent this cycle from causing problems for you. Too much worrying about how it is going to affect someone else just makes it worse.

The non-creative types seem to both envy and barely tolerate the creative people who are close to them. This kind of confusing relationship can occur while the non-creative person worships other creative people and indulges in enjoyment based on the creative activity of others.

"In the evening following one of his tirades against creativity," the wonderful Ms. D told me, "my husband was annoyed because I'd been up all night making reeds for my bassoon, while he had read several magazine articles, finished a book, watched a film, and listened to a live broadcast on the radio. So I reminded him that if everyone did what he wanted me to, he wouldn't have been able to do any of the things he had done because those people would have been spending time with their husbands and wives or family or whatever and wouldn't have finished the movie, article, or whatever."

The non-creative type grants greater freedom to creative people who can be admired and enjoyed from a distance. They don't have any interaction with them other than enjoying what they do. There isn't exactly a balance of trade on this issue, because creative people don't really get to enjoy the fruits of the labors coming from the non-creative camp, unless we get a kick out of all the sad things they've done to the world. The envy comes from the assumption that the creative person is in on some sort of free ride. Remember the song "Money for Nothing" by Dire Straits? "That's the way to do it . . . playin' your guitar on MTV . . . get your money for nothing . . . get your chicks for free."

The creative person is selfish and always out for themselves. The creative person is obsessed with hearing the praise of others, practically wallowing in it. The creative person just goes through life doing whatever the hell they want. The creative person gets to paint butterflies on walls while someone else builds the wall and worries about keeping the roof from leaking. The creative person flits through life barely remembering their own name while someone near and dear picks up the pieces and keeps track of all the mundane but important chores.

Creative people reading these thoughts will recognize them as being riddled with a lack of understanding of creativity and what the creative person is going through all the time.

It is a lot to expect understanding for the creative person, I realize. Frankly though, I would be more tolerant of the lack of understanding if non-creative people wouldn't insist on being in charge so much.

When non-creative people think about things that require a lot of thought and hashing out, you can sense something on their minds other than the immediate environment. Why, then, can't they understand that this is how creative people act when they are working on a project? Because they are unable to experience creativity as a real force. They just don't get that channel on their antenna.

They find the arbitrary nature of the creative process irritating. "One minute Miss F was doing this, the next moment something else," was the sad reminiscing of Miss F's ex-boyfriend, who left her to find someone who "wouldn't always be doing really bizarre stuff."

A portrait of a musical father by Molly Chadbourne at age 8. She misses me when I'm on tour but still has an upbeat attitude about what I'm doing.

Don't be discouraged by people who tell you musicians can't have families or be good parents. These thoughts are often expressed by people who have already given up trying. Often their next step is giving up music. Don't follow them.

A musician on the road is not always there for their children. This is something that you will never be able to fix, but you can find various ways to compensate. I always tried to make my music world open to my children, whatever their ages. They have always been allowed in my studio space at all times and have been free to hang out in the office with me when I work. I have even taken them on the road with me. Sometimes this involved putting them to sleep onstage.

One night in Spartanburg, South Carolina, I was about to begin my set while Molly, then 7, was settling into her sleeping bag in a corner behind the amplifier. I overheard a classic conversation between a creative and a non-creative type.

"Shame on him! Hauling that poor little girl around!"

"Shame on you! That's how I learned music myself, 'cuz my daddy dragged me around to every bluegrass club in the county."

If you devote yourself to your craft and remain sincere and committed to high standards of creativity, your work will possess an inner strength and you will set a wonderful example for your children. If they can imitate even a part of what they see from this type of lifetime commitment to a beautiful art form, they will be taking steps toward making their own lives blissful.

If someone asked me what it is that I show my children, the answer would be short and simple: I show them that creativity is possible. Part of what makes this possible is being willing to engage in a battle to keep creativity alive. As much as it is important to be strong to protect your work from being shoved into a closet, it is also important to be able to negotiate, compromise, and make time for things outside your work. It is always a balancing act, and nobody will ever be satisfied. Don't feel that this is because non-creative people are pigs. It is just a problem of time. This is something that everyone, no matter how their mind works, has in common.

A happily creative person will usually be working on so many projects that a typical day can involve a merry set of choices of things to work on. When you get tired of one thing, take a break and move on to something different. Some days, energy will just bubble up, and you'll feel a sense of accomplishment. Other days nothing seems to go right and a depressing sense of questioning sets in. Why am I doing this?

If the non-creative person senses this, they might try to be sympathetic or they might try to influence you. Fights sometimes ensue. Meanwhile it is all the usual tick tock. You run out of time, you run out of energy. How time is used is the focal point of probably 90 percent of the creative/non-creative fussology. Creative people seem to pull stamina out of a hat when it comes to finishing projects or pulling off complex happenings, but they may be hard to waken when the baby is puking.

Resentment can build about the face the creative person wears when indulging in a career activity as opposed to the one worn in the "family" or "personal" mode.

The creative tendency to interconnect all phenomena doesn't help matters when one is put on the defensive about their choice of personal mode. "Well, I was taking a break from music here and just lying on the hammock remembering a scene in a Gene Hackman film . . . then this bird sang a series of three pitches and it was so exquisite I started thinking about music."

Back in the '80s there was a lot of talk about "quality time." Luckily, this expression was worn out through overuse. Personally I have problems with adding two truths and expecting a third. Sure, there's not enough quality. And there's not enough time. But that's about as far as I go with this idea.

The composer Mr. H, mostly known for his TV show themes, married a lovely starlet who absolutely hated seeing the guy sitting around writing music. She would go into a tizzy of sorts figuring out how to distract him from this inane scribbling, no matter what he was working on.

One of her favorite emergencies was the toilet. She always thought it was plugged up. She would want him to unplug it before it overflowed because, with her luck, he'd be at one of those endless recording sessions when that happened! The family plumber was no help, either. "I don't know about women," he'd tell Mr. H. "Every woman I've known is the same. They are never satisfied with how much suck the toilet has."

On deadline for an important commission, Mr. H describes how he tricked his honey into thinking he was taking care of the plumbing, when actually he was composing! "I cut her to the quick this particular night by announcing after supper that I'd noticed the toilet was running a little slow, and since we had a big recording coming up, I'd better try to fix it while I had a chance. Rather than being grateful, she sneered and said something like 'It's about time, it almost overflowed this morning.'

"I set myself up in the bathroom with a supply of pens and the score paper pad tucked into the spot between the toilet and wall. I kept up a steady stream of noise that sounded like a typical plunge/fiddle job, complete with swearing. And that's how I got that piece written."

Creative people will utilize any means to get things done or to appease others they are involved with. Consider the subject of sleep from the point of view of Dr. I, who teaches Indian classical music in Ontario. "The only sort of concert my husband would tolerate would be one that was almost completely unprepared for. If we were too busy with everything else, especially family responsibilities, to get the concert really well rehearsed and take care of all the preparations thoroughly, that made him really happy, because he thought all the extra chores involved with concerts were a complete waste of time. The idea of anyone in our ensemble asking me to do anything on my own time rankled him!

"He used to say, 'Oh, you are so wide awake when they come to practice or talk about the program, but when you are with me you can't keep your eyes open.'"

Having heard this line before, and being almost desperate to introduce one of my pet subjects, Artists Falling Asleep Onstage, I wondered whether Dr. I had any theories on whether these problems might be connected.

"The tamboura player in the band, I think she tried to sleep sometimes during the performances," Dr. I speculated. "Of course, I myself had too much to do to have a nap. But the tamboura player is just waving their hand a little. It might be possible to sleep. Some people move their feet while they sleep, enough to play a tamboura or a bass drum."

I saw a video of a Miles Davis combo with John Coltrane on tenor sax. Coltrane was obviously snoring during the other players' long solos. When it was time for Coltrane to play again, the leader shouted "Trane!" and he would jump back in, right on time. So it is possible even during the creation of masterpiece music to catch a nap if you have no important obligations.

Percussionists in orchestras have known this for centuries, I suppose. Some of these people waiting for cue #567 on triangle might very well be non-creative thinkers hassled by a dynamic, creative partner for the exact same reasons: "Lack of energy! Complacency! You are boring to be around." No offense meant to orchestra or studio players, but if ever a musical system was devised that could keep non-creative players busy, it would have to be having everything written down and a conductor and/or a click track to lead the way. So the level of creativity involved really doesn't affect the basic need to take a nap and the importance of being rested in general. I heard a report of a famous singer falling asleep in the middle of a song in front of 50,000 people. He woke up when his forehead hit the microphone.

Another well-known rocker has a full-time "chip man" sitting in the spot on the piano bench normally used by a page turner. This guy keeps up a steady stream of chocolate chip cookies; they're the only thing that can keep the star awake during his set.

Mr. J from down Panama City way says his band needed a bassist so he hired a local legend named Mr. M, an older guy who had played a lot of sessions. "This guy's wife kept him so busy fixing things up around his place that he always fell asleep during the last set of the night," Mr. J says. "It was cool, though, because Mr. M had this way of wiggling his finger in his sleep. It was funky!"

An eccentric violinist and composer, Dr. O, recorded a nap taken by Miss N in his living room in Amsterdam, releasing the snores as part of musical pieces on several CDs, as well as a solo on its own. "I have collected a total of 600 guilders (about $300) in royalties," reports Miss N. And she has gotten nice reviews, not only for her snoring but for instrumental passages actually played by others, which critics insist on attributing to Miss N because they don't believe anyone would appear 100 percent asleep on a CD.

There are no doubt many other examples of creative artists figuring out how to fit rest into their productions when a squeeze play is made against

them resting in their homes. It is all part of creative adaptation.

Take equipment invented to suit the public demand for bigger and louder noise. Please. The electric guitar was not invented because anyone was looking for a sound like that. They just wanted more volume so the noisy dancing audiences would be able to hear the instrument along with all the other louder ones in the orchestra.

The British drummer Dave Ross invented a sliced-off, "quiet" drumstick at the request of bossy, non-creative neighbors. The jazz legend Wes Montgomery came up with his finger-plucked octave style of playing for exactly the same reason.

Jazz drummer Art Blakey was originally a pianist, and only got on the tubs because a gangster in a bar pointed a gun at him and said, "You play drums." And he wound up being one of the greatest drummers in history. This leads one to speculate that not only can drastic adaptations wind up being the best thing for the creative mind in the long run, per-

WALTER MALLI

Sleeping on tour requires knowledge of yoga.
Camper Van Beethoven drummer Cris Pedersen demonstrates.

haps even the non-creative bosses are serving the muse with their orders!

It does go both ways, seriously. Listen to your non-creative partners and their demands. In the long run, much of the time you spend away from your creative pursuits can turn out to be beneficial not only to you as a person but also to your creations. Make sure you stay connected to pleasures that come from outside your little creative realm, even if what you are doing seems as broad as the universe. I can't stress enough that a perfect balance is an unreasonable demand to make on yourself or for anyone to make on you. It will just seesaw back and forth as the years go on and various commitments will come and go.

At the point in my life when my children were little and needed a lot of attention, I had a relationship with a booking agent who was my age and in the same family situation. It was an interesting dichotomy because, although I was looking for people sympathetic to the give and take of life with small children, I personally would rather have had a booking agent who could devote most of his time obsessively to his work, rather than watching a dust-gobbling two-year-old all afternoon.

Through reading interviews with many musicians, I have noticed that the ones who make sweeping statements about the need to give up music time to be with their families are also the ones whose careers, although not altogether undistinguished, tend to be on the wimpy side and are usually marked by long periods of non-productivity. The syndrome of settling into a "soft" university job rather than pursuing more creative endeavors provides more security for a family, but removes a player from the artistic stream.

It is this area of creativity that is always in the most treacherous position, overall, in most societies. The commercial music business is not only an exploitation of creativity, it is a self-created musician's nightmare in that its survival is so closely linked to individuals adapting their situation to keep playing music.

"Well, I don't like the bar I'm playing in, but at least I get to play once a week."

"I would rather not play in this cheesy orchestra, but I am too poor to turn it down."

"I helped her cut a really lame demo because I got $1000 out of it."

For this really creative stream to keep flowing, there has to be a certain number of players willing to throw themselves completely into it. These are the people that persist after others have decided they are better off staying home or they can't afford to keep trying to make it, don't like playing live, or can't make it without something that pays a lot better. Persistence means successfully negotiating all these lifestyle confrontations or, if necessary, keeping the non-creative hordes at bay by force.

Biographical details indicate that while the ranks of the great musical innovators consist only of the full-time creative set, at least some of these unique individuals lived perfectly miserable lives. Do some of them seem like creeps? Sure, because the creative muse doesn't make exceptions when passing around little bolts of genius. One has to guess that, since happiness is of little real interest to anyone, the great musical artists whose personal lives haven't really been revealed must work some sort of way to balance out their time and energy. So there is at least

an existence of hope that such a thing is possible for the rest of us. "I'm just a soul whose intentions are good. Oh Lord! Please don't let me be misunderstood."

I want to make sure that many of my closest friends don't misunderstand me. I am not putting down non-creative people and putting myself and every other weirdo above them. I am not saying one way of thinking is better than the other; I wouldn't because I know we need everybody just to keep things going. And keeping things going is of interest to the creative and non-creative alike. Having so much in common makes it easy, not hard, to share lives and ambitions.

Sometimes I think of people like myself as old bicycle tires. Creativity is maintaining the proper amount of air pressure, that's all. Otherwise the tire is flat, and thus useless. Or it blows up in your face, which gives you lots of separate pieces of tire, all of them also useless. Tires need strong, solid wheels to fit around. Perhaps this is the proper symbol for the non-creative folk. A perfectly round, spinning wheel with all the spokes in place, each one representing a time when one of these people has "spoken" to one of us.

Establishing the right pressure between tire and wheel wouldn't be the only big problem solved if everyone could just get it straight that it "takes all kinds to make the world." War, racism, intolerance, religious persecution . . . these could all be corrected with the help of that cute little expression.

P.S. By the way, it takes a creative type to think up cute expressions like that!

CHAPTER 6

True Happiness: The Flawed System That Destroys Weaker Minds

Self-improvement courses, seminars, and so forth have a large captive audience that keeps growing. When I was a journalist in Canada in the early '70s, it was considered quite innovative of Calgary to offer combined training and therapy for people who wanted a radical change in careers because of a mid-life crisis. You had to be over 40 and sick of your job to qualify for this program.

I was too young for a mid-life crisis then and hadn't ditched my journalism career, so I was assigned to write a feature about the evening seminar. This consisted of a counselor with expertise in psychology and job training lecturing to a group of people who all seemed like lost souls.

The counselor said he could help them become interested in some other career, but the most important thing was to develop the proper attitude about work. I heard him say to one person, "If you had the proper attitude, you wouldn't be here in the first place."

Having the right attitude is as important in music as in any other profession. We've talked about taking yourself seriously, or not taking yourself seriously, depending on what time of day it is. It is also important how one perceives the professional world.

"What is a professional musician?" Ed Cassidy asks in his *Musician's Resource Manual*. And if anybody should know, it should be him. "My definition of a 'pro' is a person who dedicates his or her life to being the best he can be in that profession. No matter what the odds are against him, he does not give up," Cassidy says.

And you will feel like giving up sometimes. You will feel like taking the instruments and smashing them to pieces. And that's when you're in a good mood. You will feel better if you develop a good attitude, though. One musician who played with me recently said she liked the pieces I had written for our group because they each had such a "good mood" to them. "That's because I'm in a good mood," I said. Later I was thinking about this and remembered something I had decided back when I was 16! "I am going to be in a good mood because I have decided not to worry about being popular anymore."

Back then I was thinking about high school. And I was pretty immature and stupid. I am not going to tell you how to have a good attitude in or about high school. If I were going to try to accomplish the impossible, I would pick something easier, like cleaning up all the garbage in the world.

Most musicians I know seem unsatisfied, always striving for something that seems out of reach. What is it? It is many things, starting with a bank balance that doesn't involve a "minus" sign. Ideally, this positive bank balance would also be part of a long-time, secure insurance package. The existence of this bank balance becomes like water in the well at Desert Pete's place outside Phoenix. If you can get a drink from the well, you know all is well in the universe.

No matter what you play or how well you play it, you will wonder how on earth you are going to keep the well wet, year in and year out. The culture all around you seems to be providing only one answer: Make it big! Popularity might be what everyone thinks they want, but it doesn't work. This is crucial for musicians to get into their heads because as long as they try to be popular, they will judge themselves as failures and their music will also start to fail.

If they ever do open Pandora's box and become popular, then the *real* trouble begins. Popularity is like the game where the fastest runner gets a nice car to ride home in. Only the prize car doesn't run, and the winner winds up walking home. If the system were really working, so would the car. (And if you own a car, you know what I'm talking about.) Success would be a wonderful thing, and failures in the music business would have something to whine about. As it is, they are just another example of people who have it good and don't know it.

Seeing these flaws in the system can alter your perception of yourself. Why strive for a goal that isn't worth anything? If you can be happier as a failure than you would be if you were popular, you can feel satisfied all the time because you've met your goal. And you will be relaxed because being a failure is easy. And easy things tend to make people happy.

The musician motivated by success looks ahead and sees an endless road of roadhouses lit with neon. However this is a hallucination. Imagine that the one who accepts failure does not have these hallucinations, but instead sees what is really there: a bottomless bog of gunk. Mr. Success charges into the roadhouse thinking there's a gig. Bye-bye.

Mr. Failure heads off down the road and avoids these traps, becoming more and more adept at seeing what is really there each time a new vision appears. While the others pity themselves for not having "made it," the happy failure begins to profit from the whole system of stardom not functioning properly.

How can we even continue to call "success" by that word when there are so many problems associated with it? For example, once you are a success you have to worry about remaining one. This can be more stressful than becoming a success in the first place.

We are told that in this new climate of rapid-serve celebrity, having been a success already makes it much more difficult to become a success again once your stock has dipped even slightly.

During this period of success, the musician inevitably loses control of the small aspects of what they do. The daydream of the success-hungry is to have a minion ready to do all the little things: carry stuff, make phone calls, check out the dressing room, do the sound-check, schedule the interviews, and so on. The act of doing these small things becomes something the star dreads. In the meantime, the celebrity lolls around smelling roses and cleaning lint from a sparkling bellybutton.

When "success" fades, then everyone whispers, "He's back to driving himself around" or "He had to give up his manager" or "They are doing their own booking now!" All of it basically meaning that the slaves have gone packing and Queen Esther has to wave her own fan now! Horror upon horror!

I like that lyric by Willie Nelson, "Yesterday's loser is the winner today," except I would leave out the references to days, making it "Loser is the winner." And as another song goes, "This isn't sometimes, this is always." Not because there is anything romantic about "losing." And not because it is better to be a good sport, like your parents and the gym coach told you. No, this has nothing to do with that. It's because the flaws in the system are too big for an intelligent musician to overlook, and more than big

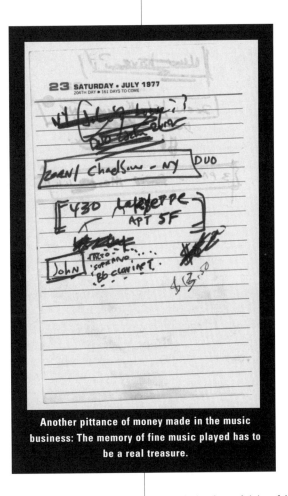

Another pittance of money made in the music business: The memory of fine music played has to be a real treasure.

enough to support thousands of us failures.

Ed Cassidy presents what he calls a flexible rule that the professional musician should always try to work with in a music-related field. Although he probably wasn't thinking along the same offbeat philosophical lines as me, his advice is to try a number of different professions: work in public relations or acting; working as a roadie, rehearsal hall manager, or librarian; or a job with a recording studio, lighting company, or TV station. This makes sense if only for the opportunities to study different aspects of how messed up the music business is.

If your firsthand knowledge of the music business includes practical experience in any of these sidelines, you will be far ahead of the pack. It is strange how few young musicians realize this. Tell Young Joey, the hotshot bassist, that he ought to work for a couple of years in a music library and he might tell you to get lost, even though it is he that ought to get lost in the mountains of material he would have access to in this situation. This is not the only benefit of the music-related employment maze, so hang on. We will be jumping in deeper in a moment.

Maturity makes smart musicians realize they have lots to learn. Even then you find people who become bitter because of that ever present minus sign on the bank statement and what seems to be a lack of interest all around them. Really they should consider themselves lucky no one is interested, considering what we've established to be the criteria for interest in this society.

Looking at the available opportunities in the music business and the type of problems that develop can send cold shivers up your spine. Instead of getting frightened or overwhelmed by it all, learn how each problem can be used to your advantage.

It is common for musicians to talk about how the leaders or most distinguished artists in certain fields never get any recognition or respect. It doesn't mean these players never achieve anything. On the contrary, we just established that many of the most obscure players are the most brilliant. Everyone is afraid of being obscure, but look around you: Being obscure or unnoticed is really being troublefree. It can give you tremendous freedom.

When nobody is paying attention, you can get away with just about anything. Never forget this. Look at some of the great controversies in the music business from the last decade. Most involve some kind of censorship, either because of obscenity or so-called "violent" lyrics, or publishing and/or copyright disputes based around the technology of sampling or mixing in bits of other people's recordings. Sometimes the attention is unwanted, although just about anyone who finds their work under legal attack

attempts to make the negative publicity work for them.

Be an obscure failure, on the other hand, and nobody will pay the slightest attention to anything you do. You can be as obscene as you want, carry out the most outrageous violations of the copyright act, and it will draw as much attention as driving 70 mph across the center of Idaho at 4 a.m.

Remember a group called Culturecide? A few of you might, but I bet most people have never heard of them. Ten years ago, they released a hilarious album in which they sang parody versions of hit songs by simply singing their own lyrics with the original record playing in the background. They did Bruce Springsteen, We Are the World, Madonna, etc. Nobody sued them. Nobody cared. Nobody heard it. Isn't it grand?

Before 2 Live Crew and Roy Orbison tangled in the supreme court over what constitutes legal parody, I had done parodies of songs without permission from the original artists. My attitude was why should Johnny Cash or anyone else have anything to say about what I do? If your kid sister wants to sing a filthy version of "Mickey" in the shower, should she have to ask Toni Basil for permission and submit the proposed lyrics? Nix! Why should it be any different in the recording world? I was able to exercise these freedoms for only one reason: Nobody was paying any attention.

Tom Petty is not allowed to sing "roll another joint" on MTV, he has to "roll another tnioj" or something. Because he's famous, he can't say what's on his mind. Meanwhile it would be impossible to count up all the obscure failures who get to say what Tom Petty doesn't.

Is it better to not say what you really want to a big audience or to say what is really on your mind to a small audience? This question is the heart of the entire matter. The success who has "made it" has often abandoned almost everything they were interested in doing, unless there never was any content to their work in the first place.

Failures on the other hand have content to spare. Obsessive/compulsive, dedicated musician types seem to have a cosmic muse that serves them smorgasbords of creative and sometime martketable musical ideas. German composer Karlheinz Stockhausen compared it to some kind of cheap radio receiver.

And speaking of Stockhausen, maybe what we need to create is a stereophonic version of this complicated argument along the lines of some of his groundbreaking work in electronics. Instead of seeing success and failure as opposite ends of a spectrum, make them the left and right channel, respectively. Now you know why so many musicians get so worked up about who is on the mixing board at a gig!

Stockhausen's "successful" left channel meant he earned as much grant money, released as many albums, played in as many galas and exotic locations, and received as many honors as any composer of classical music alive or dead.

So if I left my house today and started strolling down the street, would I find anyone who had heard of Karlheinz Stockhausen in Greensboro, North Carolina? Let's find out.

> *When nobody is paying attention, you can get away with just about anything.*

My first stop is three blocks away, where a man builds giant tubes for pipe organs. It is easy to find his house because he has added extra stories onto his workshop so he can work on these things. He didn't know who Stockhausen was.

No sense stopping at the bluegrass/heavy metal music shop or the build-your-own-dulcimer place across the street. But maybe the shop with percussion from all over the world will have a clerk who is Stockhausen-savvy.

I want to lie and say I skipped the hot dog stand, but I didn't. I went there to get some homemade ice cream, and the scooper thought I was talking about a flavor called Stockhausen—which they didn't have. (Ben and Jerry's does carry both Jerry Garcia and Phish flavors, though.)

I wound up in the University music building, where names such as Haydn, Mozart, Beethoven, et al. have been chiseled into the granite facade. It didn't take long to find someone there who had heard of Stockhausen; the challenge there would be finding a musician who doesn't harbor either readily apparent or neurotically camouflaged aspirations of being as famous as Stockhausen, if not more famous.

If you do find the rare individual not obsessed with getting to the top of the heap, you can feel sorry for them. Because unless they live like hermits, they will certainly get involved with someone who will question their attitude and push them to change it. That is, unless they already have and are suffering serious soul damage as a result.

The right channel? Failure.

Let's fade back to the left channel, please. Why is Stockhausen such a success? Because he gets lots and lots of ideas, which he says come to him in dreams, sudden visions and so forth. I know what's he's talking about. This is the same way I work. Music also comes to me in dreams or sudden flashes of imagery. Sometimes I close my eyes and see notation in front of me. Once I was sitting in a restaurant, listening to a bunch of servicemen argue about where the best hunting was, and it agitated me so much that I started making musical staffs on the tablecloth and writing down pitches and chords with no sense of what I was doing and no sound in my head other than their inane chatter. It turned out to be a very pretty ballad, but it was almost as if I were receiving signals of a contrasting nature from the reality I was in.

If you can't deal with this kind of thing, maybe you should get out of the music business. I know people like you are out there. I've heard of composers sweating it out trying to get a page of music written. And I've heard improvisers spend the whole night trying to find one good thing to play, then agonize over their failures for hours in the dressing room. (By the way, I thought it sounded great!) People like this have it tough because they have to observe others who have an endless flow of ideas that just appear at their fingertips. All they need is the will, the determination, and the stamina to bring them to life.

People that create this kind of work have to do it, that's it. They don't alter the content to make it more appealing. They shouldn't, anyway. The resulting musical integrity provides an appeal that is much more long-lived than work tainted by commercial manipulation.

I have several gimmicky names for this process. I used to call it "fairy dust" until I heard a tape of the rock band the Troggs trying to reach an agreement with a new producer when their self-produced sessions began to flounder. "Fairy dust?" this gent scowls at one point. "You want me to sprinkle fairy dust on the tapes? I'll piss on the tapes if you like!" That turned me off to the idea of fairy dust. Now I call it "Praetorious Powder," named after the noble Dr. Praetorious in the film *The Bride of Frankenstein* whose aim was to create life. By faithfully turning these musical dreams and visions into actual music without compromise, a musician sprinkles Praetorious Powder and winds up with music's eternal life.

Recently I had the pleasure of visiting Fantasy Studios in Berkeley, California, for the purpose of remastering my second solo album for CD re-release in 1997. This entire experience was covered with the powder that I'd call "P.P." for short if it didn't remind me of the previously mentioned Troggs tapes incident. First of all, the mastering guy didn't panic when he heard that the tapes were 20 years old. "Those aren't the oldest tapes we've had to work with," he laughed.

Of course not. This firm has been re-releasing music for decades. They even helped invent a clever marketing technique for such ventures: the double-album "two-fer," combining two LPs by one artist that are thematically related.

It was funny to sit and think about all the hassle and insults I had received over this music when I first recorded it 20 years ago and how some part of my personality was allowing me to see various ideas through to a sonic conclusion. Twenty years later, not only did the music have the life of its vision but it was receiving an injection of new life based on continued interest.

While I was basking in all this glory, a fellow from the accounting department came downstairs. He was smiling about how wonderful his job was. "I write checks all day. To Bobby Timmons. To Lou Donaldson. To all kinds of great people."

"It's good they are paying them," I said.

"They do now," he laughed.

"Now" and "then." Both eras when this music was happening. Twenty years from now, it will still be happening. Is this success? Not in the eyes of the public. Not according to our system. The girls in my sixth grade class liked the Beatles because they were "cute," not because they had wonderfully creative ideas. This is the reason I started playing guitar.

Musicians become popular because of their looks or their identification with certain trends and fashions. The Beatles and other groups of their era were allowed to be avant-garde and do weird stuff because this kind of "guru" thing was a fad back then. This kind of activity is clearly out of fashion now. One thing that is never really fashionable are creative ideas. Looks and so-called charisma are infinitely more appealing and marketable. An "idea" person must develop an ego that will allow them to get past all the advice they get to dump their ideas or at least water them down with scented eau de Trendy.

Once you have confidence, then you can start looking for ways to profit from everyone else's confusion. Remember what Ed Cassidy said about music related fields. Often music is just a tiny part of the whole picture.

My experience as a music journalist confirms this. Wherever music is included as just a partial offering, such as daily newspapers, school systems, libraries, stores, and so forth, it always gets minimal attention from the overlords. Yes, we are back to one of my favorite things: operating in an area where nobody is paying attention!

My newspaper gave a tiny amount of space to music, basically only enough to please the advertisers.

Someone probably had an inkling that the public "liked" music and wanted to read about it, but judging from how much space it received in relation to everything else, it was obviously considered to be about as popular as stale crackers. Filling this tiny bit of space meant paying people to write. But this was done as cheaply as possible. Nobody did music full-time. All the critics also covered other areas.

When rock music started, the promoters begged for reviews. At first they used copyboys, who worked for $75 a week, to do the reviews on an overtime basis.

> The girls in my sixth grade class liked the Beatles because they were "cute," not because they had wonderfully creative ideas. This is the reason I started playing guitar.

Later they hired younger writers who could deal with rock music and it became part of their beat. I reviewed classical, jazz, rock, and country, as well as wrote features on whatever else they wanted, ranging from the origin of pizza to how allergies were treated.

Nobody really paid attention to the actual content of the articles about music. This meant that the editor, who was supposed to read the copy and get rid of extraneous stuff, pretty much just corrected spelling.

I wound up in charge of the record review section. This was the first instance where I used what some had perceived as failure to actually create an environment of success for myself. (Or maybe it was the other way around. Maybe the left speaker has gone out.)

The previous record review editor admitted that the whole experience had been horribly depressing. "Nobody reads the reviews," he said. "We haven't gotten one letter about them." He opened a closet stacked high with review records. "I can't find anyone to write reviews. It isn't like the book reviews. They won't pay."

Book reviews were a scam at the paper. The management envisioned the book review section as classy and tossed a bit of money at it. The kind of review you could rewrite off the dust jacket was worth $15 and a longer review was an easy $100. Record reviews were paid nothing. You had to love the music because that was all you got, plus the records themselves were all awful. One of them was a double-LP rock opera about the history of Canada. Would you want to review that?

When I took over, my first move was to write letters to every company I had ever heard of that released jazz, informing them that the paper's record review section was going to be expanding and they should send jazz releases. Those chain letters that promise you'll receive luck or money if you send out 12 of your own letters have nothing on my operation back then. I sent out a couple dozen letters and had boxes showing up at the newspaper and my house for years. Some of these shipments had to be cleared through customs. The accountant got tired of my having to explain why customs had records for review and set up a system to automatically ease my shipments into Canada.

So I had loads of jazz records coming in. I even had the paper paying customs duty so obscure labels could ship me stuff. At least half the reviews in the record section were of jazz of some kind, with a heavy accent on the far out. This was in a town where there were maybe 10 people that appreciated this kind of music. No one ever said anything about the content of the column because, of course, this activity was going completely unsupervised.

From here, I decided to find out if publications that actually specialized in music also ran such loose ships. Sure enough, they did. I got in touch with a major jazz magazine and convinced them I was a jazz specialist. Their problem was that, while they could always find people willing to dip into the review pile, many of them wouldn't ever turn anything in and those who did were often poor writers. So I started getting boxes of records from them. Okay, so maybe I knew as much about the music as anybody else at this point. Then again, maybe not.

Did I deserve all this booty? No! Why was I getting it? Because two so-called major areas of the music business, a major daily paper and the record companies' promotion departments, were not functioning properly. Nobody was examining what was happening. A well-run newspaper would not waste valuable column space on some lunatic's form of a perpetual stocking stuffer, and the budget for promoting new jazz releases was too limited to be effective. Learn how to exploit weaknesses such as this for your own benefit, and you will be a happy person.

Realizing the loose standards of these publications, I decided a group I had formed shouldn't wait to get a good review, we should write our own. They were interested in the band review for their live concert review section, so the bandmembers and I wrote a rave review for ourselves. We made sure each player got elaborate praise. Of course we threw in a few criticisms to avoid being too suspicious. Two months later the review ran, and it led to several decent gigs! Strangely enough, it was the only review this particular band ever got. Is there anything wrong with this? Maybe, maybe not. Who is better to review your music than you? Wadada Leo Smith laughed when I told him this story, "Musicians *should* review their own music. When a musician comes to town, they should turn the column over to him."

Instead we have a critical establishment passing judgment and promoting whomever crashed at their place last week. The standards in this area are so nonexistent it boggles the mind. There are two standard record review formats, for example. One is a glib paragraph or two, easy to write without ever hearing the album. The second type is the long review granted an album that is deemed "important." These reviews have a built-in safety catch: Hardly anyone reads them all the way through. I have found several with hidden messages and unrelated texts buried inside them.

No one really supervises what is being written in these reviews. It is as if the public wants a critical establishment to guide it and prevent it from wasting time on unenjoyable art, but doesn't actually care whether the advice makes sense or not. I've seen no improvement in critical standards in the last 25 years.

Five years ago, there was a magazine publisher who acted like he was morally superior to everyone. This got on my nerves. When he asked if I'd review some records, I decided to see if he had any standards. I took 20 albums, and he published reviews I'd written without ever having listened to them.

"There were people that could have reviewed these that would have listened to them," he said to me. "What you did was really disappointing."

"I think you missed the point," I said. But since he was a journalist, not a musician, he probably never would get the point. Why should a profession we take seriously and devote our lives to be written about like this? There are few texts in existence other than ones written by musicians that make any sense at all.

Record labels often pad re-releases with liner notes they don't bother to edit. A '60s bandmember told me that one of the old LPs they did had been re-released with liner notes written by one of the other bandmembers in which he had accused the band's producer of extortion.

"I'm surprised the company lawyers didn't cut that part out," I said when they told me the story.

"I'm surprised at you," my friend said. "You know nobody reads that stuff."

Check out broadcasting situations such as public access cable, as easy to take over as a small duchy. I've seen hippies with guitars mount massive jam sessions and broadcast them over a cable channel with no censorship of any kind. A few years ago in Greensboro, some local enthusiasts started broadcasting sets from one of the punk clubs. I thought it was amazing how many people came up to me on the street, saying, "Hey! I saw you on TV!" The cliché is that no one watches these shows. But in actuality, nobody watches what is going on at the station itself, especially if it has to do with music.

It used to be the same with college radio, but the FCC and congress have made this a somewhat tighter ship. You better look over your shoulder if you want to freak out on college radio these days. Beyond the subject of artistic freedom, however, the college radio offers great potential in terms of free copies of recordings, access to contacts at record companies and concert promotion outfits, meeting musicians, doing interviews, and much more.

On the creative level, look for situations such as live, late-night broadcasts or specialized music shows that have a cult audience. It can be easy to worm your way into guest shots in these types of environments, wind up playing for three hours, record the whole thing, and get a free copy of the tape. It isn't really stealing. There would be no thieves if the whole world was like music, where the fine details are always given away for free.

Every good record someone finds in a bargain bin is proof of someone not paying attention when the item was marked at full price. At least this is a good way to approach your own recordings when you find them, because of someone's foolish mistake, in the cutdown pile. Buy them at the discount price, then mark them back up to full price for future sale.

Dutch folkie anarchist the Hat recently came across three copies of his debut album, circa 1973, in a used record pile at the Hannover flea market. They were mint. One of them was also particularly embarrassing. Inside was a crudely written letter, to one of the top critics in the world, begging for a review by sucking up to the critic. The Hat thought back about how he'd written that letter and sent the copy out to the critic personally. And now, here it was in the used record pile, oh so many years later. And in perfect condition. Obviously the critic hadn't shown the slightest interest in his project! Needless to say, he snapped up the records.

"You must really be into the Hat," the sales guy said as he stuffed the three copies into a recycled sack.

"I am. Even if he is a failure," he said, tucking the records under his arm.

CHAPTER 7

Big Label

There are big labels and then there are "major labels." I suppose these are labels that are bigger than the labels just called "big."

I wouldn't want to offend any of these enterprises by trying to determine who was big and who was major, but I can certainly tell when a fellow musician thinks they are onto either of these because they get sort of excited. Once again, an old expression about size comes to mind. "It's not how big it is, it's what you do with it." Would this be true about record labels?

"You really should be on a new label I am starting," Paul McCartney was supposed to have said to the illustrious, totally bizarre Captain Beefheart (Don Van Vliet) during a chance encounter in Paris.

"The bottle I'm in has no label," Beefheart was said to have answered. My encounters with major labels have been brief, rare, and sporadic enough to bring to mind bottles with messages in them floating at sea.

Any kind of music might have a chance at getting the attention of a mega-label (this is an all-purpose attempt at grouping together the big and major without diminishing the size of either) if the sounds float around long enough. It isn't that mega-labels ignore certain types of music. Just about every kind of music is represented in some way as the various record companies will try anything to make big bucks. Some of the best music ever made is on mega-labels, selling billions of copies or hardly any. And the same can be said about the worst music, and everything in between.

Perhaps the artist is better avoiding encounters with larger firms, simply because it can be dangerous business. The bigger the company the more ruthless. And, in many cases, the more colossal the blunders that will be made in attempting to carry out the very things that make musicians so excited about these kind of deals. I heard about a band that signed with a major, then didn't get any promotion. I heard about one that sold more copies when they were on an independent label.

Since dealing in opposites is standard in business practices, perhaps we should call the mega-labels dependent labels. They are dependent. Dependent on making as much money as possible on the musicians they sign. I know this because I have read a lot of articles and talked to many bandmembers. When I say that it is not based on firsthand knowledge, I am admitting that at least one thing has gone right in my career.

Archivists of my material or anyone dabbling in career gossip might point out certain contacts I have had with dependent labels, so I will save them the trouble and try to remember them. In 1974, I was encouraged to submit a demo to ECM. It was rejected with a personal, not a form, letter (see Introduction for details).

Jump to about 1984 before the dependents had anything to do with me. The Shockabilly band was asked to do a track for a Thelonious Monk tribute that Hal Wilner was putting together for A&M. Being on A&M was exciting. It meant a trip to New York to record. Of course I wanted to know, "Where's the money?"

My business-savvy band manager was afraid to ask the producer about the moolah because he didn't want to offend him. I said I would call him and take the heat by saying I was neurotic about making ends meet. Besides, if I was recording something for a dependent, I really wanted to be paid something for it. Well, the businessman found out that it was going to be double scale, which was great.

The session took place in an enormous RCA studio, with one guy on staff just to do stuff like go for sandwiches. The room was big enough to handle a studio orchestra. Jazz greats Elvin Jones and Steve Lacy cut a track right before us, and Jones made lemonade for everyone, then rubbed oil all over his bare chest. Meanwhile a roadie set up his drums. In other words, this was a night to remember. Later, A&M would try to kill our track completely for being "too weird." Wilner fought it out, but the track wound up only on vinyl, not on either cassette or compact disc.

And that's the end of that story. I learned a few things about the dependents, I suppose: They can make magic things happen, and they don't like "too weird." But if the right person makes "too weird," then no problem.

It always bothered me that the "Revolution #9" track became so popular. You'd think that based on this, everyone would have switched to weird electronic musique. If our band was as cute as the Beatles, than A&M might not have minded.

"What is this thing with you and A&M?" a college deejay asked about six years later when once again I ventured into dependent territory. The New York club the Knitting Factory had made a deal with A&M to, among other things, help them distribute their syndicated college radio show. This meant tapes of certain shows were being printed on cassettes with A&M labels.

"Did that live show with you and Camper Van Beethoven come out on A&M?" the same guy asked me when he saw one of these Knitting Factory shows. Well, no. And, yes. I keep a copy of the tape around in order to show people I've been on A&M.

Right around the same time I got a letter from a lawyer. He said he was helping musicians "shop" for dependent label deals. Would I mind if he tried on my behalf? His letter was full of glowing praise for my work, my commitment to ideals, and so forth. So I wrote him back and said, "Not if it is gonna cost me anything. And by the way, don't charge me for reading this letter."

"I will represent you completely on a speculative basis," he said. "There will be no charge for either writing or reading letters. However, if I get a deal, I will get a percentage."

All he wanted was a half dozen demo tapes to send to the list of dependent A&R types who were known to be sympathetic to artists of my ilk. I pre-pared the demo tapes, keeping in mind the dependent mind set. For example, I made sure there was a completely different song on each channel. Since he said one would go to Atlantic, I put an Otis Redding song as the opening track since I knew they liked his stuff over there. I don't mean a cover version, either. I sent them a tape of their own record.

I never heard a word about these demo tapes, but I did get a bill from the law firm. They wanted $100 per letter for a grand total of $600.

> *[The word] mega-label . . . is an all-purpose attempt at grouping together the big and major without diminishing the size of either.*

You can see why I say the dependent situation might be dangerous from the musician's point of view. Read any music business how-to book these days and they will tell you that you need a lawyer to shop for a dependent. Dependents won't listen to tapes that don't come from law firms, I have been told repeatedly. Many record company moguls deny this in their interviews. Still, it is a fact that they do their business with lawyers, and if you do business with a dependent, you are either going to have to become a lawyer or get one because lawyers like to talk to each other.

I wrote the law firm back and sent them a copy of the original letter in which the lawyer had said he would work for nothing. I received a note from the firm thanking me and telling me the reason they fired this particular joker was because he was making too many arrangements like this.

Some people will tell you dependent labels are worth avoiding if only to stay away from lawyers. There's some truth to that. I have only had a few business conversations with lawyers in the past 20 years, mainly about my will and a car accident my wife was in. But you will also hear that for true success, to really reach the top of the heap, to sell the most records, to become a household word, you have to make a deal with a dependent.

Since the above trail of anecdotes represents my total involvement to date with dependents . . . Oops! I forgot the mechanical royalty check from the IRS.

One day my wife tells me there's good news, which is nice because I am brooding over another stinker gig. "The IRS records called! They say they have a mechanical royalty check for your song, and it is going to be good!" The Monks of Doom band had recorded the sweet ballad "Voodoo Vengeance." The woman from the IRS had said, "Tell us where to send the check. It's a good one! Your husband will want to have it!"

Right! When it finally showed up after two months of anticipation, it was for $8. Eight crummy bucks! There was a statement along with it that indicated the company had sold about 100 copies of the album. The most amazing thing about this dependent label release was that I have never seen a copy of it anywhere, apart from the freebie the band sent me. I have never come across it in a record store, and it is never in the band's section if they have one. Let this be a lesson in the powers of dependent label distribution.

Another place I have never seen it is in the Used Record Pile. This is surprising because used record stores are the easiest place to come across dependent label products. The amount of promotional copies of dependent label releases that automatically get resold to used record dealers is such a problem that the dependents have gone to major efforts creating warning labels to indicate that the CD is not the property of whoever has it. It still belongs to the record company, who is "loaning" it out for promotional purposes. This system specifies that at any time someone might come along and demand the CD back, and you would be required to give it to them!

The spectrum of music industry jobs that rely on selling promotional copies for some extra pocket cash have not reacted favorably to this and other used record pile obstacles. A mysterious sub-strata of shops that "still buy demos" (this is usually muttered *sotto voce*) has come along to pick up the slack created by nervous clerks intimidated by the dependents. If you have actually purchased your copy of a dependent release and want to dump it, fear not. This is still legal. Which is where our trail leads us next.

THE COSMIC SECRETS OF THE USED RECORD PILE

The Top 50, Top 100, and many other Hit Parade variations originated because the fledgling performing-rights collection societies needed an accurate gauge of which songs were being played the most on the radio.

BMI and ASCAP developed their "sampling" strategies when the task of monitoring every spin of every record became overwhelming. They began to track record play much the way pollsters attempt to gauge public opinion at election time. From studying random airplay, they say they can determine what is played everywhere, and most people accept this as being reasonable.

Hit Parades themselves have always been under assault from interested parties who see the connections between chart placement and sales. Rather than the chart indicating just what records people are buying, the dizzying energy of conformist trend-mongering indicates that people buy what other people are buying, and this is determined by reading the charts!

One way payola, or the art of inner music business bribing, came about was through buying numbers on charts. Many trade magazines inch a record up the charts if the company or artist is good about buying advertising.

On a much bigger scale, and not involving any direct payola, is the practice of basing chart activity on record store orders rather than actual sales. In this way, a certain album can leap to the number one position in its first week of release if the record stores have been hyped into stocking thousands of copies. If there are lots of promotional displays of such a number one album, it could actually turn into a real hit, though there are many cases of massive numbers of albums being returned. The charts, usually full of releases from dependent labels, never admit that a certain album actually sold in numbers that wouldn't have even gotten it on the chart.

These are criticisms I've read in books about the music business and magazines focusing on dependent label activity, such as *Maximum Rock and Roll*'s issue devoted to dependent politics, highly recommended for detailed insight into what financial fiascoes some of these deals turn out to be for bands.

I hope to be the first to unlock the secrets of the Used Record Pile and how they relate to all this, although I'm sure all of us have gotten our fingers dusty from probing said pile. What is in this pile? That is what interests me. People sell records to get a little cash, but the state of mind when thumbing through the collection at home looking for turf-out titles is strictly negative. Like the friend you never pay attention to. Rejection time.

I've also seen these people turned away from trying to sell these records with an excuse such as, "We have too many of these." And it is not happy looks they have on their faces. They act like they've just seen the boyfriend they thought they had gotten rid of standing under their window. It was actually watching such a rejection, in this case a stack of '80s new wave albums such as Bananarama, that made me think about how many huge dependent label hits are returned in equally huge quantities.

"I just had to get rid of 50 copies of Springsteen's *Born in the U.S.A.* album," a Washington-area used record dealer told me.

I asked if this was unusual.

"Nah," he said. "The only strange thing is they still buy the CD."

I put the latter comment in out of fairness to Bruce Springsteen. Nonetheless, 50 people in one area—let's not forget there are a dozen used record piles in this ten block area alone, all of them full of Bruce—is a lot of people looking at that color picture of Bruce's butt and saying, "No thanks."

> Some people will tell you dependent labels are worth avoiding if only to stay away from lawyers.

Since the music industry regards the initial sale as being important enough to chart, actually extending that to the concept of the record store order being chartable, then certainly it follows suit that the customer's rejection of the record should also be chartable. Then and only then would we have a true gauge of popularity.

We need to subtract the albums returned from the albums sold or we have absolutely no standard of judgment. Perhaps a record that sells 2500 copies only has 25 of them returned! This purchase to return ratio needs to be examined closely, by skilled mathematicians. It might raise the status of records thought to be highly unpopular based on the fact that most people who bought these records felt they were worth keeping forever.

Compare this to a popular record that many people buy and later get rid of. Many of these albums wind up in "give-away" bins that sit in lonely rejection in the fronts of stores or near the piles of free magazines. In a giveaway pile in Gainseville, Florida, there was Van Halen, Black Sabbath, Anne Murray, Liza Minnelli, Linda Ronstadt. All big names, big careers, and a big group of consumers who say, "Be off with you! You are hereby banished to the Used Record Pile!"

Based on the number of these recordings that are rejected, one could build a case that popular music is really as unpopular as several viruses I've heard about, except the latter can't be gotten rid of quite so easily.

Checking in with many of my pals in used record stores, the so-called overlords of the Used Record Pile, was a real pleasure.

Boris: Champaign, Illinois

"I don't think I could make a list, the whole idea frightens me. But the record I have seen the most in 25 years in this business is *Going Places* by Herb Alpert. In fact, me and some of the guys that work record conventions were thinking about putting together a traveling show to take to the conventions, set up like a typical record dealer except it would only be copies of this album, hundreds of 'em. 'Cuz I got literally 350 in the basement. And we knew that would make a hilarious table. We might even sell a couple dozen, and that would be good for all of us."

Bobby: Wheaton, Maryland
1. Spin Doctors
2. Green Day, *Dookie*
3. *Waiting to Exhale* soundtrack ("In every pile!")
4. Counting Crows
5. Dave Matthews Band
6. Beastie Boys
7. Madonna ("They make the most negative comments about her records.")
8. Bryan Adams
9. Phil Collins
10. Bruce Springsteen ("Especially *Born in the U.S.A.*")

Lulu: Amsterdam, Netherlands
1. Green Day, *Dookie*
2. Rolling Stones ("The newer the album, the more the copies.")
3. *Mick Jagger Solo* ("A strange phenomenon because I don't remember selling any.")
4. Mike Oldfield, *Tubular Bells*
5. Madonna
6. R.E.M.
7. Grateful Dead
8. Bruce Springsteen ("Mostly *Born in the U.S.A.*")
9. Michael Jackson, *Thriller*
10. New Kids on the Block

Mr. Pointy: Chapel Hill, North Carolina

"The used record pile is dominated by the last wave of hit records before CDs came in." This clerk described most customers as buying records "like underwear, and when they're through with it, it is like last year's shirt." This comment reinforces my feelings of being out of touch, since I still wear last year's shirt and last year's underwear.

1. Genesis
2. Kenny Loggins
3. Green Day, *Dookie*
4. Aerosmith
5. Aerosmith ("Should get two numbers for the sheer number of copies. Mostly the last few releases with big radio hits such as *Get a Grip* and *Pump*.")
6. R.E.M., *Monster*
7. Hootie and the Blowfish
8. *My So-Called Life* soundtrack
9. first Collective Soul
10. Any rap ("But we make sure not to buy it, there is no resale value!")

Papa Jazz: Columbia (aka Cola-town), South Carolina

First, let's mention that this store owner, whose used record pile has been going strong for 25 years, doesn't agree with the cynical previous quotation comparing used record pile stuffers to style-conscious underwear sellers. "There's only one reason people bring their records here. To get money!"

1. Beatles ("By an incredible stretch, nobody else comes any where close, hardly a day goes by when we don't see a few.")
2. Led Zeppelin
3. U2
4. Bob Dylan
5. Hootie and the Blowfish ("A lot, but not as much as Dylan." Note: this is Hootie's hometown and the band's management office used to be above this store!)
6. Byrds
7. John Cougar Mellencamp
8. Wynton Marsalis
9. Paul McCartney
10. John Lennon

Perry-scope: Gainseville, Florida

1. Nirvana ("The entire catalog")
2. Aerosmith
3. Blues Traveler
4. Stone Temple Pilots
5. Red Hot Chili Peppers ("Daily")
6. Beatles ("Almost never!" This is listed because his reaction was so different from the previous store owner's.)
7. Hootie and the Blowfish
8. R.E.M. ("Last four albums")
9. Harry Connick (When asked about jazz returns, he said "None. Harry Connick . . . if you call that jazz.")
10. U2 ("Last three albums")

RRRRRon: Lowell, Massachusetts

This astute record store manager agreed with the concept of this chapter, making comments such as this without any prompting: "The more famous the artist, the more records people get rid of. The more successful the record, the more copies get brought back."

1. Billy Joel ("If I see one more, I'm gonna scream!")
2. Bruce Springsteen
3. Elton John
4. The Police
5. U2
6. The Who ("Bad '90s albums")
7. Foreigner
8. Journey
9. Aerosmith ("But it sells again.")
10. J. Geils Band ("Constantly")

Some of the used record pile honchos felt my poll was an attempt to prove a ludicrous point. "It's obvious, the more copies that are made of something, the more will get returned!" one guy told me, making me feel like an idiot.

Others were sympathetic when I said I was trying to prove that perhaps there were reasonable alternatives to the dependent label route of many sold, many returned.

"Is it better to be truly loved by 500 people than rejected by 50 million?" I asked RRRRRon.

"That's a wonderful thought," he said.

CHAPTER 8

Chicken Public vs. the Avant-Garde

Most of us are familiar with Chicken Little, who thought the sky was falling when an acorn hit him on the head and just had to tell the king. Music history is full of occasions when the public reacts as if musicians were making the sky fall, upsetting them enough that they'd complain to a king if they could. These days, they just complain to each other, or worse, ignore the whole phenomenon. Being ignored might be the worst threat to composers and artists who have used all grades of shock, horror, and indignation to promote their work. After all, nothing gets attention faster than the outrageous.

Unfortunately for those attempting to begin careers right now, so much hustling has already been done to make certain artists seem radical and so many bizarre events have already taken place that shocking the public is becoming more and more difficult. In countries where there is continual exposure to non-mainstream activity (I hate that "avant-garde" description and I'm gonna tell you why in a minute), the artists themselves often remark, "Well, it's hard to get a rise out of this audience! They've seen everything!"

It's much more enjoyable to play to an audience who is unprepared for anything even slightly abnormal. It's a chance to preach to people who are not yet converted. You have the opportunity to do this at free outdoor concerts, building-lobby events, festivals held inside a bank for all the customers to gawk at, or open-air events in a public downtown arena at lunchtime.

But what is this really about? Why is some music considered avant-garde, and why do some people hate it? And why do many so-called experts or lovers of such work judge it by the superficial gauge that

each successive event or performance must be more avant-garde than the one last week? Can anything be more avant-garde than a cellist, appearing nude, playing the instrument with a dead fish? Come back next Sunday.

What about a piece of music where nothing happens for four minutes and 33 seconds? How avant-garde! Many listeners entirely miss the point of the latter: John Cage's "4:33." Asking a classical music audience to consider its own coughs, seat-shuffling, and any other sounds that happen to occur as "music" is an act of revolution and a wonderfully unforgettable insult.

In the meantime, audience participation is taken for granted in many other forms of music. Folk singers stage sing-alongs and seem depressed when the crowd doesn't respond well. Soul and rock performers have made classic records drenched in crowd noise. ("Fingertips," "Everybody Needs Somebody," and "My Ding-a-Ling" come to mind, all spiritual brethren of "4:33.")

During the early days of the so-called British invasion, a time period in rock history similar to the baroque period in classical music, it was common for the audience's screams to completely overwhelm the music. This is the foundation for the entire rock music scene as it exists today. So what is so audacious about "4:33"?

Avant-garde literally means a precursor of something to come, something ahead of its time. This is preposterous when one is describing what is currently happening. Is the example above avant-garde? No, because it didn't happen in a time machine or on some kind of time-travel trip. In many cases, so-called avant-garde or "post-modern" work is actually something from a past decade and is older than the people who label it as such. The first Futurist concerts, in which "music" was created on stage by machines, took place in the 1920s. Jazz from 30 years ago is so far out that jazz educators today can't figure out how to teach it, and mainstream players can't figure out how to play it. When the first serial music pieces were composed, they were also considered avant-garde.

If you're told that you are ahead of your time, you should realize that you've been cursed. Prepare to deal with it. What, pray tell, do we have to do to get ready to listen to a piece of music? All a person needs is a set of ears. It is not required that one study for years just to listen to music. In some cases, a more studied individual might get more out of something they are experiencing, but since there's no competition to "get the most" out of a piece of music, who cares?

What it really means to be ahead of your time is that, although you will not feel that the public accepts you, they will turn around and accept the same ideas in some other form. This process will happen almost immediately, not in the future.

When Ornette Coleman brought his jazz band into a New York club for its first extended engagement, the event caused an incredible stir. Musicians from many different fields, some as famous as Leonard Bernstein, came to see what all the hoo-hah was about. Coleman was dubbed an avant-garde rebel, ahead of his time. This was truly post-modern jazz, they said, the music of tomorrow.

Tomorrow has come along and another tomorrow and another and another. Ornette Coleman is still considered avant-garde jazz. In the academic jazz environment, it's as if he doesn't even exist. Nothing about his musical language or concept has filtered into mainstream jazz.

But listen to a soap commercial and perhaps you'll hear Ornette Coleman. It's the same as people designing floor tiles imitating Jackson Pollock while art experts were calling him "avant-garde." Everyone knows there's nothing avant-garde about soap com-

mercials or floor tiles. They are not post-modern, they are now. So are horror movies.

Anyone in the film business knows that if you can make even a reasonably entertaining film, this is one of the easiest ways to make money with a small investment. Part of their entertainment value is the typical horror movie score, most of which consists of ideas lifted from avant-garde composers such as Schoenberg, Berg, Webern, or Messiaen. Yet I've never seen anyone in a horror movie audience put their hands over their ears and gasp, "My lord! I can't take this music! It's too avant-garde." They are perfectly

Some performers require gagging because the effort of listening might injure the audience.

willing to have this music in the background if someone is about to get their head bashed in with a meat tenderizer.

Horror movie producers will not even release a film that doesn't include such a score. *The Texas Chainsaw Massacre* has a wonderful score in which the director and several friends make weird noises on percussion instruments. The chance of a large audience sitting through music like this in a concert is almost nil, but as the backdrop for a story about a family robbing graves and making household knick-knacks out of the remains, the music suits a large audience just fine.

The public seems to tolerate certain sounds if they hear them used to sell soap or linoleum or as a background to murder and mutilation, but they cannot accept this music on its own terms. Is it because too much concentration is required? If the public is unable to actually listen to artists they say they really

GLEN WHEELER

like, how can we expect them to concentrate on the unfamiliar? The answer is: Don't expect it. They won't. But they will pass judgment on it because for some reason people feel they have a right to an opinion about music even if they haven't really listened to it.

They pick up some of these cues from critics. Even people that aren't that interested in music read the occasional music review, and we know that reviewers sometimes go to print without having actually listened in-depth to the music they are writing about. In some cases, they might not have heard the entire recording or concert or even listened to any of it.

So, an opinion can be based on nothing or, in the best of cases, only a superficial impression. On top of that, you have the abstract nature of music: Nobody can really say what music is all about, anyway. And you have the democratic philosophy that music is for all people, different strokes for different folks, and people should certainly have the right to not like whatever music they don't like. And they should also have the right to these superficial impressions. And they do.

Some critics spend their writing careers as missionaries winning over converts to music judged by most to be too weird. Others do the opposite, attacking the careers of various players who are "ahead of their time" but are lucky enough to be subject to critical assaults in the present day. By studying writing careers in library stacks, I've noticed that some critics flip-flop between both approaches. Some hope nobody will remember they used to hate so-and-so whom they love now, and others write whole articles to justify these important changes in opinion. This latter style of writing is a kind of artistic offshoot of the post-Watergate confessional style of political speech. None of this really makes clear why some music is removed from its present context and banished to misty futures. In other words: Why do people think some music is so damn weird?

There is music that tries to be weird, and there is also music that has no intention of being weird but gets judged out of context. In the latter case, I am thinking in particular of ethnic music recordings. A recording of pygmies surrounding an animal with weird noises in order to frighten it might sound strange, but nothing these pygmies do could ever really be avant-garde because they don't think along these lines. The sounds they make, in the context in which they are made, are normal for them. If they had been playing a copy of *Born in the U.S.A.* on a boom box while tracking their game, now *that* might have been weird.

There is music that doesn't really want to be weird but picks up the stigma anyway because of audience reactions. The '60s style of free jazz was a highly motivated, sometimes almost desperate attempt at communication. "It's about feelings, not music," said Albert Ayler, who has to be one of the most unconventional jazz performers to ever record. If you study Ayler's music, you will hear many aspects of normal folk music, marching band music, and children's songs mixed with approaches people consider outrageous.

Why do certain sounds, no matter how sparingly they are used, overwhelm everything else? I've had experiences where a lone squeak, feedback sound, or strange noise in an otherwise normal piece of music

What it really means to be ahead of your time is that, although you will not feel that the public accepts you, they will turn around and accept the same ideas in some other form. This process will happen almost immediately, not in the future.

is enough to panic an entire audience. If a long section of feedback and squeaking was interrupted by a tiny bit of normal music, would the whole thing be more accessible? I don't think so.

Clearly certain types of sounds and musical proceedings have a powerful ability to alienate large segments of the audience. This is one of the phenomena they talk about when the term "freak out" comes up. "God, they really freaked out when you hit those high notes," I heard a fan tell a saxophone player at a gig. It reminded me of another concert, where the Japanese trumpeter Toshinori Kondo stepped on his distortion box and began playing in a false, high-squeal trumpet register, causing the entire front row of elderly ladies to practically gallop out of the hall.

I once heard a group playing at an open-air University show where they attracted a diverse crowd. One of the players began blowing a blade of grass and making a high, annoying sound. He kept it up until only one tenth of the audience was left. One of my

I Hate the Man Who Runs This Bar!

friends remarked, "I don't think this is weird. What is weird is the fact that if he had played a really bad cover version of 'Take Me Home, Country Roads' instead, the audience would have sat through it."

The public feels threatened by music they don't understand and becomes hostile to it. To understand someone who is talking to you, you have to listen to them. Deciding that they don't like some types of music is not always something the public does at the same time as listening to music, although this does happen on rare occasions.

One thing I've never understood is when someone says to me or any musician, "Will you explain your music?" This is usually asked with slightly veiled hostility, as if the questioner has decided to show their tolerance by giving you, the offending artist, a chance at redemption. Why would a good explanation make the music sound better? If you ate food you didn't like, would an explanation of why it is good make it taste better? Not in my experience. The difference is that in the case of food, there is more of a tendency to actually taste the morsel in question before passing judgment.

I am fond of comparing taste in music to taste in pizza toppings. As serious as I am about this, one can't honestly say a positive or negative opinion should be formed about someone's music as quickly as somebody can bite an anchovy. The taste palate can change, and people do develop tastes for certain types of food just as they do for music. But an anchovy is an anchovy and really has the same taste whether you eat one or 200.

Music, on the other hand, really needs to be experienced in-depth to be judged clearly one way or the other. Anything else is unfair. It's also unfair to expect critics to have the time to do this. Compare their work to that of a restaurant critic: Even in a large city, if one added up all the possible establishments that could be reviewed and all the dishes that might be served, it is still much less material than the average music critic is exposed to in a week's time.

A restaurant critic will normally visit a place he is reviewing three or four times and sample several dishes each time. This is standard procedure, as is at least the appearance of anonymity, so that management doesn't make especially good dishes for these pundits when they show up.

A music critic, on the other hand, is free to dismiss someone's music on the basis of one piece of music or even just part of one piece. And most critics I know make their identity clearly known to everyone in the business so they can schmooze backstage, get free promotional stuff, get sucked up to by certain artists, and maintain a feeling of power over the music scene. Musicians who really examine public

and critical opinion may want to head for a safe hideout in the hills. A performer could watch the audience walk out because their music was "too weird," then turn around the next day and read a review criticizing the performance for "not being avant-garde enough."

A top New York critic who later became a composer himself dismissed an early performance by myself and saxophonist/composer John Zorn because he said he'd "heard it all before." This is a typical critical reaction. If one added up all the possible notes and sounds on instruments and all the possible permutations of them that two people could make, the total would run into the infinite. Nevertheless, a writer can get away with comments like, "I've heard it all before," despite the fact that such a claim is totally preposterous! It would be more reasonable for the critic to say he is a direct descendent of the god Thor and can make smoke and fire come out of his nose. Which would probably be more productive.

In addition to being discouraged from playing music that is too weird, the "not weird enough" syndrome discourages musicians from using more accessible musical forms and concepts. On a typical avant-garde scene, for example, someone who uses pretty melodies might be laughed at. Use a well-known rhythm and you are a sell out, especially if such an approach becomes mainstream. The public, on the other hand, thinks that such touches are proof that the musician in question can really play.

This used to drive me up the wall when, in my early twenties, I began promoting concerts for so-called avant-garde players. The perception that someone doing this sort of music was faking it seemed almost universal. I heard it from my mother, who knew nothing about this sort of music; from people that came to the concerts; and from local musicians.

When Sam Rivers performed at the University of Calgary in the mid-'70s, I was extremely impressed with his ability to improvise an entire concert on tenor saxophone, flute, piano, and soprano saxophone. He used no written material and no repeated themes or recognizable "songs," but there were different rhythms and a lot of interplay between Rivers and his bassist and percussionist. "He can't even play," a local saxophonist told me the next day.

I immediately made two arguments. The first was that someone who couldn't actually play a saxophone could never in a million years get through even a portion of a live set without their lip giving out completely. Don't believe it? Try it sometime. The second was that so-called jazz masters such as Miles Davis and Dizzy Gillespie had hired Mr. Rivers. I got sarcastic with the local hotshot. "I suppose you know better than Miles Davis," I said. This made no impression.

"Yeah," he said, "Miles has really lost it."

I am proud that in my capacity as a critic during this era, I was the only writer to give a certain Miles Davis touring band a good review. Since many ideas Miles was dealing with back then did surface and gain mainstream acceptance in funk and rap music years later, it can be tempting to buy into the "ahead of his time" concept. But this is just typical lopsided thinking that accepts the opinions of the public, too-busy critics, and other musicians over the ideas of the artist.

Do yourself a favor as a musician and look at these ideas as part of the here and now. It is safe to say that nothing anyone plays is completely new and modern. Pick any kind of weird, extended instru-

> *There is music that tries to be weird, and there is also music that has no intention of being weird but gets judged out of context.*

mental technique, and a knowledgeable enthusiast who has studied musical history will tell you which century it actually came from. Haydn was considered nuts in his era because, among other things, he used too much space in his music when the more popular, romantic notion was to fill in every hole. Go forward and backward and you will find other examples where use of silence in music makes audiences uncomfortable and they react against it.

I keep reading that it is an avant-garde guitar technique to knock on the body of the instrument, yet I learned it from folk/country player Doc Watson and 12-string blues picker Blind Willie McTell, both of whom made knocking sounds to illustrate various lyrics. And Albert Ayler is hardly the only post-modern player to use the most basic forms of folk music. They all do! Players and composers in all musical genres reference and pay tribute to the past, yet they still get described as doing precisely the opposite by both critics and the public.

You are bound to hear someone tell you, "My kid could do that," in relation to some kind of music they don't understand. I was always fond of this well-thought-out critical philosophy and became more so when I began raising my own children. My snappy

retort—"Give me your phone number, maybe next time your kid can open the show"—remains a good one.

Kids actually can and do play some of the sounds people associate with "weird" music, sometimes better than professionals. This is something that can be appreciated in any kind of artwork in which children are involved. This is partly because children have less of the inhibitions that adult musicians tend to develop after being in music school and dealing with musicians and the audience. But an unskilled child fooling around on an instrument and coming up with odd sounds doesn't have the ability to throw in a flashy musical phrase and thus appease the audience the way a "real" player can. "At first I thought you couldn't play and were just fooling around until you threw in that blues thing," is a typical reaction I've heard.

Group efforts by flocks of geese and crows, a busy hive of bees, an orchestra warming up (constantly pointed out as the favorite part of a symphony concert by many composers and performers), and various combinations of urban sound phenomena such as power tools become more and more appealing the more one listens. Begin to enjoy enough solo saxophone concerts utilizing extended techniques and sound effects, and you will begin to appreciate the sounds of canaries, dogs, wolves, and anything else capable of delivering an extended monologue in sound.

Does a duck have to know how to play a Bach cantata to be worth listening to? What about a child playing the piano? What about an adult musician who begins their career with some kind of avant-garde music, maybe to develop other skills in more accepted genres later on and maybe not? Should such traditional skills really be required before the public accepts you as "really" being able to play? If you think the answer is yes, you are not alone; but you might not be right. There are many problems in logic with this notion. Why should some musical styles have this onus placed on them? Does anyone expect a classical musician to be able to break into a Hank Williams number before they can "really" play? Does the synthesizer player in a Flock of Seagulls have to be adept at Irish jigs? Is anybody asking Ice-T to "prove himself" by singing "I Left My Heart in San Francisco"?

If you answer "no" to all these questions, then think about why people expect players of so called "weird music" to demonstrate capabilities in other genres. It's probably because people are fond of picking on this kind of music and will look for any excuse!

Often the conduct of the musicians themselves goes well beyond backstage bad mouthing. For some reason, totally unprofessional behavior by hired players brought in to do large scale "modern" works has

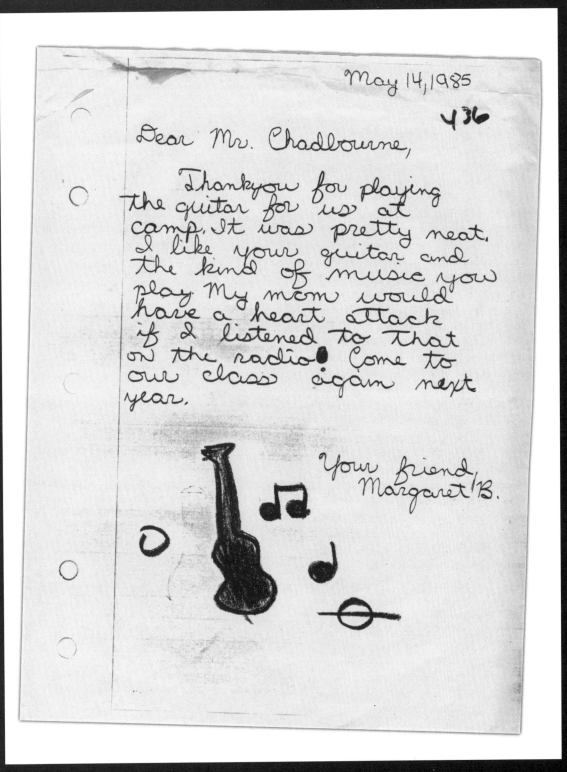

May 14, 1985

436

Dear Mr. Chadbourne,

Thankyou for playing the guitar for us at camp. It was pretty neat. I like your guitar and the kind of music you play. My mom would have a heart attack if I listened to that on the radio! Come to our class again next year.

Your friend,
Margaret B.

Here I have clearly scored a success getting my music out to a new audience. And the impression was an important one. This particular child was so charged up by my appearance that she became a musician and now has her own punk band.

been tolerated for decades. This goes for classical, jazz, and studio players. Frank Zappa describes the nightmare of paying London Philharmonic players top dollar to rehearse and then watching them get plastered during the break, for which they were also paid.

Other composers describe orchestras getting drunk at the actual concerts, while still others wish the orchestra *had* gotten drunk because it might have kept them from leaving. A recent performance by Canadian "cut-up" composer John Oswald at the prestigious Angelica festival of Contemporary Music in Firenze, Italy, apparently involved half the orchestra storming out midway while the conductor made sick faces so the audience would be sure he didn't approve of the music.

Composers in the jazz idiom, such as Carla Bley and Anthony Braxton, report similar behavior from hired players in concert and studio sessions. Snickering, smirking, and making silly comments all seem de rigueur. Why is this kind of behavior allowed? If someone acted like this at a Nashville country recording session, they would be fired and probably beaten up, too.

This might mean nothing to you if your music isn't in any of these contested areas of sound, but you'll find in most styles of music there is a lot of backbiting about different styles, different eras, who the real innovators are, and so forth. Watch out for this. Don't let yourself fall into these negative traps.

Accept certain givens. Anyone who gets up and plays music is "really playing," because that is all that is required. Listen to what the person does, not to what they don't do. If you want to hear something different, go find it. It exists. But don't ever dare say something isn't "really music." I've yet to hear any sound on earth, whether it is intentionally made as "music" or not, that can't be conceived of or appreciated as music when placed in the right context—which, admittedly, in some cases might be the mind of a madman.

Whatever kind of music you play, make an effort to expose it to the public. Look for those children who are capable of such carefree musical expression. They are quite often able to listen to music more clearly than adults. I've seen many elementary school, middle school, senior high, and college classes exposed to new types of music. For every questioner who doubts someone can "really play" or who wants to hear an "explanation," there is someone who gets turned on and becomes more and more interested in staying that way their whole lives.

Be a part of this process as a musician. Maybe if enough of us are out there doing it, there will cease to be those ignorant people heeding Chicken Public's cry that "the sky is falling!"

CHAPTER 9

Publishing

If you are serious about making any money out of music, then this is the one chapter you'd better not skip. That is, unless you feel you are totally incapable of ever creating—on your own or in a partnership—anything that might be considered an original published music work.

Almost every musician I've met over the years has, at some point, had to officially publish something. You don't have to be a songwriter or a symphonic composer, a lyricist or a poet to have something you need to publish and potentially collect publishing royalties. You don't have to read and write traditional notation or even know what a G chord is. You can record your five-year-old son banging on tin cans for five minutes, record it on a cheap tape recorder, call it a composition, register it, and who knows, maybe even make money off it 35 years later.

The only way to ensure that you *won't* make money on original compositions is to not publish them. Of course, publishing them is no guarantee that you'll make anything, but at least you will be part of the large fraternity of published songwriters whose state of mind is often a combination of elation and paranoia. The former state comes on those occasions when publishing checks are much larger than normal; the latter should be an ever-present state of mind. This is because when you talk about the international publishing empire, you are talking about a wealthy and powerful bureaucracy that makes the big record companies look like the corner magazine store.

There are dozens of performing-rights collection agencies in every corner of the world. But before we clash with these monstrous tycoons, let's try to explain what is represented by a musician's "publishing rights."

These rights indicate a certain private ownership of pieces of music that are deemed to be original compositions. These terms are intentionally vague because, as you will see, what constitutes an original composition is less straightforward than you might think.

You don't have to have hair like Beethoven and spend hours writing down notes to be a composer; although if you do that, you certainly are one. Improvise your own music straight into a tape recorder and it can be registered as your composition and published in some form. Make up a song and teach it to a band, and even if the drummer throws in some original licks that he's made up, any recording of that song will be considered your composition, not his, unless you decide to share the rights with him.

If the drummer took the same licks, played them into a tape recorder and called them his composition, then he could be considered the composer. The way the publishing business works, the same record could contain the drummer's licks published as his composition and the song in which the licks appear published as someone else's composition, and nobody would care—unless the two composers decided to sue each other.

Or the guitarist could record the drummer complaining about how the band isn't making any money, call that a composition, and collect royalties on it for generations. And the drummer can sue the guitarist, claiming the conversation/composition was, at the very least, a collaboration.

This actually happened with the late Frank Zappa and the members of his first band, the Mothers of Invention. Members of this outfit, drummer Jimmy Carl Black and keyboardist Don Preston, will tell you that some of the communally composed music was credited to Zappa as his sole composition, which meant that he got all the money from it.

This is a common complaint in many bands. Trombonist Julian Priester told me that during his stint with the Duke Ellington Big Band, he noticed the Duke and his collaborator Billy Strayhorn would nab riffs that players in the horn sections were coming up with off the cuff and then write them into the

> [The disposition of] published songwriters . . . is often a combination of elation and paranoia. The former . . . when publishing checks are much larger than normal; the latter should be an ever-present state of mind.

scores as their compositions. If you took the notion that the score was worth XXX dollars and each written passage a part of that total, it would only make sense that whoever actually wrote each part should get paid for that part.

The problem came up again for Priester in the Herbie Hancock *Sextant* Sextet, where there would be long, group-improvised recording sessions that the trombonist felt were group compositions and should be credited as such. But the bandleader edited those pieces down and called them his own compositions.

Zappa went so far as to secretly tape the bandmembers discussing their problems, then put these out as album tracks that were credited to him. When he asked Jimmy Carl Black to "go out in the studio and say something, anything," and Black came up with, "Hi, boys and girls. I'm Jimmy Carl Black, and I'm the Indian of the group," Zappa published the text as "his" composition. Is this going too far? Maybe not. Black might have made the comments, just as other bandmembers made comments about the band not working enough, but it was the "composer" who decided that this material would be interesting to record listeners. Shouldn't Zappa get credit for this?

An obvious solution would be to distribute the credit, but this is done too rarely. Lately, more and more groups who play in genres where improvising and group composition is encouraged are devising ways of manipulating songwriting credits and publishing registration so that income is shared more equally.

Everything about composing and publishing is a state of mind. Some states of mind, however, are clearly illegal, such as intentionally copying too much of someone else's published composition if it is the text or the melody. The way the publishing business is set up, important parts of recordings, such as the chord changes, the exact way the rhythm is played, or the improvised instrumental solos, are completely unprotected as compositions in themselves. This is why in jazz music so many published compositions by Charlie Parker and others are based on the chord changes of previously published works.

We are pointing out these confusing discrepancies in the publishing world just to set the proper tone. Music publishing is intense, confusing, and full of lies and ridiculous double standards. Get used to it! You can't even *think* about publishing for five seconds without some fib creeping in.

Dealing with publishing as a musician is a lot like being in love. It is best to try and live with it, not without it. Nonetheless, aren't there a lot of aspects of love that seem corrupt? Do you wonder why you even bother? This is just like publishing. You will find out, somewhere along the line, that you are being cheated on, and there won't be a lot you can do about it other than move on and hope it never happens again. I have been cheated on my publishing, but I have also had the happy experience of ripping open envelopes and finding checks that surpassed my wildest expectations.

The great thing about publishing money is that it keeps coming in decades after the work has been done. This is a rare treat for a self-employed person. Even better, the royalties are not subject to the same social security tax as self-employment earnings. However, don't start thinking that it is some kind of free ride. Not only is it an unreliable source of income, it requires constant surveillance. Theoretically, the more time you spend researching what publishing money might be owed you, the more you will get. If you could afford the time or the manpower to have someone monitor radio broadcasts all over the world, for example, it would be worth it in the long run. The cold reality of the situation is that even the Michael Jacksons of the world can't cover every possible publishing pay-off base. Money will go uncollected. Who likes this? The performing-rights societies, that's who.

A published work can be any form of recording: a tape of a concert, a commercially released CD or LP, or any other medium. It can also be a score for a piece of music, but there is no legal requirement that the score or the composition has to exist on paper at any time. The whole thing can be in your head.

To become a publisher in the USA, you have to set up shop with one of the three major companies that collects and distributes publishing income: ASCAP (American Society of Composers and Publishers), BMI (Broadcast Music Inc.), or SESAC (Society of European Stage Authors & Composers). You need to name your publishing company something that has not been used before, and have a writer whose work you can publish. Publishing income is split between writers and publishers. If you own your own publishing, you get 100 percent. Of what? Of whatever gets collected and distributed by the society representing you, whether it's ASCAP, BMI, or the foreign equivalents of these societies abroad, as well as whatever foreign subpublishers you might have dealings with. (We'll explain what a subpublisher is later. It has nothing to do with printing pictures of U-2 boats.)

"Foreign?" you might ask incredulously. "What if you've never left the States?" If you are doing original music of any kind, chances are that most of the publishing income will come from outside the United States. This situation has improved slightly in the last few years since college radio began paying broadcast royalties, but the radio media in the USA practices a virtual blockade against any music not specified as worthy of broadcast (and this specification often depends on whatever cozy relationships a radio station may have developed with the big record labels).

If you live in Nantucket and write a punk song or a song for a chamber quartet, publishing royalties for broadcasts are more likely to filter in from Sweden than from your home state.

Many people confuse publishing with copyrighting, but it is possible to collect publishing without having copyrighted anything. On the other hand, you can copyright all your works and never collect a penny. Copyright is simply a form of protection, although whether it is necessary or not is up for debate.

Publishing registration is a system under which anyone can try to collect money that has been paid to publishing collection societies for their works—or at least, work a composer has claimed was theirs with no one questioning that claim.

I bring this up because I currently collect money for several songs I had nothing to do with writing. I have seen, over and over, cases where record labels registered a song to someone who was not the actual songwriter, thus diverting the flow of royalties like a lock across a canal. That is, unless someone successfully questions the situation.

In my own dealings, I have found many aspects of the world publishing empire to be impenetrable and impossible to question or change. Oh, sure. You can write all the angry letters you want and you can even scrawl insulting threats across the bottom of official forms, but it won't get you a nickel.

I became an official publisher when I put out my first album. I learned about publishing while investigating copyright. In the process of figuring out how to copyright the music on my first album, I got in touch with BMI and was advised to set up a publishing company for myself. Of course, my first reaction was fright, thinking that setting up any kind of company would involve financial outlay, particularly to lawyers who had to do the paperwork involved and perhaps also to branches of the government for licenses and so forth.

Luckily, I received good legal advice. "You don't need to set up a company, register anything, or do anything to put out a record like you're talking about," the guy told me. "What you're doing is on such a small scale that nobody will care." This was fantastic advice. Years later I watched an associate scrambling around doing everything by the book for an equally small-scale release. All for no reason.

The publishing registration, on the other hand, was something I couldn't neglect or I would never get my hands on certain money that gets released into the publishing collection system.

On my first album, all the pieces were original compositions. I sent out dozens of these albums to various radio stations here and abroad. Disc jockeys who were really into unique music looked for just such stuff. If they happened to reside in a country where the publishing collection was efficient and honest, even one broadcast of one of my pieces meant money. And that is just what ended up happening, much to my surprise.

When I set up Nukem Music, my publishing company, and signed myself up as a writer published by Nukem Music, I was completely confused by what was happening. I kept thinking that for Nukem Music to truly exist there had to be an office somewhere with a sign that said Nukem Music. There had to be something official, right? Something tangible? But there doesn't. There is just the name and supposedly a flow of published works behind it. That is the whole thing. You write music, and you register it.

I ended up registering every composition I had in my notebook. Later, I wound up abandoning at least half of the pieces—at least I thought I had. But during one of my first trips abroad, when I was in Italy with the percussionist Andrea Centazzo, I noticed strange sheets of paper circulating around backstage after the concert.

Before I met up with Centazzo, I had done a few small gigs in London at a musician-run venue of the sort that is never covered by a performing-rights society collecting for "live performance" rights. England is very much like the United States in this respect, and you must perform in an extremely large venue or festival before the performance-rights societies take notice. "Taking notice" means their agents collect an annual or per-performance fee from the venues in question, and this money is in turn distributed among the composers involved once the organization's operational fees have been sucked out.

One night I saw Andrea crouched over an official form in the dressing room. Although there were quite a few lines to be filled in, he had only written one phrase in Italian, his signature, and his address. He didn't like me looking over his shoulder, but being a snoop is an aspect of musical survival that should never be underestimated. I couldn't figure out the Italian, so I asked what it meant.

"The Dream of the Impossible Fish."

"What's that?" I asked.

He was getting more and more annoyed. "It is a composition."

"Of yours?"

"Yes," he said with a look of pride.

"Why are you writing it down now? What is this form?"

There was no turning back now. He had to tell me. "Is publishing registration for tonight's concert."

Then we discussed why he was writing down the title of this composition when we actually played other things. Most of the music we played together we made up on the spur of the moment. I had no objection to him naming these improvisations after a fish, imaginary or otherwise, but I didn't like the idea that he was taking all the credit, not to mention the money.

"I have my own publishing company," I told him. "Why don't we split it?"

Then he explained that there would be no point. If I didn't live in Italy and speak Italian, my chances of collecting anything from the Italian performing-rights societies were probably lower than getting invited for a personal audience with the Pope.

He could have offered to pay me out of his own pocket when and if he got the dough, and he did do that in a way. He invited me to tour in Italy. He also took me into his home and his mother's and grandmother's, all of them full of Italian food that ended up on a one-way journey from the stove to my stomach.

From this I got an early picture of the publishing world. The most important lesson I learned was that when registering material from a live performance, there is no need to write down anything that has to do with what you really did. That was where those "abandoned" compositions came in.

As I started filling out my own forms, I sometimes found myself unable to remember what I had played. Or I might have played something new that I didn't have registered yet. Or, when I started playing more and more "cover" versions, writing down what I had really played would mean I wouldn't get paid. (This rhymes. Perhaps it should be registered as a lyric.) So I started writing down certain titles that were registered under my name, honing my skills at defrauding the publishing societies as I picked up more tips on how things worked.

Don't get me wrong! Writing down my own registered compositions when I had actually performed versions of songs registered to other people is a complex issue, and I'm not just trying to make myself appear more honest than I am. If you know anything about improvised forms of music, you will realize that neither publishing nor copyright legislation has come anywhere near being able to deal with reality. Musicians in these fields must figure out ways to more closely approximate what is really going on, though most of them appear underhanded on the surface.

Let's look, for a minute, at the great master John Coltrane and his multiple recordings of the song "My Favorite Things." Have you heard Coltrane's group play this sweet song from *The Sound of Music*? During, let's say, a short 25-minute version, the group plays the Rodgers and Hammerstein theme for maybe three minutes maximum, including the theme statements at beginning and end. Coltrane does not use the lyrics to the song, which in a typical songwriting team division is 50 percent of the royalties. He also gives a different feeling to the song by changing the rhythm and eliminating most of the chords, casting it instead in a mode influenced by Indian ragas.

The improvising that dominates every version of the song that Coltrane has recorded has absolutely nothing to do with the Rodgers and Hammerstein tune or at least nothing that is legally binding from the compositional sense. Nonetheless, every published recording of this song by Coltrane bears the publishing credits for Rodgers and Hammerstein. This is a result of publishing legislation set down to provide protection for certain types of music and performances.

My own approach to cover versions of songs is heavily influenced by Coltrane in that I radically change the songs and each performance contains a lot of improvisation. I should be able to register these improvisations in some way, just the same way a drummer who comes up with tasty fills on someone else's songs should also have the opportunity to make these composed bits official. Remember, the same fills in a different context, say a five-second "out" theme on a public radio show, would be considered published works, so this is not nit-picking.

The fact that I have been paid anything at all over the years proves to me that the system is less corrupt than some people think it is. One very interesting site on the Internet describes the horrors of the big performing-rights societies with an intense mania. Between the accusations are various offers for employment in the music business as songwriter, producer, record executive, and so forth.

There is plenty of reason to mistrust the BMIs, ASCAPs, and SESACs. The aforementioned exposé artist on the Internet, who calls himself General Bobby Farrell, thinks the system of monitoring the big societies use is suspect. He has a point. They don't go

> *Dealing with publishing as a musician is a lot like being in love . . . You will find out, somewhere along the line, that you are being cheated on, and there won't be a lot you can do about it other than move on and hope it never happens again.*

out and monitor every radio broadcast. It's more like a glorified political poll: They do a sweep of this area and that area until they have a general picture of what is being played. They then supposedly extrapolate this into royalty payments that are equitable for everyone.

If a song is really popular and goes above a certain number of radio plays, the pay rate is doubled. I have never understood the reason for this, and neither does Farrell. He thinks the big artists at the top control everything and are taking everyone else's money—with maybe a few has-beens getting tossed a nickel or two so they'll keep their mouths shut.

So why do I get paid? I hardly keep my mouth shut about publishing societies, but it is with a mix of chagrin and relief that I admit nobody much is listening to me. Why pay me off? It would be easy for BMI to give me as cold a shoulder as GEMA (the German performing-rights society). So why don't they? I am definitely a marginal artist if there ever was one. I write down the name of something that will get me paid for the stuff I have composed and created for each piece I play, regardless of how each piece would officially be recognized by a performing-rights society.

Let's say you have turned a previously published song into something almost completely different and the publisher of the original composition listens to what you have done and has an opinion about it. Why should this opinion mean anything to you? Sure, the publisher might own the rights to the song you started out with, but whether or not they think what you have done is "original" and worthy of a share of the royalties is an opinion that cannot be taken seriously.

First of all, they have a vested interest in trying to keep the full share of the piece. Second, and perhaps more importantly, they might have no experience with the type of work you are doing. There is no branch of the publishing world set up to determine whether the original composer knows what they're talking about or not.

In fact, the societies that collect for publishers are unable to deal with any division of composing credits beyond a two- or three-way split. Perhaps the whole idea of a songwriting "team" came about not because writing music is particularly intimate but because nobody wants to get left out on payday.

Music publishing is confusing because so much is set down in stone or else made official based on whatever some joker happens to write down in a dressing room. I'm not suggesting that there is any way BMI or even a performing-rights society in a small European country such as Slovenia can possibly check out everything people write down or claim to have composed, by the way. The problem exists because it's impossible to monitor, not because corruption or stupidity dominate the world of composition and publishing. (This is my opinion! We'll air the grievances of those who feel otherwise as we go on.) Here are some more strange things I've learned.

When I started recording, my music was considered avant-garde (see the chapter "Chicken Public vs. Avant-Garde" for an unclear understanding of this phenomenon) and thus accepted in the overall genre known as "serious" music. Performing-rights societies all over the world seem to agree on one thing: There are two kinds of music, serious and not serious. If it is serious, it gets more money, that's the main thing! Music from the serious genres—classical, avant-garde, opera, and so on—is paid at a higher rate than popular songs. Except, of course, in the case when a song is a huge hit and gets the "double your money" treatment mentioned earlier.

Since most broadcast and performance royalties are based on the duration of the piece of music, obviously a 30-minute symphony will get more dough than a two-minute bubble gum song. The "serious" music situation goes well beyond this, though. The basic rate of pay is higher. I noticed this when I began songwriting and made the mistake of registering some of my rock band pieces as "serious" works.

Despite "serious" sounding titles such as "When You Dream About Bleeding" and "City of Corruption," a BMI honcho contacted me immediately to set me straight. From that point on, I was told to register songs as songs and serious works as serious works or they would come around and tear off my arms and legs (serious exaggeration here).

During this same period, I came up with the idea of improvising solos on an amplified metal garden rake. What does this have to do with publishing and composing? Everything. These pieces of music,

> *If you think a mechanical royalty is something your car repairman should get if the van makes it through a tour with no problems, you are just the type that gets exploited by record companies, despite your possible appeal to grease jockeys.*

called "The Rake," would probably not be considered pieces of music at all by most people who hear them. A television station actually gave me an award for noise pollution based on an electric rake solo I did at an outdoor festival. Meanwhile, BMI awards me generous payments for solos on "The Rake," because they consider it a serious, or classical, piece of music. What is this all about, anyway? Compounding the strangeness is the fact that similar solos played on homemade instruments such as a plunger, a bird cage, a cooler, a shopping cart, and a toaster all get the same high-priced treatment.

From a compositional point of view, these solos are unique because there is no composition other than the invention of the instrument. After that I just wing it, often fueled by the ravings of drunks in the front row. Nothing could be less like classical music than an electric rake solo, yet classical music it is to the performing-rights societies because, once again, they are unprepared to deal with reality.

In a fair system, something as obnoxious as a rake solo would be paid at a rate even lower than that of a pop song. However, I am thankful there is nothing fair about the publishing world. I asked drummer David Licht, who toured with me for several years, how he could stand listening to a rake solo every night. "Each one is a lil' different," he told me, which made me regret that I hadn't registered each rake solo as a different serious piece.

When I first started out, BMI and ASCAP required a composer to submit recorded copies of published works, which meant that someone could actually "check" to see if a so-called composition actually existed. But at the rate these submissions came in, the performing-rights organizations were advised that unless they had secured control of some prime real estate for their future expansion, say something the size of the state of Texas, there would not be room to keep all this stuff. They dropped this requirement, now all you have to do is send in forms.

What forms and how you fill them out is not really worth going into here. This information is easily obtained from the societies themselves. They get many requests for information, since most musicians are ignorant about the publishing world. Ask for the free *Songwriter and Publisher's Handbook*, which has everything in it you need to know (except the weird stuff I am talking about).

If you live in the United States or Canada, study the information in this book about so-called mechanical royalties. The German and Dutch performing-rights societies, GEMA and STEMRA, also collect mechanical royalties, as do many other European organizations. BMI, ASCAP, and the Canadian SOCAN and PROCAN do not. If you think a mechanical royalty is something your car repairman should get if the van makes it through a tour with no problems, you are just the type that gets exploited by record companies, despite your possible appeal to grease jockeys.

Try saying the phrase "mechanical royalty." Roll it around on your tongue. Now use it in a question, such as, "What about my mechanical royalty?" As your career progresses, you will see that this can have the chilling effect on some record company people that a question like, "Will you have sex with me tonight?" might at the beginning of a first date. Although you may be pleasantly surprised a few times, you will often find that this is the last question you are allowed to ask. Record companies wish that mechanical royalties were never invented.

Believe it or not, for years it has been law that any company printing copies of a musical composition must pay the author or authors of said work a royalty rate, the amount of which is set by congress, with regular raises written into the picture. The composer/publisher and record company might negotiate a lower rate, but whatever happens, the company is required to pay something, per song, per copy pressed. At this writing, the mechanical rate is just under six cents for a normal length song. In many European countries, a rate is set for an entire CD or LP, and this total is proportionately divided among the composers of the release.

In North America, mechanical royalty collection is ostensibly turned over to the Harry Fox Agency. This New York-based mega-bureaucracy has the field pretty much all to itself. Do they do a good job? Well, they send a few bucks my way every year, so they seem to be collecting it from somewhere. They obviously have no idea what is going on in the world of small labels, however. I did a few projects, including many cover versions, for a record company who admitted they'd never paid Harry Fox a dime because, "Why the hell should I send Paul McCartney $50? He doesn't need it!" Unless alerted to the existence of a non-payer, the Fox Agency makes no attempt to follow who is recording what. Even if they are alerted, there isn't much they can do besides send a letter.

With small record labels it is up to the artist, if they are their own publisher, to establish a business deal that includes the payment of mechanical royalties, either up front, on an accounting basis, or in the form of merchandise. Make sure you get something! It is the only money you are required to be paid by law. Although there really isn't that much you can do, short of taking frustrating legal action, if a recording is pressed and you aren't paid. It is a good idea to find someone to put out your records who is willing to deal with this requirement. In some situations, I have told labels that if they refused to pay me mechanical royalties, I would only record cover tunes for them. Let Paul McCartney worry about his own problems.

The attraction of writing your own music and recording it should be obvious already, but one charm is the mechanical royalty. You can make more money recording your own music. That's the way it is supposed to work, anyway. Labels will go to extremes to keep from paying this money. One band I knew kept the mechanical arrangement separate for months while they were negotiating a 200-page big label contract, only to find out their manager had caved in and tossed the mechanicals in with the other royalties as an expense the record company was allowed to recoup against. Don't do this! The songwriter that does will find that money they thought they had coming has gone down the negative chute.

You will no doubt be told from time to time that the situation is "much better" in Europe, but hold on. Despite claims that mechanical royalties are required to be paid up front to the mechanical societies at the pressing plant, I found out when attempting to col-

lect such funds that many established labels (and they don't need to be very big to do this) are able to work up relationships with the performing-rights societies that allow them to pay later, when the records are accounted for as sold.

"We make the money, you find it," thus becomes the prevailing system in record companies as well as many other businesses dealing with profits and royalties. Music publishing is a two-step process: writing music and then searching for the money it made. I have spent years looking for certain publishing money. If you keep pounding your head against the wall, a check may eventually show up, but never for what you are fully owed. These kinds of publishing disputes and missing moolah searches should become ongoing projects. You should "keep the pot boiling," as a friend told me once, explaining why he had written a letter about capital punishment to the local paper.

For every biography of a music artist, there ought to be two volumes about their publishing deals. The following excerpt from Chuck Berry's autobiography, *Chuck Berry*, makes my head spin:

> December brought Phil Chess to finally acknowledge in writing that no songwriter royalties had been paid for three years on my Chess Records product. In a settlement it was agreed that ARC Music would make these collections from then on and I received a check to make up the difference . . .
>
> I was surprised to learn that I had been paid the same songwriter's royalties for an LP as I was receiving for a single record. Chess claimed to be unaware of this "mistake," as if they had never noticed that LPs had between eight and ten songs on them. I also suffered the surprise to find, during the audit, that foreign royalties, which were supposed to be collected through ARC Music, were claimed mysteriously delayed in transit from important countries such as Germany, France, and Japan. This meant that my share of songwriter royalties on U.S. receipts just accumulated (with interest for others) until whenever "received" in the U.S. Further I was told that the German subpublisher, which was delinquent in paying, was really just a subsidiary and was acting under the directions of ARC Music.

Chuck Berry was also the victim of a publishing scam that became household knowledge. Disc jockey Alan Freed wormed his way into becoming one of the "writers" of Berry's first big hit, "Maybelline," because he convinced the greenhorn rocker that the tune would never get played on the radio otherwise.

If you look at the way things are on today's music scene, with a healthy oldies market just about anywhere you go rotating only a few hundred titles, you would think that an artist such as Chuck Berry would have it made. Indeed, he probably never has to work again if he is careful about what he does and, more importantly, if he constantly keeps on top of each title in his publishing catalog. Don't ever let your guard down, though, or that publishing money will find it has "No Particular Place to Go," and then it's "Roll Over, Beethoven," for sure!

Here are a few examples of situations I have run into, and I'm no Chuck Berry (thanks, Lloyd Bentsen). This is by no means an attempt to describe every possible horror story you might find yourself starring in. Look at this as you would a late show you tune into while channel surfing.

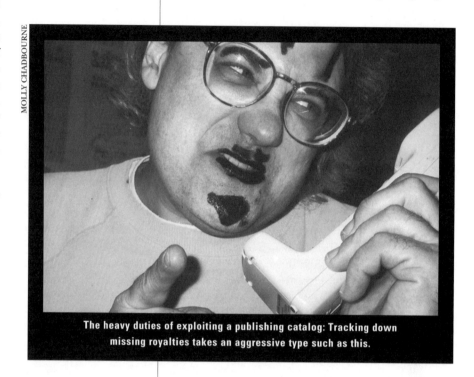

MOLLY CHADBOURNE

The heavy duties of exploiting a publishing catalog: Tracking down missing royalties takes an aggressive type such as this.

First let's talk about subpublishers because whenever problems develop, one of these creatures is usually hanging around. I didn't even know subpublishers existed until I made my first album for a large British indie rock label. Before then I had released stuff in Europe and had been filling in the performance payment forms at festivals and concerts as if I was totally my own enterprise wherever I went, which is the way I thought it was. I had gotten some decent checks from BMI, and the money was coming from all over the place so it seemed like things were okay with my publishing rights.

When Rough Trade put out the first Shockabilly LP with original songs on it, I was told I had to sign a subpublishing agreement either with them or someone else in the UK. If I didn't, they said, it would be impossible for Nukem Music to collect a dime. This includes the mechanical royalties which, in England, can be paid directly to the publisher or subpublisher by the record companies if such arrangements are made.

At first I was totally defiant about this issue. I felt since the money was clearly owed to me as a publisher under the international legislation for recording, broadcast, and performance royalties, I shouldn't be required to sign away part of it in order to get any of

it. Unfair as it is, though, countries like England do this in order to prop up their own publishing enterprises. It is known as a nationalist trade arrangement, and it is certainly not rare.

I changed my mind as soon as the subpublisher told me I'd receive a cash advance upon signing. It was at the close of a tour that had netted each player about $200 profit, so it was either sell my precious Fender Deluxe in London (where it would be worth as much as a dented Rolls Royce) or take the publishing advance.

Publishers work on the premise that the money that actually comes in will far exceed what they advanced you, and they'll make out like bandits just from doing a little paperwork and sending out a few letters. This is what attracts many to publishing, and like lots of things in the music business, it is true to a certain extent—but it's never as easy as it sounds. Intriguingly, sometimes when I thought I'd been cheated, I wasn't even sure if the cheater actually got anything out of their dishonesty.

Take the record company that managed to sign me to a British publisher who in turn resold the rights to my entire catalog, or at least what they thought was my catalog, to a German publishing company. The British firm approached an American record label I was dealing with and offered to buy publishing for all the records that had come out on the label. This was a nice deal for the label, and they in turn sent checks out to various songwriters, including me.

The money was halfway decent for what was supposed to be just the British publishing rights. However, I was having a German publisher help me locate missing money when they notified me that the German rights to the music were not mine to collect because someone else already owned all the songs. Who? I had never sold the publishing rights in Germany. But the British company had, claiming the American label had authorized it, which they had no right to do. The guy at the American label denied doing it. The British firm sent a copy of the letter authorizing it. It was such a light copy that the signature could easily have been forged. They didn't even make an attempt to provide a good looking fake!

The next step was to get the list of titles that this German firm supposedly owned. (The publishing business is full of such lists of songs.) To my surprise, the German publisher's list not only had the original titles I had written for my records on the American label, it had all the cover versions I had recorded, including titles by Charles Mingus and some '60s songwriters. All of these were on the list as being my titles, giving the German publisher the rights to them!

Despite all my protests and angry letters, there was nothing anyone could do about this nonsense except wait for the publishing agreement to run out. We never found out if the German firm collected a dime on my songs, by the way, but the indications were that this publisher bought and sold so many lists of songs that they didn't have time to even try and collect on anything except hit songs that were bringing in big checks without much effort on their part. They just bought everything so no one else would have it.

"Exploiting" a publishing catalog—i.e., working it to the point where all the money circulating on the titles is grabbed up—takes a lot of effort and a mind prone to details. Something most people in the publishing business don't seem to have.

For example, the Rough Trade subpublisher promptly took the list of 12 songs from the first LP I did and screwed up several of the titles, left names off the jointly written tunes, and credited a Roger Miller country song to me (although I never collected on it). When you consider that the defining factor of publishing is keeping an accurate record of composers and song titles, mistakes like these give you as much confidence in a publishing firm as you'd have in a doctor that didn't know how to take your temperature.

One way we knew the Germans hadn't collected anything on my titles was because, as I mentioned, I had another publisher working on them already. This was a publishing firm and record label working under the Warner Bros. umbrella in Germany. This gave them clout, as well as access to computer scanning and so forth. They were asking GEMA not just for uncollected mechanical and publishing royalties, but also for live performance royalties based on literally hundreds of official forms I had filled out during five years of heavy gigging in Deutschland.

At every club, from a big 1,000-seat showcase in Munich to a tiny punk squat covered with anarchy symbols in a small mountain town, the GEMA people came, saw, and conquered. Every organizer came up with the pale yellow GEMA form, usually grimacing about the large amounts they had to pay for the right to present live music, and asking me, "Do you ever get anything?"

"From SUISSA [Switzerland], yes. From Scandinavia, always. France is good. Holland is excellent, they even have a small consolation fund composers get if royalties go astray," I said. I always built up to the answer they wanted to hear: "I can't seem to get my hands on even five marks of this GEMA money you are paying."

This news would make them even angrier about shelling out. And it ought to. GEMA told the Warners-affiliated publisher that I was ridiculous and off-base, that none of the venues a pipsqueak like me played were big enough to require them to collect. Yet I had been given forms at each place and had been told that the venues were paying GEMA! Finally the publisher gave up. We had managed to find out, however, that GEMA had not paid the big German publisher the performance mechanicals they might have received if GEMA had been doing their job and looking out for whatever money my music was bringing in.

When a catalog goes unexploited, it means that even when money is owed on a title, nobody gets it because the publisher that has the rights doesn't bother to collect. Other interested parties pestering performing-rights societies are told to go away, they don't have the right to collect!

Bizarre situations develop as a sort of consolation sometimes. In the case of the British/German rip-off, I wound up collecting some royalties for the '60s hit "Psychotic Reaction" simply because I recorded a cover version and it got on the sloppy list the British firm put together.

Nonetheless, more and more businesspeople get into publishing, especially the companies putting out records. Since they are already publishers by virtue of publishing recordings, there has been a natural trend for many years to also acquire the publishing rights to original compositions recorded by a label's artists.

Jazz labels such as Blue Note and Prestige were famous for coercing artists into signing over publishing—or not coercing, in the case of the ones that didn't know any better, which was most of them, apparently. The math in this case is simple: 50 percent writer, 50 percent publisher. Give the record company the publishing, you give up half.

Should you ever do it? In many types of music, record companies might make a convincing case that they cannot survive without the publishing revenue. You might feel that the opportunity to have the music released will not be there unless you turn over the publishing. Half of something is better than all of nothing. And of course it is half of something combined with all the benefits of having a recording released.

In some cases, you may decide to let a company take the publishing or subpublishing rights (the latter takes a smaller cut, between 25 and 35 percent usually), especially in a foreign country where as sole publisher you are not going to be in a position to collect a single centimes, shilling, or guilder.

In the big label world, publishing becomes the mega-battle of greed. This stems from the time when radio became a medium for popular recordings. Prior to that, the publishing business was mostly concerned with making sheet music for piano players. Out of this burst of radio activity came a need for "charts" to help track what was really getting the most play. Then broadcasters could be made to shell out to BMI, ASCAP, and SESAC, and they, in turn, could pass on the publisher's share once their expenses came out (a cost, I have read, that has risen from 16 percent of the total to more than 80 percent!). These expenses include the costs of the admittedly limited monitoring they do, administration, and little perks such as the glossy magazine BMI sends out full of photos of various publishing executives drinking cocktails with songwriters in tuxedos.

In many ways, the songwriters are the real moneymakers for the labels, whether they are the recording artists or not. Tin Pan Alley has grown into a highway that stretches from New York to Nashville to L.A. to Tokyo to Paris to London then back to New York. Everywhere there are anonymous faces groaning with the strain of writing songs. You must have heard the popular Nashville joke: How do you find a songwriter in Nashville? Just yell, "Waiter!"

"Everyone is writing songs with someone," a Nashville recording engineer told me on his way out the door to rendezvous with, you guessed it, his new songwriting partner, a dietitian.

Once I got a call from Nashville's famous publishers, Tree Music. Some of the best country songs have been published by Tree. I got really excited and made what I thought was a great demo of only three songs. Months went by before I finally got the nerve to call and inquire about my tape.

I spoke to the guy who had initially called me.

To my surprise, he started whispering. "Listen, I have to tell you I fooled you. I am only the janitor here in the building. I just wanted to get a free tape from you. Frankly, if I played that tape for anybody here, I would lose my job." The strangest thing was that this didn't discourage me. After all, Kris Kristofferson had been a janitor in a recording studio. Maybe this would be the beginning of something. "Next time don't play such weird guitar on the songs," was his final bit of advice. And it was good advice.

If you make demos for a publisher, don't spend any time on the instrumentation or actual playing. Do the song solo on piano or guitar with pretty much just the chords and vocals. Publishers want to know you can write. Send an average of seven hours of original songs. If possible, bury the publishing building in your cassettes. Some of the publishers in Nashville are located in little one-story houses, so this might not be so hard.

I heard a story about the author of a recent hit who had given up her publishing to make her first big label record, believing that nobody would ever put her music out without her giving them the publishing as a sweetener in the deal. When she realized that losing half a million dollars was much worse than giving up half of $250, she tried to get the seemingly sensitive, liberal record company mogul to give the publishing back. "No way," he told her. "It's as if I bought some land that people thought was worthless, and I discovered oil on it. Why should I give it back?"

Business is business. But don't let anyone convince you that any piece of music that can be published, be it a solo on electric rake, a song about a girl named Maybelline, or Symphony No. 6, is worthless. As far as the publishing business is concerned, that's the one piece of music that has never been written, and never will be. And that's serious—"serious" or not.

CHAPTER 10

Band

Had a bad band bonding? You might want to call this chapter "banned," or maybe you wish bands were banned. Weren't travelers in days of old wary of roving "bands" of robbers? Did those bands have vans full of amplifiers? Being in one of those so-called new wave bands that roamed the countryside in the '80s made me feel like a band was some variation on a gang or mob, especially the way bandmembers liked to sneer in their 8x10s.

Then there are bandleaders. Sidemen. Cooperative ensembles. Each is a kind of conspiracy, but thankfully none are covered by the RICO statute against organized crime (in some bands you can drop the "organized" part completely).

There are many different kinds of bands. Maybe your band is an ensemble, combo, marching unit, or even symphony orchestra. This chapter is a collection of information about the intense musical, social, economic, and sometimes unhealthy human conspiracies that anyone forming any kind of musical combination will be drawn into.

This subject deserves a book of its own—and it has plenty. I can think of several I have not read, but their titles sound like they are definitely about bands: *Gone with the Wind*, *War and Peace*, *The Brothers Karamazov* . . . Even Mickey Spillane seems to have gotten into the act with *Survival . . . Zero*.

Think about a piece of music you like and remember that you never would have heard it if it weren't for someone's compulsion to bring musical ideas to life by working hard, either as the "boss" of a combo or through the collective bargaining of a co-op band.

Making music in a band can keep you constantly busy just contacting people to find places to perform. If you are doing a good job at this, you will find that you don't really have time to do the performances themselves. It's a virus that's common with many of the I-did-it-myself types. They're so exhausted by the time they hit the stage, they barely have the energy to go on.

If your career is on an international level, you can work all day and all night if you want and stagger to consciousness in various time zones. Music business types love to brag about such working schedules in their interviews, and it goes without saying that us actual musicians need to work harder than these jokers in order to succeed. Heat up another pot of Joe!

STARTING BANDS

Anybody starting a band will find someone to play with them. This is a basic rule. (I'll explain the obligatory "exception to this rule" later.) As for whether you are a bandleader or a sideman, let's not think about that right now. Lots of bands are started by people that get together to play first and only later decide whether they are going to have a leader or be a cooperative venture. These decisions might change within a band from week to week, if they meet that often. Sometimes one person will make a few phone calls to other musicians and get them together to practice or just to fool around, a sort of bandleaderly thing to do. This unit might then develop into a cooperative group. Then someone might quit and another member might take over. Sometimes a new member will take over. This can mean a complete change in musical direction.

When your band is newly formed, savor the absence of such band politics. This is the only moment in your history when there is no inner dissension and no important decisions to be made, because nothing has happened yet.

Surely everyone has seen those signs on music and record store bulletin boards. "Drummer wanted. Must be serious." What not everyone knows is that all of them are written by the same person who has been wandering around the country trying to start a band since the first railroads were built. He's the exception to the rule that anybody can find someone to play with. But seriously, these signs are a traditional way of finding players or whole bands to join. Papers run ads

> "Blues? I don't know if I've heard of that . . . I play heavy metal."
> —B.C. Hippie

that are different versions of these signs, especially in the big music towns. Phone calls with the people who run or answer these ads save you the trouble of meeting and rehearsing with other musicians because talking to some of these geniuses will tell you a lot.

When I got the bright idea to pick up a little extra money playing rockabilly guitar in the '70s, there were columns of ads begging for such players in New York papers such as the *Village Voice.* "What does your hairstyle look like?" was the most common question from these bandleaders, followed by, "Do you own a lot of good outfits?"

Bands are sometimes advised to skimp on the cost of making a demo tape but not on their 8x10 publicity photo. This reality of the business has to be swallowed immediately, even if it seems like one of Dr. Hackenbush's horse pills. You need to decide whether you are in music for the "look," the "sound," or both. I'm not going to pass judgment about what you should do. I'm just pointing out that it is best to surround yourself with people who think like you do or there will be conflicts. I know this because the truth is, no matter what you will do, there will be conflicts. In fact, finding the right people to start bands with is the easiest part of the whole enterprise.

There's a story about blues singer Georgia Bill, who was driving up to Toronto for a gig at the famous Colonial Blues Tavern. Bill liked to have a backup band but was such an eccentric character that no one

stayed in his band long. (Just watching Bill eat one of his normal meals was enough to inspire walk-outs.) A hitchhiker caught Bill's eye somewhere around Sudbury. Bill picked up the kid, a typical greasy, heavy metal guy, the type that gets called "B.C. Hippie" in Canada. The B.C. saw the guitar and asked "You play music, man?" Bill affirmed the B.C. hippie's suspicions.

"I play, too," the kid said. "I play bass."

"You play blues?" Bill asked, keenly interested.

"What? Blues? I don't know if I've heard of that."

"Heard of blues? You haven't heard of blues?"

"No, I play heavy metal."

Then Bill offered the kid a job at the upcoming gig. "I got a bass in the trunk, just in case," he coaxed. This shows you that, when worse comes to worse, a bass player can always be found if your standards are nonexistent and you have a spare bass in the trunk.

At the club, the booker, a blues purist, was absolutely disgusted with Bill's hiring policy. When he heard the heavy metal guy fumbling around on the bass, he fired both of them. This illustrates another basic lesson: If you are a bandleader, try to have some standards. It might not seem like it, but someone is listening. Sometimes.

Let's assume you've contacted some people and made a date to get together and play. These get-togethers happen all the time with variations on the number of people and the instrumentation. Sometimes people show up carrying reams of music. Others might not talk about what they are going to play at all but just set up the instruments and start making music together. Someone who is sure they are a bandleader might assemble some musicians and try to teach them some music.

None of these approaches should be considered the only way to do it. Miles Davis' technique was to invite potential players over to audition or rehearse and then retire to his bedroom, where he relaxed and listened to their jams on an intercom. After I read about this, I always attempted something similar when I got new players together, although never on as lavish or classy a scale as Miles. I might pretend to take a phone call or have to go to the men's room, but I am actually listening to see if the musicians get into anything interesting on their own. I've noticed that players who can't do anything but fudge around during these breaks can never get anything going among themselves onstage either.

As I look back on the first few bands I was in, I can see that each provided important learning experiences. It all began with what we called "features," where various groups of friends and I would gather together all our records by a certain artist and then pretend we were playing along on tennis rackets.

Eventually this progressed into miming on actual instruments, including a bass ordered from a Sears catalog.

In these features, we weren't actually playing any real music, so it didn't matter who was in the band; it was fun whoever showed up. There were never any arguments other than a brief discussion over whether it would be a Kinks feature night or Cream or maybe the Beatles. (The latter not a real favorite since they had stopped playing live by then—we were into realism.)

The lack of tension in the typical feature shows that the real destructive factor in a band is the actual creation of music, not alcoholism, egomania, narcotic addiction, greed, sex, religion, or any of the other things that normally get the blame (and we were heavily into all of them as kids).

People just pretending to play music are more relaxed than real players. I make this point in tribute to such popular enterprises as karaoke; personal appearances on *American Bandstand*; well-loved bands such as the Monkees, New Kids on the Block, or Milli Vanilli; and the '90s concept of veterans touring with anonymous "pro" back-up units.

In my first band that actually played instruments (although we never performed), the only real crisis was the hot competition to land a certain drummer because he had a shiny Gretsch kit and could actually play. Two of us in the band had an old friend nick-

> *A bass player can always be found if your standards are nonexistent and you have a spare bass in the trunk.*

named the Cheese who could play drums well but owned only a snare drum. We were intensely disloyal in our sucking up to the other drummer, who shafted us anyway and joined another band with amps bigger than ours.

Then came my first performing band, where every step of our too-short career was an important music business lesson:

1. I had to bribe the leader with illegal drugs in order to get into the band. That was in 1969 during junior high school, so I hope the statute of limitations has run out on this flagrant violation of the law. Based on the career of this group, let me stress that any band that requires you to do this is not worth joining!

2. I wasn't even considered for the group until I managed to get an amplifier that was bigger than the leader's. He was able to admire it without being devastated because his amp was at least a brand name, Fender, while mine was from a mail order company. This is an important part of band politics, kind of a small-time version of the weapons pacts that brilliant leaders such as Reagan and Gorbachev hammered out.

3. The main reason there was such reluctance to hire a guitar hotshot like myself was that I was a totally unpopular dweeb, while the leader was handsome and had loads of girlfriends. Nonetheless, the music combo has always been a place where nerds, dinks, and even people with zits could create their own niche—mine was an ability to remember my wah wah pedal and step on it from time to time. (The psychic power of a wah wah pedal in 1969 cannot be overemphasized.)

4. Our band's sense of importance was born at the second party we played, when an older guy who played in one of the more popular "grown up" local bands showed up, heard us jamming really well, and got so jealous he created a drunken scene.

5. We fantasized about the gig at the senior prom but were shafted out of even auditioning, probably because the principal couldn't live through more than one rock band audition. This frustrated the leader so much that he forced the band to break up. There was a long discussion in the lunchroom during which all the bandmembers and some friends tried to talk this joker into giving it another chance and not letting this one setback get to him. But to no avail.

Here you have typical band personal dynamics. You had this leader, who was Mr. Cool in the school and the quarterback of the football team. Because he was in it, the group became popular overnight and everyone at school wanted the band to play at their parties.

There was the drummer, who had been playing since he was a little boy. He never had the kinds of strong opinions that the leader and I did. While we constantly locked horns about the music, the look of the band, the equipment, and everything else; the drummer just set up, played his drums, and was transported away to some personal nirvana. He had sort of grown up in the band life because his older sister always had musician boyfriends, and their tolerant parents allowed many a combo to set up and practice in their living room.

And there was me, the social pariah who was finally able to get in the door at the big parties as long as I carried a guitar case, plugged into an amp in the corner, and stayed there for the duration of the night. Just walking into one of these parties with all the popular kids hanging around used to frighten me, so the band setup was kind of a sanctuary.

I've thought about this off and on over the years as I've shared the stage with players from many generations. As we travel the road from gig to gig, bandmembers often seem like lost souls. You'll see it in someone's eyes as they stand on a train platform or watch someone else gas up a van out the window. It's a pleading look that says, "Please get me there."

A rock band leader told me about a well-known bassist approaching him for work, saying, "I just like to play, the money doesn't matter. All you have to give me is $10 a night." This was not in 1924 or something, by the way. This happened just a few years ago. There are players out there who just like the lifestyle and the feeling of playing. You can tell who they are immediately because they're the ones who look the most lost.

Some players have no ambitions to make a career, and some would like to but don't believe it will ever happen. Some people don't want success but get it anyway. Every player you meet will have their own personality with variations on all these different principles, philosophies, and desires. Each is unique but similar in much the same way each day of your life has little variations, some standing out more than others.

Sometimes a group of people feels right and an ensemble is born. Or maybe no one feels right and they forge ahead anyway. And of course, many bands are formed for purposes that don't require feeling right about anything. When you play at a wedding, you shouldn't be worried about whether this is a happening bass player or not because nothing is going to happen anyway, other than the cutting of the wedding cake.

Right, wrong, or irrelevant, the group is together and they all have each other's phone numbers—if they've got phones. The No Consistency Rule comes into play when requiring bandmembers to have phones. It might be harder to call someone with no phone, but don't forget the line runs both ways. It makes it harder for them to call you, too, which in some situations might be a blessing.

RUNNING BANDS

When a band begins, there will be ongoing get-togethers, with the eventual goal of a successful first gig, then more gigs, then the chance to tour and record, followed by a lifetime of such activity. This summarizes the reality for most bands in the fields of rock, jazz, country and western, gospel, chamber music, salsa, polka, classical Indian music, and so on.

No matter what the style, the pattern's the same. Some bands exist only as local or regional units. Some remain "jam" or rehearsal bands. Others are formed specifically for gigs and never rehearse.

A group interested in rewards beyond the simple pleasure of getting together and playing usually tries to get in on something: the new music series at the library, the blue-collar bar that has gone new wave, the local blues society, the party house, the frat

The psychic power of a wah wah pedal in 1969 cannot be overemphasized.

scene, the Deadhead network, the baroque music society, radio broadcasts, commercial jingles, songwriter demos, backup for other artists, house bands. All worthy aspirations.

Or you can just get together to play in a friendly fashion. A neighborhood drummer used to tell me about jams that had been going on for ten years in a house down the block; the band still had never played "out." This is positive music energy that has nothing to do with the business scene. It is music made for the enjoyment of the participants. Nobody makes any artistic judgments, critics aren't given the task of interpreting or placing a value on it, and there's usually someone standing on the sidelines whining, "Do you really have to do this?" (See the chapter entitled "Understanding the Non-creative Mind.") The other end of the spectrum is the bands that get together only for money reasons and would never play just for fun. Anything wrong with that? No, and you are passing judgment if you think so.

The "for fun" band doesn't really need to concern itself with much of what is in this chapter other than to feel good about what they are missing. Personally, I have always felt the real fun is the gigs, not the private get-togethers or rehearsals. So if fun is your motivation, don't assume the professional music world is the wrong choice for you. Enjoying something you do is a sign that you are meant to do it. When a novice at touring told me recently that she thought the over-organized, hard-working schedule full of fuzzy, late nights and bleary early morning departures was "fun," it meant that she was another character cut out for this kind of work.

It's an established fact that looking for work and pulling off the jobs you manage to get is a complicated and unrelenting process. When you start out, you'll experience devastating frustrations. The public you will deal with will seem to be a cross between a wolf and a lamb. When you are unknown and unpopular, the public will be happy to turn on you like a pack of wolves. "Who is this band? They suck!"

But become popular—or enlist the high school quarterback as your singer—and everyone will follow you like a flock of sheep. The equivalent of the shepherd might be the club booking people, festival organizers, disc jockeys, record company honchos, or critics who create opportunities and help decide in which direction the stream of gravy shall run.

When you first start booking your band, you will probably wish you could deal with a shepherd who would simply hit you over the head with his staff when he wants to be left alone. These people just don't want to be bothered with you. Some of them receive a personal thrill from having the power to say yea or nay on a subject as dear to everyone's hearts as bands. But bear in mind we are not just talking about the rock world here, with its battling roving bands. Try to get started booking a group in *any* genre and you will get the same kind of treatment. Many musicians talk about wanting to find someone to do the booking. "If I only had a good agent," they begin. "Then you wouldn't have to deal with all the disappointments and abuse on a firsthand basis," is how I complete it.

Understand that a good agent will not be interested in a new band. If they are, it is not a good sign. (Of course, remember the No Consistency Rule.) We will soon discuss a band personality type known as the Svengali, and these also exist in the world of wannabe agents. Someone might approach a new band hoping to mold them into superstars. It sounds like the plot of a bad TV movie, but thousands of musicians dream about it, as well as people who don't even play instruments. The fact that this concept isn't easily recognized as a nightmare says a lot about the seductive image of power that people associate with big music stars.

In the small-time music world, bandmembers have to realize that they will have to book themselves if they can't find someone to do it for them—which they won't. I strongly advise booking yourself. It's a way of retaining control of what you are doing and keeping track of the green wrinkled parts. It's also a way of learning enough about the business to know when you have found a good agent, a dunderhead, a crook, or all three at once, which can be quite common in music.

Tex-Mex bandleader Hank Gonzalez: organized enough to have become a success in politics.

DAVID NIKLAS

No matter what you to do to book your band, no technique is as effective as the tried and true method of finding a home in some club. A cynic might compare this to a child who would rather have Mommy's breast but will settle for his own thumb. But all that poor, homeless, itinerant musicians want is to have a once-a-week gig in the same club. If there's any chance to develop a following, this is the way to do it.

If a band is ahead of the trends in town—for example, if they start a salsa band when the music is not well-known—their once-a-week gigs often become hits as both the band *and* the novelty style develop a following. My oldest daughter told me a few weeks ago that some of her friends were launching a revival of '70s disco with a once-a-week gig. It hasn't happened yet, but I did pray extra hard that night.

You can even wander cities looking for places that are open to trying out live music as an experiment. A small bar or restaurant, a community meeting hall or coffeehouse, the library or planetarium, campus facilities, other schools . . . the possibilities are limitless. With a little bit of public relations skills and a smooth collection of boasts and lies, you can find yourself writing down lots of dates on your calendar. The best thing is that your band will get a chance to practice and get better at what it does.

Successful bands need to have more than one organized, motivated type. In the words of Tex-Mex combo honcho Hank Gonzalez, "There has got to be someone organized enough to be able to tell when the one who is doing the organization isn't organized."

I was in a band where the three main tasks were divided equally, with next to no overlap, between three members. In this type of band structure, which I call triumvirus, there is:

Role 1: The Creative Force. In charge of songs, arrangements, lyrics, actual content of the music, and the band's creative philosophy, if there is one.

Role 2: The Producer/Booker/Manager. This one counterbalances the Creative Force with business smarts, common sense, the dare to stretch the budgetary imagination, and the will to hustle. "Even if I am the biggest crook in the world, I am still on the phone eight hours a day telling people you are the greatest musician in the world. That can't hurt your career," is how this one justifies his actions.

Role 3: Motor Pool. The final part of the triangle supplies the van to go to the gigs Role 2 books. Also, in the case of my band, Role 3 never shared the driving—except for two hours, once.

Flaws in this system? Role 2 wanted more input into Role 1, and Role 1 was totally selfish in this area. Role 2 also had too much access to band funds, diametrically opposed to Role 3 who was in the position of fronting and never recouped dough for engine repairs and so forth. If you think a pizza delivery guy who burns out his car earning seven dollars an hour in tips is a financial genius, then by all means join a band and ask for Role 3.

Role 3 does sometimes get to keep the vehicle, as in the case of a certain eclectic sextet. "I wanted a band but I got a van," was how one Motor Pool member described his situation.

In a British chamber music quartet I know, they have a division into four basic jobs.

1. The cellist has a knack for graphics and takes care of promotional brochures, programs, and posters for concerts, as well as CD design when and if such an opportunity exists.

2. The violist, being a recording bug with an interest in doing her own productions, works on projects like the potential CD. When the group has time, she organizes and sets up recording sessions and, if all goes well, winds up with a good tape. Her responsibilities include duping and sending out letters and cassettes on speculation to addresses she finds through research.

3. One of the violin players is in charge of looking for grants. Many groups hire someone from the outside to pursue this possible lucre. Ask yourself whether you're playing music that you could get some kind of grant for. A chamber music group is a good bet, a heavy metal band doing obscene satanic songs is more difficult but not impossible. "The more notes written on paper, the more grants," is how the grant-dripping composer John Hate thinks it works.

4. The final member is like Role 1 in the rock band. He puts together the repertoire for the group, chooses the pieces, and makes sure the scores are available.

All members must meet regularly to exchange ideas, since none of them can act without affecting what the others are doing. Programming decisions can impact grant potential, for instance, or cause engagement cancelations. In the complicated world of ensembles, where nothing is consistent and taste is completely arbitrary, the potential for complicated disagreements is endless.

The band experience can be a helpful lesson in the art of compromise, particularly because of all the bargaining that goes along with a cooperative situation. Others find that compromise is something of a euphemism for giving up what you believe in; they would rather be the boss. The non-compromisers are often capable individuals who have been in many bands where they were the only member willing to do anything besides jump onstage at the gig. These people decide that if they are going to work this hard, they might as well be in charge. It has the ring of logic, but so do some suicide pacts.

There are other jobs associated with bands that are sometimes shared among bandmembers, sometimes not. Many bands hire people to carry their equipment. Others find they can do that themselves. Then there's the question of running the soundboard. A self-contained band often sets up their own sound system and has the running of it down to a science.

Or you might be of the opinion that it's best to just get to the show and hope there's some kind of P.A., because as long as somebody pays to get in and you get paid, how technically perfect the sound production is doesn't matter. In fact, it's a good idea to be able to put on a show with no P.A., if worse comes to worse. There is no consistency of success with either approach.

A bandleader will find that whatever philosophical ideas he has about presenting music, someone in the band is bound to disagree with him. Healthy discourse about these subjects is, of course, how we all learn and get the impetus to try new things. Bandleaders can decide whether they want to be surrounded by "yes" types or go to the other extreme, sometimes known as "the asshole syndrome." In this syndrome, a band must have someone who has the ability to stink things up by being overbearing or letting some other negative aspect of their personality take over. This can give an ensemble a certain type of energy that may or may not be attractive.

Cooperative bands are often set up in such a way that the members' weaknesses, whatever they are, counterbalance each other. One of the best examples of this could be the Beatles, if you are of the school of thought that the overall work of the group makes up for each area that the individual members overdo it— Paul McCartney is too sentimental, George Harrison too laid back, John Lennon too fakey experimental, Ringo Starr too good a drummer.

If you are a bandleader, you can deliberately set up such a balance, or you can choose to do without certain people's weaknesses. Fire 'em! I admit I fired a drummer once because he admitted he had never heard of the great jazz drummer Philly Joe Jones. I thought about it and decided I could not, in all good conscience, pay money to an uneducated musician when there were so many others out there who were taking the time to study. (This same drummer, at age 26, complained about not having roadies.)

Of course, my decision was snobbish and severe. As a bandleader, though, you get to be that way. It is a small payback for all the hard work you do that other bandmembers don't have to even think about. Such arbitrary judgments, based on purely artistic trivia, can really be what makes the difference in a group's musical content. Or they might mean nothing. If the bandleader himself is never really sure, how can anyone else be?

It is more fun to hire than to fire, and we'll get to that in a minute. First, more reasons for firing sidemen, as brought to you by some of the world's great bandleaders:

Drugs! When they start wearing ice cream scoops around their neck for coke spoons, it's time to let 'em go!

—Rompin' Ronnie Hawkins

Beards! You've got two weeks to get rid of the beards. I want to see all clean faces.

—Buddy Rich

Stealing. We had to let the drummer go when he got caught trying to take ten thousand francs worth of gongs out of the Paiste convention under his raincoat!

—Andrea Centa, conductor
of Cazzo Orchestra

When they write their own songs. Once a sideman writes one song, they think they're another George Gershwin. That's when you gotta take 'em aside and remind 'em, "Georgie Gershwin was no goddamn sideman!"

—Rompin' Ronnie Hawkins

Being late. When I went to pick up this saxophone player and I showed up right on time and he was not even out of bed, and he made me wait while he took a bath, I figured out right there why Miles Davis had fired the cat last year!

—Norman Connors

Johnnie and Ebby were vividly showing increasing deficiencies in their performances due to their drinking. Johnnie would become quiet and clumsy when intoxicated, while Ebby would get loud and silly. This annoyed me to the point where I began to set drinking rules for them . . . My restriction against drinking in the station wagon was followed—Ebby and the bass player who rode in the rear seats would hold the jug of wine outside the window and swallow. Which I would protest. Ebby would confidently reply, "Not in the car, boss—just as you said," and take another swallow . . . From then on, I mostly toured solo.

—Chuck Berry

Getting to make a bunch of "hire" calls has got to be one of my favorite things to do as a bandleader or organizer. Whether it is an old friend you just can't wait to tell the good news to or a chance to hook up an idol with a nice job, it feels great.

One job I've landed a few times is a German festival for which the bandleader gets to hire 11 other players for a three-day, loose as a goose, casual get-together of improvising. An afternoon spent calling musicians and asking, "Hey, want a free trip to Germany? A grand or two?" really can't be beat.

Super bandleader, the great Duke Ellington, wrote the following priceless commentary about the hiring process in his autobiography, *Music Is My Mistress.*

When a man is needed, I personally scarcely even know which way to look for a replacement. I haven't the slightest idea whether the grass next door is greener or leaner. So someone suggests So-and-So and we send for So-and-So, and we get him. We play together a day or two, and then I inquire whether or not the new cat likes what we are doing, having already watched his reaction in the band. If he likes it, he is invited to stay.

As a rule, he is usually a very good man for our purposes. He's a good musician, neat and clean and with good manners and stage deportment. Of course he has his own idea of the dramatic aspects of his sole responsibility.

Everybody agrees he's a nice guy until one day, sooner than expected, one of his other selves breaks through, or one of his more eccentric sides shows. Then I confess, or one of the other cats in the band hollers, loudly, "Duke, you never miss!"

Let's wind up this discussion about bandleaders by talking about money. Some bandleaders pay themselves less than they pay the rest of the band; some don't pay themselves at all, pouring funds merrily into some kind of black hole they think is required to keep a band running. Sometimes these people are doing the only thing they can, sacrificing today for what might be happening down the line. And it's true that you have to be willing to think in these terms if you are going to get anywhere running your own band. But it's also a simple truth that any leaders who don't pay themselves more—at least double—what their sidemen make are nuts.

At the same time, other leaders insist their members do what is called "paying to play." This boils down to an economic imbalance between what is available as a wage to the total band for a concert and what each individual in the unit is able to pocket. With payment to bands by bars locked in at the same levels they've been at since the days of my first facial hairs combined with the expenses of playing skyrocketing, there are as many pay to play opportunities as there are loose cold germs. Thus, the bandleader who really wants to have a band out there working has to learn how to make a profit out of very little and to put some money in the players' hands each night.

Paying other musicians is enjoyable when there is something to give them. Many players are relatively carefree and extremely easy to deal with about financial matters. The opposite is the nebbish who wants to

know every breakdown of every financial deal concerning the band. These people suspect that the bandleader is making more than they are and resent the fact. Or else they want to make sure everyone is making the same amount as everyone else.

All our little lessons about merchandising come into play here. One of my longest running band experiences, the infamous trio known as Shockabilly, would have been a money-losing experience had I not sold my own recordings on every tour and made money from that.

Finding people who will work for little or nothing can be an important part of launching a band, and it might not be as bad as it sounds. I've had peo-

> *"How much do we get paid? When do we get paid? And where's the beer?"*
> —*Jimmy Carl Black*

ple join groups because it meant a two-week break from a day job and free travel. I don't feel these players are on the same level as the full-time, pay-me types, but they can still be pretty good. And considering how little the pay was for some of those gigs, I could hardly complain that some of the sidemen weren't on the level of Miles Davis.

For the band as well as the bandleader, the profit and pay situation is simply like gas in the tank to get the whole machine rolling. What a tour is really about is intense, steady practice in a setting much more serious than a basement practice room. It means you actually have to pull off the music the bandleader has been daydreaming about, perfect it further, polish it, turn it into the Ultimate Version. If you are lucky, it will also be about the individuals in the group collectively developing a kind of enthusiasm for the music that becomes infectious to the audience, in turn pushing things to even greater heights of musical quality.

Not every musician is born to be a bandleader. Some don't realize this until well into their careers, and by then it is too late. If the group in question has any kind of activity going on at all, the job of bandleader is likely to be too much to handle. To properly deal with all the aspects of organized band activity, a bandleader has to simultaneously organize music (which often involves scoring, transposing, arranging, and the time-honored art of stealing ideas) while also making travel arrangements, tracking down band personnel, designing and distributing publicity material, attempting to create recording opportunities, and when recordings exist, getting them finished and ready for release in some form.

While all this is going on, the bandleader is staying in contact with everyone in the band, deciding when it's necessary to let people know what's going on—people who might be problems to deal with or at any time might decide to quit the band. Is this unique? Only the music—sometimes. Dishwashers walk out, so do bass players.

Delegating responsibility is a big part of the bandleader's life, but this process is better described as the relentless attempt to find someone, anyone, who can both play an instrument and take on even one-tenth of the load the bandleader has shouldered. Drummer Buddy Rich wasn't even asking his young band to make flyers, call the travel agent, or create a new CD design when he yelled at them that it was "too much for them to play and tap their foot at the same time."

In the Duke Ellington big band, much of the road managing and financial business was taken care of by the Duke's son, Mercer. In other bands, it might be the leader who does this because in the words of Gonzalez, "Otherwise it's too confusing figuring out how to rob yourself." It is said that Mercer liked the businessman role, but it may also be true that he penned the classic tune "Things Ain't What They Used to Be" when he was spending more time adding columns of figures than blowing sixteenth notes.

Bandleaders thrive on finding a Mercer to take on some chores, but they in turn have got to be thriving in order to pay the salary. Someone starting up a band or trying to keep one going is no doubt going to wind up wearing as many hats as they can, rather than paying someone else to wear them.

Louis "Satchmo" Armstrong was a pretty relaxed character who had a wide audience and Top 40 hits right up until he checked out. (In fact, the song "What a Wonderful World" was a hit for him after he died.) As soon as Satchmo could afford it, he turned over the day-to-day band business to others. He liked this so much that in most cases he preferred being the "leader" of a band that was actually directed by another musician, the latter taking care of musical arrangements, rehearsals, hiring and firing, and miscellaneous static. Especially the static. According to the biography *Louis* by Max Jones and John Chilton, "Armstrong could never be bothered with all the extra musical headaches of keeping a band together . . . especially the complaints . . . Besides, he often observed, it makes a man too many enemies."

When a conductor visits a symphony orchestra to perform, he is the "leader," although he doesn't have to do any of the administration chores of the small bandleader who also conducts. Top star conductors communicate to the players through the first violinist, who then gets to be called the leader, a bit of barter many hassled bandleaders envy.

"I wish just for once I wasn't the bandleader," is almost as common a comment backstage as drummer Jimmy Carl Black's famous "How much do we get paid? When do we get paid? And where's the beer?"

We've described bands as always looking for a good booking agent. However, one of the most important talents a bandleader must have is the ability to step in and save a tour when the world's greatest booking agent turns out to be inept. And of course, unless a booker has actually been on tour extensively, the experienced bandleader will always be miles ahead in terms of experience and practical knowledge. The experienced bandleader should always be the one telling the booking agent what is going to happen.

The bandleader takes on all these responsibilities because he has an inner drive to control musical events. This drive expresses itself in the unending stream of ideas for instrumentation, combinations of personalities, songwriting canons, stylistic merrymaking, and just plain fun that we all take for granted.

Bandleaders not only contact people, but they work them, developing a creative public relations skill with other musicians that distinguishes the really great bandleaders from the riffraff. Duke Ellington's long-running big band is a model for the ambitious, creative bandleader. The Duke was a master at drawing the most incredible music out of his players, creating entire programs of music around them and complete bodies of music for the best soloists. Because of this, he had some of the same people working for him for more than three decades.

Okay, not every band is the Duke Ellington Orchestra. We're not just talking about geniuses that can lean against a window in a studio and write a song like "Sophisticated Lady" in ten minutes. The dude who throws together a garage band in order to sing ditties such as "Your Shoe Is in a Baby's Butt" is also under discussion here.

Of course, the No Consistency Rule is in force, always. There are bandleaders who are absolute tyrants, don't ever try to make anyone working for them feel good about anything and are actually abusive. Needless to say, there are always talented players lining up to work with these types. Sometimes it's because these leaders are musical geniuses of one sort or another, inventors of systems that cannot be learned any other way than through direct contact with them. In this case, listen to everything but bring a shield.

Among these user-unfriendly bandleaders are also total losers who have nothing at all going on musically. (Of course, the No Correct Judgments rule means it's a matter of opinion about which ones are the geniuses and which ones are the losers.)

RECORDING BANDS

Whatever the ambition of your band is, even a just-for-fun jam band, you are bound to get around to making tapes. Making great music with a band and making a great tape of that band making great music doesn't always happen at the same time, easily, or at all. Although there are instances of lightning striking the stage and the VU meters simultaneously. Most musicians have at least one story of a fantastic band they were in that never got on tape, or else they made and released a tape that was just a shadow of what they were capable of.

Everyone also has the experience of their pretty useless band somehow knocking off a tape with the essence of genius, or making up a fantastic song, taping a great version of it, and then never playing it again. (Jefferson Airplane's "Coming Back to Me" is supposed to have been such a ditty.)

When they came up with the term "recording magic," they weren't kidding around. The art of making a tape really comes down to being prepared. On the other hand, it can be the ability to transform what is unprepared into something someone will want to listen to over and over again.

Start with recording your own rehearsals, using whatever equipment is available. There is no such thing as "too bad a recording." Everything provides some kind of sonic record of something. Learn how to make a decent recording with a boom box. Or make horrible recordings. It doesn't matter. It is like the advice the coach gives you about shooting baskets: Each try makes the next one better. Guitarists who hate sports can bypass the coach comparison and heed the words of Chuck Berry, my choice for Best Guitarist Ever. Reminiscing about one of his first studio sessions in his autobiography, *Chuck Berry*, he writes, "I was well aware of the patience it required to come to a satisfactory cut from my own trials and errors in trying to do a perfect tune on my home-made tape recording machine."

Try to find ways of getting the equipment to you, rather than the other way around. But however you get the equipment, try to arrange it so you are using it for free or barter or on some kind of extended arrangement, often called a "lockout." Paying for a week or weekend at a time or a 48-hour burnout period is always better than an hourly rate.

One of the first things studio newcomers gasp about is how fast the hours fly. Remember the first time you made out with someone and then looked at your watch and realized three hours had gone by? It's just like that. I have learned to work fast in the studio, mostly as a reaction to how quickly the time races by. In one Nashville studio I set a record for cutting songs: 20 in one three-hour session. One song was literally cut while the producer was urinating. The previous record of 12 songs in one day had been set in the same studio by country singer Steve Earle.

More than working fast, though recording is about a state of mind. Like Chuck Berry, I am glad I spent so much time fooling around with tape recorders as a kid because it really prepared me for the mental state required to make creative, exciting music in studio conditions.

Let's halt a second here and point out that many big record company producers and executives would have an extreme allergic reaction to using adjectives like "creative" and "exciting" in the same sentence as "recording studio." A different frame of mind is required to work under such conditions, but it's not one that I understand much beyond the suspicion that perhaps the "mind" part is best left at home.

For you, a player who's just trying to practice your musical craft to the best of your ability, many studios will seem intimidating. The recording nerds that have fooled around at home with equipment for years will have the edge in these situations. But after some of the situations I have been in, the relief of knowing that the machines will run and that the microphones will pick up sounds without me having to crawl under a house and connect wires balances outweigh the intimidation of being in a big, "pro sound" studio.

No matter how many problems develop, one always reaches a point when everything is running and you record something that has the purity and brilliance of completely unfettered creativity. But you need to do this as much as other people need to boil water in order to really cook in the recording studio. When taping music like this becomes second nature, you will know that the magnificent tape recorders and massive speaker systems in a recording studio can make everything sound fantastic, including the garbage you have recorded at home if you bring it along to the studio with you!

"How did you get that sound?" I've had many a studio owner with $250,000 invested in high tech equipment ask me. The answer is simple: Poverty. The best recorded performance of your music really has nothing to do with the rich vs. poor equipment debate. Getting a really good performance is about being totally prepared. This is stressed in any book about recording. It's as logical as staying out of the rain if you have a sore throat. Getting a good recording means everyone in the band has to be totally pre-pared, and you have to keep all of them out of the rain if they have sore throats. In this case, raising children might be good practice for band membership or vice versa.

"I told you that you should have kept your toque on!" was a comment I overheard from members of the Alberta rock group the Stampeders when one member got the flu after dilly-dallying around in the -30° climate. (For non-Canadians, a toque, pronounced "toook," is a wool hat.)

When a band gets ready to record, it should really have the music down cold, not *have* a cold. You should be able to repeatedly play whatever it is, all the way through without any mistakes (and with nary a sniffle). If it is still one of those numbers you have to stop halfway through every time you play it, you are never going to be able to record it.

Some types of music are exceptions to this, most notably simpler structures or concepts that a band can latch onto quickly and come up with a good spontaneous version of. Nonetheless, a band who plays the same song live in concert a few hundred times first could make a much better recording of it. Try to plan things so that your band is recording music it has played over and over and over but is not sick of. And for the sake of the band, hope it is a song that you are not ever going to get sick of. Because if anyone likes the recording, they are going to want to hear it live.

Don't let yourself be affected by what engineers or studio managers think if you are producing yourself. These people have usually burned out on music by the time they hear you. Teach yourself not to need any kind of reaction to make you feel good in the studio. You can expect more enthusiasm from the attendant at the gas station on the way there. I knew I was onto something unique with my solo guitar music when I noticed strong reactions from couch potato studio types. Over the years, many studio engineers have thanked me after a session, saying, "You wouldn't believe all the stuff I have to listen to normally." The reactions will not always be positive, but if you're doing something different than what they have recorded before, take that as a good sign.

If your band is working with someone who has dubbed themselves a producer, make sure you look at the situation carefully. This is one of those job titles in which responsibilities vary drastically from situation to situation. It is also a field of employment that just about anybody can walk into regardless of experience or inexperience.

Sometimes it's someone from the band that is doing the producing. A producer can assume much more control from behind the mixing board than

from playing live onstage. That might be fine with everyone in the band, but it's stupid not to be aware of the power of a producer.

Outside producers are sometimes brought in with the logic that a producer who worked on one popular record can make any record popular. Do record buyers grab titles because of a producer's name? Somebody seems to think so. But the truth is

> *Remember the first time you made out with someone and then looked at your watch and realized three hours had gone by? [Recording is] just like that.*

that while some of these producers could assemble all the equipment in the studio from scratch if they had to, others need to hire someone to twirl the knobs for them. Some producers make brilliant records with monkeys and others take fantastic groups and create drivel with them. Sometimes the collaborators meet halfway at a point of mediocrity.

Do you need a producer to make a record? No, never. You need someone to point a microphone in the right direction and press a few buttons. Period. And a ten-year-old kid can do that. (An appendix of ten-year-old producers will be provided.)

"Producing" is a fancy word for "make." Worry about "making" a tape first. Then worry about the sub-creation potential: 7- and 12-inch vinyl, CDs, mini-CDs, cassettes, 8-tracks, DAT collectors' editions, CD-ROMs, yogurt packs. The first step is to make the tape. Why dwell on this? Because too many people think you should have a fully conceived album inside your head when you tape a band. They'll even record it in sequence and will become tremendously discouraged if the chore isn't completed in two hours. Maybe you think you are clever enough to do this and make a decent recording of the band at the same time. But why push the odds? A better approach is to take it song by song and just try to get clear recordings. By this I mean without distorted levels, unless that is what you want. (I saw a good British recording engineer put duct tape over the VU meters at a mastering session once. Yes, the record sounded awful.)

Don't put any effects on these recordings unless

the music simply can't exist without them. In other words, don't try to do too much at once or impart too much significance to any recording. And don't be too critical of what is going on at the time.

I have been in countless recording sessions and have yet to meet anyone whose judgment at the time of recording can really be trusted. Discourage participants from mouthing off because it can bring you down. I can now laugh off the ultra-critical reflex twitch we all experience during a session, and that seems to relax the more nervous players. Give the recording some time to get out of your head, and take your time judging it.

Play these tapes for lots of people. Put them on whenever possible, in as many situations as you can. See how people react. For instance, when do they start and stop talking? People will always talk over music, so any time you get their attention, even if it's for five seconds, you know you are on to something. Listen to what people say after these rare moments of musical concentration. In one band I was in, we had a messiah producer who wouldn't let me touch the equipment even though I had been fooling around with tape recorders when he was a baby.

"That's the whole problem," he used to tell me. "You just fool around. I am going to make us rich." He then mixed the vocal so low that on one ballad involving an affair, a robbery, and murder, I couldn't hear the lyrics! "Nonsense," he said. "I can understand every word."

Thankfully, a local lass wandered into the mixing session while we were making a cassette of some of the songs. "I can't hear the words anymore," she said. "I used to like that story with the murder." Only then was he willing to remix it.

Make lots and lots of tapes. After you've listened to them endlessly, start figuring out how to arrange them as completed albums or whatever you plan to do with them. You are going to be sending demonstration copies off until the people at the post office seem like members of your family, so you might as well keep yourself amused by producing as many finished works as possible.

For many bands, that first tape is usually made to send to club owners to get bookings. This leads to many strange tangents, some of which show just how bizarre the music business is.

In some styles of music, bands are advised to make sampler tapes. I am told a Top 40 cover band should make a tape containing the first 20 seconds of 15 or so songs and should update it every few months. So-called creative bands rack their brains trying to figure out what their "best" song is. Or what song, if not the best, has the best opening ten seconds. I've got news for everyone: Don't even bother sending the tape!

I've been conducting a research project for years now. It involves making friends with club owners until after a few repeat visits, they are willing to part with the smelly, overstuffed boxes they have under their desks that are full of—yuck!—cassettes from bands. I take all these home, dub my own music over them, and redistribute them. But not to club owners! They've already had their chance to own these tapes.

This appeals to me for two reasons. On a kind of science fiction level, I feel like I am taking over the world with my music. I take a box of tapes of other bands, then destroy them with my own sound. Hey, it's better than going to a bar and picking a fight with someone smaller than you! The main reason that I take these tapes, though, is to find out how many of these tapes have been played for two or three seconds and then dumped back into the box. The results so far are 100 percent.

This actually came as a surprise to me because I assumed that club owners never listened to them at all. It's disappointing, but I'm happy to pass my findings along if it can save my fellow musicians time and money. It's far better to sell these tapes to people who like your music!

Unfortunately, to follow standard operating procedure and get gigs, you can't just be Chatterbox the Dilettante and stop sending out tapes cold turkey. Explaining your reasons to club owners—"It is based on the research of Dr. Eugene Chadbourne!"—is not going to get you any sympathy. Any time you take an attitude like this, people start thinking you are a pain. They want you to merrily send a tape along so they can have that full box under their desk. If they do book you, it will be for another reason. To them the cassette is something like a peasant bringing one of his goats to the king as a gift. If you're making cassettes anyway, let these club people take a few and put them in boxes. The thought of this shouldn't really kill you.

Some people take a creative approach. Mykel Board, who has fronted bands such as Artless, used to send out tapes of reggae bands to get bookings for his own group. I liked the idea and tried it with a club in Raleigh. I sent them a tape of Charlie Feathers, the Memphis rockabilly legend, and pretended it was me. Unfortunately, the club burned down, but it was that rare instance when a booker actually listened to the tape! "You have a more rockabilly direction now," she said. "I like it!" There is no way to check the tape to know if she was shooting the bull because her box of tapes melted in the fire.

Bob Log of Arizona's down home blues duo Doo Rag said you can get the attention of bookers by wrapping the tape in a bag of guano (bat excrement). "One guy we did this to told us he thought it was drugs, and he smoked it!" Bob said. All right, maybe he didn't listen to the tape, but getting the booker to smoke the package is some kind of accomplishment.

Stuff like this is fine, but making a tape specifically for bookers to listen to is a contradiction in terms. I know in interviews these jokers like to get really serious about how they sit and listen to every tape they get, but come on, don't kid around with me!

Don't worry about them when you are making a recording. If you are taping a band with the intention of sending the tapes to record companies, do think about what each company, A&R person, or record label head is enthusiastic about. This doesn't have to change your music, it just gives you some guidelines or perhaps concepts about different ways of organizing the music, sequencing the songs, deciding which pieces to include, and so on.

There are countless possibilities when you're making tapes, none of them more right than any other, so be receptive to ideas wherever they come from. Try them out, if only to be amused by how different your perception of what a record company might want is from what they really do want. Sometimes you will hit the nail right on the head. More often, you will have no idea because you will never receive a response. A state of limbo will exist over the tape and its potential. Time to make another one. Or send the same one to someone else. Or change it. Just don't sit around brooding about what happened to the tapes that you have already sent out to record companies.

Okay. If you don't think you can live without knowing, I'll tell you. Another one of my related research projects involves befriending A&R reps or owners of record companies until they can be pressured into parting with—yes you guessed it!—the box of cassettes under their desk. This research is a bit more time consuming because the demonstration cassettes from bands have to be weeded out from the unused promotional tapes from the label itself or from other companies. There are usually dozens of these. These tapes all have one thing in common: Nobody has listened to them. (Again, I doubt anyone at a record label sits around rewinding.)

Unlike the club tapes, however, many of these demo tapes have not been put into a machine at all. Will A&R people call you up long distance, at their expense, ask you to send a cassette, and then never listen to it? Yes! Why? I didn't sign on to this project promising to solve the mysteries of the universe.

By the way, don't think this "no listen" policy is reserved for unknown acts. In one box, I found a demo tape from an act that used to top the charts. This singer was portrayed as an abusive, wife-beating drug addict in a popular Hollywood film, meaning he might

be quite appealing to the public with a comeback move. I am talking about the great Ike Turner! There was his demo tape, complete with a card from a Hollywood lawyer. Had anyone listened to the tape? Nope.

If a record company employee does listen to your tape, their feedback might not be worth hearing, anyway. If you get dismissed critically by someone, take it as a good sign. All the really successful music business acts were turned down by everyone. For several years, the Doors' record company wouldn't release all the hits they recorded because they thought Jim Morrison had "no charisma." Most turndowns are the result of how you look in your 8x10, anyway, according to the knowledgeable insiders.

Positive feedback is actually cause for suspicion and disappointment, not champagne. One label honcho told me my demo was "the only tape of good music we've gotten in here all year," and then, of course, went on to say that this meant it was impossibly uncommercial and they would lose money releasing it.

In the final analysis, it doesn't matter if anyone listens to the tape other than you and your band. Make a tape that you like, then throw it out and make one you love. If you do anything serious with the tape, you will have to listen to it so many times that you better make it as lovable as possible. There is consolation if you fail, however. The tape can be filed away and rediscovered as a lost masterpiece when you are graying. Or you can get it released anyway and then never listen to it again.

Many of these band principals also apply to solo projects. And for both band and solo projects, wise use of time, comfortable facilities, and an open feeling will help you make music that's exciting.

Through experience, players should be able to learn how to get the most out of whatever is happening. Be adaptable. Learn how to work cheap, but be comfortable and productive in a first-class studio. Toss the clock out the window. Keep personal problems out of the recording sessions. If you can't do that, figure out how to keep the people causing them out of the session. Once, when cutting a record with a well-known band backing me up, I arrived at the studio to find the singer delivering hate letters to the other bandmembers. It seems there had been a fight onstage the night before. The singer was resigning and had spent the morning typing up his reasons. Instead of a sound check in the studio I had a band reading letters. Luckily, I was only paying $12 an hour for it!

The solution? Coordinate special recording sessions for the singer and have him do his tracks privately. It worked, except that he didn't quite finish on time and had to be ushered out the back door while the rest of his ex-band was coming in the front.

It is particularly frustrating and sad that in so many cases even a well-received band is impossible to keep together or keep active, putting the bandleader back at square one, thinking up an idea and making phone calls.

Some bands sort of fizzle out rather than break up. They hibernate and wait for offers. Meanwhile, the players get entangled in other things. Then there are real band break-ups when, for one reason or another, the group stops working together even though there is plenty of work to be had or at least good potential for work.

Fans and particularly journalists like to ask musicians why this and that band broke up, knowing full well the reasons are usually hot and steamy. Nine times out of ten there is an argument of some kind, stemming from what lawyers in divorce cases like to call irreconcilable differences. This basically means disagreements about everything.

Comparing band break-ups to relationships ending is almost a cliché. Both can be sad and an incredible release of tension. For the diplomats who head a pack of hotheads, a band can be just as stressful as a bad marriage. And just like romantic attachments breaking up, ex-band members find themselves realizing things they hated about the others all along but had been burying inside somewhere.

In the end, being in a band isn't about making music. It's about making friends and then losing them. But, though friendships are nice in bands, they're not really necessary for making good music. This is something you learn from experience after many instances of seeking out pals to bond with in your band when what you really need is someone with talent.

One of the greatest performing groups I can think of is the Dutch jazz duo of drummer Han Bennink and Misha Mengelberg. One night Bennink said to me that he had no idea what was going on in his partner's private life and, furthermore, doesn't want to know. "It is already 25 years playing music with this man. The rest of his life I don't want." The more intense the friendship, the more intense the breakup and the more distractions you'll have from the music.

To be in bands means being with lots of different people. You have to learn to get along with as many of them as possible and figure out ways to deal with personality traits that bug you. It is a lesson in developing tolerance, even though you might continually find yourself questioning why it always seems to be at the expense of your own peace of mind!

A hit new wave group from the '70s told me why they finally canned their original drummer. It sounded like a classic erosion of tolerance. On one hand, the guy was an obnoxious person. For example, on the road he never contributed his share of the restaurant bill. The others tried every trick they could think of and even wrote to the "Ask Dr. Chad" column for advice (see "Road Bad? Ask Dr.Chad!" chapter). Nothing worked, but they tolerated him. When he couldn't keep up with learning new music, though, they decided, "It would be one thing if he was a stingy jerk and the world's greatest drummer. Or if he was a mediocre drummer but a really nice, generous guy." Negatives in both areas were just too much.

We live in a world of maybe three dozen basic personality types, all combined in different and sometimes not so different ways. In this context, we find certain types that show up in every band. I began thinking about this after a humorous discussion with longtime bandleader Col. Bruce Hampton (retired) who has led or been a member of the Hampton Grease Band, the Late Bronze Age, the Aquarium Rescue Unit, and is currently in the Fiji Mariners. In the film *Sling Blade*, Col. Hampton is the nutter at the jam session who recites his poetry.

We were talking about a guy in one of his bands, the organist Daryl Shamer. "Every band has its Shamer," the Colonel sighed. From this I came up with my theory that if every band expanded to a ten-piece, it would have one of each of the ten types of basic characters. I call this group the Ten Most Unwanted List.

1. The Svengali. Able to turn each member of the band into an absolute genius, if they would only listen. Listening to the Svengali is required because in his words of wisdom lie the plan for all future success. "Listen to me, I will make you a star, never mind if it makes no sense."

2. The Rasputin. Related to the Svengali but more interested in bossing everyone around just for the fun of it. The Rasp does not set forth any great musical path to follow but can predict the future —and does: "We're not going to get any gigs!"

3. Sammy Shy. The greatest player in the world at rehearsals, S.S. falls apart as soon as the first member of the audience bumbles in. "I get freaked out by people watching me."

4. King Edward III of Extrovertia. Separated at the hip from Sammy, this joker just can't seem to focus on anything at rehearsals, when he manages to show up. However, if the band ever gets a gig, watch out. No matter how much pressure or who is in the audience, the King takes off on great flights of musical inspiration. He doesn't get a chance to say much because he is surrounded by people saying, "You were burning!"

5. Connie Competition. Why and how all these other people in music got so famous, from Bach and

Beethoven down through Black Flag and beyond, is something sad old C.C. will never understand. Every concert performed by someone else, every record released without her name on it, is all part of a fantastic misunderstanding on the part of the public. "I can't believe they didn't call me! What's their problem?!"

6. No Comment. Just doesn't say much. Sometimes these people play bass. It should be stressed they are not mad, unsatisfied, or paranoid.

7. All Comment. No is sometimes preferable to long-lost brother All because the latter never shuts up when directions are given. He never shuts up, period. The good side of All comes out in situations such as boring interviews and all-night drives when the driver begins to develop an attraction for the cement barricades on the road. "And then do you know what happened?"

8. Sir What I Did. Here is the bandleader who everyone wants to work for because of all his great accomplishments in the past. I mean, the guy has really paid his dues. Like what, you ask? "Well, let me tell you about the first time I headlined the Newport Folk Festival . . . "

9. Lust for Life. The guy that adds the "olo" to the gig, this person's entire purpose in performing music is to find a sex partner. This is the musician who hangs around restroom doors to see what the prey looks like. One such L.F.L. played in a surf music group, which is where I overheard him telling a woman autograph-seeker that he'd be "more than glad to give you a lot more than that!"

10. The Shamer. Practically a one-man band, or at least you wish they were, the Shamer combines attributes of all the other Nine Most Unwanted. "To get somewhere with your music . . . I can tell exactly what is going to happen . . . [ten minutes of talking later] . . . You're attractive, and I'd like to get to know you better."

Just being in a band with one of these, or all of these, is no reason in and of itself to break up. The reasons come later, and they're usually something one of these people do as a byproduct of who they are. The evocation of meat byproducts is intentional. You didn't ask for those unpleasant music byproducts but you're served them anyway, sometimes concealed within an attractive plate of food.

Financial pressures push the privacy envelope. Go on the road with any type of band and this will become abundantly clear. You are constantly expected to make budgetary considerations that result in a loss of privacy. It costs hundreds of dollars more to put everyone in separate rooms. There's no way to measure what is lost when people who could really use some privacy are forced to be together.

Counting the money in your pocket can make you peeved at everyone else in the band, particularly bandleaders or organizers and agents that you think are letting the band down. Or maybe it's you yourself that you are worried about. Maybe the rest of the band is mad about that. People can, and do, get mad about absolutely everything. And people in bands need to let off steam. As annoying as the complaining types are the keep-the-lid-on-it, Pollyanna types that want to solve every problem and cool everyone out.

Unresolved spats kill nine out of ten bands. The main exception seems to be those bands that break up because a crucial member dies or no longer wants to play in the band. Certain bands do need to have certain people in them, and I've nothing but respect for groups that know they've reached a point when they can no longer carry on.

Of course, this principle is one of a triad of "Absolute Musts" I've developed for a really classic band. This will be my final comment on bands because if you find yourself in a band like this, you should pinch yourself to make sure you are not dreaming.

1. If the drummer is replaced, the sound would change so much it would be a different band.

2. If there is a horn section, it sounds really great whenever the members are playing together.

3. Whoever is in charge of playing the chords—piano, guitar, bass, accordion, banjo, whatever—never gets drunk.

That might be the last word on bands, but let's end the chapter with a question that, if asked at the beginning, might have saved us all a lot of trouble: Do you even need a band?

Never underestimate the value of working up a solo performance you can take on the road. Even those who failed math class must realize it is easier dividing up money this way. This isn't a joke. Easily two-thirds of the money I have made in the music business has been from solo performances and their related income.

Also take a look at various players that work as singles. Many jazz players travel around to work with local groups, bringing their own music with them as well as choosing from the large standard jazz repertoire. The same goes for some touring soul and blues acts. Of course, many classical players move around playing with various groups all over the world. In all these cases, there is still a band happening, there is just no one trying to drag the members all over the place—an experience one saxophonist I've hired describes as being "like a concentration camp."

I've already picked out Chuck Berry as my favorite guitarist, and one reason is his status as a single who, through most of his career, has gone wherever he wanted to and picked up a backup band. Despite his legendary temper and strange moods, he never has a problem finding backup because he created a style of music and playing that has been adopted around the world.

Critics of Berry who find this approach haphazard and sloppy are completely missing the point, which is typical. Players such as Berry–and there are others in many fields—have just managed to make the whole world their band.

CHAPTER 11

Putting It Out Yourself and How I Did It

Releasing and promoting your own music is the essence of artistic creation. I *could* claim that someone who never does this isn't getting as deeply into the music as the people that do, but one of the main reasons people put their work out themselves is desperation. I suppose we have to give the well-heeled, the overnight sensations, and the charismatic hustlers a break—even though they never have to pack boxes full of their own CDs and send them off to exotic locations such as Taiwan, Traverse City, Toronto, and Trenton.

You really have to love your own music to want to pack it into boxes yourself, and there's nothing wrong with that. You *should* be making music that you love. You should be madly in love with your music and want to listen to it all the time. That should be your main motivation for finishing lots of master tapes. Your next goal is duplicating this material into whatever formats are available (if this was another millennium, we'd be discussing scratching up rocks, but stick around and we'll talk about scratching up old records and CDs) and making someone else fall in love with it so that they will buy it.

If you honestly have enthusiasm for your music, someone else will, too. This is only logical. First of all, there are only so many types of people in the world with only so many interests. Sooner or later, somebody will share your point of view. Sometimes it is several somebodies. When I decided to combine traditional country and western and avant-garde improvisation—neither of which were popular at the time—I had no idea that lurking in every town were four or five guys with huge record collections who thought this was a stroke of genius. These people

were duplicates of me, in a way. Or I was a duplicate of them. Anyway, one trait we had in common was our ability to interest others in our passions.

Bear in mind that millions of advertising dollars are spent each month in the music business to get someone interested in certain recordings. The people who fall in love with your music and begin spreading it in their circles completely outclass this type of cash advertising. If you are putting out your own music, you should completely forget about any kind of paid advertising. Even one dollar spent on paid advertising would be better spent on, well, anything. The only kind of advertising that matters is creating fans for your music.

Why wait to get desperate before you start manufacturing it in some way and selling it directly to people? It is obviously the smart business thing to do, and it will improve your music. (My experiences going into a third decade of self-manufacturing may or may not bear out the latter opinion, depending on your critical point of view.) Even when I started finding record companies to put out my music for me, I consistently tried to maintain, and still do, outlets for self-manufacturing.

The importance of the cassette movement will be trumpeted here as if it were the heralding of gilded angels. In the big music business terms, cassettes are nowhere. Sales are dwindling, market share is crumbling, blah blah blah. For the independent musician digging around the underground, though, they are like nuggets of gold. We will see how the mass production of vinyl and CDs ties musicians up in a frustrating lifestyle of writing checks, watching bank balances dwindle, and dunning distributors who have sold your product and spent the proceeds on sports cars. In the meantime, the nifty little cassette elf has a bag of gold coins.

Let's start at the beginning with my first album, *Solo Acoustic Guitar: Volume 1* (an auspicious title!), which I recorded and self-released in Calgary, Canada in 1975. Was I desperate? Well, I felt strongly that I wouldn't be able to find a record company to release the music I was doing. In reality, I'd only sent out one demo tape to a record company in my life, and that was to ECM of all places (which probably doesn't stand for Exclusively Chadbourne Music).

It was more pride than desperation, and copycat pride at that. I wanted to be like my musical heroes, many of whom were putting out their own records. Just for the sake of reference, let's list a few people who have started their own record companies. In the mid-'70s I was worshipping these artists, and I am not ashamed to admit that I still do.

Charles Mingus. Acknowledged as one of the geniuses of jazz and American music, this bassist, bandleader, and composer was one of the first jazz artists to put out his own album. He made a big deal about the politics involved in his breaking away from the establishment music scene. There were many foul record company practices of that day, such as trying to control repertoire, stealing publishing, manipulating band lineups, and of course, scamming royalties. Mingus took them all on.

Sun Ra. Sun Ra and his various interstellar, intergalactic Arkestras roamed the world in their frayed costumes, and the self-produced debris they left behind in fans' collections is legendary. Hand-painted covers, tiny editions, intentionally confusing discographies—it all came from good old Sonny Blount of Birmingham, Alabama. Whether you think

Sun Ra is a total crackpot or a musical genius, you're not going to find a musician alive who wouldn't envy a career like his.

Johnny Paycheck. Years before "Take This Job and Shove It" came along, original outlaw Johnny col-

BRIAN HORWITZ

These pictures were taken in a suburban Washington, D.C., record store where I appeared with my oldest daughter, Jenny, then about 12. She enjoyed signing autographs for several of the album and cassette packages she had designed art for. The packages seen on the signing tables are typical cassette packs of that era: sticky-back paper folded over a recycled envelope.

laborated with Aubrey Mayhew, who ran the little Starday record label and also co-wrote and co-produced many of the Paycheck singles. Because of the lack of big record company interference, these recordings are some of the most experimental and innovative ever to come out of the country genre.

Andrew White. If one of the finest saxophone players alive (who once played for 24 hours and released LPs of the entire session) has his own label and puts out his own records, what is the point of all these inferior hornmen mailing out their demo tapes? Answer: These hacks are the ones the big labels want to sign because they sound a little bit like David Sanborn.

Wadada Leo Smith. In the '70s, Mr. Smith was telling interviewers that no musician should record for any label other than one that they owned. Furthermore, he thought all musicians should stop allowing critics to review their productions. He still fights for the rights of musicians to express themselves through the media rather than constantly being filtered through the preconceptions and prejudices of various writers who are sometimes better-known than the musicians they are writing about. To him, self-production is much more than just a way of surviving and perfecting your own music—it affects all music positively by wearing down the stranglehold of the establishment.

Carla Bley. This pianist, composer, and bandleader—another true American original—not only started putting out her own records, but she also helped found an entire distribution company devoted to selling such releases, and the existence of that company was encouragement enough to many players to go ahead and do it.

The Beatles. When the world's most successful band got to the point where they could do anything in the world they wanted, what did they do? They started their own record company! So don't tell me it is about desperation. And if you see what happened to Apple Records (a big flop), don't tell me achieving success at such ventures only requires money, popularity, and talent. These moptops had all three and couldn't pull it off.

Derek Bailey. This British musician, on the other hand, may have played session guitar on singles released in the Beatles' era (rumor has it he played on Petula Clark's "Downtown"), but the Beatles' worst selling enterprise (their German-language single) has probably sold more copies than all the Derek Bailey recordings ever released. When I discovered this genius of the guitar, it was on a record he had put out himself. His partners on the record, drummer Han Bennink and saxophonist Evan Parker, are acknowledged as some of the best musicians in the world.

There we have it. The best musicians, the most popular, the geniuses, the innovators. You are in good company when you put out your own record. I wanted to be like all these people when I put out *Volume 1*. The idea of making an album appealed to me, anyway. I had dabbled in self-released productions through various high school enterprises when I duplicated reel-to-reel and 8-track tapes of my own songs. That was on a tiny scale, of course, but it was clearly the beginning of what would later develop into a life-long interest.

I had always fantasized about making my own album; I even had my own made-up Hit Parade of these fantasy albums. This seems to be something many creative musicians share, long lists of album ideas, sometimes with titles of songs and complete artwork. I have seen such collections in scrapbooks of people who never got around to really making any of the records as well as in research on noted and prolific recording artists such as Spike Jones.

People that make lots of records are obviously compulsive, and usually well past the point of being neurotic. Spending a lot of time in a recording studio has been compared to being walled up in a mental institution minus the nursing staff (although that would depend on who was engineering).

Anyway, by 1974 I had one project that had actually made it to the "demo" record phase. This was a live recording by a trio (sometimes a quartet) that I was in, the Western Music Improvisation Company.

My full-time job at that time was at the Calgary *Herald* newspaper, where one of my entertainment department perks was getting wined and dined by the record company promo men. The joker from Polygram, representing Deutsche Grammophon and ECM and thus inclined to talk about "cultured" music, took an interest in the WMIC album tape. He was the one who talked me into the ECM submission.

Eventually I started playing solo. I got a lucky break when the organizers of a concert series in Toronto gave me a chance to play a solo show at an early, important date in a series they were launching, even though I had very little reputation and had done practically nothing. This concert was taped, and even though I thought it was a horrifying failure, there was something there that tickled the ears of someone who heard it, the one and only Anthony Braxton (see "Introduction" for the details).

Anyway, Braxton was barely on his flight out of town when I made my decision to release an album in an edition of 500. A few people suggested I shouldn't contemplate suicide if these were all still sitting in my bedroom ten years later. I got the name of a pressing plant, RCA Special Products, who said I had to bring them a master tape, and if I wanted to, I could sit in on the mastering. I didn't know what they were talking about, but I made plans to go out there and deliver the tape and sit in on the mastering.

We recorded the music in two nights on a Dokor-der 4-track, mixing down directly to 2-track. One friend put the entire cover together and another who was a printer printed them. Nobody in Calgary manufactured albums at that point, so we did everything piece by piece. The jackets were folded and glued together by some children at a local institution. They also inserted the little flyer I had printed up.

I saw from this first effort that even though people would say "Chadbourne put out his own album," I really did it with heavy assistance from several peo-

Spending a lot of time in a recording studio has been compared to being walled up in a mental institution minus the nursing staff (although that would depend on who was engineering).

ple. Fellow WMIC member Clive Robertson, one of the first people I knew who published and sold material on cassette (in this case an audio magazine entitled *Voicespondence*) took care of doing the recording, typesetting, and layout of the cover and folder. My printing company friend, Peter Moller, took much better care with the project than the average for-hire printer would. A girlfriend, Vivian Jean, took the cover photo, and my pals in the photo department at the newspaper took care of printing her negative and enlarging, cropping, and superimposing some writing on the photo.

When I did a second album, a deejay friend helped record some of the tracks, and a CBC recording engineer also got involved, sneaking me in late at night for many sessions. In short, producing recordings is a collaborative endeavor that one cannot really do without talented friends.

Back to *Volume 1*. I dashed out to Toronto with the master tape. Luckily, I found out that I didn't need to go to the pressing plant itself, which was located practically in Montreal. I went to the RCA studio in downtown Toronto. It was the dead of winter, and I still laugh when I think that we almost drove all night to make the mastering appointment.

As it was, I had the wrong format. "You need

half-track," they said, making me feel like an idiot. But they stopped me just short of going all the way back across Canada to re-record the album. It turned out that they could transfer my tape to half-track on their own machines. (I couldn't understand why the guy had acted so frustrated since it was something they charged extra for and meant extra dough for them.)

Soon, I was watching them make a master lacquer disc from my tape. It was fun. I learned the next steps would be making a metal plate, then a stamper, then a test pressing, then the album.

I went back to Calgary and awaited the test pressing. It was thrilling to get it, but even better was the word that the LPs themselves had arrived at a shipping depot. The album got a few good reviews, mail orders started coming in, and I was on my way. By the time I started work on the second album, I only had about 100 copies of the first one left. Nowadays, if I can find one, I sell it for about $75.

Let me linger over a few of the thrills that releasing this record gave me. I clearly remember opening the envelope from a small record store in Vancouver that contained the first check for an order in it. I don't remember the amount of money, but I do remember feeling that my idea was working and it was possible to get people to buy my music.

The first check that came from overseas was another big thrill. It was from a now long-defunct distributor called New Sun or something like that. Knowing people were going to buy my record in France made me very happy.

I was lucky to get a good review in *Guitar Player* magazine on my first album. It is a cliché for musicians to say that reviews count for nothing. The old symbol of justice is a lady balancing scales; for the musician, it's a five-ton collection of press clippings in one hand and an empty checkbook in the other—and no sense of balance at all. But in some cases, a review can help. This particular one was like flypaper—it connected me with several important contacts. Although I must add, *Guitar Player* never reviewed a single one of my albums after the first one!

A recording studio guy in Calgary contacted me when he heard I was working on *Volume 2*. He'd hit on the idea of offering a package to bands that came in to record. With much less overhead per-profit-dollar than he got running the studio, he could take completed master tapes and album artwork to manufacturers and make a percentage off each step in the pressing and printing processes. He could do this and still offer the artists a lower rate than they would get on their own, so it worked to everyone's advantage.

He offered to get me 1000 units for $1000. This worked out okay. I knew more about the process with this second album and recorded the music in six different sessions, then had an engineer splice together the stuff I wanted. The first album had actually been played and recorded in what was to be the final order, including the pauses.

When *Volume 2* went off to Toronto to be mastered, this recording studio guy enclosed a note that I later intercepted when I got my master tape back. It was full of condescending and obnoxious comments about my music, claiming it was signaling the end of the world as we know it. This hurt my feelings at first, but later I was glad that someone like him had a reaction to my music at all.

By the time the second album was out in an edition of 1000 copies and bringing in even more mail orders, I decided to leave Calgary and seek an environment more hospitable to experimentation in music.

The *Guitar Player* incident repeated itself when I showed up in New York. I got a mention in an article by big shot New York *Times* critic Robert Palmer when I scheduled my first New York solo concert. Palmer has not written a word about me since, but this first mention helped elevate my status slightly.

Most of the best releases were still on artist-owned labels at this point, and the era of punk rock and do-it-yourself labels from this scene was just around the corner. During a five-year stay in New York, I took part in releasing 14 different albums, squandering my life's savings in the process. Making an album was always the same and required a great deal of patience to see the project through from concept to some semblance of the idea on tape, make covers, get a decent pressing, yell at pressing plants until they finally admitted they had the boxes sitting there waiting to be picked up, and finally, the most fun of all, yelling at distributors if they bothered to take your call. It was a pain in the ass, but exciting.

The lack of funds always made it difficult to do anything but the most basic, rushed job on the albums. Then I'd have to put up with various pundits who badmouthed the sound, the artwork, the labels, the fact that the catalog number was written in a weird place, whatever.

By the time I moved to Greensboro, North Carolina, in 1981, my life had changed drastically. I now had a child to support and no spare money to throw into recording projects. By then I had done the country/avant fusion "There'll Be No Tears Tonight" and was going through a mid-career rejection of the self-publishing process, a syndrome as common as the cold.

The band that would develop into Shockabilly was kicking around, and we were looking for someone to put out music for us since I could no longer

take it on. One bandmember, the eventually notorious producer Mark Kramer, came up with the idea of a cassette label and asked me to make some projects. I listened to his pitch. You only printed as many as you needed. No dough was tied up in overhead. New music could be released immediately. Lots of releases could come out. It all sounded great, except the part about him taking half the money. Since it was all stuff I could do myself, why not just do it myself and keep all the money?

Cassettes had been kicking around a while, but they still weren't seen as "real" releases. Do-it-yourself records were fine, but a cassette was substandard. I soon realized that this was part of a subtle, music industry brainwashing that everyone who gets into music is exposed to. It's part of a plot to keep you down if you are a lowly, unpopular sort with a cheap cassette deck. You are made to feel success on any level is unattainable unless you buy it at the high price of fancy equipment, hourly studio rates, and 1000-plus pressings of albums that look really "professional."

My financial pressures at this time were so great I couldn't afford to create a new tape unless I was assured of some financial return, even if it was just $50. Kramer was frustrated because I was pushing to get paid for the Shockabilly recording projects we were licensing to the Rough Trade label and others. He thought it was ridiculous that I was holding out for something specific because at that time, we actually had to negotiate rather than just schmooze. And talking about specific financial advances to record label people is often the quickest way to end the whole deal.

My attitude, however, was that my music was the only possible resource I had to create income without having to take on other kinds of work. If I gave the music away for free, there was no chance I'd make any money from it.

I gambled about three bucks worth of stamps mailing out flyers about some solo cassettes I was releasing. The two titles advertised actually didn't exist except on paper or in my mind. About a week later, some old friends in Calgary sent me a $50 check for copies of the tapes. I was on my way! The project, as yet to be recorded, was already turning a profit.

Creating these two tapes, *Guitar Freakout* and *Solo History*, taught me how to edit. This kind of thing should be an ongoing process throughout any good music career. You figure out ways to pay yourself to learn things you want to do. I was tired of being at the mercy of engineers' razor blades. Cutting up tape suited me perfectly. I liked looking at the pile of discarded snippets on the floor and thinking about the "less is more" philosophy.

Guitar Freakout sometimes had as many as nine splices in a minute. In the process of learning how to splice for myself, I saw that the editor who had worked on my orchestra album, *The English Channel*, had misled me about what was "right" and "wrong" in editing. He had told me to change my ideas because he said they weren't possible in editing. I learned that as long as you have a sharp razor blade, anything is possible. (By the way, this editor was Les Paul Jr., son of the great guitarist and inventor, whose strange use of recording effects was a heavy inspiration for most '60s-era psychedelic guitarists.)

In the first year of cassette production, I sold a small number through the mail. Advertising was not much help, since publications at that time paid very little attention to cassettes. Business picked up dramatically when I decided to start making a stock of each cassette, 10 or 20 copies at a time, to take on the road with me. At that time we had two cassette machines in the house, and I made copies one at a time. Slowly we expanded until now we sometimes make eight at a time, all in real time from the same master signal which, since about 1995, has been a DAT production master.

Packaging has to be the most fun element of cassettes, and you could argue that the cassette-buying audience enjoys creative packaging on a level that's rarely reached by mass-produced mediums. An early design we used involved recycling envelopes by printing artwork on the sticker paper available from Xerox places or printers, folding the stickers over the envelopes, and then cutting an opening at one side for the tape to go in and out.

Fans love these packages, and in my opinion, they look much better than commercial plastic CD and tape packages, feel better to the touch, and are certainly more durable. (Old leaves are more durable than plastic.) But the peeling was too much work.

For a few years, I switched to a combination of Xeroxed artwork with the tape folded up inside, and the whole thing shoved inside a plastic newspaper bag. Tying the plastic bag tightly prevented shreeves from ripping off tapes (this had become a problem with the envelopes, because it was easy to open them and palm the tape if you were a light fingered-Louie), but it was an aesthetic downer of sorts compared to the envelopes. Still, they were quick and easy to slap together.

Recycling is a happy tie-in of the cassette scene. A few years ago, I started taking certain types of food containers out of the recycling container and using them to package tapes, creating my own artwork by combining the stuff on the package with my own stickers, glued-on parts salvaged from old flyers, and so forth. The overall look of the thing was inspired by Australian anarchist artists who specialized in defacing advertising.

Fans love these packages because they are big and sturdy enough to hold lots of extra junk. Homemade booklets, photos, bonus posters, flyers, and so forth all fit in easily. The idea of each package being different is appealing and, in the opinion of some, means you can raise prices. "These packages should be selling for a half million at an outside arts fair," I've been told.

Meanwhile, in today's economy where we deal with a sometimes impoverished audience, having an item on sale for $5 and still making a 200 or 300 percent profit is handy. Why is the profit so high? Because it is possible to buy good quality cassettes in bulk. After that, if you are ingenious enough, your only costs are a few cents here and there for printing.

The size of the cassette makes it suitable for packaging in many different types of containers; many of them available for nothing. Other successful Chadbourne cassette packaging enterprises include:

Dirty Sock. A trio of live tapes with Camper Van Chadbourne, all packaged inside one of my socks. Or one of my kid's socks. Or anybody's sock. Actually never a dirty one, though. Legend that the sock was dirty helped sell it, though, as did the inspirational credit on a Camper Van Beethoven LP that I had left "one dirty sock behind in Albuquerque." This little bit of free advertising was printed on more than 50,000 albums.

My Shoe. Inspired by an incident at a They Might Be Giants concert on the Rolla, Missouri, campus. Someone heaved a shoe at me during my opening bit. Incensed, I announced that the party better be prepared to call home tomorrow and beg for a new pair of shoes because they weren't going to get this shoe back. A sobbing teenager approached me later with a security guard, begging for the shoe.

"She threw the shoe at me, " I argued. "I am considering charging her with assault." I asked the security cop if a shoe was considered a deadly weapon in Missouri.

"My shoe! My shoe!" the girl cried. "I didn't throw it, some drunken boy took it off my foot! He did it! It's not my fault. I want my shoe!"

I had to give the shoe back, but her plaintive cries rang in my ears. I knew then what to do with the pile of odd shoes that had been accumulating in a plastic garbage bag on my back porch. During one tour in 1994 in Italy, Austria, and Germany, I made nearly $500 selling copies of *My Shoe* to fans at concerts. Nearly every dollar was profit. The triple tape package used only discarded tapes from nightclub booking agents, all of varying lengths. All the artwork included was leftover stuff from other projects, things that had been found in the streets and so forth. Of course, the shoes were free.

Coffee Cans. These sturdy containers could hold all manner of gunk. A ten-cassette set? No problem. Filled with memorabilia? Could be worth $100 if someone is enthusiastic enough about your endeavors. And the actual tape will smell like coffee, which in the Joe-heavy music scene, has got to be a plus.

"Think how cool it would be if Thelonious Monk had gone through all the leftover junk around his house and given it away with his records," the producer of the *Electric Rake Cake* package said to me when he saw the finished design. In that case it was a double CD, but the packaging idea came from the cassette series. We used a small cake box purchased from a packaging outlet that serviced bakeries among many other things. There was loads of room in there for goodies.

Big manufacturers can spend tens of thousands of dollars creating groovy packaging for new Pearl Jam releases but they could never create packaging like this. Their products may be listed on charts in magazines read mostly by disc jockeys, agents, and managers, but the stuff *you* can create will be held dearly in the hearts of fans. What's more important? We'll give you some time to think about it and go on discussing the packaging of cassettes inside old take-out sushi containers, fried chicken bags, McDonald's Styrofoam sandwich boxes that were donated for a supposed "school event," metal bandage boxes, cheese packages, and cookie boxes.

The cassette scene is a combination of everything in music, like a temple of possibilities that no one knows about. If there was incense burning in this temple, it would be Essence of Chaos. And of course, an important facet of the temple is that if you don't like the way it looks, push a button and you can "erase" it and put up a new building of your own.

Anal retentive procedures of documentation in music history get completely skewed when it comes to home cassette producers. Complete discographies of artists? Impossible. Ever-escalating collector's prices for rare items? Forget it. Anybody can dub a copy of anything. Copyright registration and interference from international performing-rights collection agencies? Dream on!

If someone releases an LP and later goes back and changes a track or adds another one, it is something of a big deal to these historians, who duly take note. On the cassette scene, it is possible to make every copy of a release different in some way. Getting recognition for such hard work is nearly impossible, however, because hardly anybody knows that it is going on, and the people that do can't keep track of it all anyway. So the entire impetus for creation must

be the artist's love of their own work. Nobody is offering anything else. This instills into the cassette scene a quality of genius.

Of course, since anybody can make and release a cassette—my collection includes ones done by ten-year-olds—it is impossible to enforce music business quality controls. Magazines that pride themselves on printing a wide range of obscure reviews often brag about anti-cassette policies. Who is going to take the time to listen to all this stuff, they ask. And how can they possibly have an opinion about it after it burns them out? Which it will, because there's so much of it.

This once again proves how brilliant the cassette movement is. Like the self-perpetuating, self-creating, automatic mechanical factories written about in Philip K. Dick's science fiction, the cassette scene has within itself all the mechanisms required to dismantle the establishment music scene, including a virus-type effect on music critics: If they are exposed to this mountain of cassette productions, they will burn out. They will no longer have opinions. Good! Let it happen! It's about time.

Cassette material seems to be more revolutionary because people include things nobody would ever put on an album—drunks jumping onstage and singing, children screaming at birthday parties, as well as performances that are unique but were recorded without benefit of high-tech equipment. When material like this does appear on a CD or album, it is because the artists are attempting to recreate the freedom of the cassette scene. Nice try.

The cassette sound, whether heard at home, on a blaster, in a car, or on a beach, lends itself to so many levels of low-fi and hi-fi that it is indeed possible to do just about anything. The "low-tech" label that has come along recently is simply saying what many listeners have said all along. All music is sound, and there are many ways of capturing sound. A lot of cheap, low-budget, junk, or a-step-up-to-bargain equipment can produce sounds that are pleasing to many listeners.

As an artist proceeds to document ongoing activities through cassette releases, loads of volunteer help will come out of the woodwork in the form of bizarre individuals with tape recorders who will tape events or jam sessions and pass along the recording just to help out. Instead of being some sad sack scrounging $500 to record two songs in Eddie's 16-track Shack, you can be squirming under a mound of cassettes of yourself you haven't even listened to, all suitable for release in some form.

The prestige of a CD or LP release is much greater, it's true. And having the help of someone who is running any kind of record company, even if it is just a couple of cartons kept under a bed, is career help for you that you didn't have before. It is a mistake not to get things going on all tracks.

But think of what is going on in the mind of the discerning listener, the person who might really follow your music. To them, a cassette purchased directly from the artist could be the ultimate. On an artistic level, it might be more real because many artists water down their music when they're putting out a prestige item. How many times have we heard statements such as:

"This is for a record! Let's make it sound really slick."

"I like that, but I don't want to put it on the record."

"I'd be scared to put that on a record."

"This is my first CD, I really have to impress people."

"I'll put out something like this later on, but for now I have to do such-and-such to get a record deal."

All these are common attitudes, no matter what kind of music is being contemplated for release. But cassettes? The most common attitude is, "If you don't like it, dub over it." And after decades of documenting music, that's the most exciting thing I've ever heard.

Others in the music business are no doubt much more excited by the supposed profit ratio of CDs over albums. Getting the public to pay more for their music is something of an art form within the industry—or it's about as close as these jokers can get to art.

The real artist is preoccupied with making things cheaper, not more expensive. Thus, we begin to distance ourselves from corporate entities such as the Beatles, whose first move after realizing they were too spaced out to run their own record company was to help invent "selective pricing," thus setting the stage for the entire CD revolution (which was a revolution in higher price tags and nothing else).

Why do most people hate the color Day-Glo green? It's because this was the color of the sticker most stores placed on *Abbey Road*, indicating that it would cost a buck more. From here it was a short jump to realizing that if consumers are willing to pay a buck more for the same product just because it was by a top band, they'd probably part with the entire contents of their wallet if a brand new format came along and it was the "top" format—i.e., CDs rule.

There is now a demand for "Indian scouts" within the industry, the kind of intrepid souls who used to lie down on top of hot buttes all day, watching for the telltale rise of horse dust on the horizon. But now they are looking for signs of new formats developing so nobody remotely connected with music will fall victim to the dreaded "down time."

The CD era has seen a boom in the establishing of independent labels and self-publishing. One reason for this is that on paper it looks like the CD manufacturer will stand to make a big profit if 1000 copies of an item are sold. Most small companies are finding now that it can take more than two years to collect from distributors on these sales, if they can collect at all. Distribution companies have been accused of

> *The cassette scene is a combination of everything in music, like a temple of possibilities that no one knows about.*

intentionally sabotaging the livelihoods of small labels, under orders from the big companies that often secretly own the distributors.

Other distributors are not so secret about the fact that they run their own labels, give them top priority, and will sabotage other small labels just on the off-chance that decreased competition will be good for somebody. Whether one believes any of these paranoid theories is irrelevant. The point is that small label business is in jeopardy.

What kind of small business can wait two years to collect on accounts? We'd all love to try this with our rent or car payments, I'm sure, or even at the grocery store. "How about 90 days?" would be a good question to ask the cashier next time you check out with a watermelon.

Small labels have to be steeped in cash coming from somewhere else. Often they are sidelines of people with thriving businesses. The Leo jazz label in England has a proprietor who works for BBC radio and translates advertising for the Russian market. Another label owner pays his bills by making signs for casinos in Louisiana. These are typical examples. Labels aspire to reach a state where they can have a large catalog, keep everything in print, and sell about 200 copies each year of each title. This may not seem like a grand goal compared to your typical rock star's dream of world conquest, but pulling it off without going bankrupt is more than most labels seem able to do.

In my own case, raising three children with no medical coverage while having a business and plenty of lapses in cash flow means it is too difficult for me to sink money into printing stocks of CDs, although I do investigate the idea from time to time. Usually the opportunity to release the material through someone else comes along. From a business sense, it is sometimes better if you can get someone else to take a risk and pay you an advance based on money that is supposed to come in down the line from CD sales.

For someone to give you this money before the tape is even recorded—or even once it is—is a big leap of faith. An important part of the successful music profession psychology is being able to talk people out of this money and accept it graciously when it arrives, even though, deep down in your soul, you might know that the chances of the person recouping it are practically nil.

However, it is never a mistake to print the material yourself. A group on the road with a stock of CDs is set up to recoup all kinds of travel expenses, if nothing else. There are many ways to divide and account for money as it comes in, but the important part is to have people handing it over to you.

Compact discs are also small enough to provide room for experimentation with packaging, although distributors are mostly clinging to the much-hated jewel box format that was pushed on the industry by plastics manufacturers. But the artist must be like Marco Polo and find their own trade routes.

By the way, never count out a format that is hyped as being out of date. Vinyl never really went away when they said it would, and on the independent production scene it is back and better than ever. You can even charge more for it because consumers familiar with the drawbacks of CDs are willing to pay more for their beloved vinyl now. Even a format considered as ridiculous as the 8-track has its own legion of fans who publish a magazine and espouse a convincing philosophy: How can you go wrong when you can get the top-of-the line player for a buck? You don't make money, you simply eliminate entire areas of expense by sticking only to 8-tracks!

People will argue about whether today's technology is making it easier to self-publish or not. There is a lot of hype about how simple it is to create slick-looking products these days. But if the content is the real point of the endeavor, being able to access a million typefaces isn't any different than Beatrix Potter hand-lettering her own Peter Rabbit books because nobody would publish them. No matter what era we are living in and what the machine of the day might be, self-production is always a rewarding and necessary outlet that clever and hard-working artists can get going for themselves. Meanwhile the other half rots away in hot tubs.

CHAPTER 12

Living Under New Machines

"Oh, I like that title," a friend reading over my shoulder said the other day. "I get this image of a bunch of people crushed under a machine, trying to survive." The image is apt. It isn't like a car or train wreck where they wait for that "jaws of life" contraption to liberate them, either. Members of the consumer public, and that includes just about everybody in some way, have to be on their guard or they will wind up buried under all the latest stuff that everyone just "has to have."

Musicians have to think about the dangers of our consumer society just as much as anyone else. I won't say more, even though equipment is at the heart of everything. Without instruments, how could anyone play? Without recording equipment, how could any music ever be commercially released? Without the sound equipment known as a P.A. (who is your M.A., then?), how could bands blast their sound out to 60,000 people gathered in a coliseum? Hmm, maybe we're onto something. No, musicians don't have any more of a dependency on technology than anyone else with their cars, kitchen appliances, video players, and what not. For once we have a situation where musicians are not removed from public or mainstream perceptions.

Selling technology to the public is an ongoing campaign that makes the presidential election look like a middle school competition for student council. If you consider advertising a form of brainwashing (in other words, if you are perceptive), then what happens with new gadgets is something dictators such as Hitler and Stalin could only daydream about. So much depends on getting the public hooked on buying certain items that advertisers carry the art of hype, otherwise known as spreading misconceptions, to an extreme.

During my lifetime, I've seen some huge changes in sound equipment, recording technology, and most notably, the actual format of recordings sold to the public. If you are, say, 18-25, you can expect to see many more of these technological upheavals. You can recognize them by the big cardboard boxes in front of people's houses and by the onslaught of lies from the media about the contents of said boxes.

Don't dare call me skeptical, you whippersnapper! Just think how tied in all the players in the media game are with each other. Television, radio, and print media all rely on advertising to pay for their programming. Advertising sells, among many other things, the new forms of technology being offered to the public. It is only natural that, as a favor to their clients, the media outlets create and distribute misleading stories about what is happening.

"Vinyl is dead!" everyone was declaring a few years back. Situations like this, where everyone is expected to ditch perfectly good possessions they have spent years and hundreds of dollars accumulating simply to buy them all over again in a "new format," is what advertisers dream of. They would be thrilled if everyone on earth had all their teeth yanked out every few years and replaced with some new invention. (I really shouldn't write this kind of crazy stuff because I might give manufacturers new ideas.) Every time new technologies develop, someone is exploited. Who gets exploited in the music business, you ask? Anyone who plays music or even likes to listen to it, that's who.

I blame the Beatles for the invention of the CD because they are credited with the concept of "selective pricing." Other popular artists followed suit. That's when the germ of the CD began to spread. Business types realized assigning such value to particular artists was good, but shifting the price up on an entire new format of recording and convincing the public that the old format was dead, well, that would be better. Look how many people bought into it!

What musicians need to realize is that they are part of a low-income segment of society. Economizing should be part of the musicians' everyday existence. This is especially important when it comes to equipment. A drummer's wife I knew used to moan all the time about how he was constantly upgrading his equipment even though, in her opinion, he owned two perfectly decent drum sets. Another couple I knew split up because the musician in the family had the "gotta have it" syndrome and couldn't stop herself from going on buying sprees. First it was the entire family of saxophones, including the pricey contrabass sax. Then it was the computer era and a complete state-of-the-art set up.

It is no coincidence that these types rarely create new and better music on their new and better equipment. If they don't have the sophistication to realize they don't need all this fancy stuff, how could they possibly possess the more complex creative ideas that they *really* need?

Now, there are some people who are just plain rich and never have to worry about running out of money. Music stores and manufacturers of equipment like those people, maybe even love them, but they don't target their propaganda campaigns at them. They know they'll have their business anyway because those folks love getting the latest equipment and have no reason to cut back on expenses. But it's the poverty-stricken players that ad campaigns are aimed at because without convincing masses of folks to spend, spend, spend, most of these companies would go under. It is like gun manufacturers insisting

they need freedom to make whatever weapons they want for the deer hunters when what they really want is plenty of business from armed robbers and Third World insurrectionists.

The subject of terrorism is not irrelevant here, because it is a sort of terrorism that technology practices on the arts with, thankfully, a victory here and there on the side of consumer security. Whenever

Czechoslovakian music store, circa old regime:
Here is where a musician could find some real bargains.

there are improvements in home recording technology, for example, it makes it easier for musicians to create their own recordings without having to go into hock to pay for overpriced studios. This helps make the working situation more secure for the musician, but of course, the manufacturers always try to retaliate.

For example, it is commonly known that the DAT-machine, although still a bargain by recording equipment standards, could be available to the consumer for much, much less than what it is currently priced at. Overpricing it prevents people from bypassing both the studio and recording industries. Yet we have survived individuals being able to make their own master-quality tapes, which the industry predicted would be catastrophic. It wasn't.

Since it's so difficult to earn money playing music, it's useful to spend some time attacking the column of debit figures from the other side. Hustling for new jobs and trying to get paid more for the ones you get are worthy ambitions, but your overall profit can be increased in many cases if you spend less. This usually means economizing on equipment, looking for bargains, keeping old equipment going, and learning to live under the new machines. By this I mean developing a bird doo-doo sensor for advertising and media campaigns, learning to make up one's own mind, and not getting swept away by fads.

Anyone that studies the music scene even superficially for a year or two will see that a lot of attention is given to making the newest products seem like things no one can do without. An important part of this philosophy is kicking whatever is down. A few

> *You have to worry when a pack of razor blades that costs a few bucks is replaced by a system that costs thousands of bucks to set up.*

years ago we were told that traditional instruments such as the guitar and the piano were going down the tubes. Much effort went into making new electronic keyboard versions of these instruments. Remember the old Casio guitar? The point to remember is that you should be out looking for one now that nobody wants them. That's how you make money in the music business. Wait for something to be so out of style that nobody wants it, then buy it cheap. All these things are simply created to make sounds. If you have any originality or creativity, you can make these sounds interesting to someone else, who in turn will become interested in what you are doing.

Don't worry about the kind of audience that is turned off if you don't have a state-of-the-art Furshinglugger-synthi-mop. You can't depend on that kind of audience if you are trying to make a living from music because they will ditch you just as quickly as they become interested in you. You might feel successful with all your piles of equipment, and you might bring in ten times more pay per night than Joe Shreeve with his beat-up six-string guitar. But if Joe Shreeve is spending ten times less than you, he might have the bigger bank balance. This concept is important in every area of musical equipment.

Here are the Ten Commandments of Equipment, brought down from Mount Techno by the Moses of Low Tech. The expression "low tech" is something of a misnomer, by the way. I first heard it

on a grand scale when artists such as Beck started having chart success with home recordings. The media was typically misrepresenting the situation as a new one, because there were always artists who played with minimal equipment. This brings us directly to commandment number one.

1. *If you have spent more than $2,000 on equipment in a year, kneel and pay attention: You are not worthy!* Chuck Berry recorded the song "Memphis" on a $79 reel-to-reel in what he claims was a $145 studio. I'd like to hear his justification for that extra $65, by the way. For what, a microphone or something? A stool to sit on? Anyway, check out this song the next time you hear it. Can't wait to analyze it? Turn on an oldies station and wait an hour, you'll hear it. It is one of the best records ever made, in rock or any other genre, with some of the best guitar sounds ever put down. It's a brilliant rendition of a truly touching, timeless song. This is proof that a talented artist can create a really good recording on equipment that is deemed "worthless." Talent and a good song are what you really need, and neither can be bought. This fact probably keeps equipment manufacturers awake at night.

2. *Anyone can afford state-of-the-art if they are willing to live in the past.* What would you pick as one of the best rock albums of all time? Many would choose *Sgt. Pepper's Lonely Hearts Club Band* by the Beatles. Maybe you have read about all the wonderful fun they had putting this together using an Ampex 4-track reel-to-reel machine (which at that time was a state-of-the-art recording machine).

And what about the 8-track? Early works on this model include the classic *Strange Days* by the Doors, another beautiful piece of work. If you were running a state-of-the-art studio these days, you would probably keep a 4- or 8-track machine in a closet somewhere, maybe with a stack of *National Geographic*s on top of it. Like those magazines full of interesting maps and photos of places hardly anyone goes to, the old recording machines seem to still be valuable enough that studio owners won't get rid of them. But they don't exactly keep them on display either, because they might give potential clients the wrong impression.

If you've owned a studio for a while, you'd probably like to find someone to buy your old equipment, but nobody ever offers anything close to what the machines were worth when you bought them. There just isn't that much demand for them. People that come to a studio want state-of-the-art, which these days means 16-, 24-, 32-, or 64-track via computer hookups.

I own an Ampex 4-track, which I bought almost

ten years ago now from a studio old-timer. I don't want to make this gentleman, Phil Nelson, sound like a dinosaur or anything, but he has run a studio of one kind or another since the *Sgt. Pepper* days. "When I bought this it was state-of-the-art," he said of the 4-track, which is the size of a sawed-off VW bug. "Having this is what made me have a fancy studio. People came in just to look at it."

These four tracks not only allowed a person to record four separate tracks and synchronize them, but they could also bounce around from track to track using the "sound-on-sound process." A guitar part on track A could be moved to track B alongside a bass part, and with the levels set correctly, they would blend perfectly, freeing track A again for something else.

The 4-tracks each had plenty of room. This is why, for example, the guitar solos on Beatles' albums have a clarity and bite to them unlike anything recorded these days. Phil's machine ran at 30 ips, which also added to the brilliance of the sound. (Generally, the faster tape moves, the better the sound. On the other hand, slow speeds are sometimes intentionally used to create distorted, rumbling bass. This is currently a popular technique with grunge and hard rock bands.)

"I sure would love to find a good home for this," Phil told me one day when he came across it while digging in a closet for a homemade voice effects-thing that I wanted to try out. "I almost had a karaoke place ready to buy it," he went on. "But the guy figured out it was cheaper and easier to get one of those 4-track cassette machines." Technically, the difference between the Ampex 4-track reel-to-reel and a home-tape high-speed cassette setup is like comparing a sports car to a little red wagon. But anyone who has been in a karaoke bar would agree that a little red wagon will do just fine.

I asked how much the karaoke guy had been willing to pay for the machine, and Phil told me two grand. I knocked him down to a grand and a half and explained that there was no way I could pay it all at once. "I will be happy knowing this machine has a good home," he said, being quite fond of my adventurous studio ways.

This worked out great for everyone. What a fantastic machine! It comes from an era when equipment was made to run indefinitely simply by oiling it now and then and tightening a few screws. It has had a total of 50 dollars in repairs since I bought it, and the electronic nuts that fixed it were so excited to come in contact with it that they probably would have done the work for nothing. "I think my band must have cut a surf music demo on this machine back at Phil's place in the old days," one of them said when they saw the 4-track.

I still use this machine constantly; there is always some kind of complex project going on involving it. It has paid for itself 20 times over. Every time an album or CD is assembled with tracks from various sources and it includes work on my 4-track, I find that the stuff from other studios has a much less vivid sound. This includes tracks done in top-grade modern studios.

If a piece of equipment is really state-of-the-art and not just pretending to be (as so many machines do), then it has unlimited potential for the artist, and a lifetime can easily be spent learning how to use it. One will always be able to discover something new about such a piece of equipment. Logically, if we live in an era when something recorded on such a machine can have just as much appeal as a track from a studio currently considered state-of-the-art, then one has to ask what that expression really means, anyway.

Take advantage of the trendy nature of the society we live in. Studios will always be upgrading their equipment because they think they need to in order to attract clients. They are probably right—most of the people who go into recording studios are too naïve to realize they don't need all this monkey-tech. Find a great machine that a studio has dumped or is willing to dump, and take it home with you at a great bargain price. Use it, use it, use it. You won't regret it.

3. *Don't ignore today's technology.* Pay attention to what's going on as if you were attending Jesus' Sermon on the Mount. In other words, don't think you are so brilliantly behind the times that you don't need to concentrate on the now. From time to time technology does come up with something that can save a musician money. Watch for it, and be sure to get in on it.

The best example at present is the DAT machine. I own several now and use them by themselves or in conjunction with the Ampex. Their main benefit is that they save a fortune in tape. A reel on the Ampex at high speed costs about $2.50 a minute, whereas the perfectly acceptable 90-minute DAT is a little over ten cents a minute. This is a big saving for players. Like recording live? A DAT recording can get the whole set down, continuously with no breaks, for $10. The major drawback of the DAT is that, unlike analog equipment, there is no way to adjust or tweak digital recordings so that distorted levels sound good. This is something even an electric rake player should be able to live with.

4. *When they tell you technology has made life easier, run for your life.* Along with the DAT came the development of digital editing on computers. I don't want to complain about the projects I've been involved with that used this technology, but you have to worry

when a pack of razor blades that costs a few bucks is replaced by a system that costs thousands of bucks to set up.

Studios immediately had to computerize, not only to get in on the game but to help out clients who were DAT-ing at home but couldn't figure out how to assemble master tapes from what they had done. Editing is not just about shortening a track or taking out the lousy out-of-tune cello solo; it is an essential part of the final production. The same set of songs arranged in a different order can have a huge impact. Thinking that a finished project can be recorded in sequence is a little high fallutin' for most of us.

When I saw that a fellow with a computer studio was charging $330 an hour and claiming it was a competitive rate, I realized I had to figure out my own way of editing directly on the DAT machines. I knew it wouldn't be impossible after years of fooling around with cassette machines and their pause-button apparatus. Nevertheless, the early DAT equipment had all the finesse of an awkward home video machine with gaping, yawning holes between edits.

I have developed many systems of DAT editing, some of which are quite perverse. I like the idea of first filling the entire DAT tape with background noise that immediately drops in the moment you hit the stop button on the tracks you are recording on top. This and other secret techniques have gotten me DAT masters, which have the desired effect of mastering labs. In other words, they call the record company and/or me in a total panic, wondering, "What on earth is going on?" And it is no fun making records if you can't get this to happen.

Still, I miss the old razor blades. Film editing has also changed over to computer, and my friends in that business tell me it's an improvement because footage no longer gets lost on the cutting room floor. This is important in an era of director's cuts, uncensored versions, out-takes, and so forth. In the old days, this stuff was just swept up by the janitors unless the film artists went to extra trouble to hang on to it.

The main thing I miss about the old style of editing is the pile of tape snippets that would accumulate on the floor as one cut down a project. The shorter length of LPs (as opposed to CDs) meant you were always weaning out a few seconds here and there, hoping it would add up to a minute or more by the time you got to the end of side B. I used to call this "the ca-ca pile," and it used to make me happy although it is hard to understand why since I am such a cheapskate. The little bits of tape I sliced up were really cold, hard cash!

5. *Don't dismiss fads, just wait until everyone else has.* This includes fads that never catch on. I mentioned the Casio guitar. What a piece of junk! Regard-less of whether everybody or nobody in the music business buys what they come up with next week, why didn't anyone buy the $14 Casio Rap Man? Sometimes an attempted fad's failure is a mystery. Here was a machine that enabled *anyone* to be a recording artist in the rap genre, at least to my ears. Some of the rhythm tracks on the Rap Man still show up on rap records.

Only $14 for a machine with sampled drum tracks, keyboard sounds, plus various sound effects such as barking dogs and even a cheap imitation turntable scratching sound. This is a bargain that rivals the acquisition of the island of Manhattan. But it's typical of what happens when supply is greater than demand. And this happens all the time.

Two concepts about the nature of fads need to be understood. One is that almost anything that creates music or sound can be used as part of some kind of really good music, regardless of how popular or unpopular the device is. When the Fender Rhodes electric piano came along in tandem with its cheaper quality buddy the Wurlitzer, it swept certain styles of music like a California brush fire. Everyone had to have that Rhodes sound, until listeners got completely sick of it. Then for a while, you could get the keyboards for next to nothing. The keyboard player in one group I was in during the '70s was actually given a Wurlitzer by a guy in a music store who said, "You want this? Really! Take it! I'd feel bad charging you anything for it." A few years later, the same guy was given an early Moog synthesizer for the same reason: The dufus behind the counter saw no future in a piece of equipment that was going through what he saw as a downward spiral in popularity.

Nowadays, there is a demand for such equipment for a variety of music including rap, house, and techno. Many players simply acquire as many cheap keyboards as they can and are satisfied if they find one usable sound on each one. (And give these instruments the benefit of the doubt. Let them lie around for a few years after you're sick of them because one day you will put in fresh batteries, turn it on, and—eureka!—find another sound you like coming out of them.)

In addition to being able to ignore fads, a musician should study them closely to see what it is about them that people like. Even if it is mainly the look of a product that sells it, there is usually something musical hidden in there, too. Even a stupid gimmick is worth studying and attempting to understand. If people like it once, they will more than likely like it again. This process might take 20 years, but that shouldn't deter a serious player who is in this for the life experience. Many of these fads wouldn't die out so quickly if they weren't overexposed. This leads us to the next commandment.

6. *Thou shalt not covet thy neighbor's video.* Music videos are not technology or equipment in themselves, but they have achieved their widespread popularity via other technological developments, particularly the upgrading of cable TV systems and the resulting proliferation of new channels.

The sick result of this is that acts starting out in any field where there is cable TV video representa-

> In addition to being able to ignore fads, a musician should study them closely to see what it is about them that people like.

tion are force-fed the concept that producing a video of a song is a must. This has, in turn, led to music industry A&R and production people thinking in terms of the video rather than the song. Recently, a producer complained to me that the records he had grown up with, like "On the Boardwalk," allowed his imagination to create visual images, whereas nowadays consumers are presented with video images and find they cannot escape thinking about them every time they hear the song.

The guy is right, but before we go further into this theory let's quickly retrace a little history of the music video. If you read or hear somewhere that music as a visual entity was invented by MTV, don't believe it. There is a long history of this kind of thing in a variety of fields. Many rock videos these days are imitative of the visual spin groups used to receive when they played "live" (usually lip-synching) on various TV variety shows. I remember seeing the Byrds on the *Smothers Brothers Comedy Hour* doing one of their psychedelic numbers with a lot of cheesy video effects tossed in. Nowadays the oldies rock video shows recycle many of these clips, and youngsters wonder why they look so much like the stuff on MTV.

Predating these clips are the musical shorts they used to produce for use with jukeboxes. These days, some high-tech bars have video jukeboxes, but many don't realize this idea is quite old. Strippers from the old burlesque days used to make what were sometimes called "videoscopes." So did a variety of performers from various genres including jazz, rhythm and blues, and Broadway show music.

I distinctly remember going to eat Moroccan couscous in a seedy dive in the Parisian Latin Quarter

back in the '70s. The men were gathered around watching a music video featuring a boy and girl duo singing in Arabic while a tale of lust and murder was shown on screen, sometimes with the performers crooning and dancing around in the foreground. It was of a quality perfectly suitable for MTV broadcast, maybe even better.

Obviously, people are interested in watching these things, but are they necessary for a career? I think not. In fact, my opinion is that they *ruin* many careers! Exceptions are the people whose videos are actually better than their records. An artist such as Weird Al Yankovic, for example, makes hilarious videos of some of his songs such as "Amish Paradise" or "Like a Surgeon," and the visual images one retains actually augment the process of listening to these tracks on CD.

For most bands, however, the continued visual exposure through music videos seems to make the public sick of them far more quickly than Top 40 used to. We used to get sick of songs back then, too; it's bound to happen even when a song is a masterpiece such as "I Am the Walrus" or the unbelievable "They're Coming to Take Me Away Ha-Haaa!" (That song doesn't really belong in here, I just like typing the title.) It seems to me, though, that back then one of the reasons fans bought concert tickets was the chance to see the act in person.

I remember looking at the few pictures of the Byrds that were printed on their various albums and being fascinated by their personal appearances. My older brother and I bought tickets to see them and part of the fun was seeing the people in the band, even though from where we were sitting you couldn't make out details like the color of their eyes.

Nowadays, a new band puts a video on MTV and you get to see *everything*. You see armpit hairs, nose hairs, zits; you see them in their underwear; you see them in dozens of changes of clothing, sometimes in the space of a four-bar guitar solo. You get totally sick of these people after seeing a few videos, at least that's what I've observed.

And the trend seems to be accelerating. Industry big shots whine about how quickly bands go from being popular to being nobody. The management of the once super-hot Spin Doctors said in an interview that it would be easier to book a totally unknown band than one that has peaked and declined on the current market. I have to blame videos for this state of things, especially when so many of these now-ya-see-'em-now-ya-don't bands rise to the top through heavy video exposure!

When you factor in the heavy expense of a video, like most of the big label expenses that are eventually sifted out of the band's real earnings (i.e., money they would have in their pockets if they hadn't tied in with a big label), the entire idea seems nuts. But this is all part of the philosophy so many new players buy into in their lust for success: Even if it seems crazy, do it anyway because you have to. You don't have to do anything. This is the essential rule of creativity that we call the No Consistency Rule. It is as true about technological developments as it is about anything else.

7. *Good players need good equipment, but good equipment doesn't make a player good.* A musician needs to come to grips with this very important concept. If you are on any kind of budget, trying to support a family, or even having trouble making ends meet for yourself, you will have to figure out how to own decent instruments without spending a fortune.

If you play well, you will be able to get a good sound out of just about any piece of equipment. This doesn't mean you ought to own a piece of junk. It is just something worth realizing. Sometimes I borrow guitars on the road in order to have less to carry, to save wear and tear on my own gear and equipment, and for the fun of trying out different instruments.

I gave up bringing an amp to most gigs years ago. It seemed insane to buy an amp and then destroy it carrying it around. Just getting vibrations all day in a moving van is enough to trash most amps, considering how slapdash the construction is, even from the better firms. (And I'm talking about vibrations from the road, not "Good Vibrations" or "Rastaman Vibrations.")

I love when I play some borrowed guitar and the owner comes up and says, "Wow, I never heard my guitar sound like that before!" That's because a good player develops technique and tone in their hands, their embouchure, or whatever it takes to play an instrument. I love the way a master pianist can sit down at any piece of junk and immediately get "their" sound. (I also like it when a lame pianist sits down on a $60,000 grand piano and sounds like Randy Rinkydink.)

This is not to say owning a good instrument is unnecessary. On the contrary! What the inexperienced player doesn't notice when I borrow their instrument is that if I detect intonation problems, I instantly make an adjustment. Or if there is a tone insufficiency, I make up for it by doing things like holding the pick differently or playing a little harder or softer. When I play on a good instrument, I don't have to make all these little adjustments and can concentrate on other things.

I'll never forget the first gig I did with the used Deering Deluxe five-string banjo I picked up at a good used instrument shop in New England. Up until then I had been using the poor quality banjos one finds in the $150 and $300 range, full of tuning prob-

lems and what I call "crap spots" on the neck. Suddenly I had an instrument that played beautifully no matter where I was on the neck or what I was trying to do. The only limitations were my own. This is how it should be.

Players who are just starting out or aren't that serious don't need a high quality instrument. If it ends up lying around under someone's bed, it's an insult to the art of music. Learning players need to struggle with crappy instruments in order to get better, although not to the point where they can't make any progress. Try to find music store clientele who can help you out in this area, but don't expect that to be easy. Music store clerks that discourage beginners from wasting their money on top-of-the-line equipment usually get fired. A better avenue is to find a professional player who can help you pick out a good beginning instrument. I do this all the time for people. And when I do, I try to never let them break the eighth commandment.

8. *Thou shalt not buy new.* Used instruments are always a better deal. No matter what. This is partly for the same reasons it's better to buy a used car. So much value is lost on a new instrument the moment it leaves a shop that a used instrument has to be a better bargain.

Another reason is that most instruments were made better in that vague era known as the "old days." As more and more instrument companies shift to impersonal overseas manufacturing situations and the supply of good raw materials dwindles, older instruments are more and more appealing. This is the case for guitars and many of the other instruments I've checked out.

Good players on saxophone, trumpet, drums, and bass, for instance, always seem to be looking for vintage instruments that incorporate some feature that was stupidly dropped or lost its appeal with the mainstream players. The big manufacturers always imitate their past glories, meaning they are either incapable of new developments or have no confidence in them.

There are companies that have retained their integrity by purposely keeping things on a small, controllable scale. I mentioned Deering before. This San Diego company that's run by a bluegrass banjo player is in a good position because, although the banjo's popularity might vary to some extent, there will never be the same demand for them as there is for electric guitars, for instance.

Even with guitars, you can look for craftspeople and small regional outfits who work out of their own shops. That is, if you feel you *must* have a new instrument! You'd be even better off finding a used instrument from one of these smaller outfits. Used instruments are not only cheaper, they have already been through their time of seasoning and adjustment. If the instrument was a lemon, and many are, it is not going to be sellable in a shop ten years later. Most instruments that survive the breaking-in period are going to be worth owning.

9. *Burn hype in Hades.* Learn to ignore hype. Hype would have you believe that only name manufacturers make good instruments. So often players will spend much more than they need to. Again, let me stress that finding a good instrument at a good price can be the equivalent of scoring five good club gigs! Learn to think like an accountant—but only for a moment or two.

An example of this theory is what happened with various guitar makes over the years. Instruments such as American-made Harmony guitars or the Czechoslovakian Framus were once considered completely inferior. Now, players realize these were well-made instruments at totally reasonable prices. If you were smart, you would have bought one of these back when nobody else knew about them. Now it's too late. But keep your eyes and ears ready for the instruments that haven't been discovered yet.

10. *Thou shalt pick up junk.* Finally, watch for stuff people throw out. When it comes to technology, learning how to repair things and deal with scrap equipment is essential. I am a slow learner with electronics, so I know this is only too true. It has taken me years to take advantage of freebies.

Once, while sitting around on a park bench in New York City complaining to an associate about how I never got a break, I looked down under my feet and saw that someone had left two perfectly good cheap hand-held tape recorder microphones there. Why? The cords were frayed. A quick repair and they were good as new.

I have picked up a half dozen guitar necks on the streets of various towns over the last three years. All of them were in trash cans. Some of them were from brand new guitars made by Kramer and the like. Everything is worth something, if only for parts such as the tuning peg and nut.

People commonly throw out turntables, stereo amplifiers, broken parts of drum sets, weird collections of records, recording tapes that can be used again, old ironing boards that can be used as keyboard stands, sheet music, and all manner of *kvatch* (that's an old Yiddish word for supposedly useless nonsense) that can be used in recording and percussion setups, for example. Go to yard sales and spend a few bucks. I bought a Japanese nylon-stringed bass for $50 from a family some 15 years ago, and it is still going strong with the same strings on it. Yes, it is a piece of crap, but that hasn't stopped several bass luminaries from asking me, "Hey! How did you get that cool bass sound?" This kind of excitement really does come cheap.

I love to haunt the back alleys of music stores. I have picked up piles of broken drum heads and cut out sections to use for repairing smaller drums. I have also picked up bits of broken electronic stuff that I have no idea what to do with, but they look pretty cool and who knows, maybe one day . . .

Never assume something is broken or useless just because someone throws it out, anymore than you can assume something is worth buying just because it is new and has a price tag on it. And that last sentence is really what it's all about if you don't want to wind up condemned to rot under piles of expensive equipment.

CHAPTER 13

The Musical Shoe Salesman

"If you tour America, it is a good idea to join up with someone who is considered by the press to be a new Bob Dylan. This will mean good crowds and big money. But just don't wind up with Eugene Chadbourne, or you'll spend your days running around endlessly. He's like a shoe salesman!"

—Jo "Doc" Rosenberg from *USA Travails* (Rose Press, 1986)

When my first carton of homemade albums was delivered, one of the first stops I made was a friend's neighborhood record store. They bought a few copies in advance to make me feel good and then struck a deal to keep supplied in the future.

It's all very simple. Take records or CDs. Put them in boxes. Take them into stores. Talk. Accept money or leave. When you run out of records or CDs, make new ones. Stop in at recording studios if you have time. (There's usually a pot of coffee brewing.)

Not every musician will sell directly to stores. Labels of any size will forbid you to do this. Label honchos without the clout to get a CD stocked three blocks away from their house have called me up and warned me to stop selling to shops two time zones away. Meanwhile, when you enter such a place, you'll hear the refrain, "I'd love to carry your stuff, if only I could figure out how to get it."

So don't let record company people talk you out of doing this. If they are doing their job, your record will be in the store anyway and you won't have to worry about schlepping it around. If you are any good at your job, it will not be the only CD or album you have ever created. You'll no doubt have something that the record store doesn't have, and they'll be inter-

ested either on their own or with help from your spiel.

If you have a back catalog of titles, chances are good that some store somewhere will have your old titles sitting there that they will gladly trade for something new. And they'll usually take a shower on the price. Then you can resell these items full price at concerts or to some other shop that has had requests for them or just wants a better selection. I call this form of moving stock from shop to shop "shape shifting." There are more exciting adventures to come in this chapter about this process.

Some musicians won't run around to record stores because they see it as being uncool or degrading to their image. They are right, of course. There is nothing cool about going around selling your stuff to record stores. After all, Jo "Doc" Rosenberg was one of the original cool cats and you see what he thought. This is the essence of musical survival. These basics come back no matter what subject we're talking about. It is cool to be cool, to hang around somewhere cool, to look cool, to say cool things, and to be part of a cool thing. Just walking down the street, someone might point me out to a friend and say, "That's a musician," or "He plays banjo," and in the spirit of that moment, just walking along, I can look, feel, and be cool.

Actually working at something, though, is never cool, particularly not if someone cool compares you to a shoe salesman. It is an activity that makes you a salesman, yes. If you are talking about tempos and counting time, you should talk to other musicians, particularly conductors and drummers. That is a music activity. Selling is not. To swap stories or find sympathetic ears, you can go hang out with peddlers of shoes, maga-

126

zines, hardware supplies, what have you. One difference between you and those peddlers, though, is that you are supposed to be selling something you really believe in, something really special to you. Your music is you, right? You are selling yourself.

The record store people who like your music will enjoy seeing the face behind it and will remember you as someone who walked in and acted like a normal human being (except that most humans are handing out money before they leave the store rather than accepting it). In merchant terms, you have been elevated to a loftier level. So that's that for the idea of being degraded. Never mind that you are only a few

guidance, it is possible to completely avoid places that are going to reject you. But even hot tips about a really great shop that likes to buy stuff can turn into a humiliating stare-down when someone tells you that you're blocking access to the house section.

The telephone is a time-saving tool of the trade. From a cozy nest in a motel, nightclub, or guest room, you can call local record stores and get insulted over the phone rather than in person, and it's one-tenth as painful. You can also find out when the person with the power to buy stuff is actually going to be there. Thus you avoid the time-wasting trip to the place, knowing you could have made a sale

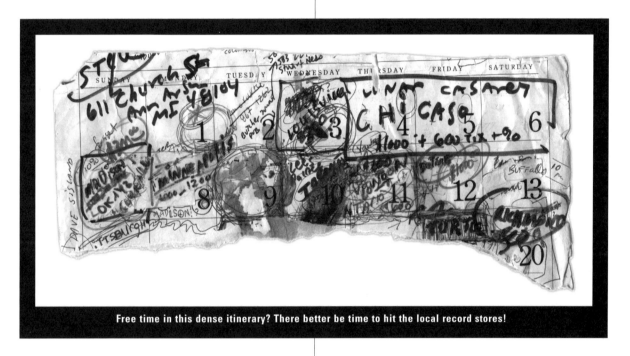

Free time in this dense itinerary? There better be time to hit the local record stores!

bucks ahead of the joker that just dumped a bunch of old Bananarama sides.

The record store people who do not know who you are and have no desire to carry your records will think you are some kind of scum. Not quite as bad as some street person coming in to beg quarters off customers, but close. When you come into the store, you destroy their carefully cultivated image of musicians being angelic images that float like mist out of their advertisements, appearing in the flesh only long enough to be judged "sexy" or "cool." (Can you imagine an MTV video of some clown going around selling records?) People give you the evil eye, and you can tell they see you as a huge failure. When they hand your stuff back to you, they touch it differently, as if it were diseased.

On any given sales day, you might have one of the first experiences described and two of the second. Or the other way around. Sometimes with the right local

if you had been there when Mike or Jay or Keera was on duty.

If you are into creating independent productions, the idea of hitting the record stores shouldn't be viewed as mounting an expedition. In most fair-sized towns, there are only going to be one, two, or three stores that will carry anything interesting and is managed with the kind of flexibility that allows them to buy from some goofball who staggers in off the street unannounced. In the major meccas of art and commerce, such as Berlin, Chicago, New York, Los Angeles, San Francisco, Paris, and so forth, though, getting around to all the shops can be a research and development project that can gobble up the good part of a week. But you should make some money doing it, so there's a reason to put in the time.

We are totally disregarding the big chains, Tower, Discount Records, Peaches, and so forth. These places are corporately run and management has no right to buy anything. If Sir Lancelot rushed in with the Holy Grail and wanted only parking lot change in return, the manager of a Tower would not have the authority to make the deal.

Some smaller chains will see the positive side of getting music from a freelance musician/producer that they can spread around their shops, particularly if it is someone who has any kind of following in their market. Small chain managers know that as long as they can pull off selling one copy of something in six different stores and repeat the miracle all day long, they'll have a job. You are just providing another opportunity for them—that is if anybody wants your stuff.

We are taking for granted here that you are doing a good job with your music and have found some people that like it. The people that work in record stores must have a strong suspicion that someone is going to buy your record or they are not going to give you money for it. There are only so many ways they can come to this conclusion. They already know it from having sold your previous stuff. They have heard people asking for it in the store. They might have gone to one of your shows and seen it selling off the stage. Or you might just be very persuasive about selling your recordings.

If the person buys your stuff without a hunch that it is going to sell, they are pretty stupid. This is going to happen. You will be out there striving to get intelligent people to take an interest in you and give you some of the money they have amassed through their intelligence, and instead, stupid people will give you money as a result of their stupidity. The record store scene, however, is one of those settings where you should take the money anyway—if only to see if it feels different than intelligent money.

If your music is completely uninteresting to everyone and you have had no luck selling it, then go ahead and roam the globe hoping someone stupid will buy it for their store. You will make a few sales, probably; but in most cases, this type ends up still holding a full box of merchandise at the end of the day, unless they have fallen into the deadly trap sometimes called "consignment." (More on this danger coming up.)

To really do well making the rounds of record stores, you have to have "made it" in the music business. Everyone will wonder exactly what this means. I used to myself until comments made by several of my friends defined it for me.

One day, I was pawing through a mound of rejected promos in a record distributor's office with a pal. This stuff could not be given away. Some of it by totally world-famous people who hadn't really "made it" in the right way. This was obvious because in an environment where there are always people who want free merchandise, these new releases were unclaimed. In fact, the future of these releases was to be a part of a cruel monthly game at the distributor's in which employees pile up such dredge in the parking lot and drive over it. "You wouldn't see one of your CDs in there," my friend said, suddenly delivering one of the biggest compliments I'd ever received. This was reinforced in a San Francisco record store a month later.

> *You will be out there striving to get intelligent people to take an interest in you and give you some of the money they have amassed through their intelligence, and instead, stupid people will give you money as a result of their stupidity.*

A friend watched me sell one copy each of three CDs to a clerk and remarked that this was a sign of success because so many artists would only be offered a consignment deal. Even if the clerk thought only one copy would sell, this was a sign of faith. That's what it means to have made it! You made the record yourself, and you are even willing to sell it yourself.

Sell it, though. Don't leave it on consignment. This is a rule to establish early in the game, before we get into the more amusing world of vaguely educational anecdotes. The exception to this is the local band who has a steady relationship with a local store. However, the following experience makes it impossible for me to even recommend this type of arrangement without reservation.

You see, I decided to bend my no consignment rule with someone I had known for a long time, a quite successful restaurant owner who had branched out and opened a book and record store. Her new operation was in the heart of the campus area, in the spot where there had once been an alternative record store that had sold my stuff. It only made sense that the new store would stock my stuff, and I expected it would sell because of the campus clientele.

I Hate the Man Who Runs This Bar!

Because of my long-standing relationship with her, I saw no reason to make a big deal out of an advance sale. I knew if she had to pay up front, she would only take one or two discs because she was a good businesswoman. I had a large catalog in stock at that point and thought it would be more impressive and result in more sales if my section in the new shop had a whole slew of titles.

A few months after the shop opened, I checked in and saw that some of the titles were already moving. "I don't have time to collect right now," I told the girl at the counter, "but I'll come back later and settle up when the boss is here."

"Good," the girl told me. "I don't know how to do the consignment thing anyway." Ding! There's a signal. If you do sell stuff on consignment, you are going to run into people who don't know how to take care of it. The consignment business is such a dinky part of most record stores and employee turnover is so great, no manager in their right mind is going to waste time training someone how to do consignment sales.

I kept checking back, and what I eventually found out was that the manager hadn't worked out, so he'd been canned. The new manager remembered that there had been a box of my CDs in existence, but now nobody could find it. "They've either all sold, or we don't know where they are," is what I was told.

"If they've all sold, I should get paid," I said. But since the place was run by an old friend, it was necessary to give them time to find the missing CDs. "Or else I'll get the money for them and then they'll show up," I laughed. I eventually collected on the consignment debacle at my friend's store, but because of our relationship I was socially obligated to discount the total. I wound up with a check that was for less than I probably deserved had they really sold them all—and certainly less than I would have made if they'd given the box back to me and I'd sold them full price at gigs.

A variation on this incident happened in a looser era when the local Peaches management was actually allowed to buy off people like me. I had sold them a bunch of stuff that seemed as if it would be sitting in there forever, until one day a local paper did an article on me. I got a call from the Peaches manager: "People are asking for your stuff because of the article," he told me.

"Good, you've had it there for a while," I said.

"I know, but I haven't seen it lately. We're thinking it all sold. Can you bring some more by?" Can I? With wings. Of course, a week after they bought more stuff, they found the missing stuff and called up to whine.

Making consignment deals means you are deciding never to be paid for your stuff. It's like giving it away. Sure, there are some exceptions. One guy told me about a record store owner who actually sent a check across the country when some consignment stock sold, but someone else in the room had a heart attack while the story was being told and I never got to hear the end of it.

Some local bands will put their music out in hometown or regional shops and collect the loot, although I can think of someone who is having trouble collecting from a record store where he also works part-time.

If you put your stuff on consignment in another town, figuring out when you are going to go back is just the beginning of your problems. If you go back through that town a year later and try to collect, you might have to deal with the following scenarios: the store is closed; the store is in the process of closing and everything, including your stuff, is marked down, way down; the store is open but the person working there doesn't know how to do the consignment thing; the merchandise is still there, they think, they know how to do the consignment thing, they think, but they can't pay you for the merchandise you think they have sold because they can't find any of it right now.

Unless you have a method of printing and pressing the merchandise in your pocket as you drive from gig to gig, the limited supply on hand means that any consignment activity is a waste. There's a basic law about not allowing something to be part of someone else's cash flow until it is out of yours. Why have stuff sitting around somewhere that you haven't been paid for? Why put yourself in the situation of not getting paid for your stuff unless you are there at the exact moment it sells? Look at the first three letters of consignment. See what that spells? Had enough? No? Okay, now take out the word "sign" and the "nt" at the end. Now what do you have? Get it?

That's about it for important guidelines. In summary:

1. Make some music somebody is going to want to buy.
2. Call ahead to weed out potential time-wasters and buffer the insults.
3. Don't do consignment.

FAVORITE RECORD STORE SAGAS

Frankly, selling to stores lacks the pizzazz and potential danger of nightclub engagements or record company entanglements. You just won't find as many wild anecdotes about days spent selling records. When a video director came to me with the idea of a film about an artist going around selling records, my first question was, "Can we put a werewolf in it or something?"

Nonetheless, there are a few stories I'd like to

tell about selling records. Some of them might not really have much to do with how to be a success selling records to stores, but they illustrate what kind of an experience it can be. Sometimes these experiences can provide revelations that positively affect one's outlook for years. If these things happen because one is out selling records, then we have to appreciate the experience for providing a setting for such nifty little dramas.

COLUMBIA, MISSOURI

The night before, I had been pelted with pennies by a rude and angry college crowd at Iowa City State University. My initial reaction was fury. I tried to insult the crowd by suggesting they call home for more money because "these pennies you ripped off from your parents aren't enough."

The next day, I had to drive to a campus in Rolla, Missouri. It was a They Might Be Giants tour and I was filling in for a week or so after the contracted opening act had dropped out. I cruised into Columbia, Missouri, midroute because I knew there were a few record stores there that might snatch from my box.

What is interesting about this incident is not the common stuff that happened in the stops: the cold shoulder warming up to a consignment offer in a new age shop, the fiend behind the counter in another store buying $100 worth of stuff for himself before even starting on the store's share, or even the check from another place bouncing. No, the miracle occurred when I tried to park in this typically auto-saturated area.

For some strange reason, the meters in that part of Columbia only take pennies. Everywhere I looked there was somebody digging around in their pockets, getting frustrated. But not me. Thanks to Joe College, I had pockets full of pennies.

Confucius says: "Hatred of last night's audience pay your way today." And these words are worth a pretty penny.

AMSTERDAM, NETHERLANDS

Generally, my rule about anecdotes is that nobody is interested in the pleasant ones. But I'll risk the reader's boredom by mentioning my typical activities when I am in Amsterdam six or seven times a year.

Like anywhere in Europe, record distribution in Holland is hit and miss. The mass culture goes for musical fads that often come and go before anybody knows what they are back in the states. The "Macarena" record was a hit in Holland two years before it was popular in the states, for instance. You can go in record stores abroad and not know what half the stuff is.

Often stores can't get a new release because no distributor is bothering with it. If you have records coming out on small labels here, there, and over there, it is most likely that no one distributor is putting it all together and organizing effective combined sales in a country like Holland.

Thus I found out a few years ago that record stores would carry my merchandise if I brought it right to their doors. This was particularly true in Amsterdam but also in other large Dutch towns such as Eindhoven, Utrecht, Rotterdam, Den Haag, and

Actually working at something . . . is never cool, particularly not if someone cool compares you to a shoe salesman.

Groningen. So I began keeping record stores stocked in Amsterdam. At this writing, there are more than a half dozen I visit regularly. I know the clerks on a friendly basis. It's interesting to see how my business grinds to a halt and then picks up again at some shops, while doing the reverse at others. Some shops will suddenly look for a bunch of back titles, while others will want to get rid of ones they've been keeping.

I usually do these sales calls on foot or on bike. In a pleasant environment such as Amsterdam, these add up to delightful days of mixing business and pleasure. Even on a bad day, I at least pay for all the eating and drinking that a normal tourist would mine from his own wallet.

One day I had to record a live radio broadcast for Dutch radio. The interviewer who did the show was a real fan and had a stack of CDs that I recognized as having sold to a shop in the neighborhood. I figured that the shop would want to get new copies since the radio guy had bought them all to prepare for the show. And I was right.

LITTLE ROCK, ARKANSAS

Here's a town with usually two or three good record stores going at once. I had a rough experience the last time, though, funny on several levels. I'd made an earlier call to an old customer, a cantankerous sort. "I still got much of what was here from last time," he said when he got on the line.

I always try not to let this bother me. "I'll take it back," I said. "I can always sell that stuff." I had no idea what he had but figured it was pretty old. He said he had vinyl, and any vinyl title was probably out of print, which meant it would be just a matter of time until I could run into someone who would want it.

He mentioned having to meet some record buyers from abroad. Arkansas is one of those areas that Japanese and European collectors like to hit hard because the used record stores tend to be loaded with treasures, and you can find just about anything you want.

We made a loose arrangement to make a trade either face to face or via the clerk that would be there if he wasn't. The latter turned out to be the case. A girl who said she was "still in high school" when some of my records first came in was working there and went through the stuff with me. Even after I took everything back, there were three CD titles she wanted for the store, so I got $30 and headed on to the next stop.

This is where the first manager tracked me down. He was in a rage that the clerk had spent $30 on new CDs and had been yelling at the poor girl for a half hour. "I don't like you coming in here tricking me into buying your stuff," he said.

This misunderstanding had a positive side. The fact that he'd called me at another record store meant the owners there knew what was going on, laughed about it, and probably bought more than they had planned to make me feel better—and also to one-up the other guy. They even bought all the stuff I'd gotten back from his shop. I figured out I'd made a $35 profit alone just driving this stack of old sides across the river.

NASHVILLE, TENNESSEE

These two sales calls are among the most disappointing I've had, and having them happen back to back is enough to put anyone off from selling records in Nashville forever.

This is a unique market because record stores could get by selling only country collector's recordings to music tourists. Nevertheless, some stores make a pretense of keeping up with other developments, like the one I talked to that said, "We're big fans! Come on down! We'll take some of your stuff!" I showed the clerk five copies each of seven different titles.

"Let me show my manager," he said, taking the box of CDs away. Then the bad vibe set in. All of a sudden, I knew I wasn't going to get anything. The clerk came back looking sour. He knew there was going to be trouble. "I'll give you three dollars each for them," he started.

"What? That's less than it costs to manufacture them," I said.

I'd mistakenly gone into a "cleaver shop," where new products are purchased by the store for extremely low prices and, even though they are then marked up by 200%, are still cheap enough to be a bargain for the consumer. There are lots of opportunities for shops like this in bigger cities, especially anywhere a music industry thrives. Imagine all the promo copies floating around in Nashville, for example. The rule of thumb with promo copies is that nine out of ten copies are sold to cleaver shops or used record piles, even when the big labels wire them up to land mines to try to prevent such heinous activity.

People selling music door-to-door have the freedom to take cash offered at cleaver shops, even if it is well below what they should be getting. It is cash in their pockets. Unfortunately, most people have to account to someone else, such as artists expecting royalties, partners expecting to be paid off, or pressing plants and printers with outstanding bills. There's nothing left for these interested parties if all it sells for is three dollars per CD.

After a little arguing, the price went up to four dollars per CD. I was disgusted because I knew that by asking for five copies each of the CDs, they were confident that they would sell. I decided to sell them copies of one particular CD that I was well-stocked on and for which I had been paid totally in merchandise. That way the 30 minutes spent in the place wouldn't be a total waste. On the way out, the clerk told me I ought to check out another shop up the street that was less of a bargain place and would be more likely to pay full price. This turned out to be a perverse vendetta on his part.

In this other place, the first clerk to look at the box was a young guy who started pulling out a few titles and setting them aside, one of the steps in the final purchase phase but not the last step by any means. Then the big boss walked in, and he was such a straight and uptight fellow we both knew we were in trouble.

The clerk quickly put back all the titles he'd taken out, as if he was afraid he'd get in trouble for *thinking* about selecting something that was a no-no. The boss looked at the CD titles from the side, then grabbed the one called *Jesse Helms Busted With Pornography*, a 1996 release on the Fireant label out of Charlotte.

My oldest daughter who was with me at the time thought the guy grabbed this title because he thought it was by Jesse Helms or was some kind of tribute to him. He became completely disgusted when he saw it was a lewd attack on Helms. He handed the whole box back. "I don't think so," he said. There was something special about the way he touched the box, though. If you believe that memories can be golden, then the look that he gave me made the whole trip worthwhile. I don't think anyone has ever looked at me with such disgust, except maybe the Catholic priest who caught me washing my hands in the holy water when I was six.

And those, believe it or not, are all the interesting stories I can remember about going to record stores to sell my music. Like I said, there's just not a lot of intrigue. Like practicing, it is something one can choose to do endlessly if advancement, self-improvement, survival, and spreading a musical gospel are important life goals.

My wife pointed out that on family trips, a stop at the local record store can produce more than a supply of cash. It can be an introduction to some nice people in the community. They may end up pointing you toward a good restaurant or hotel or even inviting you over for a home-cooked meal or comfortable place to hang out during your down-time.

The finale to this analysis of the shoe salesman lifestyle is a summary of excuses people will offer you for not buying your records. You are going to hear these over and over. I can always tell when one of these statements is going to be uttered; it's something in the way the person takes a breath before speaking or in their body language. When I know these lines are coming, I follow a philosophy of escaping into Never-Never Land. I start thinking about a new composition, the first pictorial I saw of Racquel Welch in *Life* magazine when I was early into puberty, or an incredible meal some promoter put out one time. Think about whatever you want. The point is not to devote one's full attention to lines such as:

"I've never heard of this."
"I've never seen this."
"Nobody has ever asked for this."
"I know you were in the paper, but I am going to wait till someone asks for this."
"We can do consignment."
"We don't stock local artists."
"We buy from a one-stop."
"We buy from a central warehouse."
"We only buy used CDs."
"We only buy CDs people will want."
"We can't take a chance on something like this."
"What will happen if it doesn't sell? I don't want to be stuck with it."
"I've never sold this."
"I never will sell this."
"People don't like this kind of thing here. I hate to insult you."
"I don't want to put you down, but I don't think anyone will buy this."
"I'd take one, but the boss is in a bad mood."

"The boss is in a good mood today, so I wouldn't want to do anything to jeopardize that."
"Sorry."
"No thanks."

I Sold 300 Records in 25 Years!

. . . on as many labels, I should add!

In the early '70s, I had the assignment to interview the rock legend Rompin' Ronnie Hawkins who was coming into town for a week-long nightclub engagement at the infamous Den of Satan. By then, he was in his early fifties and had been associated with a lot of so-called rock history. He'd put together a back-up band (The Band) so talented that Bob Dylan took it away. But even that wasn't good enough for the Band, and they left Dylan to go out on their own. Ronnie never made it to that level; he was still rompin' on the small club circuit.

At that point he had no new record coming out, but he was philosophical: "You know they give you an award when you sell a million records. A million copies of one album, you understand?" he Ozark-drawled. "Now what about an award for someone who makes a million different albums, sells one copy of each? That would be worth an award, and that's one I'd be eligible for, sure would be."

Rompin' Ronnie's words of wisdom have followed me through the first quarter century of my musical life. His remarks are scattered through this book not only because he is hilarious, but because he is provocative. This is his theory of million sellers. Imagine an individual who is able to create one million different records, let alone find one million record companies (or madmen) willing to release them. (As this chapter will illustrate, the terms "record company" and "madmen" are interchangeable.) This prolific artist would be worthy of respect on many levels for such an achievement, regardless of musical quality or sales levels.

If only a handful of each issue were purchased, it would still be considered no small feat to have made one million records. If only one copy of each sold, this artist would be in the record collections of one million people. Just about anyone starting out on a musical career would find such a plateau of success totally out of reach.

An artist such as the late big band leader Sun Ra, for example, put out his own records and sold them almost exclusively at his shows and in person to record store buyers. There were dozens of these Sun Ra records, many of them with handmade covers. Sales figures for these various albums have not been published; in fact, a complete list of all these titles doesn't exist, despite extensive research including several book-length discographies. Nobody would be less impressed by Sun Ra if, say, it was discovered that the his LP *Nubians and Lovers on Saturn* sold only 25 copies the first time it was released.

In his long career, which he insists is just an extension of a previous life that had begun on the planet Saturn, Sun Ra had only a few fleeting contacts with major labels, most of them near the end of his career. A Sun Ra or a Rompin' Ronnie Hawkins is more likely to release records through companies such as the ones that I'll describe in this chapter.

The purpose of this chapter is to clarify the nature of the independent record label in our culture. In a society like ours that guarantees publishing freedom, any person or group of people can become a record or book publishing concern. (In the old USSR, all records were released through the state record label, Melodiya. Private releases were illegal so, despite the fact that there were probably madmen galore in the USSR, we can't say they were interchangeable with record companies.)

Independent publishing is such a time-consuming, unglamorous, and compulsive lifestyle, it tends to attract, if we can be allowed a few generalizations, loner types that would be uncomfortable in the hyper-socializing bar atmosphere. The profit-motivated types that foggily drift toward the bar business also sometimes start record companies, but they are usually not the ones that stay in it for very long. In terms of making profits, record companies have a distinct disadvantage over the bar business: There's no tie-in to liquor sales.

Record labels are the dominion of the dedicated types who want to document music that they really appreciate or make their own mark on the music scene. Often they subsidize these desires with inheritances or better-paying outside jobs.

A combination of the punk scene and the inextricably linked European squatter's scene allowed many young record or CD manufacturers to put out impressive catalogs of titles while living almost completely on the edge. These catalogs can rival the work of small corporations run by so-called experienced music industry types. Some of them do this while still living in their parents' home, maybe even still in high school. These labels are on such a small scale, with so little distribution and overall sales, that they can be impossible to even locate during their existence and can disappear without so much as a ripple in the pond.

Players trying to pay their bills will watch mailboxes for checks, make endless phone calls for money, and give up trying to understand the complexities of merchandise distribution in the world. Even if you have made two million separate albums and sold two copies of each, it still won't be worth the frustration of trying to collect every nickel you are owed.

HOW I SOLD 300 RECORDS

These stories are told in no particular order. The final story tells the tale of the first involvement I ever had with something that was technically a record company. It was just as much a record company as all the rest of the enterprises described.

Back in high school, to have sold 300 copies would have seemed an incredibly amazing feat. Furthermore, it would have impressed the high school snots who used to say stuff like, "The Beatles are overrated." Part of the destructive side of music business hype is this very notion of what constitutes impressive sales for recordings of music. We only rob ourselves of thrills this way. If it is exciting for a teenage band

to think of 300 people hearing a tape of their music, why should it be less exciting for an older musician? It's because they've been beaten down by public perceptions.

This same syndrome shafts the mighty as well. The pop icon with the white glove wanders the halls of his mansion, disappointingly sniffing out the latest sales figures. Only seven million? Tsk, tsk. "I'm a failure." Sob, sob.

In the course of my relationships with various record companies, more than 300 copies were sold of each record. Sometimes sales were in the tens of thousands. (The name of this chapter is designed only to get a cheap laugh—and as a tribute to Rompin' Ronnie. If one copy each was good enough for him . . .)

Here follows the sagas of record companies, big and small. The businesses spill over into record distribution, and the action includes all the things that happen behind the scenes of a record being made, from the recording sessions themselves to a frightening trip into "the hot place" where the vinyl discs are stamped out. You will meet people you wish would come take your best tapes away and come back in a few months with steaming boxes of CDs. And you will meet people that ought to be tied up and buried under these boxes. But you won't meet anyone real. Once again, these are fictional portraits based on mixtures of various circumstances. The point is to illustrate through anecdotes the nature of the type of activity that occurs when you deal with a record company or distributor.

LABEL: KING OF SYRIA

NUMBER SOLD: 28
The Swinging Blacksmiths were a mid-level local band specializing in country and country rock. They would start their shows early and sober with a wide selection of C&W material, much of which was penned by bandleader Anvil Smith. By the third set, the group would go into their "long jams," which were as horrible as the band was drunk. One soundman would experiment with turning off the channels of various bandmembers each night to see if anyone in the audience would notice. The gaps between gigs were so long, however, that it threatened this kind of scientific research.

When the band put out their first album on Blacksmith Records (sales: 15), they made a poor choice of material, favoring the jams rather than Anvil's C&W material.

King of Syria Records belonged to Jack Morgan, a big country fan. He had put out a dozen rock records because he'd heard this was where the profits were. He had followed a trail of cardboard boxes into the record industry, a noble path. As a teenager in Philadelphia, he unloaded (and sometimes ripped off) freight shipments. Sometimes the boxes contained records or 8-track tapes. This was his first connection to the music industry. Morgan often sold off this box or that to record distribution warehouses

> *"What about an award for someone who makes a million different albums, sells one copy of each? —Rompin' Ronnie Hawkins*

for stray $20 bills. It wasn't difficult to do the same thing with cartons of records put out by the bands he knew. Eventually, he was manufacturing the records himself.

One of his grandparents had died recently, and an estate down in Alabama passed into the family's hands. It was a nice spot, down on the "Redneck Riviera" near Panama City Beach. But aside from the benefits of its locale, it could also be refinanced to provide a fat business loan for the record company. Jack liked the feel of it. He had the dough to finance ten releases and hire a secretary and a promotion man. Thinking about it over a glass of Jack Daniels, he realized he had nothing left to do but think big thoughts.

Now he was an impresario, roving the country looking for promising bands. Since he was into country music and it was getting popular again after a glut of rock and roll, it was smart business sense to sign country artists. He'd managed to hook up with a few promising performers who were getting attention in Europe. This meant he could go to Europe and poke around for licensing deals and partnerships with small labels and distributors. One of these partners was a British guy named Harvey Okeh who had made a lot of money running a Leeds game room where patrons re-enacted medieval battles, jousts, and tortures. Okeh also liked country. Okeh would tell Jack, "Get a good country songwriter. That way, if they write a hit and we own the publishing, we'll get rich. A country songwriter never has to work again." And Jack had a story that reiterated this philosophy.

Tommy Boyce was sitting in a Music City bar. A

hack songwriter recognized him. Two hours later, they were both still in the bar but the hack was drunk enough to think he was a big shot.

He went to Boyce's table and asked, "Hey, you Tommy Boyce?"

"Yeah."

"You the one that wrote 'Last Train to Clarksville'?"

"Yeah."

"The Monkees song?"

"That's right."

The hack leaned down. "And what you done since then?"

"What?" Boyce asked.

"And what you done since then? I know you wrote "Last Train," but how about writing another hit? When you gonna do that?"

Boyce just smiled at the guy. "You dumb hick. I wrote "Last Train to Clarksville" so that I would never have to do anything again." Except drop dead, which he did about a year later.

They considered signing Anvil, but the record he had submitted had a 14-minute jam on it that nobody wanted to listen to. Still, Morgan was going through a town where Anvil had a gig, and they'd agreed to meet. "You need better production and more country," the record mogul told the songwriter. "I'd be willing to hear another tape. But since I don't have much confidence in that first record, I won't finance the session myself. I don't feel sure we can release the result." It wasn't what Anvil wanted to hear.

"I was hoping you'd put us in the studio and pick up the tab," Anvil said. But Morgan preferred his own "arrangement": The musician would give Morgan a tape. Morgan would promise to pay royalties within the year if they sold 1000, earning a profit. Then the record company would wait on the distributors, who would rip them off for several possible reasons:

1. Just to get the money.
2. To put the little record label out of business because the distributor was actually a front for the little label's competition, i.e., another little label.
3. Same as (2), except they're a front for a big record label.
4. They lose the money.
5. All of the above.

This meant it would be impossible for Morgan to pay the musicians royalties within the year even if he had wanted to.

Anvil would have been glad to do an album for no money if it meant getting to put out some of his original country songs, but there was no way he could afford to record. He still owed the studio where the first album had been cut. They had wanted to record more of the originals even back then, but they had gotten drunk and jammed instead.

Anvil had planned to kick off with one of his better numbers, a George Jones-style ballad. The soundman had been instructed to put on this defective Jones cassette they'd found. It was Jones singing backwards, pretty far out. Anvil stepped up onstage, strummed a chord, began the song, and then puked. Jack couldn't believe it. "That's a great move!" he shouted. "Do it again."

> *The terms "record company" and "madmen" are interchangeable.*

Anvil's performances had been getting worse, and he wasn't coming up with any good new songs. That night he made it through the second set, then went to the parking lot to moan and groan. Jack went back there to stand around grinning. It was clear that Anvil and his band had no chance of getting on his label now. Anvil and his band could see in Jack's eyes that he thought they were a bunch of losers. This made Anvil feel aggressive. He kept yelling at Jack, and none of it made much sense because he was drunk. But Jack was also two sheets to the wind. Anvil could have been reciting the Magna Carta in Greek, and Jack wouldn't have known the difference. He started to get mad at the stuff Anvil was saying—whatever it was.

Soon they were shoving each other. Then Anvil grabbed Jack's T-shirt, tearing it. Jack stepped back, tore the shirt off completely and let his sweaty chest gleam in the glaring light of the alley. Then he took a couple of quick steps, socking Anvil in the jaw. Anvil collapsed. "Ripped my shirt," Jack told the small audience for the event. "Man shouldn't do that."

A Dutch partner, Rob, jumped on board, a distributor who had made a lot of money with house music. He told Jack to set up a whole U.S. label on a grand scale. You know, hire another PR guy for the West Coast. "That's the way they do it in America, isn't it?" Rob asked. "One guy on each coast. Because the difference is too great." Then he told Jack to set up a special phone and fax line for the company. Make plenty of long distance calls, the kind you do when you are promoting. "Spend the week calling the stations in every state, just to say hi. It'll be good for

business. Start an ad campaign," Rob told him at the airport. "Put ads in all the music magazines."

Jack was taking notes about all this stuff. It was going to run into doolah. He'd run up completely unmanageable bills just hounding the distributors for money and linking up with the occasional deejay. In fact, he was planning to rob Rob and use the money meant for expanding the office to pay last month's bills.

Jack initiated some of these projects, and soon the new enterprise was deep in debt. But the Dutch guys kept saying a bank transfer was coming. Then, one day, Jack got a call.

"We've decided to drop the American label we were talking to you about," Rob said abruptly.

"But, why? I'm just gettin' it goin'."

"We don't see the progress."

"Progress? It's only been one month." There was no arguing. They pulled out completely. Not another guilder was seen from those boys.

The amazing thing about King of Syria was that it actually survived. Jack drove around the country, selling the stock out of the back of his van. In some stores he'd hear rumors like, "King of Syria's gone out of business, hasn't it?"

Thanks to the old southern mansion, this hadn't happened. But the family and the bank had recently announced that there would be no further refinancing because everybody was at the end of their tethers in terms of Jack's record business.

Jack had been living out of his truck. The company had to have a phone number, so he used his folk's place in Newark. With King of Syria there was a unique mechanism for fielding complaint calls. Dial the label's number and you would get Mrs. Morgan, Jack's mom. She would then talk your ear off about what a louse her son was, completely distracting you from your own complaints. Or, she would encourage you to complain if you stayed on long enough. Lame things her son might have done in business with you would remind her of dumber things he'd done as a kid. That carton of records he forgot to send? That's nothing compared to the tricycle he left in the road, the one the neighbor totally wrecked by running over it. *And* it dented the neighbor's fender. And we had to pay for that.

The two country bands that Jack had picked up after the Anvil incident weren't paying off, so Jack put his antenna out for punk rock bands that could bring in big money if promoted properly. This led to an alliance with the unfortunately-named Butt Wipers, whose two CDs and one 12-inch vinyl release still hadn't sold enough to pay the motel bill the band ran up when their van broke down in Montgomery, Alabama. They had been given 12 hours to pay or they would be introduced to the sheriff and his handcuffs.

The bassist had spent the week flinging a martial arts weapon at the walls of the hotel. It was a razor-sharp disc and imbedded itself into the drywall. Because of noise complaints, the band had changed rooms on several occasions, thus destroying the walls in four rooms. They had also charged hundreds of dollars worth of food and another small fortune on the phone before the wise man in charge cut them off.

Jack had to put on his suit, drive to Montgomery, and deal with the big redneck in charge. But his redneck act didn't impress anyone in Montgomery. He told the band, "I'm no good with this guy. I can't barter him down. He knows I'm not really from Alabama."

The Butts told Jack not to worry about the bill. "You'll make it back in CD sales. The tours have been really going well. A lot of people want to buy the CD. If you can get it in the stores, we can sell it," they told him.

Oh, and by the way, the Butt Wipers wanted to renegotiate the old contract, which gave them 12 cents on every dollar that came in. There were seven Butt Wipers, and they wanted a new arrangement where Jack would be counted as if he were the eighth member of the band. This would mean that Jack would be getting an eighth of the profit instead of the seven-eighths he was now receiving. Since he was barely breaking even with the old arrangement, the new one frightened him to death. So he cut loose from the Butt Wipers. "They won't get anywhere," he told everyone. "Not with that name."

A couple of years later, they were the top attraction in the independent rock scene, averaging ten grand a show. Another several years after that, they were a Top 40 band, doing about 50 grand a show. Meanwhile the word "butt" had become an acceptable word. Jack hadn't counted on that happening. "I'm just as happy not to be involved with them. They're communists," he told everybody.

He was more peeved about the political argument they'd had long after the contract discussion had ended than he was about losing the band's business. Jack had blurted out, "I'll tell you one thing that was great last year! Desert Storm! We sure kicked their butts." The seven band members passed sick glances back and forth. They knew Jack was conservative, but this was too much. So, for three hours, they made fun of Desert Storm until he was blue in the face from arguing.

"I tell you what," the bandleader Lipso said. "Look at this stack of records you've released. All of them got anti-war songs, songs against Desert Storm!"

"So?" Jack asked. "What's that got to do with anything?"

"If you really believe in Desert Storm, why don't

MICHAEL MAGIOCE

The notorious British psychedelic band Shockabilly: The exploits of this band loosely inspired the Deal So Smooth saga.

you put out a record about how great it is? Can't you find someone to record that?"

Jack admitted he hadn't come across anyone with such a song, and he wouldn't put it out anyway. "It wouldn't sell." Then again, if he dropped the price down to $3, it probably would. He'd noticed lately that when sales were off, he could move a bigger quantity of CDs by dropping the prices radically. He would still have enough money at the end of the day to eat, drink, pay for a motel room, and gas up. And his partner in England would never see the disappearing money if Jack did a good job on the books.

He hung around long enough to take a few night accounting courses, than took off selling in his van. Meanwhile, bands would break into his house while he was gone to get their hands on the stock he'd promised but had never send out. One of the musician/burglars claimed he got the idea from Jack's mom.

For every artist who got sick of the King of Syria and swore never to work with him again, Jack was fat with concern. "Hey, there's plenty of songwriters who want to do records," he would say. "They're chasing me down everywhere. And there's always that Anvil guy, the one I K.O.'d. He's probably still writing songs."

LABEL: DEAL SO SMOOTH

COPIES SOLD: 11

Dusty swaggered around the East Village telling everyone about it. He'd gone to England with his personally produced masterpiece of psychedelic music. He'd gotten the head of Deal So Smooth, Keyes Bikel, so excited about the music that when the tape ran off the spool, Bikel had said, "I've got an idea! Let's go master it! Now! I'll call the mastering place, I know somebody there."

Now he was awaiting release of the material on a 12-inch, 45 rpm single, all the rage at that time. When it came out he sent it to relatives who, thinking it was an album, played it at 33 rpm. "Gosh, it's so long! And your voice is so low," was the common reaction. Oh, well. No matter. Bikel had just okayed the proposed $1500 advance for a full album. Even his great-grandmother would hear that on the right speed.

The band recorded the album in a warehouse on somebody's 4-track reel-to-reel so they could pocket most of the advance. They had no monitor or headphones, so they had no choice but to let the tapes play over stereo speakers in the room while they were overdubbing vocals. Bikel called the overall sound "a revelation soaked with acid—the true essence of psychedelic! This one will hit the top!"

He meant the top of the British Independent Top 10, published in *Melody Maker* and the *New Music Express*. The 45 release had made it to number six on this chart. Dusty loved calling people and saying, "I've got my first record on the charts." The LP pushed past that to number four and then dribbled away after a few more weeks. It was a good showing, and Deal So Smooth suggested that perhaps the band do a European tour.

"We're doing our first European tour," Dusty announced as visitors dropped by. "The album finally came off the charts." Members of the band were told to stand by and take a breath, Dusty was going to

make them big successes. So far they'd had spent less than $100 on recording, including overseas postage, and had hit the charts in England.

This chart was compiled each week after conversations with a handful of record store clerks. These guys in turn had conversations with the record labels and there were indications that they sometimes discussed what would be picked for these charts. "We want to get the chart buyers," Bikel explained. "Most British record buyers get a record when they see it has charted."

It seemed easier just to hang the chart on the wall of the stereo den and not buy the records. But in England, the chart was particularly easy to control because a sort of socialized distribution system was in place for the independent labels. They'd divided the United Kingdom up into various sections, and in each section there was an independent label acting as distributor not only for its own releases but for all independent labels. This way there was no competition. Furthermore, each label had incentive to sell the releases of the other labels with vim and vigor because if they didn't, the other labels would slough off other releases in their territory.

Deal So Smooth was king of this situation. Their territory was London and environs, which went on and on and on. Their office and warehouse setup was enormous. When the band dropped by late at night, Dusty stood way up on a balcony, looked down on rows of shelved records, and watched two of his bandmates pilfer stacks of releases because nobody from the company bothered to keep an eye on them as they wandered through. They were really loading up on sides. It wasn't just a collector's thing, the guys hoped to turn this into money via the used record pile at home. If not, the tour would come up zero.

"Don't expect to make money on the tour," Keyes had warned them. "It will be a record company promotional effort. The group will not be so well-known, so the fees will not be large."

But the band found out that the fees actually were large and somebody was getting some rich, deep gravy off the tour without giving much to the band. They discovered this in Germany, where the majority of the gigs had been set up. Even though Deal So Smooth had branches of the company in Germany and California, Deal So Smooth Deutschland and Deal So Smooth USA insisted on being completely independent, especially in terms of artist rosters and releases. Whereas Deal So Smooth Deutschland had released the new LP and was doing all right with it ("almost 200 sold, a hit by German standards for independents!"), the much-needed California connection had bailed out.

"Please send us a demo tape," the Deal So

Smooth California manager had told Dusty when he'd called to hype the new release and set up a record-company sponsored tour to promote the act in California like the one they did in Europe. Dusty didn't have the heart to tell the band that the West Coast branch of this great company wanted to hear a demo tape before they'd even talk to an act that already had records released on the UK branch label.

> *As a teenager . . . [Jack Morgan] unloaded (and sometimes ripped off) freight shipments . . . This was his first connection to the music industry.*

Meanwhile, the guitarist had pillaged the Anvil attaché case belonging to Johann, a guy who announced he was the band's road manager the evening of the first gig. "Road manager?" the drummer had asked. "I didn't know we had a road manager."

"Oh, yes. Hired by the record company," Dusty said. He actually hadn't known about it, but he didn't want to appear out of it.

This guy's salary was coming out of the band's pockets. Lots more was, too, the guitarist found out while rummaging through the attaché case. It contained all the contracts for the tour, so Dusty began his research with these.

Dusty had told everyone that, like most of the gigs, there was only a 300 deutsche mark guarantee for the Bremen show, which back then, during the Reagan era, was about $100. However, the Bremen contract indicated that West German radio would be recording the concert for broadcast and was paying the record company 3000 marks.

Then there was the promoter, who would come into the Bremen dressing room and make an impassioned speech about how he was totally dedicated to the arts, never made any money on his shows, and would rather spit on his mother's grave then take money out of hard-working artist's pockets. He had a deal worked up to take 100 percent of the door receipts minus the 300 marks he was giving the band, and he was getting a 500 mark fee from the radio for promoting the concert they were going to record. Plus, as owner of the venue, he was getting a rental

fee from the radio, although this wasn't detailed on the contract.

More than 300 people paid 15 marks each to get into the event. When confronted with this gargantuan rip-off, Johann tee-heed and explained that the profits from the Bremen concert were going to pay for the rest of the tour. But reading through the other contracts made sauerkraut out of that explanation.

The German record company people whom the band met in Dusseldorf said they were simply "following orders."

"I know you don't like to hear that from a German," one of them grinned.

"We were told to book the tour this way, by Keyes Bikel."

"Yes, it is the standard procedure."

"It is good promotion. From the second album, there might be 300 sales. That would be a very big hit for Germany."

The only thing to do was talk to Keyes about the situation, but Dusty told everyone it had to be done tactfully. He didn't want them to mess up their chances to do a second, higher-budget album for the label, one perhaps in the $2500 realm.

Keyes was in New York, looking for new bands to record. The label had gotten pretty hot with one of their acts, a light folk-rock trio called Jones & Jim. Keyes was getting daily messages to find other stuff like that. It rankled Dusty that Keyes was in New York looking for groups when the ultimate group was on tour in Europe getting embezzled by a branch of his company that kept insisting it was independent.

"There is no real connection, only the label name for promotional purposes," the Germans kept telling Dusty.

"But you booked a tour for us."

"Only because Keyes told us to."

When Dusty reached Keyes, he was full of sympathy. "You don't say? I don't believe it. I have never heard of such a thing!" he kept saying. When told the information had been uncovered by rummaging through private property, he was most accommodating: "Bully for you!"

Meanwhile, the Germans said, "This is a standard tour, organized the way they always organize them. The only difference was that you had a spy that snuck into Johann's suitcase."

Maybe the obsession with money would have been less if the gigs had been more fun. On a typical night, someone in the audience would pelt the band with potato salad (and it wasn't even the good German variety—this was fast food stuff).

Keyes offered to subsidize the return trip home, which was supposed to have been the band's responsibility. However, this was probably less an act of generosity than a case of the Deal So Smooth organization being afraid that the American band would get stuck in London and end up welching off the label, hanging around every night stealing more and more records. "I shall meet you in London," Keyes told them. "We will arrange everything there, and of course, make plans for the next album. We can begin work on that immediately. We shouldn't wait!"

This thrilled Dusty, and he was willing to forget about the tour problems. But the rest of the band still wanted the label to make up the difference between what the local promoters had paid the record company and what the record company had paid the band. It was a significant amount of money. Even a small percentage would be more than the band had made.

The tour took them to Paris, then England. When they arrived at UK customs, they were told that the work permit Deal So Smooth was supposed to have arranged had been rejected. The band was not allowed into the country. After three hours of interrogation and threats to send the band back to Paris, the immigration guy winked, stamped the passports, and let the band in for three days. "I suppose if you do your little gig nobody will be the wiser."

Keyes was delayed in New York negotiating with a big new folk act. He called Dusty in Paris and soothed the hurt feelings, promising they would be treated wonderfully when they arrived in London. They had lots of press stuff lined up, would meet with the accountant to settle the money issue, and would meet everyone else with the company. He told Dusty he could get $3000 for the next album and the label would release it as soon as they got the tape. (The label waited two years to release the album, and they never sent the final $1000 of the advance.)

The press stuff turned out to be just a taped interview the label said it could use all over the place later on. And as they were getting started, a frenzied individual burst into the room to tell the press agent, "You've got to come help. They can't find a hotel for Phlegm, not with a big enough bed anyway."

Phlegm was a world famous funk guitarist. He'd arrived at Heathrow with a beautiful woman on each arm. Now he wanted a bed in a London hotel big enough for the three of them. The man himself was so big the beds were ruled out even before the women were added.

"Derek has been working on it, he has been going around to hotels since last night when Phlegm arrived from Copenhagen."

The press agent, microphone still in hand, slapped his other hand against his leg. "But sod it all! I must interview this band."

"We really need you to help with this. Nobody else will deal with Phlegm."

"What about Ramona? Can't she help?"

"Ramona had to run off and sign on." This was a British ritual, signing on for another month of dole benefits.

The solution: The band would interview itself while the record company went out and searched for the right bed for Phlegm. The interview turned out to be a lot of useless horsing around. Nobody would have published it, anyway, because the UK music

> *On a typical night, someone in the audience would pelt the band with potato salad (and it wasn't even the good German variety—this was fast food stuff).*

press was now totally hooked on the Jones & Jim trend.

This was the end of the company's interest in Dusty and his band. If the accountant had known this the day he met with them, he might not have given out *any* money. After all, he said, "I am the only one who knows anything about where the money is going in this company. Really, I am the only one to speak with, not Keyes or any of the other people that manage the company. They have no authority to sign checks."

Dusty was confused. "So you are more than just the accountant?"

"No, I am just the accountant. But there is no system here for dealing with anything. I have authorization from Keyes to pay for your plane tickets and provide a voucher for excess baggage."

"What about the tour problems?" Dusty asked.

"What tour problems are these?"

They went into a long explanation of the rip-off. The guy acted like he wasn't paying attention. He didn't have to, because he knew about it the whole time.

"That request was denied," he told them.

Dusty asked when the $3000 advance would be theirs.

"We must have a label meeting about this."

"But Keyes said it was happening," Dusty said.

"Keyes must meet first. There are other projects," the accountant said.

The band made the album on Dusty's dime because he was sure everything was cool with Deal So Smooth. Five months later, a $500 transfer came to Dusty's bank. It almost covered the phone calls he'd made trying to track down Keyes.

Nevertheless, Dusty still thought everything would be great once Keyes heard the fantastic tape the band had made. A complete change in direction! A masterpiece with better studio sound this time. Dusty spent nearly $1000 on recording the thing, and some of it still needed to be mixed.

Playing the tape to the record company was a disaster, though. By this time, Keyes was the only person connected to the label who had any affection for the band. First, their music was so far from the Jones & Jim trend it was almost an insult. Second, the accountant really hated the band, as he did anyone he had to write a check to. Third, anybody in the company who had it in for Keyes—which was almost everyone—could use this tape, perceived to be wimpy, as a sign that this once with-it record company dude was losing it.

"I mean, really, Keyes! Where is your taste?"

"I think the tape has potential," Keyes argued weakly. He spent a weekend listening to it, trying to feel enthusiastic about it. He felt sorry for Dusty, so he managed to squeeze out a bit more money from the label by agreeing that once this album was released, not a dime in promotion would be spent on this piece of crud! If some critic wanted a free copy, they could just forget it. No radio airplay. And it certainly wouldn't be allowed on the charts.

Strangely enough, accounting figures for all the releases were about the same. Sales were at a certain level regardless of whether the record was promoted or not. They got lots of reviews for the first one and none for the second, but there was no difference in sales.

LABEL: PARMESAN RIP-OFF

NUMBER SOLD: 21

When Peggy Lee got hungry, she would sit in a restaurant and eat whatever she could off the table. She specialized in parmesan cheese in Italian places. A good score and she'd be full of protein all day. "I lived for a week on a nickel," she said. "The nickel was still there at the end of the week." She did this by relying on friends and credit. The latter is what brought her infamy on the independent record scene.

When Peg announced her first dozen releases on the Parmesan Rip-Off Series, it was not only the sheer number of releases but the impeccable quality of each one that made the whole thing so impressive to advertisement readers.

Mastering labs, print shops, pressing plants, and fabrication plants all want their money up front, sometimes 50 percent in advance, balance due on delivery. To get credit at any of these places was a dream, and Peg was living this dream, thanks to her close relationship with Harrison Lacrosse, an old friend of her late father's who owned a record pressing plant.

Lacrosse was cashing in on the new punk scene, that's for sure. The type who collected baseball cards and knew all the information on them by heart, Lacrosse had no trouble keeping the entire punk rock scene straight—bands, players, personnel changes, song lists—even though he didn't actually like the music—or any music for that matter. "Happens to everyone in this business. Worked quality control for ten years," he would apologize. In quality control, he listened to the record sides as they came off the manufacturing line.

A few of Peg's releases were so odd that quality control screwed them up. One of them was a double record set a guy did of his bathtub drain, only they printed side 3 on side 4 as well. Nobody listening to it could tell the difference until 500 of them had gone out. The effort to straighten this out cost Lacrosse's plant about $500, which was a shame. They shouldn't have bothered; the release only sold four copies, total. "My worst seller," Peg said. "But a classic of its kind."

She had five releases by Shard, a band that had made an album a day for the past six years. It was a dream of Peg's to have a new release every day, so if anybody could accommodate them it would be her.

Some of her other titles were actually selling pretty well, and she might have had a chance to really accomplish something if she hadn't gotten a little too fast and loose with the credit situation.

She was approached by a punk band that wanted her to take care of the printing of their album; once the records were in boxes, the band would take over. They were too spaced out to go through the whole manufacturing process, and they knew Peg could pull it off, even though there was no way she'd ever put them on her own label. They had a grand saved up, which was enough to make 500 albums. So Peg banked the grand and got their project going on credit with Lacrosse.

When Lacrosse found out what was going on, he told Peg he didn't want to do business with her anymore. "And unless you pay me back the ten grand I fronted, I am gonna sit here, press your records, and then sell them to distributors until I recoup!" he threatened.

To her this was a hysterical joke. "And you're going to find people that understand this type of music and can sell it? I really don't think so! This isn't the same old garage band stuff you've been pressing. This is great art!"

They had their little standoff and that's how things stood when Roy Puye, the leader of Shard, came to Los Angeles on a solo tour. Peg had organized the tour, the first such trip out west for Roy. In Newark, he found that the flight had been canceled, and the passengers were treated to a night on the floor in the cold, dirty terminal.

The next morning, he sulked about his lack of finesse with career moves. Here he was, ten years into the business, with 1350 albums made, about one-tenth of them released, and about one-sixteenth of those still in print. And here was another typical low-budget tour, organized by a complete freak. When would it ever end?

Of course he was on the cheapest, most uncomfortable type of flight. But he looked down the aisle and saw a face that seemed to have floated off the album cover, *Blues From Laurel Canyon*. It was John Mayall, wearing fringed suede with a beaded purse hanging around his neck. Roy thought, if this flight is good enough for John Mayall, quite a music business veteran, well, then it wasn't so bad after all.

He was still feeling good when Peg and her buddy Gina fetched him at the airport quite early in the morning. Peg said that it was a good time to crawl through the back window at Lacrosse's pressing plant and snatch a few boxes of Roy's new solo album.

Roy was aghast, but Peg didn't beat around the bush. "That's the situation. That's the only way I'm going to get the records. You're really on Lacrosse's label now, Roy. He's taken me over. He's pressing them, and sending them out of there. For all you know, he could be putting his own music on them."

"Does he play?" Roy asked.

"No, but why should that stop him?" She was clearly upset, but the successful rip-off cheered her up. The back windows in the place were hanging open limply, not even fastened shut anywhere. It was as if Lacrosse wanted to be ripped off. They decided to raise some dough selling the discs around town. That's when they noticed they'd mistakenly stolen a case of Aerosmith cassettes.

"These should really sell," Peg said. At each stop, Roy hawked his solo and band releases while Peg sold the Aerosmith cassettes. Everything was moving. By the end of the day, they'd each made about $200.

Roy stayed at the building where Peg had a room, a factory in the warehouse district downtown. Lots of artists and designers and printers lived in this building. There was even another record label there, the Individual Design.

Peg's record company was strewn across her bedroom—all the mail, press releases, glossies, magazines, artwork proofs, test pressings, demo tapes, and so on were scattered everywhere like the remnants of a volcanic eruption.

Presley Hearn of the Individual Design was the complete opposite. He had his own print press in the basement so he could fabricate and print his artwork, and his office had a meticulous filing system. His contacts were all instantly within reach. His record company was a professional, efficient business.

"He's a dufus," was Peg's opinion. "Imagine micro-managing anything to do with music."

As nutsy as Peg's arrangement was, things got worse when she vanished from the scene and all the record company property was in the hands of Lacrosse, who still harbored a grudge, claiming he'd recouped less than half the credit he'd laid out. He refused to let any of the artists have access to anything having to do with their projects. When the bathtub drain composer left rude messages demanding cartons of records, Lacrosse dropped an old, rusted bathtub on the guy's front porch.

Roy thought some of his classic recordings were in this held-for-ransom catalog and regretted his involvement with Peg. Every five years or so she'd call him. One time she told Roy she was back in the business. She'd been hanging around a bus stop, all alone when she happened to notice an address book on the ground. She picked it up, found the owner's address, and decided to return it. It took about four hours to walk all the way to his place.

He was so happy to have the address book back he invited her in. He asked what she did, and she mentioned having a record company, which she still talked about even though it had been a decade since she'd crawled through the back window of Lacrosse's plant. It turned out that he was a Serbian film composer who had done a soundtrack for a low-budget film in 1953. The film was just marginal, but the soundtrack had merit. He'd assembled a small jazz band to record it, and since that time the individual members of the group had individually become big names.

Peg couldn't believe her luck. This tape outclassed everything she'd ever done. It was quite an accomplishment.

To celebrate, Peg disappeared again.

LABEL: SMUGGLE-O DISCS

TOTAL SOLD: 9

They were brothers, Joe and Bo. As for their last names, you could pretty much take your choice. When first contacted by Smuggle-O, bandleader Kendrick Dithers was told he was speaking to Joe

Amari. A week later, when Bo called and mentioned that he was Joe's brother, Kendrick assumed he was talking to Bo Amari. But when the guy sent him a piece of mail, he signed it "Bo Sveeters." From his accent, he sounded more like an Amari than a Sveeters; but Kendrick was so happy that somebody was going to put out his tape he didn't care if his last name was Schicklegruber.

The Dithers *Heavy Lung Action* album had been kicking around as an unwanted tape for six years, and it was long past the point of attracting an advance payment . . . or so Kendrick thought. The check for $500—a 50 percent deposit on the advance—was signed by one Joe Sveeters.

The main act on the label was Rampbooth Phantoms, and it was selling well. It was the brainchild of Donnie Fargin, who had been into skateboarding a long time and electric guitar almost as long. He'd gotten into the habit of bringing his portable Pignose amp to the ramp and playing some of his skating-inspired tunes. Many of the skaters liked the tunes and asked him if he had a tape for sale. Once he'd sold about 20 tapes, he figured if he could do that in every town (20 tapes multiplied by all the towns in the USA), he'd be rich.

His tape got around to the two brothers, who heard a good thing and knew the skateboard thing was spreading. They asked Donnie if he wanted to cut an LP.

He quickly agreed, and when he called his friends, he said, "Guess what? These two brothers, the Olivers, they want to put out an LP of the Phantoms!"

The checks Donnie started getting were signed by the Olivers, so there was no confusion there. But when he was at their house once, he noticed mail for Bo Sveeters, Joe Amari, the Smith family, Bo Donner, Joe Phrant, Bo Willebrand, and the Amari/Henton Foundation. However, he didn't think twice about it. Another time he was snooping around one of the brothers' bedrooms and opened a chest of drawers. There were three rifles in it. Once again, he didn't think much about it. This was Arizona, after all. "Coyote might come up. Or a rattler," Donnie said to himself, "and you'd need three rifles to get rid of the thing."

Various houseguests found these weapons and other gun caches over the years. Most of these houseguests were recording artists for the label and other labels. They were all so happy to have found a label willing to release their stuff and pay a modest advance that they decided not to mention the arsenal they found, including the large machine gun mounted on the back of a truck in the garage.

Various theories came out over the years about the true identities of the brothers. According to one story, their family had lived there since being involved in the building of the railroad. Another story had them mixed up with the mob, who supposedly were thick and fast in the Phoenix area. It was the mob who had gotten them into a lucrative gun-running operation.

The brothers weren't into this stuff, but they did seem to get their hands on the odd firearm. And they liked creating confusion about their identity. "Once you get in the music business and get connected with clubs, musicians, liquor suppliers, the media, hey, it's good to have an extra name or two," Joe confessed when one of the acts finally got too curious. But it was not the brothers' mysterious lifestyle that did in this record label, it was good old-fashioned capitalist high jinks.

Donnie had come up with a new design for a skateboard that was being produced by the record company, which despite a few hits such as the notorious album *Which Is Bigger, Your Mind or Your Shoe?* by Dipswitch, was making a much greater profit from the boards. These profits even helped pay the legal expenses when the label put out an LP by a local heavy metal band that credited "Alice Cooper" as producer.

The showbiz legend Alice Cooper got his lawyer on the case, but it turned out there was nothing that could be done. The producer was a young lady named Alice Cooper. As producer, she'd done nothing but go for sandwiches . . . and provide her name, of course.

The board profits were so fat that the manufacturer told the Whoever brothers that they were having delays in production. In actuality, they were bootlegging the design and selling the knock-offs out the side door. There was nothing the brothers could do because they could not invest in all the machinery needed to make the boards themselves.

While their skateboard business deflated because of these shenanigans, one of their main distributors for the LPs and CDs had a little problem. The manager of the company had been writing funny little checks to himself, with the end goal of buying a Rolls Royce. The distributor went bankrupt thanks to this embezzlement and the ensuing tax troubles. Any assets left were tied up in a legal battle. Bo and Joe were out $22,000.

So, they went into a much more secure business: ticket scalping.

COPIES SOLD: 16

The conga drummer for the Art Ensemble of Balzac stood in the lobby of a hotel in Quebec, watching people load onto a bus outside. But these weren't just any people. He poked his bandmate Bobby Boom in the shoulder. "Bob, man, check it out. Check out that bus."

Boom squinted. It was a little early in the morning for him to check out anything.

"Man, that bus. If it crashed, that would be it."

"That would be what?"

"It would mean no more festivals, and nobody would have a record label anymore."

This sounded serious. Boom went outside to smoke a cigarette and take a better look at this bus. He watched various people settle into their seats. Some of them noticed him and waved. There was Tiv Palo from the Norwegian Go Kill festival and Kill Go improvisation label. Sitting next to him was the Quebec organizer, Jean Decouers, whose label, Chansons, had released three of Boom's trio's CDs. Going down the aisle was Clive Robrook, founder of TOACNV, whose catalog Boom had yet to crack into, but who had invited him to this year's Toa-Fest, a very good sign.

These festival organizers all enjoyed the fact that their annual festival budget would pay for them to attend everyone else's festivals. If you were invited to play at one of these festivals, chances were good you'd meet the honchos from all the other fests. Many of these organizers also ran their own record labels. And many of them had impressive catalogs after as little as three to five years.

It is safe to say that the activities of these festival organizers provided some of the best available work on an annual basis for many top players, musicians whose work just isn't commercial enough to break into more mainstream markets. The players are happy for the opportunities to perform at these festivals, to return on a regular basis, and to have an ongoing series of recording projects scheduled, sometimes on several of these labels at once.

These musicians are happy not only because this work ensures their survival, but because the atmosphere is stimulating and offers the chance to meet new people and catch up with old associates. In addition, those who are also in the recording business make the best music from the festivals available to fans worldwide (or at least anybody that can figure out how to get their hands on those hard-to-find, poorly distributed, overpriced imports). So, the people on the bus provided a lot for the musicians in this scene.

"Just about everything but the music," Boom admitted to an interviewer. Still, the relationship between musicians and festival organizer/record label owners wasn't only about admiring each other through the window of an idling bus. When a musician comes face to face with an organizer at one of these festivals, it's safe to assume that each musician has a project to sell. The organizer has to sift through these project ideas like a successful film director who finds everyone running script ideas at him.

Every musician has a different level of success or difficulty dealing with these individuals. Some can merrily hobnob with organizers until the roosters crow. They develop special relationships and bask in hot tubs in the organizer's private house. While others are left to sponge down in the sink of a small hotel room because they can't stomach the thought of having to sell themselves in such a casual face-to-face meeting. Very few ideas are proposed in formal, sit-down meetings. Someone gets on an elevator and by the third floor have intrigued someone else with the concept of a band consisting of a tuba, a Chinese zither, and a rainstick.

Each festival is viewed in the same way by everyone in the course of their careers. First, it is the elusive wish, the conquest you hope you can make. This can lead to the first engagement at the festival, after which the players hope they will be invited back. In the case of the Toulouse Action Positive festival, the mayor of the town begged the organizer on his hands and knees to stop inviting a certain American avant-garde composer and bandleader. The ideal is a long-ranging relationship with as many festivals as a musician can keep going: steady work without over-exposure.

Cynics see this as the corruption of an art form. One of the great philosophers on this subject was the Belgian, Frederich Satog, who ran a small performance center out of what was once a Flemish torture chamber in Ghent. He prided himself on his absolute lack of contact with any of the larger festival's organizers. When they tried to "network" with him, he would look the other way. "They are creating the context the music has to move in for the musicians. So the musicians, they come up with these ideas in order to get work. Is it what they would do normally?" He shook his big black beard free of cheese specks. "No, I don't think so!"

What was worse to him was that these projects were then picked through by a bunch of organizers. "And these are not even musicians! Why do they get to decide what is going to be performed? What gives them that right?"

On the other hand, there is Liz Quench, who started out on the punk rock scene before getting into avant-garde music. "Before I was invited to these festivals, we used to play in the worst little bars, and when we made a record it was always horrible. Or if it was a good studio and a good tape, the guy who was going to put it out would get murdered or he'd vanish with the tape. Sometimes when they did come out, it was worse than if they hadn't. The record looked like somebody had parked a car on it, and it would sound like that, too."

Then Liz entered a new world. "For the festival Tiv promoted, we were at a really fine hotel with private rooms. The concert was at a really wonderful old

> *Donnie had come up with a new design for a skateboard that was being produced by the record company, which despite a few hits . . . was making a much greater profit from the boards.*

theater, and Tiv had set up a full buffet banquet upstairs in the dressing rooms. Everyone was hanging around up there, it was a blast.

"When I did the solo album for TOACNV, they used the best studio in the entire country. I've never seen a studio as good as that. It's where the orchestra records. Halfway through the session, Clive and his assistant Marie showed up with several fine wines and a silver platter full of gourmet cheeses, smoked fish, and freshly baked bread.

"I've never received treatment like this. In America they get you to eat an oily rag on a bun at a recording session. Then they say, 'Keep going, we got 14 more songs to cut and mix by the morning!' "

Jean Decouers liked to advance the players recording with him as much as possible because he knew this would help them survive. "The music business environment is hostile to creativity. This is one thing I can do so that it is possible for these players to continue," he says.

One such player was the saxophonist Nicholas Association, who spent the first 20 years of his career on a freezing street corner in Buffalo, New York. Association now has hopes that the next 20 continue to lead him through a maze of buffets, first-class hotel suites, complimentary bottles of French wine, and monthly CD releases with cash advances, one of

which was more than his income for the years between 1957-1964.

"We had an incredible problem with Nicholas because at the recording session he decided to record a piece concerning his political philosophies about abortion, the situation in Kurdistan, deforestation, and something to do with computer technology and Satan," Jean recalled in his soft voice. "We had to have a meeting with the recording engineer and everyone on the festival and recording staff to see if these philosophies of Nicholas were offensive to anyone. Of course they were. I didn't know what to do, because each person was upset about something.

"It was very bad, we had the investment from the studio, the tape, and the agreement with Nicholas. We had some of the music, which was fantastic, but he refused to release any of the project without the spoken part. Finally, we decided to release everything. We put something on there about it not representing our opinions. And that we are supposed to be supporting a free kind of expression so we don't feel we should censor the thoughts of this man. He has his own point of view."

After agreeing that this was admirable, all the record label heads said they wouldn't record Norman again, except for Clive who had never recorded him at all.

Clive had spent the early part of his promotional career working for the German festival organizer Hans Hunchen, the man behind the Jazz Hippie Festival held in the town of Bad Krankenhaus, Germany. Clive's opinion was that "Hans is the example of everything you shouldn't do in this business."

In the early days, Jazz Hippie was the epitome of chaos. One year, the players arrived to find that the festival site consisted of a pile of mud and a smaller pile of beer crates. No sound system or stage ever arrived. But by the '80s Hunchen had created an empire with help from the Bad Krankenhaus burgermeister, and the Jazz Hippie Disc catalog had over 500 releases. When he loosened up, Hunchen would admit he'd "paid royalties on only a dozen of these titles, mostly because the artists sent gangsters to collect from me."

This wasn't Hunchen's first label. Clive had taken the name of TOACNV from the backwards spelling of VNCAOT, Hunchen's label when Clive first went to work for him. Back then there was an old pressing plant outside of Bad Krankenhaus, which the BASF company finally bought and demolished. Hunchen's crony, Fritz Mockler, owned the place, so Hunchen could wander in at night and press records of whatever he wanted to, usually tapes he'd made of bands playing his festivals.

These were recorded on cassette players or

145

Chapter Fourteen

cheap reel-to-reels, sometimes with a microphone Clive was told to clip to his jacket. Not realizing these tapes were intended for release, sometimes Clive would wander off to the bar, leaving the stage area. Hunchen grimaced at these sections of tape where the band would sound a million miles away, but he didn't think the problem was that big. "We'll still release," he'd say.

None of the musicians were consulted. They learned about the records when they found them in record stores. Many wanted to maim Hunchen, but they'd think twice about it because it would mean no more gigs at the Jazz Hippie festival. The pay was too good to pass up, even if Hunchen was a cheapskate in other areas. For example, there was never catering at his events. If a musician wanted to eat or drink, they paid for it out of their own pockets. "I make good money on the coffee," Hunchen would boast. "Sometimes the fee is paid back from this, if the guy is drinking a lot of coffee."

Clive says Hunchen practices the "erosion" method with his recording artists. "Once he actually started getting people's permission to release their records, he noticed if you put out the record at the time the artist was doing the project, they would be entirely too fussy and demand too much control. Hans didn't like being criticized for every little thing he did that wasn't to their liking.

"If he sat on a tape for five years and put off the musicians who were clamoring for it to be released, by the time he got it out they wouldn't give a damn—they'd either have lost interest or just be too damn desperate to get it out. So he developed a system of sitting on everything, which he called 'erosion.'

"Actually he may have copied this system from a guy named Munich Karl. I'm not sure of the last name, though," Clive said. "Karl is an art speculator who got into music. He runs a club, not a festival, and a record label. Except he doesn't really run the record label. He's never released anything because he's waiting for all the artists to die. Then he will start the label.

"Karl believes the value of the music an artist records isn't even worth considering till they die. He books an act and plays tricks to keep the audiences away, such as advertising the wrong date, spreading the word the club is closed and so forth. He feels they will play better to a smaller house, which is often true. But more importantly, he can then beg the artist to take less money because there is nothing in the box office. But he really wants something else. When they refuse less money, he makes them give him the rights to the recording he has made of the concert, or else they get no money. He wears them down with this argument.

"So far he has released nothing. But he has 600 reel-to-reel tapes of concerts. He is waiting for everyone to die."

Hunchen really admired Karl, according to Clive. "He would be like Karl, Clive would say, except he does not have the patience."

LABEL: CURLY JOE DISCS

COPIES SOLD: 33

Hal Herck started this label when he was 17. The first release was his pal Murk's band on a special one-sided seven-inch. Then the band changed its name to Severed Foot and really took off on the East Coast punk scene. Three singles were released through Hal before they got "too big" for his label.

By his 19th birthday, Hal had been ripped off by one indie rock distributor for every year of his life. He didn't care, though, because his new job at the sanitarium looked like it practically came with tenure; nobody ever got fired there. He was so mellowed out after three or four years of punk shows it didn't frazzle him to deal with groups of disturbed individuals. After all that loud music, stage diving, and moshing, nothing bothered him.

Putting out records continued to be a hobby and got him into relationships with a few more local bands. Some were heavy drinkers, as was his new girlfriend, a nurse at the sanitarium.

The drinking seemed linked to both activities. The bands that got really drunk at their shows seemed much looser, and went much further out of bounds in their actions and relations with the audience. For punk music, this was good. At the sanitarium, Hal started noticing that the staff also indulged in alcoholic drinks. Maybe they didn't get smashed, but they at least got to where they were feeling good.

By the time he was 21, Hal was an alcoholic and showed no signs of getting sick of booze. He was getting sick of punk rock, though, since his own behavior had gotten so woolly and wild that none of the clubs would admit him anymore. This hurt his activities as a talent scout for Curly Joe, although he had friends who would tell him what band to sign.

His dad had been a folk singer who had never had much luck recording, although he'd done a little. Hal always thought his dad's songs were great so he decided to record and release a CD of them and expand his label activities. This became the only thing he was doing that wasn't alcohol-oriented. Hal had been so plastered taking a group of patients to a museum that someone had phoned in a complaint. The supervisor told Hal, "This is it. One more incident and you're going in the drunk tank. And when you get out, you will sign your resignation." Hal responded poorly to this threat, but the test copy of his dad's CD came in the same day and took the edge off. His dad came by to hear it.

Around the time the pressing plant said the new Curly Joe CDs were on their way, Hal got in trouble at work for drinking. "Caught you red-handed!" the supervisor shouted. He had opened a closet to find Hal tilting a bourbon bottle back so it would gush down his throat.

They put Hal in the hospital to dry up. Meanwhile, the boxes of CDs were waiting at home. Hal's dad and some of his friends came over and opened everything up. To save money, they'd ordered CDs in raw stock form, which meant they'd come with no artwork or packaging, just the CDs shrink-wrapped into a tube that looked like a giant laser beam bratwurst.

Hal and his volunteer squad had planned on putting the CDs and some artwork and information into cheap little plastic sleeves. It was the most economical way of releasing CDs. After putting a few together, they decided to wait on Hal. After all, it was his label.

Once the hospital sobered Hal up, the supervisor demanded that he resign, which didn't suit him at all. He wanted to hang on to the job because it was supporting all his music activity. He thought if he made the boss feel sorry for him it might save the situation, so he threatened suicide. But the boss had been attending a tough love seminar and simply said, "Fine. Go blow your head off."

Hal went down to a sporting good shop and got a shotgun. By lunchtime, he was back in his apartment with the barrel down his throat, which was how his girlfriend found him when she came home for lunch because she'd forgotten her vodka bottle.

She couldn't get the gun from him, but she managed to chase him outdoors. He was twirling around in the yard, blasting the gun in the air. It was the middle of summer and kids swimming in a nearby backyard pool got hysterical. Their parents called the cops, who showed up about 90 minutes later.

By then Hal was face down on the back lawn. He'd dropped the gun in the bushes. They grabbed him, bound him, and searched his house, where they found several things they didn't like. One was a syringe for drugs that some lowlife at a high school graduation party had stuck up there. The other was a handgun on the top closet shelf. This belonged to his dad but had never been registered. It was one of those guns they sell in Florida, next to the lollipops.

In this state, a "get tough" law demanded automatic jail time for possession of any unregistered handgun, no matter what the situation. About 48 hours later, Hal was finally out on bail. His dad was adamant: The first thing they had to do was get those

CDs put together. Everybody who was there for the assembly job tried to cheer Hal up.

Hal's girlfriend's sister came over to help later, and the gals got drunk. But everyone else was cooling it with the booze out of sympathy for Hal, who was under a court order not to get drunk and to stay away from any place where anybody was getting drunk. "They should have told me not to go home," he thought to himself later when all the CDs were stuffed into boxes and the volunteer crew had departed.

He was sitting on the living room floor, his back against the sofa. On one side of the room were the girls, slumped against each other and snoring. An empty vodka bottle was stuffed into the crook of one of their legs.

On the other side of the room, he saw the accumulation of stuff from the new release: shipping boxes, garbage bags full of the plastic that the raw CDs had been wrapped in, Styrofoam shipping gunk, and cartons of his dad's CDs wherever there was a flat space. On a shelf, he could see the arrangement of Curly Joe releases on display, a sight that always looked good to him. It surprised him how many there were and that it was something he had made happen himself.

His dad had told him a story about the time he was in Austin, Texas, and went out for a walk. He was looking at plants in people's gardens; it was spring and everything was really pretty. The street he was on dead-ended at the base of a hill, and he recognized the tower in the distance that was part of the university skyline. Charles Whitman had shot a bunch of people from this tower.

"Son, I could look down at the wildflowers and it was like I was seeing everything good about the earth. Then I could look at the tower and it was everything bad. It was just a matter of turning my neck slightly," his dad said.

Hal now realized he was in a similar situation. He could put his energy into the record company and all the work that went with it: bugging distributors, stuffing boxes, hounding record stores, calling radio stations, and hanging around bands. And it would be good and would save him, even if he only sold five copies of each record. Or he could put his energy into drinking and that would kill him.

He drifted off looking at the CD cartons and knew everything was going to be okay. As long as he could stay out of jail.

NUMBER SOLD: 1

Bosnia Pudding—his real name was McClain Frankenhof but everyone called him Bos—had made a small fortune before his 30th birthday simply by writing a half dozen of the most offensive songs in history.

With titles unprintable in family journals, these songs had become anthems in a genre that lay somewhere between heavy metal, reggae, polka, and electronic music. Sales figures attracted major labels, but the number of obscenities, averaging three per four-bar stanza, would clearly keep this stuff off Top 40 radio.

There were a few run-ins with overseas independents and publishers who tried to rip off Bos by claiming the royalties were impossible to collect because the performing-rights societies had refused to enter the obscene titles into their computer logs. This led to Bos' decision to start his own label: Miscellaneous Intestine.

A repackaging of all his hits plus extra collector's stuff sold enough to earn a gold record, if anyone had been keeping track. But Bos kept the accounting and business end of his enterprise pretty low-key. He put out the word that the aggressive music business hustling was not to his liking, and it would not impress the new label manager he had hired, Katherine Labwork.

Bos and Katherine took an investigative approach, sniffing around for new bands or individuals that could create money-making and, hopefully, highly offensive projects. This is what led them to the rockabilly artist Maurice Cabinetti, who had already made about ten albums and was something of a cult figure.

"Can we sell rockabilly?" Katherine asked Bos.

"We're known for genre smashing," Bos reminded her. "Besides, this guy is something of a production genius. Let me tell you about what he did for Gonzalez Martinez."

Martinez had played lead guitar in a '60s act, Frozen Fire Blues Band, who had four or five chart hits. Since these glory days, he had floundered around on the West Coast, sometimes showing up when the band did a reunion tour, sometimes not. Frozen Fire had been one of those faceless acts so they could hold a reunion with none of the original members and no one would notice.

Anyway, Martinez still had something of a reputation in France, where the music of the '60s was being reappraised. A French label that had released a few of Maurice's albums called him one day and asked if he would like to produce a Martinez Gonzalez album.

"Martinez? Man, he's a legend! Of course I'll work with him," Maurice answered.

Martinez was known for playing everything on the guitar with only one chord position, the D chord, but sliding up and down the neck. So Maurice figured that even if Martinez had forgotten everything, he could teach it to him during the weekend and still come out with gravy.

The first thing he asked Martinez when he picked him up at the airport was, "How many songs you got ready for the album?"

Martinez was a tall, skinny man with a beard down to his bellybutton and hair down to his ass. His eyes—if he had any, nobody ever got a good look—were stashed away behind dark sunglasses. "Man, yeah, I got one tune done," he told Maurice.

"One? Man, we gotta cut a whole album!"

"We got the one song, it's a good start. I know it will sound good with a horn section, chick singers—you can line that up, right?"

Maurice took the guy out for breakfast burritos, which Martinez ignored in favor of six or seven margaritas. "Let me explain something to you, we got a small budget for this," Maurice told him.

"Yeah? So, you know a lot of people around here. You can get a horn section and chick singers to come down to the studio and cut the track for nothing, right?"

"That's not the way it works in Austin," Maurice tried to explain. "You see, there's ten thousand bands here. They all want gigs and there's only six clubs, so they can get the bands for the door, and nobody makes any money.

They only make money on a recording session. If I call any of the horn guys or singers around here about a session, they are going to have their hands out for money, at least $100. As it is, I gotta pay the drummer, bass player, and myself," Maurice said.

Sessions started that evening. While Martinez stood around looking lost, Maurice plugged in his Gibson Firebird and came up with some kind of funk/rock/boogie lick. Martinez picked up on it, then they jammed around for three minutes or so.

"That sounds pretty good," Martinez admitted.

Maurice agreed. "We oughta cut that. It can be a co-writing deal."

"Yeah, sure. Let me get a drink before we cut," Martinez said, then staggered slowly to a Mexican restaurant down the street. While he sat there drinking straight vodka and whisky, Maurice checked out what they had just recorded. The little jams didn't sound half bad. A couple of overdubs here and there, and they would be perfectly acceptable.

"It's a cut!" Maurice shouted in jubilation. "Now somebody go down there and get Martinez."

They pried the guitar legend off his barstool and returned to the studio. Martinez had forgotten that they were about to cut something, and Maurice started another jam. It went on this way for the weekend, and when the studio time ran out, Maurice had more than an hour on tape. "That's a CD right there. No reason to give them all of it, they ain't paying that much," he told the engineer, who was listening to reruns of the *Andy Griffith Show* with one ear and mixing with the other. The song Martinez had wanted to cut with horns, singers, and so forth was never mentioned again.

> **The engineer . . . was listening to reruns of the Andy Griffith Show *with one ear and mixing with the other.***

"Anyway, the CD came out," Bos told Katherine. "Sold 8,000 copies. Record company even made money on it. The budget was cheap. Around five grand." Katherine said she'd give Maurice a call.

"See if he'll collaborate with Chatterbox, the jazz guy. That could be killer," Bos said. The Chatterbox/Cabinetti duo had come out with an LP called *Cucaracha*. This had done well not only on college radio but on an international level as well. One tune, "Bo Diddley Is a Communist," had been a hit on Yugoslavian student radio.

Maurice was receptive to the idea. "We'll do *Cucaracha Dos!* Gimme a weekend to come up with a budget."

"Did he say anything about his health?" Bos asked when he got the news. "I heard he'd been sick." What they didn't know was that Maurice had gone from a rowdy and robust semi-madman of the stage into stereotype of the dying old bluesman, crippled and blind.

First he'd gotten cataracts in both eyes, a family ailment. Then he'd fallen down some stairs loading out of a gig, which had messed up his leg.

"Now don't stay off this," the doctor had told him. "The only way you are going to help this leg is to exercise it."

Maurice's form of exercise was to lie down and listen to the television. "I know the programs so well I don't have to see the picture." He only got up to answer phone calls from record companies, which

happened enough to make him feel good but not enough to keep his leg from turning into a powerless, hanging mass of flesh. Now when he gigged he had to sit down, which was a radical change from his old Jerry Lee Lewis days. He also had to have Rabbit, a bass player who had hung with him since high school, hop him around. By continuing to drink, he'd managed to go 90 percent blind.

"Now Rabbit's my eyes," Maurice would say. "And he takes me everywhere."

When Chatterbox flew in for the session, Rabbit picked him up and drove him to the little house where Maurice was couched watching *Dragnet*.

"We got an $8000 budget out of those boys," Maurice said. Chatterbox had already cashed a $1000 advance check last month.

"We'll do it quick and split the leftovers," Chatterbox said with casual greed.

"Now, hold on there just a minute, Box. I done spent a lot of that money already on the production. I had to hire a drummer, Marty Cash. He's the best. And we gotta pay Rabbit here. And we got the studio time and the engineer—"

"We been through all that, we added it up already," says Box. "There's still no more than $4000 even with all that added up." To make a record and spend more than that would have been an affront to Box's religious beliefs.

"Well, we'll see about that. Right now let's get some beer. Rabbit! Get a case of that Busch beer."

Box went into a depression about his old pal Maurice. The guy had degenerated to the point where cutting the session was going to be a hassle. Unlike the Gonzalez Martinez project, Box was armed with tunes. But it took three hours of rehearsal to clue Rabbit and Maurice in to what was happening.

The next day the sessions began, and Maurice was unable to remember anything that they'd rehearsed. "You sure we played that? I never have heard that song of yours before. It's a good 'un, we oughta cut it, but not without a rehearsal." And so it went.

Luckily, Rabbit and Cash, the drummer, were pros. All the tunes were cut in record time. Cash had been expecting two sessions. But it was all done in one.

"Here's $100," Maurice told Cash.

Box took Maurice aside. "Is that all you're giving him? I thought it would be more."

"No, I talked him down some."

"You budgeted a grand for the rhythm section, right?"

"Well, it's about $1100."

"So, now it's less?"

"No, it is still $1100."

"But Cash only got $100."

"I gotta give the Rabbit a grand."

"A grand? That's the same as the advance I got, and I'm the leader of the session."

"Well, I hope you're gonna get more. There'll be some left."

"But it doesn't make sense. Rabbit's an okay bass player, but for a grand you could get anybody! You could have gotten Leland Sklar or Jack Bruce."

"I'd rather have Rabbit, he's my eyes."

But Box thought it was cheapskate stuff hiring Cash for two sessions and then sending him off with $100. "Cash cut the session in half! You saved on the studio time–you should still pay him for two sessions! That's the way it's done."

"That ain't the way it's done in Austin," Maurice said.

The session continued running ahead. Mixes were done on the day set for overdubs because those had been completed during what was supposed to be the second day of basics. Maurice found a nice couch facing the TV set in the studio manager's office and helped mix the record from there with *Andy Griffith* in the background.

Maurice was out of it for the mix, but then again he had his moments of clarity. Just when Box and the engineer were at the end of their rope trying to find the right vocal effect for a rockabilly/swing style number, Maurice barked from the couch: "Give that number four Hard Rock Gunter echo!"

At first they didn't quite understand. "Hard Rock Gunter! Number four!" he repeated. This turned out to be a brilliant move and gave the vocal a fantastic sound.

The tracks were all finished except for sequencing, editing, and artwork. "And that's all stuff the label will do!" Maurice laughed. "We are done with our part!"

"So how much money is left?"

"Well, not much probably. I got to check at the bank."

Several afternoons went by with the repeated phrase, "I got to call the bank, let me just take care of something here. I gotta call Bos and tell him how the great the tape is. I gotta call Ernie about the photos they wanna shoot. I wanna get me another one of them barley waters." Around dinner time it would be, "Damn, the bank is closed! I thought they was open till 7 tonight."

Rabbit took the nervous Box aside. "Listen, I know Maurice. All that stuff about the bank is crap. He could drink six of them cases of Busch and still know exactly how much doolah he has in the bank, down to the dollar!"

So the morning of Box's departure, they had a final business meeting. Box wound up with an extra $300. At least he had gotten more than the bass player.

He got in touch with Bos, whom he knew a little. "So I guess I send the tapes out to you to finish the album," Box said.

"Wait, wait. What do you mean? What about the sequencing, the editing, and the artwork?"

"Maurice said you guys would do that."

"Well, we can do the artwork in-house, that's true. But the rest of it, well, send the cassette and let's see if I can help you with the sequence."

But instead of sending a cassette of the proposed sequence, they told Box to actually make a finished version of the sequence and dub a cassette of that.

"But that will cost money," Box said.

"Isn't there something left of the budget?" Katherine asked.

"Not according to Maurice." Maurice had told him that the record company said if there were additional expenses editing the project, they would write the check.

"I never told him that. Let me check with Bos," Katherine said.

"This pisses me off," was the reaction from Bos. "I never told you to tell Maurice that we would come up with anything above the eight grand. That's already top-end for a project like this."

"I never told him that you told me that," Katherine said. Nevertheless, she paid Box $300 studio time for the first edit. Bos listened to it and fell asleep, so it was rejected. The second edit was deemed a winner, and Box got another check for doing that one.

Another place the skinflint Box noticed money being wasted was in the daytime phone communication from the company. There was a different person on staff for each job—art, advertising, radio contact, touring tie-ins, merchandising, publishing—and none of them were willing to pass a message along to someone else at a desk ten feet away. Instead, another call was made, sometimes about something you had just finished talking about.

All this money was just being flushed down the commode, as Box's grandfather loved to say, because the album barely sold 1000—at least that's what Bos said. "We don't really keep exact records."

"When do I get a statement?" Box asked.

"Well, we haven't been doing them regularly. You should ask Katherine." Katherine said the accountant did that and she would try to pass along the message. Mostly Box was concerned about his publishing royalties. He'd written about two-thirds of the tracks.

"That was all in the advance," Katherine told him after checking with the accountant, who checked with the girl who did the publishing stuff, who checked with Bos, who checked with Katherine.

"How could it be in the advance? We didn't

know exactly what songs would be used until the sequencing and editing was finished, and he'd spent all the money before then! He never put any publishing in the advance."

"Well, you got paid something, didn't you?" Bos said, a little frustrated.

Oh, that annoyed Box. It was such a typical thing to say to a musician. "I didn't get my publishing!" he said.

Katherine called a few days later to tell him not to worry. The accountant had told the publishing lady that he would work out a system for Box to recoup royalties from future sales. Six months later, if Katherine could have pulled up a statement for *Cucaracha Dos,* it would have shown that 11 copies had been sold in that period. If anybody had been keeping track. And if Bos hadn't already fired her.

LABEL: ROOTS MUSIC

NUMBER SOLD: 0
(Record not released)
"You ought to be on Roots Music!"

Nobody knew how sick Launch Lynch was of hearing this. Since he'd become known for his avant-garde, leftist field-holler style, and even back in the days when he did calypso, there was always some music business know-it-all who would say this.

Roots Music would be great, sure. It was considered one of the largest independents, and it had a heartwarming success story. A group of sweet, nice old folkies started it in their basements. Their hearts were bursting with love for traditional music. They journeyed into the heartland; paddling canoes; repairing tires on mountain roads; and searching for the unsung, forgotten heroes of blues, old-time, country and western, bluegrass, calypso, field-holler . . . hey, right up Launch's alley!

Line two of the "You should be on Roots Music" ballad was, "Have you ever called them?"

Oh, yes, calling them was lovely. The receptionists were sincere, positive, and encouraging. The A&R reps and producers returned his calls and never had an attitude.

"Launch Lynch! Oh, yes, I've heard of you! I'm a big fan," Marge Preen told Launch. She was one of the Preen sisters, founders of the label. "I'd love to talk to you, but I'm pregnant. In fact I could give birth at any moment."

Lynch gave her some time to give birth and polished up his current field-holler recording. He felt sure they'd go for a good demo, they were so enthusiastic.

The next time Marge called, Launch felt sure it was a good sign. "I'm back on the scene," she said.

"Your project is on my list. I have some notes I've taken about the tape."

Launch sat down and got his own pad and pen ready for action. Here is what was written on it fifteen minutes later:

Hot Mud Family
Violent Femmes
Talking Heads
David Grisman
Hank Gonzalez
Freddy Fender
Hot Mud Family

On and on it went, with Launch scribbling to try and keep up with her stream-of-consciousness description of the ultimate field-holler avant-garde record, the one Roots Music would release to both pay tribute to the art of field-holler and shatter all the misconceptions people had about this great folk art.

Launch's tape was brilliant, she thought. "I love the way you blend the contemporary paranoia with the old-time Hot Mud Family feeling."

This was the Hot Mud reference. The other names were mostly people that Roots Music said it was willing to pay to come to sessions with Launch to record collaborative "field-holler with friends" tracks.

"Having these big names on the CD is sure to sell many copies, really expose your work to a wide audience. That is what we are dedicated to," she said.

"But we'll need a big budget," Launch said, mentally thumbing through a pad of signed checks.

She told him that this was a subject for discussion as soon as all the artistic questions were answered. Well, she sort of told him that. She was off the subject so fast it was as if somebody had snatched a needle off a record mid-song. "The way I would like to see it would be what we at Roots Music call an alternation sequence. Have you heard of this editing technique?" she said.

"Well, up till now I've done all my own editing."

"We edit in-house. Listen to me. I'll explain how this works. The first track would be a field-holler; alone and short. Then we go to a track with guests and a band. Now what about Paul Simon? Someone who can make a really big splash with the track. We have a girl blues singer we just signed who's fantastic. Then that track would alternate with the next one, another field-holler. We would keep that kind of short and then be on to something else that really rocks. Then from there, alternate to another field-holler. After that, a folk song thing, and that would be with the Violent Femmes."

Launch listened to this—field-holler, short, followed by something else, then another field-holler, short, followed by a big guest star.

"Maybe we shouldn't just do it the same all the

way through," Launch suggested. "It might get dull that way."

"We find that this really works well with our audience," Marge persisted. "It would be the best way to do it."

She kept him on the phone about an hour, but at least she paid for the call. He paid for the next nine, all inquiries about when he would get a budget to start recording this masterpiece.

"We have finally met about the project and have a new plan," she finally told him.

"Okay, tell me," he said, getting his pad and pen ready.

"The budget has to be scaled back."

"We never really had a budget."

"In terms of how it affects the concept, I am saying. We can only afford to have one guest star, and that would be the Green." The Green was a light folk rock act. "The Green?" Launch asked. "Do they do field-holler?"

"Well, they would do their music, and you would do yours. In an alternation sequence."

"You mean it would go back and forth between me and them?"

"Yes. Perhaps there might be a track together. I don't know about the schedule, they are very busy this period." (This was in the dark ages, before Frank Sinatra invented the fiber-optic dial-a-duet.)

"I really don't think that's the best . . . "

"Believe me, it's the best. We've got a contract with them requiring a sort of sampler thing for free. If we keep the number of tracks that they're on down, it makes it a sampler, and then we don't have to pay them. We never needed to release the sampler we originally planned with them because they got so popular. The company decided it was a good economic move to do it now because we can use it to give the avant-garde field-holler a break."

Then followed her standard speech about how the company was dedicated first and foremost to making massive gains for all indigenous music and to improve the standard of living of the brave souls creating this music with their blood and sweat. "Believe me, I appreciate what you are doing," she told Launch.

And that was the last time he ever talked to her.

NUMBER SOLD: 13

By the age of 36, Amber Mukti had released ten full-length albums of her orchestra and chamber music compositions. She had a shelf full of press clippings, three and a half weeks worth of work booked for the next year, and $250 in the bank. Oh, and only one of her albums was still in print. So she was delighted to find that the Belgian Maltese Falcon label had progressed from their cash-soaked disco/house music phase to an interest in her.

The deal came to her through one of the American labels she'd done a few projects for. This joker wanted it to happen because he'd get a cut. He described it as the deal of the century. Maltese Falcon head Orson Heygt said he wanted to release the entire Mukti catalog on CD, vinyl, and cassette. "The publishing will be worth thousands. Think of it, Amber, you wrote all the music, and over there they gotta pay that, it's not like the States. And they have to pay it up front when they press.

"On top of that they'll come up with an advance for the combined project. We gotta hit them with a figure, that's one thing we have to come up with.

"And of course, I already told them you wanted some boxes of records. That will be part of the deal! So you'll have all your old records back in print, and you can sell them."

They asked for $26,000 but slid down to $16,000 when they realized asking for more than 20 grand had put the whole thing in jeopardy. There were to be two installments, and the first check showed up right on time.

Amber banked it and skipped out the door. "Finally! I've made eight thousand dollars without doing anything."

"If you don't count all the work you did on those records," her husband reminded her.

The second half was due after the third release. Meanwhile, they waited for the first two records, which were supposed to be released together. Amber flew to Chicago eight months later for a concert. There were still no Maltese Falcon releases, and it had turned into one of those things you get sick of checking on.

In Chicago, she went to a record store and checked her bin. There were all ten of the old titles, all brand new imports on Maltese Falcon. When the store's staff revived her, wondering whether she'd suffered a concussion falling to the floor, they were amazed that Amber knew nothing of these new releases. "It's a really good series," a clerk gushed. "Oh, we sell a lot of them."

Amber called her American label contact. "I've

been leaving messages with Orson," he defended himself. "I've got a really high phone bill trying to find out what's going on for you. I still haven't gotten my check for the rights to the ones I had on my label."

"Well, they put them out already, they're already in the stores." Amber told him. She bought copies of everything and made an early morning phone call to Orson.

"Oh, my dear, it is such a pleasure to speak with you," he said. "I have to say your project is one of the most important things we've ever been involved with here at the Falcon." He had a thick French lilt to his voice. Amber imagined him sitting there with a beret and a glass of cognac. He went on praising her and talking about the incredible promotional effort that was going on. They had hired a press agent specifically to come up with concepts for the Amber Mukti Series, a first for the company.

"Maybe you could get this new press agent to mail me some copies of the re-releases, if she can spare a moment," Amber said sarcastically.

Orson didn't catch the edge in her voice. "Of course copies have gone out in the mail. I have a record of that right here."

"And what about the cartons I'm supposed to get?"

"Of course, my dear, they have also gone out. Let me check with shipping." He clicks her on hold, probably going off to take a oui-oui at the cost of $2 per message unit. "Yes, they have gone out from the shipping department."

"And what about the remaining balance of the advance, since all ten albums have been re-released now?"

"No, only half the releases have come out. You are mistaken."

She didn't bother to mention that either way would be contrary to the agreement. "No, all ten were in the store in Chicago."

"The store in Chicago? What store? This is impossible. The U.S. distributor has yet to place the order. It is that new, the release."

This guy could really ladle it out with Maurice Chevalier savoir-faire. It made Amber think of a chocolate sauce salesman on the streets of Naples stirring a kettle full of fresh chocolate that you could smell miles away.

For a while, Amber got almost daily calls from the company. First they were from Orson personally. "I see you are correct about the release. Originally the concept was five now, five in the next year. In the concept department, however, there was the idea to make a big splash, releasing everything at the same time. When we spoke, I did not realize this was the

course we had pursued. It is certainly a great promotion! I will have our agent for the Amber Mukti Series call you in the morning to discuss the strategy."

One week later, a woman named Lariat Badamino called Amber and proceeded to tell her . . . absolutely nothing. All the while making references to radio promotion, print ads, album inserts with catalogs, transatlantic interviews, and that favorite hobby: record company supported promotional concert tours.

"I am sure Orson would authorize to pay the ticket for such a tour, it would make the promotion much easier." It would certainly make Lariat's job easier. All she would have to do is call around and offer a live interview, which they could take or not take. She wouldn't have to use the clever manipulation that was often required to get a critic to write a "think piece" about such serious music as Mukti's.

Orson did authorize the ticket, although not the second $8000. When Amber complained to her American contact, she found he'd already gone off the deep end about the deal. "Those people are liars. I'm never going to get my check for your records. And they ripped me off on something else, too. Have you gotten your cartons?"

She admitted she still hadn't even gotten the promos. The only copies she had were the ones she'd purchased. "Don't my mechanicals get paid up front?" she asked.

"You should check with Orson. I'm not sure."

"That's what you told me when we discussed the deal. Up front."

"Listen, Amber, don't get mad at me. The deal isn't with me. It's with Orson. And he's a liar and a thief!"

She was able to get Lariat on the phone whenever she called, but her days of reaching Orson were over. Lariat suggested she talk directly to the shipping department about her cartons of CDs, LPs, and cassettes.

"Oh yes, 15 or 20 cartons, they went out, they are going to you via the U.S. distributor, Coen."

Coen was a well-known distributor in Indiana. Amber called them up and said, "Have you seen my cartons from Maltese Falcon?"

"You better run this past me again, I don't understand you," the stock guy said.

"Maltese is sending me a bunch of stuff through you guys."

"Through us? They would never do something like that. I don't know what you're talking about." But he promised to keep an eye out for this occurrence.

The company bought her a ticket for the European tour she'd arranged, but it was a reservation for a day three weeks before the tour was supposed to start. And it was a no refund/no exchange kind of ticket, purchased at a price so low it made the airline rep burst out laughing when Amber showed up pleading to get it changed. Luckily, a guy at the airline took pity on her and changed the ticket on the sly.

Before she left the country, she called the American guy who'd brought her into this. "I still haven't gotten the check for your . . . " he started.

"Yeah, I know, I know," she said. "I'm getting ready to go over there."

"I found out something you ought to know about your mechanical royalties," he said. "The way it's supposed to work over there is that they pay the royalties at the factory. But what I heard is that guys who do a lot of business, like Orson, make their own arrangements with the performing-rights societies to pay later."

"Like when?"

"Like whenever they want to, I don't know."

"So they can get away without paying."

"Or they can just pay for the ones they sell," he said.

Wonder of wonders, the $8,000 check, dated several months back, showed up the morning she left. She banked it on the way to the airport.

The tour actually went fine. Lariat kept insisting Amber let her know the dates of her concerts and was always on the verge of scheduling major press events. Amber went along with it, hoping one day to catch Orson in his office.

During the second half of the tour, Lariat was suddenly not in the office anymore. Neither was Orson. Amber stopped calling Maltese. The next-to-last gig was in Brussels. It was a medium-sized crowd. She wondered if anyone from the company would come. A petite girl came up to her at the break. It was Lariat.

"I've been fired," she said. "Really, Amber, those people are very bad."

"I got the rest of my money at least," Amber said.

"Yes, but that is because my friend Quentin, who was looking for a promo pack, moved the check book, and the check was stuck inside the pages. They wrote the check but never sent it. So we sent it. Now I am fired," Lariat smiled. "But I have a key." She dangled it on her finger. "I am expected to turn it in tomorrow."

Amber mentioned she was thinking of going over there tomorrow to get some of the stock she had been promised.

"I know they never sent it," Lariat said. "The guy in the stock room, they told him to tell you the cartons had gone out. But I know where those cartons are." And she kept repeating, with a smile, that she had the key.

The gals helped themselves to stock that night, and the Maltese Falcon bureaucracy never missed it.

The company took a new approach with Amber, though. The series was set for the slag heap. Sales were poor. The company was into ragamuffin music now. Another mistake they had made was printing vinyl. Orson wrote in a handwritten note. "It is not your fault that there was this radical change in the industry. Of course we wanted to make vinyl in your series for the emotional connection with the original issues. But now there is no possibility to sell this."

He offered to sell her all the cartons that she would have stolen if she'd had a truck with her. The albums were going for a dime each. Six months later, the back room in her flat was filled to the ceiling with this booty. It was as if she had gotten back all the copies that were originally made at all these albums.

She counted 996 copies of her *Orchestra Works: Volume 1*. That set her off looking through old receipts from when she had done the first printing of *Volume 1* herself. The bill from the plant showed that she'd ordered 1000 and gotten . . . exactly 996.

"You're gonna have those around 20 years from now," her cynical boyfriend at the time had said.

LABEL: UMLAU

NUMBER SOLD: -20
A general rule of small labels is that no matter how small the sales, the total number of records sold is usually higher than the number of individual titles released.

An exception to this rule is the Berlin Umlau label, which wound up on paper as having sold in the negative—i.e., more copies were returned than were actually distributed in the first place. This was a result of an accountant who had gone mad escaping from East Germany combined with a lawsuit over the label's final release, *Rosenberg's Violin Concerto in E Minor*, which mandated that the entire pressing of the album be confiscated and destroyed.

Rosenberg was considered foremost an "action" or performance artist, but he played the viola and had been a classical virtuoso as a child. He met Diedrich Detleff of Umlau at the famous Berlin Days independent music conference. "Please, you must do a project," Detleff had begged Rosenberg. "I think my label should push the boundaries of what is acceptable."

"I need an advance, speaking of what is acceptable," Rosenberg said.

Detleff agonized over the impossibility of this request and came up with an alternate plan. "Make a tape that I know I can release, and when it is almost finished, I can get some money to you. Maybe 1000 marks, more or less."

"East or West marks?" Rosenberg asked. This

was back in the days when it mattered. As it was, the West marks had to be dragged out of Detleff. Some of the money wound up being paid, but not the full advance.

Still, Rosenberg had the project in mind when he circled the globe with his viola. From town to town, he would call whomever the most famous musicians in town were. At least half of them were willing to get together to hobnob, having heard of Rosenberg and his strange activities. Once he hired an orchestra to run up and down the stairs of a concert hall. That was his "stair symphony." What he hoped would happen was that the musicians would improvise a little and make a tape. He was packing a portable recorder in case this happened.

After a few months, he had taped duets with a dozen or more famous players. He hadn't mentioned anything to any of them about releasing the material; the musicians thought he had just been making a tape for himself. He sent the work in progress to Detleff, who liked it and told him to finish it. Cash was on the way.

Rosenberg had gotten tired of the project, though, and was no longer in the mood to hook up with the players on his list. He was afraid getting paid hinged on having these recordings done like he'd promised because he'd given some of these names to Detleff. So, he got out his viola and various solo recordings that some of the musicians had done and taped his own instant duets.

Detleff didn't notice this sneak move and put out the *Round the World With Rosenberg* album.

Calls started coming in from some of the musicians. "I didn't know I was going to be on this album."

"He's got my solo album on there."

"Well it's just a small pressing, only 500," Detleff lied. Really he had ordered 2000 on the first run.

It received good reviews and none of the critics noticed that some of the music had been pilfered off other records.

This gave Rosenberg his next idea, which he sold to Detleff over a big Greek salad. He would steal an entire album, this time from some really big cheeses, say, one of the world's most famous symphonies. He showed Detleff an album that was on the Deutsche Grammophon label. On its cover was a picture of an internationally renowned orchestra conductor waving his baton. Rosenberg had done a little mock-up artwork, mostly consisting of drawing a Hitler mustache on the conductor.

"Brilliant! We do it!" Detleff said, without even saying that he had to hear a tape first. Rosenberg taped it in 40 minutes, putting on an actual record of the London Symphony and recording his viola on top of it.

"This is a masterpiece," Detleff said. "I rush it out. It is the ultimate record we make." And the last.

Deutsche Grammophon, an old and well-established dynasty, sent its lawyers to convince Detleff of the wisdom of re-releasing this masterpiece with a new cover. The lawyers had been kind enough to do their own mock-up, crossing off and blacking out everything that was litigious about the original. By the time they were finished, they had an almost totally blank cover.

The sobbing Detleff broke the news to Rosenberg, who reacted differently. "Brilliant! This is fantastic. What a statement," he said. The record got good reviews, and all the critics assumed the orchestral background was written by Rosenberg and recorded under his auspices. None of them realized it had been ripped off of a record.

Nearly a year went by before anyone noticed, but it was too good to be true. Another set of lawyers came around and demanded the entire pressing back plus all stampers, master discs, master tapes, and even Rosenberg's brain if they could get their hands on it; all of it was marked for destruction. This fiasco, along with his distributors' refusal to pay up after a decade, convinced Detleff to flee the record business.

Rosenberg took personal responsibility for gathering up the copies that had been stolen. "I knew practically everyone that had bought a copy, and none of them wanted to keep it anyway," claimed the maestro.

LABEL: PORCO DISCO

NUMBER SOLD: 55

Richard "Ringo" Fulci lived in Northern Italy and came from a family of lawyers. It was assumed that he, too, would be a lawyer.

During his freshman year at college, he caught a bug, though. He became fascinated by disco, house, any kind of music that a turntable and a deejay were involved in making. He wasn't into dancing because of some back problems, but he liked to watch and listen to the deejays mix and get the dancers excited. He might have realized that being a deejay would be an easy way to watch cute dancing girls, but he was also concerned with the musical aesthetics. He had two turntables and a mixer set up in his small student apartment and spent hours messing around with them.

His grades began to plummet; Fulci Sr. didn't know that Ringo had picked up three deejay gigs and had a good chance of landing a whole summer's employment in Ibiza, where a lot of the house trends were coming from.

Though his family had practically disowned him

(a difficult thing to achieve in Italy, no matter what devilment one gets into), Ringo found himself in demand on the disco scene. He was getting offers all the time, although only in Italy and Spain. What he really wanted was to break into the scene in Germany, France, England, or even better, the United States. This meant making his own records. All the companies and distributors he had insisted that nobody would put out a record by an Italian deejay. The shops sold British, German, and American music, especially "black guys from the ghetto"; that was what was really hot.

Ringo married a dancer he'd met at the club, Rebecca. He invested some of their wedding present lira in his own label, Porco Disco. "Porco" refers to a style of swearing from Bologna, where "porco" (pig) is combined with various deities—God, Jesus, the Virgin Mary—to create foul epithets. This name was quite scandalous in Italy and Spain. Outside of that, nobody much cared. The first single, *CB Porco Disco*, attempted to cash in on the then-trendy CB radio scene.

Ringo sent a copy to his favorite American deejay, Why the Great. He couldn't believe it when Why wrote back. His final words set off fireworks in Ringo's brain: "Would love to come to Italy sometime."

Ringo phoned a few of the big discos he worked. "Would you like to have a really cool American deejay come and do a special show in the club?"

Oh, would they ever. What was it worth to them? "Hmm, three million lira [about $1500]." After a few such reactions, Ringo had the pleasure of phoning up his idol and saying, "You have an Italian tour!"

The American loved the idea of the all-expenses-paid trip to Italy. Ringo cooked up another great scheme along with the pasta one night: He and Why could tape an album's worth of material in his basement studio for Porco Disco.

"It would be my record with the American guest deejay. The shops will buy it then and the distributors will like it. Then I will be in the shops finally," he told Rebecca.

Why the Great was the first of a series of British and American deejays to go along with the scheme of an Italian tour and a record on Porco Disco. They all felt the same way about the project: They liked the work and the trip to Italy, but they weren't wild about making the record. Eventually, though, they figured it wasn't that bad, and the album was on such a dinky label that nobody would ever see it anyway.

Ringo knew he would have to do a USA promo tour to launch himself and his label. He developed an innovative dance music system with 100 turntables. He got the idea looking through a book about Japan.

In Kyoto there was a temple with 1000 different statues of Buddha arranged in rows. The 100 turntables was a trimmed down version of the original idea that involved 1000 turntables and demanded that the deejay create a program based on Buddhist philosophy.

Ringo became obsessed with playing more than one record at the same time. With the new setup, he sometimes played 30, 40, even 50 different albums at once. Could people dance to it? They couldn't even listen to it in Italy. But he was convinced that the USA would be different. He would completely wow them and put Italy on the dance map.

By this time, there were 11 releases on the Porco Disco label that featured Ringo with a different American deejay. Sales were reasonable as long as the pressings weren't too large. Relations with the guests varied, but a few had actually gotten chummy with Ringo and promised to find him guest stints at clubs if he made it over to the States. He wound up with something of a tour, including jobs in New York City; Birmingham, Alabama; Richmond, Virginia; and Los Angeles.

It was supposed to be a second honeymoon for him and Rebecca, but lugging around the 100 turntables and their accompanying Anvil cases made it more like torture. On top of that, they had car trouble. A deejay named Tim-Tom had loaned them a vehicle; it ran okay but attracted trouble wherever it went.

The Southern jobs were scheduled within days of the couple's arrival. Jet-lagged, they struggled, sweated, and groaned to get all the turntables into the little station wagon. Ringo had one on his lap while he drove. Rebecca had to hold several on her lap and prop her feet up on others.

In Alabama, Ringo made $400. The club had been half full and no one said a word about the massive turntable setup. It felt like a success to Ringo, though, and he was still going on and on about it as they packed up all the turntables at 5 a.m. the morning after the gig.

Ringo enjoyed driving the highways heading back toward Virginia. He did 60, 70, 80 mph, up toward 90.

"Police!" Rebecca shouted.

"Cazzo!" Ringo said. "Porco la Madonna!" He couldn't understand what could be wrong. At home when the cops pulled you over, they were usually looking for terrorists. Did they do that in the USA?

"Don't y'all believe in the speed limit?" was the first thing the big trooper said. He looked at the international driver's license. "Italian, huh? Don't you have speed limits back in Italia?"

Ringo grimaced. "What is a speed limit?"

"Didn't you see the signs?" the cop asked. "The

ones with numbers?"

"All the signs have numbers. You see, we are new to the states. The English, it's good, but . . . "

"What do you want with all them turntables?" the cop asked, looking around in the car. "Maybe you two better come down to the station."

At the station, there was a complex procedure to determine what to fine the foreigner. They asked him how much money he had.

"It is $400, everything I have so far from the tour," Ringo said.

> *Rosenberg had done a little mock-up artwork, mostly consisting of drawing a Hitler mustache on the conductor.*

"Isn't that interesting, the fine is $400 for speeding in this county," the sheriff laughed.

Ringo was so ticked off that he couldn't wait to complain when he got back to New York. He thought the cops had done something illegal and wanted to get his money back. They drove to the street that Why lived on but couldn't find a parking spot. "We double park," Ringo told Rebecca. "We just run in to tell him we're back."

In the apartment, they started talking about the $400 fine. Why interrupted them as soon as he could to ask them where the car was now.

"I make double parking," Ringo shrugged.

"You better not do that! They tow on this block!"

Towing, this was another new thing. In Italy, everyone honks their horns when there is any problem with a vehicle being where it shouldn't. Ringo ran out to find his borrowed car had already been towed. Rebecca hung out at Why's while Ringo went down and paid more than $100 to get the vehicle back in time for the evening's gig at a Brooklyn club.

The Brooklyn gig went all right considering that Ringo made some money, but his reception was not enthusiastic. When more than ten records were playing at once, the audience became hostile. They couldn't follow what was going on and threw pennies at Ringo. His deejay pals apologized. "The scene here is lame, man," they said. "You can't experiment like you can in Europe. These people are here just to party."

Discouraged, they began dragging everything to the car. Rebecca thought her arms and legs were going to fall off, packing up the car was miserable. Finally, they hopped in the car and Ringo turned the key. Nothing except a grinding humming noise. Several people wandered out of the club. "Sounds like your starter!"

"Won't turn, eh?"

"Maybe you got too many turntables in there, buddy!"

They called a cab and left the car stranded in the street, Ringo hoping nobody would steal the turntables and Rebecca silently praying that somebody would.

The starter had to be replaced and Tim-Tom said the Italians had to pick up the tab. "After all, you were driving it."

The turntables couldn't be left in the car anymore, so Ringo hauled them away to where they were staying. This required two cab trips. Both cabbies asked him what he was doing with so many turntables.

"Maybe is too many turntables," Rebecca suggested. "Do you have to take them all to Los Angeles? Is ridiculous."

"Rebecca, this is my art," Ringo said. "You must understand. You are my wife."

She dropped the matter. So did the airline they had booked their flights home with. In fact, they dropped everything to do with the couple with 100 turntables, including their reservations. "I'm sorry, this airline has gone out of business," the agent told Ringo as they tried to check in.

Ringo couldn't even buy other tickets because someone had stolen all the tour money from their Los Angeles hotel room.

"If we stack all turntables here and block traffic in airport, someone will fly us back to Italy," Ringo predicted. He was right, but it took 72 hours. One good idea came to him while they sat there: He had Rebecca take a picture of him sitting on top of all the turntables. "This is cover for my USA tour album," he told her, smiling at his genius.

One good idea came to Rebecca, too. "When we get back to Italy, I am divorcing you."

"Rebecca, this is just the pressure of the tour making you say this," Ringo said to soothe her.

But when they got home, the matter went to court. When the judge asked the reason for the divorce, Rebecca's lawyer had her assistants carry in the 100 turntables, set them up, and demonstrate Ringo's deejay concept. It only took 35 records going at once to convince the judge to grant the divorce. Ringo didn't quite get the message. He thought maybe his turntable concept had a future in family court as well as on the dance floor.

Rebecca had run the business side of Porco Disco. Without her, there was nothing. He folded the label and changed careers, becoming an orchestra conductor.

About 20 years later, he was reading about the war in Bosnia when the phone rang. Coincidentally, it was a deejay from Radio Belgrade. He was trying to track down some of the early Porco Disco sides. Some of the records with the 100-turntable set up were underground classics in Yugoslavia, considered accurate musical depictions of the horrors of war. Ringo was flattered, even though he had no idea what they were talking about. He sent some to the radio station, and the next day he cleaned out a dozen more cartons from the basement where the glory days of Porco Disco were languishing. He drove to the Bosnia Relief Agency in Udine and donated the records.

One day he was reading about one of the American "mercy drop" missions where they fly over a Bosnian Muslim enclave and drop pallets of food, medicine, and supplies. There had been an accident and one of the pallets had hit a crowd of people, killing some of them.

"Probably the Porco Disco catalog," Ringo thought to himself.

LABEL: GASSERY NOVA COLLECTION

NUMBER SOLD: 15

Jazz historian Sven Hursfaw was telling his Stockholm class about the explosion of self-produced records by musicians that had begun in the '70s.

"It seemed the major jazz labels, even the small independents, were unable to provide recording opportunities for so many of the most innovative jazz creators.

"To think that at this stage of his career, Cecil Taylor would have to print his own record and unload them himself off the truck. This is embarrassing! Yet overcoming this embarrassment was what made it possible for these artists to continue making records during this period."

As thoroughly as Sven had researched the subject, however, he had yet to unearth one of the main reasons behind the sheer number of labels owned by musicians: None of them could agree on what was worthwhile to put out. Once you had at least two artists involved in starting a record label, chances were great that it would split off into two different labels.

In Toronto at this time, there were between a dozen and 18 musicians dedicated to new developments in improvising, some was jazz and some wasn't exactly jazz. Some was composed and some was not. It was confusing. And between packing and unpacking equipment and the discussions and arguments, it was quite a challenge to make time to actually play, so

some of them didn't.

"I'll pick up the bass again when we get a grant," was the ultimatum issued by Ruggy Metrica. He sat down at his kitchen table and started writing grants, and Ontario Over the Top went without a bassist until he'd secured funding, under the "parallel gallery" program, to open their own performance space.

Marvin Quittung, master of the sopranino saxophone, was a recent addition to the group, who had been asked to join not for his playing but for his connections with record store owner Turney Barton and his label BBBB (Barton's Bunelian Brown Bag).

Quittung had joined because of the grant. The group would have a performance space and that meant Quittung would have his foot in the door to set up his projects, which included a solo recital.

"What should be my next album for BBBB?" he mulled.

"What about recording Ontario Over the Top?" Barton suggested.

"Man, they are not ready to record. I mean, their music is just not that together. You'd have to sift through hundreds of hours of tapes to get enough material for a good album, man, it would be torture," Quittung said.

"But the drummer's a genius!" Everyone agreed that Bodie Lala was a genius.

"Oh sure, man. We should do a drum solo album of Bodie if you really want to do something . . . "

"Drum solo? Ridiculous, it would never sell," Barton said. He pulled out sales figures for other drum solo albums on labels such as Sticks, Eternal Rhythm, and Boom Cycle.

"Worst selling things in the store," Quittung acknowledged. He thought it would be humiliating to record with Ontario Over the Top, but it would still mean releasing an album. If he did record with them, though, he'd want to have more control over the music.

"They'll have to record some of my compositions."

Bringing this up at the next rehearsal, though, caused a firestorm. The Over the Top veterans, including 62-year old trumpeter Hale Byke, told Quittung he was nuts.

"Tunes? Nobody wants to play your tunes. Man, I quit playing tunes 30 years ago. I haven't played a tune since then. I haven't even looked at a music chart," Hale said.

The group's pianist Louise Yollo would sit and pick out standards on the piano. But her feeling was that the improv group didn't need them. "What is original is that we are not using them," she said.

As for Bodie, he agreed. "There's no way we

should play tunes. You want to do that, Marvin, you do it on your own. And don't ask me to back you up because I'm not interested. I don't play tunes. I play like this." He started playing again, and Over the Top played with him.

Quittung was fuming and played some of his tunes during the improvisation out of spite, but nobody heard them because the electronics were way too loud.

The grantmeister, Ruggy, had been listening to the debate as he was drawing up budget figures. He took some of the key people aside after Quittung left. "There's nothing in our grant thing that says we can't start a record label. I mean, I've been looking over the budget and there's enough padding in there so we could press a record or two."

Everyone loved the idea of Ontario Over the Top Records, or OOT, which sounds like the way they say the word "out" in Canada. When anybody asked what kind of music they played, they answered "Out!" or "Oot!"

Quittung and Barton were mortified.

"I don't think the scene can support two labels, man," Quittung told Bodie and Hale when they announced the news.

"It undermines what we're trying to do," Barton added.

"Well, we got no choice. Your man here won't put out a record unless he is the leader," Bodie said, pointing at Quittung.

"Yeah, and then we have to play his tunes," Hale added, shaking the frost out of his long gray hair.

"Well, we blew that opportunity," Barton sighed.

"What opportunity? Their music is really awful, man," Quittung replied. They dropped the subject and never discussed it again because Barton had total faith in his friend's musical judgment. At least, he wasn't about to start listening to that squeaky modern jazz in order to have his own opinion.

The first Ontario Over the Top album didn't come out on the OOT label, which by then was established with a glossy catalog and six releases. Gallery manager and label honcho, Ruggy, still too busy to pick up his bass, had decreed that OOT was not in a position to release Over the Top music. It was both "too out musically" and "too in from the social point of view." His reasoning was that the group should wait. Let OOT release a few titles by other, more well-known Canadian musicians.

"That way it won't look like we're just putting out our own music, the way they do with BBBB. The Council isn't so wild about our weekly concerts, either," Ruggy argued.

"But I want to get a record out!" Bodie pleaded. "I mean, the group really needs to," he added to

sound less desperate. Personal problems had heightened the intensity of his drumming crusade. He'd been diagnosed with leukemia. They predicted he would live a year or two more but not beyond that.

When Ruggy finally admitted that he had no intention of ever putting out Ontario Over the Top on OOT, Bodie didn't take the news well, but Hale offered to take money from a separate grant he was getting and sidetrack it into a new label. He called it Gassery Nova Editions because they were standing in front of a newly opened gas station when they thought of it.

"It's an improvised name," Bodie said.

They had released three Gassery records, all by Over the Top, when Bodie finally had to be hospitalized for good. He was too weak to drum anymore and this weakened the band's spirit. It was years before a new group rose from the ashes to satisfy the Canada Council, who thought the grant applicants were performing too much in their own space.

The players splintered off into different projects individually, but each of them dropped by the hospital to visit Bodie and satisfy his relentless quest for gossip about the players. He wasn't looking for scandals and smut, just evidence of who was improvising and who was "playing tunes."

He pumped visitors for information about what concerts had happened or what records had been released, even what was going on at rehearsals. Always the same question: "Do they play any tunes?"

The only one he knew who would never play tunes was Hale. Guys would bring him cassettes, but he had to remind them, "No tunes!" Hale needed no reminding.

Quittung decided the second local BBBB production should be a solo album by Hale, who was so tied in with the Canada Council that he could get the whole production funded. It was supposed to be solo trumpet, but there was a problem with the microphone cable, and what was recorded was a combination of electronic static and CB radios from passing trucks. Hale listened to all two hours of the tape and decided it was the greatest thing he had ever heard. He told Quittung this had to be the album and it would be a double.

Barton had been trying to keep an open mind, but when he heard this tape he said, "Absolutely not," even though the Canada Council was willing to pay him $2000 to put it out. "You can't pay me to put that out! It's ridiculous."

Hale loved it so much he started his own label, Fix Records, and this was its only release for 15 years. At that point, he released the same tapes backward.

There was actually an Ontario Over the Top tape released on BBBB after all. He took one of the earlier multitrack Over the Top masters and mixed everyone out except for Bodie. Then he put out the drum solo record he had always wanted to. He got permission from Barton because a few more sales were insured since Bodie was dead.

Hale had been by his side and reported his last words: "Don't play tunes."

LABEL: SQUARE SOLEIL

NUMBER SOLD: 14

The Bellevue district was a neighborhood in Paris several square miles in size. Almost every building and every business was owned by the infamous Tang Brothers. The lone holdouts in this monopoly of power were the occupants of apartment 14 at 223 Rue Jack Hawkins: three men who bumbled into a cheap apartment rental that the Tangs seemed to have overlooked. All were music enthusiasts with tastes that branched out into many styles. The apartment's occupants spent most of their time recording, releasing, and distributing albums.

Twenty five albums had come out on Square Soleil, each in editions of 500. Manufacturing was stripped to the basics, and the records were pressed in the Czech Republic. They kept the boxes of records in the apartment, cleverly bypassing the Tang stranglehold on shipping.

The business was theirs outright, so they had no one telling them what to do, no president at a big label, especially not the Tang Brothers. All the releases sold 500 eventually, but they would start with 300 and then do a 200 reprint to hedge their bets and keep the Tangs from getting suspicious.

Being into weird music, they naturally took an interest in Shiny Alberts, an American drummer who played on the Paris streets. He was a music business veteran with roots in the New Orleans styles, and he also knew a lot about American Indian music, having grown up on a reservation. He would put a band together and play tunes he'd come up with, combining these different styles, and it would be great. He had also backed up some legendary jazz players over the years.

Alberts was a grouch, though, who would get impatient as the gig wore on and the late-night smattering of people would start yabbering with each other over the music. He would henpeck the other musicians while making worse mistakes himself, sometimes even swearing abusively, which would carry over the club P.A.

Still, the Soleil guys liked him and wanted to have a Shiny Alberts title in their catalog. They took charge of the whole affair, and the recording session went pretty well, until near the end when Shiny

thought the saxophonist had insulted him. But by then enough material had been cut for an LP. "It is a good thing we are not making CDs," the partners agreed.

When the Shiny title came out, they borrowed a friend's pickup truck for some of the local distribution. When Shiny heard about the truck, he called for a favor. "You got that truck for a while? 'Cuz there's something I need to do," he said.

They agreed that, in a couple of days, one of them would drive Shiny about an hour out of Paris to the warehouse of Magna Carta Sound, a large European distributor known for hustling bootlegs, cutouts, and other flotsam and jetsam of the music industry.

"This friend of mine works out there at Magna," Shiny explained. "He called the other day and said they got a bunch of returns from the old Petit Disques label. I gotta get my hands on them!" Shiny was no record collector, he just had an old business feud going with Petit Disques. Shiny had six albums on the label. For that he had gotten nothing. The call from the warehouse had been specific: There were boxes and boxes of Petit Disques titles. If Shiny was quick, he could sneak as many as he could carry out the back. That's why he needed the pickup truck

"This is one gig I ain't goin' to on the train," Shiny laughed.

They timed it so that they got to the warehouse when most of the work force was gone. His pal was waiting. He showed them the boxes, and after peeling back the well-worn cardboard, they saw that they had their hands on lots of good stuff. They piled the boxes mostly full of Shiny's titles onto the truck and then took off. Thirty miles down the road, though, on one of the most ghastly stretches of congested French motorway, the truck began bucking. It slowed to about ten mph and when they got up on the shoulder it sputtered to a stop. This vehicle never moved another inch on its own.

While they were sitting there wondering what to do, a tremendous downpour began. Within minutes, water was pooling up on the road and the boxes of records were getting soaked. Unfortunately, very few of the releases were shrink-wrapped. "We gotta do something to protect those records," Shiny moaned, looking at the disaster in the back of the truck.

The two of them took as many boxes as they could carry, maybe 150 out of the 1000 plus that they'd scammed and struggled down the road. Eventually they got a ride from a truck driver who refused to turn around and go back to get the rest of the records.

They finally arrived back in the Tang with their booty of 150 records. They needed drying off, but could still be resold, maybe at a slight discount. The

I Hate the Man Who Runs This Bar!

Petit Disques titles were rare, so even a mildewed copy would be worth something. As they unpacked the boxes, they found shipping receipts that indicated the entire shipment consisted of defectives. Shiny saw his young friends' look of disappointment and told them to cheer up.

"Listen, man. Them Petit Disques were the worst pressings of all time. Probably every single one pressed is technically defective," he laughed. "And if there was one that wasn't, somebody probably listened to it, didn't like it, and returned it as defective. I know it's true for my albums. I don't like them myself. But I sure like having copies of them, so I can say, 'I did this!' Anyway, we oughta get back out on the road and find a way to get that truck and all them other records."

By the time they got back to the truck, some jokers had helped themselves to the rest of the records. They all stood feeling sorry for themselves until Shiny cracked them up with a Cheech and Chong reference: "Someone ripped off the thing I ripped off!"

Then the rest joined in.

"Probably the Tang Brothers."

"At least they like vinyl. This is good."

"I hope they're jazz fans."

LABEL: PORCH

NUMBER SOLD: 16

Like many from the punk scene, N.E. Leigh started his record label Porch in order to record his own band, Not Any Good. What was unique about N.E. was his philosophy: a combination of punk disgust combined with a mischievous flair for thumbing his nose at the very scene that was supporting him. This first expressed itself when he got sick of having to deal with other bandmembers.

So, he began a series of bands that existed only as names. When he had to send a tape to a club, he would send a band's demo tape that he had received in the mail. Sometimes he sent a tape that he liked, but this was frustrating because his taste wasn't the norm, and club owners usually rejected his choice of a "good" tape.

He didn't have any better luck with the tapes he didn't like, but a tape of a reggae band would almost always snare a gig. After going out on the road with various groups of people who had never played together before and would never play together again, he found the indifference in the clubs thick enough to sustain such a fraud. Half of the places couldn't remember the band they'd booked was a reggae band, and the rest didn't notice the difference.

He also noticed that the worse these pseudo-bands sounded, the better the reception from the crowd, and the higher the likelihood that the manager would ask them back.

It was only a matter of time till N.E. had a revelation: If he could be this bad and be more successful than if he were good, surely he could find others out there that were even worse. If he got in the position to manage such un-talent, perhaps he could become a rich producer in the process. At the very least, the research would be worth compiling into an album.

So, instead of sending out the worst tapes and pretending they were his band, he began selecting the cream of the crap for himself, with the idea of a compilation album devoted to the absolute worst bands he could find.

He began contacting research assistants in various parts of the globe, asking everyone to think hard. "Do you know somebody who is really, truly terrible, without any redeeming characteristics? I'm not talking about camp," he was quick to emphasize. "I don't want groups that are so bad they're good. I want groups that are so bad that they are really bad, that's all. The worst of the worst."

The *You Don't Want This Record* album began accumulating tracks like a bad cold accumulates piles of mucus-soaked Kleenex.

"I am discovering that just being bad leads to apathy," N.E. wrote to one assistant. "To be really hated, there has to be something more."

Among the acts signed for this monstrosity:

F-F-Funt: Began the fad of lead singers rolling around in piles of broken glass. New York *Times* rock critic Hom Jopner wrote: "The only positive thing is that these lowlifes might be exterminated slowly and painfully in the process."

Poop Factor: Songwriter Piece of Wood says the band was founded to be "as annoying as possible." Their first album contained songs making fun of cripples, children, senior citizens, police, nurses, and FEMA emergency crews, but caused the most offense to hippies, who took umbrage at "malicious anti-drug lyrics" (*Yippie Times*).

Your Problem: "I went to a gig where half the audience poured lighter fluid on their jackets and then set themselves on fire."

Kathy and the Knockout Artists: A band that gets the audience so worked up that it attacks the stage. A front page story in a Cleveland paper describes "the show stopper . . . a member of the audience leaped onto the stage, slammed into the lead singer, Kathy, a wispy blonde, literally knocking her unconscious. She was carried off the stage."

Lousehead: Securing a recording of this one-man band was a trick in itself, since a court order had been issued in his hometown, restricting him from leaving his basement and "recording, broadcasting, writing, or in any other way creating entire or partial arrangements of sound and/or lyrics that can or cannot be construed as music."

Collie Lasagna: Certainly the only rock band of its type. Made up entirely of howling and barking dogs, several of them with tambourines duct-taped to their legs. "Cruel and almost too musical," commented N.E.

The Tangerines: Ex-strippers singing ditties that nearly rhyme about various ex-bosses and leering customers. "The concept is good, but luckily they are really bad," their agent wrote in his note. The tape sounded familiar to N.E., who realized he had received a demo a few years before and had used it to land a job in Boston. "The club didn't notice that we were not an all-girl band, like on the record. In fact we had no girls," N.E. reported.

Venison Hunting: Hobbyists from Michigan, this band performs wearing freshly skinned deer carcasses. They were banned from most clubs but were a top attraction at the Gourmet Game Café in Wilmington, North Carolina.

Josie and the Pussycats: Once a popular kids' cartoon band on Saturday mornings, this combo had degenerated to the point where getting a track on this record was even more than they deserved.

Pip and Bubbie: Actually one of those sugary children's groups that play songs about spankings and tearing the legs off crickets, the combo became a top attraction on the punk circuit when the manufacturing plates for its new release somehow got switched with the new album by heavy speed metal punk stars Adrenaline Victims.

It was easy for the packaging to be better than the music on a record like this, but some buyers thought Porch's packaging was better than the music on any record. The album came completely covered with fake vomit from novelty shops. It took them months to glue it onto the records, and by then the first pressing was sold out and they had to start all over again.

All the bands were invited for a gig to promote the album, and more than half showed up. (Josie and the Pussycats were no-shows.) The resulting performances were collectively so disgusting, offensive, horrifying, shocking, ludicrous, obnoxious, and just plain bad that outraged ticket buyers followed the bands back to their motel and taunted them from the parking lot. It was a modern version of the peasants storming Dr. Frankenstein's castle. All they needed were torches.

"Come on out, you rotten stinking lousy musicians!"

"We dare you to come out. We'll knock your teeth in, ripping us off like that!"

"That was the worse stuff we ever heard! Get out of here!"

Some of the motel patrons got annoyed and called the cops. A couple of squad cars eventually rolled up.

"You gotta arrest those guys," the mob ringleader told the cops. "You wouldn't believe the awful show they just did."

"They rolled on glass and threw blood at the audience!"

"They threw up on stage!"

"They called my girlfriend fatso!"

"They played the worst music I ever heard!"

"They poured tomato sauce on their amplifiers!"

"They did a song making fun of kindergarten teachers!"

One cop wrote down these and dozens of other comments. A few of the officers interviewed some of the bandmembers, the cops discussed the matter among themselves briefly and then addressed the crowd with a bullhorn. "You are to go home! You are to leave this parking lot! You will be arrested if you come back!"

The people left, grousing to the cops. "You should do something about this. I mean, you're the police."

"The fact is, we think you folks are lying. You can't possibly be telling the truth about all this. There's never been music that bad."

LABEL: SAFETY NET

NUMBER SOLD: 8

The little girl gripped her father's hand. She was frightened. He had taken her to many strange places in her three years of existence. But this time it was a deep, dark basement. And hot! Fire seemed to be coming out of the walls. They were waiting in front of a metal door that looked like something out of an evil sorcerer's fortress. Light was coming through the crack in the door, but it wasn't like any light she had seen. It was more like flames or the light you would see in the air around flames.

They were down there for what seemed like hours, both of them sweating buckets. Still, her dad kept saying, "Let's just wait a minute more. They said they were coming. If they don't come in a minute, then we'll ride the elevator back up to the top, ring the doorbell again, and find out what's going on." He was getting frustrated.

She'd heard a little bit about hell, things here and there. This must be what hell was like, really hot, dirty, dark, and scary, with flames coming out. And of course, your parents are there saying, "Wait a minute, we'll go in a minute."

How long is a minute really? This was something of a mystery. Anyway, it must have passed because, with a sigh, her dad took her back to the elevator. It was the biggest elevator she'd ever been in.

"It's a freight elevator," he told her.

Great. Freight. She didn't know what freight was. Maybe it was a kind of fruit.

When they got off the elevator, the path back to the street was blocked with piles of boxes. This was what Dad had come to get.

A big slob was standing there. "Where the heck did you go?" he asked her dad.

"Downstairs. I thought you said to go downstairs," dad said.

"I never said for you to go downstairs. That's where the plant is." The big guy looked down at the little girl.

Plant. Yes, freight must be fruit. They must be growing it in the hot place.

Dad and his friend Jeb, who'd been waiting in the car, loaded all the boxes into the back seat. Dad thanked the big guy, who grunted and shut the door.

Jeb started driving. Dad turned to his daughter in the back seat and smiled. "My new record's out, sweetie!"

He tore open a box and they started admiring it. She got one to hold, too. It had a picture of her daddy on it.

Jeb and Dad drove to a few places and dropped off boxes of records, but most of them were going where they always went: Mom and Dad's bedroom.

Mom gave her a hug. The little girl burst into tears. "Mommy! They took me to the hot place!"

Mom patted her on the back and kissed her cheeks. She fired a question at the guys. "What's the hot place?"

"The pressing plant. We went down to the basement by mistake."

"It was burning! Like hell!" the little girl cried out.

Jeb couldn't keep from laughing. "Must be the devil's music, this record."

The little girl realized they were teasing her so she cried harder.

Her mom told her dad that Frabillo had left him a message. Dad, Alexander Larn, the president of Safety Net Records, put the last box away and picked up the phone. Frabillo was releasing his first album with Larn. The various parts were all supposedly down at "the hot place," but the project hadn't been assembled yet. It was still at the proof-checking phase, and that was probably what Frabillo had called about. Most likely there was trouble.

Frabillo was hovering by the phone and grabbed it on the first ring. "Are you gonna be home a while? I gotta show you something," Frabillo said.

"Is everything all right?"

"No, you're not gonna believe it. You have to see it, though, I can't describe it." Frabillo hung up and promised to be there in an hour.

Larn then had an hour to worry about what had gone wrong. When his partner, Frabillo, arrived, he was holding a small manila envelope. He pulled out a round, white piece of paper. It was a proof for the label they glue in the center of LPs that usually says what side it is and what songs are on it.

For his album of Sicilian bagpipe music, Frabillo had decided against this and, instead, had made labels covered with the little doodles he did while talking to his mother on the telephone. She called from Palermo, every Sunday. These doodles meant nothing to anybody but Frabillo who was intense about them. Alexander looked over the proofs. He couldn't see anything wrong with them. They were just doodles.

Frabillo lost his patience. He jabbed at the edge of one of the labels with his thumbnail. "Look! Look closer!"

Alexander squinted and strained. He still didn't know what the bagpiper was talking about.

"Look! They cut off a line."

"They cut off a line?"

"Yeah, a line in one of my drawings. They printed the circle a little off center and got rid of the line."

"Yeah, but what's the difference?"

"What's the difference?" Frabillo repeated indignantly. "I want this to be exactly the way I designed it. What's wrong with that? I'm paying for it, after all."

"Maybe you should go down to the printer and get him to do it over," Alexander suggested.

"Now wait a minute, man. You told me you would take care of that." The deal was that Frabillo put up the money from his inheritance for the records. Alexander did all the hustling and manufacturing.

"Yeah, but I can't go down to the printer and ask them to do it all over for the one line!"

"The one line is really important. If it's gone, the project is no longer what I wanted. Every detail is important. When you neglect a detail, you are neglecting everything. You are saying nothing is important."

"But that's just it. If you go down there and ask them to do it over, you'll see what I'm talking about. Nothing is important to them. They'll act like it's the biggest bunch of crap they've ever seen."

They compromised and went down to the printer together. The guy threw a major fit, yelled at both of them, and then got even madder when he noticed that the doodle-packed labels lacked any indication of whether they were side A or side B.

"How you gonna know what side you're on?" was his question.

"Look, you put one label on one side of the record and the other label on the other side. It's not complicated," Fabrillo said.

The printer got up from behind his desk. "Listen, you gotta realize the people that are working in that factory sticking these labels on your records are not intellectual like you. They're not too bright is what I'm trying to say. They are used to seeing labels with side 1 and 2. Side A and B, okay? They can follow that, some of them," he said.

"They should still be able to understand, two piles of labels, one on one side, one on the other." Fabrillo looked to Alexander for support.

"Nah, you don't get what I'm talking about," the printer said. "We'll try to do this thing for you, but I'm warning you, if these labels are on the wrong side, I don't want you coming back here complaining. Because these people aren't what I call too bright."

"I don't care what side of the record the labels are on," Fabrillo said. What really worried him was the prospect that some of the discs might end up with two of the same label, but he was too frazzled to bring that up.

Alexander didn't care if the labels were glued on upside down and backwards. He dreamt that night that Fabrillo was pounding at his door, screaming, "They've ruined my record! They've destroyed it!" He was holding a record that had been completely covered with sticker labels so that you couldn't even see the vinyl anymore.

Alexander woke up because his daughter was climbing in between him and his wife. She'd also had a nightmare about a pressing plant.

"Please, Dad," she said as her eyes shut. "Promise you won't ever take me to the hot place again."

LABEL: TIMTUF

NUMBER SOLD: 0*
(*Before artist's death; number now expected to increase)

Tim Breem got his label Timtuf going with a form of artist manipulation that most working musicians will run into from time to time. Tim had a job selling computers in a Midwest college town. No one organized concerts, either on campus or in the local bars, aside from a pizza place that booked whoever happened to get the owner on the phone, and the bands were usually told to knock it off because it was too loud sometime during the first set.

A friend in a nearby big city had told Tim that some touring acts were coming through the area. His main interest was progressive rock, though he liked jazz and international stuff. As long as it wasn't too commercial, he would give it a listen.

His friends in local bands told him that he should start a label, mostly to release the tapes they'd been making in their basements. He liked this stuff. He thought it was as good as some of the stuff put out by big names. He made a cassette of some of the local guys, alternating tracks with established recording stars like Stingy Bed, Clinton Sparks, Jacques Errors, and Thrown. The local stuff held up. More than that, he liked the tape he'd made and wanted to make an album like that.

So it was artistic intent and musical enjoyment that was behind the conniving that brought the above-mentioned big names to Tim's town for gigs that he had arranged. First, he had them play in the student union, and then, when they threw him out for being weird, the pizza parlor took over as a venue. The night ended with a pepperoni-gobbling old bag taking on the sophisticated pantomime-with-electronics artist Jacques Errors.

"You can't sing and you can't play!" she kept shouting.

"He's not singing, he's a mime," her companion tried to tell her. She heckled until she couldn't stay conscious any longer. At that point, she sunk her head into her pizza and fell asleep.

Tim admitted that his hometown had too many galoots like this woman to support a sophisticated music scene. There were only about six people in the whole town who understood this kind of music. These were the cold hard facts. He had to give up concert promotion.

The big names gave him permission to tape their concerts and, if there was a song or two that was really excellent quality, to release it on his upcoming sampler, *Getting to Know Timtuf*. Oh, they had their little demands. But it was just about bits of money, figures in the hundreds, royalty advances, and the mechanical royalties paid to songwriters.

The project was well received when it came out. Of course, the critics panned the tracks by the local artists, but Tim knew they would. "If I'd switched the credits around they wouldn't have noticed, they would have praised the local tracks," he was sure. He was just hoping that the project would pay for itself, and it did. He spent a few hours every evening selling copies. He didn't have that many to get rid of—he had printed 2000—and when they were more than half gone, he started thinking about the next one. He figured that because he no longer did concert promoting, he would go to the musicians on his vacation time. The trip could be a fun thing.

When he released his fourth collection, a double CD, he was so into the whole record company thing that he expanded the catalog to include complete releases by certain artists. Some of these sold better than the compilations. Compilations are usually a more difficult item to sell, the most difficult being "a compilation of drum solos" according to Tim's friend Dill Hassen over at the Record Run.

One day, Dill was in New York on a record-buying spree. He was riding in a cab and heard a '60s legend, the Immortal Beep, blabbing away on some talk radio station. "Beep, do you have a new record coming out?" the deejay asked.

"Actually, I don't," he said in his polite Texas twang. "And if there is anybody out there affiliated with a record company, maybe they'd like to call me." And he gave out his number. Dill scribbled it down. Neither he nor Tim were fanatic fans of the Immortal Beep, but they did have to admit that he was a total original; there had never been a performer quite like him, and he wasn't the kind of act anybody could imitate.

The Beep had one hit record, a remake of "Hit the Road, Jack" sung in a deranged falsetto. There was a band on the track, but all you could hear was the snare drum mixed way up front. In the middle of the song Beep took a bugle break, one of his specialties. The way he played the horn reminded Tim and Dill of Donald Ayler, someone way out in left field. Except the Beep had gotten his material on Top 40 radio.

Nobody Tim had released was familiar to most folks. Yet when Tim launched his Immortal Beep *A la Moderne* project, he mentioned it while sending off some packages at the post office and loved the reaction he received.

"Immortal Beep? Oh yeah, I remember that guy!"

"What a weirdo!"

"Remember when he got married on the Ernie Barlow show?"

"Right, to a 17-year-old!"

"And they just had him on cable the other night, on the old *Burp Out!* show. He was on there and did that crazy song where he screams and plays the trumpet."

"The bugle," Tim corrected him.

Dill was proud of bringing the project to Tim. "You're gonna sell a million of these," he predicted.

Three years later, the CD had still not been released. The recording process had taken about a year, as it required the ever mobile Immortal to make recordings with various young collaborators. The duo with Frank Sinatra was done over the phone, with Beep in a motel in Indiana and Sinatra in a studio in Rio de Janeiro, but nobody else involved had this kind of equipment.

When it was nearly done, Tim met Immortal at the Chicago State Fair, where he was doing 20-minute sets and personal appearances (this meant he wandered the grounds signing autographs for anybody that would ask him).

A few days later, Tim was diagnosed with cancer that had progressed well beyond the point of no return. The 30-year-old was so shocked by this that he had a stroke and died that night.

As he fought the shock and the grief, Dill told himself that it was his mission to keep Timtuf going now that his friend was gone. He changed the name slightly to Mit Fut in order to establish his identity, and then proceeded to carry on with everything Tim had set in motion. This turned out to be no small feat because Tim's record company was the standard messy bedroom setup.

As for the Beep, his manager wanted to talk about contract re-negotiation. "Beep's deal is with your old partner, the Tim guy. And guess what? He's dead. Which means you and me, we got nothing," he explained. "The contract? That was with Timtuf. You changed the name to Mit Fut. Is that German? Anyway, we got no contract with the Mit Fut label, you gotta draw one up. Terms gotta be different. We drew that last one up two years ago, and since then a lot of stuff has happened for Immortal."

Yeah, right, Dill thought. He knew, for instance, that the Immortal Beep had done a 20-minute set at the high school pep rally two towns down the freeway just a few weeks ago.

The negotiations gobbled up a half year because the agent nit-picked in slow motion. The record company wasn't exactly floundering, but there were problems. The worst was a CD project that came from the pressing plant with a much longer and clumsier edit between two songs than the one they had turned in. Even after Dill yelled, screamed, and wrote nasty letters, he was left with no choice but to sell the releases as is or take a loss. The pressing plant was unwilling to make good and was unconcerned about his final decision.

Finally Beep's contract was set up, the tape was completed, and the artwork turned in, but now Dill didn't have the money to move with the *A la Moderne* CD. In the end, the deal he had signed with Beep's management was more of a licensing agreement than a record contract because Beep wanted control of his tapes. It did give Dill the right to license the material out, so he decided to explore this avenue, hoping to sell the tapes and recoup everything that had been laid out. He sent cassettes everywhere and even had a few interested parties, but their interest lessened once they heard Dill wanted an advance. The project sat. And sat. And sat.

Then the Beep's health wasn't so hot anymore. He had a strange incident in an airport when the hospitality cart he was riding in lost control and smashed into a crowd of people. He had been drunk but was not driving at the time. Then he became confused on a British tour, unable to keep the traffic directions straight. The road manager "saved his life every single time he stepped out into the street," the agent told Dill.

At another show he lost consciousness in a taxi in the parking lot of the club. The driver didn't care, he just sat there reading magazines with his meter running. Beep missed the show completely and had to pay the taxi driver more than $150. He was front page news six months later. He had suffered a heart attack during a bugle solo at a show somewhere in Pennsylvania. He didn't survive.

Jacques Errors, a friend of Dill's, read the news in *Le Matin* and called Dill up. "It is very sad. This was a great man," Jacques said. "And now, what about the release of this CD, the one you work on for such a long time?"

"Well, it is gonna come out now, that's for sure. All the record companies I sent the tape to have been calling. They all want to release it. So, I get to sit and watch them bid on it, it's great! The manager wants to re-negotiate the contract again, though, since Immortal is dead."

"Does he have this right?"

"I'm not sure. But even if he wants more money, from the sound of things there'll be plenty to split up."

Jacques smiled. It was good to hear his friend doing so well.

Dill said, "It's always this way when somebody dies. That's when the money starts coming in."

"I hope you are not planning to kill all of your artists," Jacques said.

LABEL: LAHR'SSSS

NUMBER SOLD: 7
The sign said Lahr'ssss Sssssells Usssssssed Recordsssss. It was hard on your eyes but it didn't keep the local teenagers from coming in with piles of heavy metal records. Ray Lahr had a knack for making money with their castoffs. "I make my money selling old heavy metal records," he said. And he spent it on his music hobby. To say Lahr was on the edge musically would be like saying Michelangelo was sort of a talented guy.

He dismissed everything that was commercially available. Anything played on the radio—even public radio—anything sold in a regular record store or released on a label that was like a real business was garbage. "I don't mind touching those things, you

know. I'll buy one for $1 and sell it for $4, I don't mind doing that. But listen to it? Please."

The birth of the cassette underground in the '80s was what this guy had been waiting for all his life. He knew that everywhere you went there were demented musical geniuses experimenting in their home studios. These were not people who put out records. They were not influenced by trends. They just did their thing out of a compulsion. They didn't avoid contact with other humans, but they weren't interested in having contact with the "schmooze me please" music business-types, even on the small independent artsy scene.

If some stranger sent a letter asking for a tape, though, and it wasn't some record company type, then it would be, "Why sure!" and the tape would go off, usually accompanied by its trusty sidekick, a sloppily printed list of all the other tapes this artist had made.

Lahr had other tape-collector friends who would buy everything anybody put out. For instance, cassette artists loved Ulrich because if they sent him a list, even if it was of cassettes that hadn't even been recorded, fresh U.S. cash would arrive by post a week later. But the Ulrich subsidy ran out on Aug. 9, 1989, a day cassette artists mark with black strokes on their calendar. On that day Ulrich woke up feeling strange, and by mid-fruhstucke (breakfast) decided on a lifestyle change. From then on, it was no more cassettes; he began to follow professional lacrosse games instead.

Lahr thought this was nuts. In 1989, he was more into this music than ever, and his activities had mushroomed. He was now doing a radio show. He played only cassettes and always at least three different ones simultaneously. The cassette artists adored this kind of "instant collaboration" and begged Lahr to release the results on his own label.

But instead of putting out just one or two titles, Lahr came out with 20, all mixtures of different people and none in a standard album cover. They came in strange boxes, metal oil barrels, large lab specimen bottles, and old shoes. He put them all into a mail order catalog, which listed thousands of cassettes and similar concoctions and had business coming in from all over the world.

He was bussssssssy. Some days he was pricing heavy metal rejects with one hand and tearing open mail (containing a folded check inside) from Japan with the other.

Lahr is a local legend, but he is also an oddball. "His thing with money is strange," a label artist who asked to remain confidential said. "Metal people bring their stuff in and then he makes money selling it. It all sort of disgusts him but he likes the money. He says he prefers the money he makes from the music he likes, but that also must disgust him because if your album really starts to sell well, he won't put out another one."

On the other hand, the Japanese master of explosion montages, Kindo Tariaka, has put out 18 different titles on Lahrsssss, none of them selling more than 12 copies, and he has an "absolutely wonderful" relationship with Lahr. "If you are not such a big success at selling records, it is good to have people like Lahr in the world," Kindo says. "The less success you make, the more it makes him happy. This is good. It makes me feel relaxed."

LABEL: VIBRAMANTRA

NUMBER SOLD: 13

Eddie Chatterbox entered the small Da Papa Theater, the only building left standing on the block. Everything smelled really musty, and there wasn't anyone there. A chair was lying around, so he sat down. Twenty minutes later, nothing had happened. Just when Eddie was finally ready to give up, Hank High walked in. He was a tall black man with a beard and mustache, one of the giants of the tenor saxophone. "Are you playing tonight?" Eddie asked. He'd seen a poster to this effect hung on the bulletin board of the Jazz Investigation and Arrangement Centrum.

"Sure, give me a chance to round up the cats," High answered.

Before he could leave, Chatterbox reached beneath his trenchcoat and exposed a copy of his brand new self-released solo album. "I'd like to give you my record, Mr. High."

High made an interested face and perused the LP.

"I love your playing," Chatterbox said. "The album on FTQ Records is one of my favorites."

"Ah, man, we were tripping when we cut that! Tripping!" High said. "Let me go get the cats and we'll lay down some of my new sound. I'm into a Sonny Rollins thing now." Thirty minutes later he was back with two other guys, a drummer and bass player. Chatterbox was still the only one there. High approached him sheepishly.

"There's a $4 cover charge, man," High said.

Chatterbox took out the money and handed it over to High, who stuck it in his pocket. Then he pointed at the drummer. "That's Yoyo."

Yoyo gave Chatterbox a nod. "Cool," he said.

They played about 40 minutes, announced a break and disappeared. Chatterbox disliked crowds so he went home.

Hank rang him up early the next morning. "Excuse me, man! But I'm tripping!" was the first thing he said.

Chatterbox released an incoherent sound.

"Hey man, I was listening to your record," High continued. "You got a unique concept, man. Listen, I've got a record date coming up for a new company, Vibramantra, it's going to be their first release. We're gonna do it in two days. I can pay you about $300."

It was an ecstatic wake-up call for Chatterbox, his first big break in the New York jazz scene. He was also positive the other sidemen on the date would be famous, too. This was going to help establish Chatterbox as the guitarist of the new generation.

The next morning Hank called again.

"Uh, listen, man, I been talking to Dick Farro and his partner Fatso, the guys doing the Vibramantra records, and these cats want this company to be a success, and they really want the records to sell, so . . . uh . . . what they told me is that since you aren't really famous yet, your name won't help sell the album. I'm gonna use Dizzy Jones on trumpet instead."

Chatterbox was crushed. "Listen, Hank, I'll play the session for free, just to get on the record."

"I can't let you do that. Be cool," High said and hung up.

That night he called the depressed musician and said, "Chatterbox, man. I know you feel bad, but at least come down and hang out at the session tomorrow. Check it out. Get to know Fatso and Dick Farro. Meet the cats." Chatterbox wrote down the address.

It was way down Wall Street in a private apartment. The largest of the rooms was full of Fuller Brush products, which provided the funding for Vibramantra. Both Dick Farro, a little pimply guy with glasses who smoked cigars, and Fatso, whose name appropriately summed him up, were Fuller Brush men.

"I took the job because I'm a Curtis Fuller fan," Fatso said, half kidding, although he was enough of a jazz nut to have really done that. He had filled every other space in the apartment with albums, magazines, books, and thousands upon thousands of reel-to-reel and cassette tapes, all live broadcasts of various jazz players done over the years and acquired through trade from an international cast of similar jazz fiends.

"We decided since we'd bought every record ever made, we had to make a few of our own," Farro said, describing the philosophy behind Vibramantra. But the fact that, at this time, the tax break that allowed wealthy individuals to write off any money they invested into little record labels was still intact might also have been a motivator.

The recording setup consisted of a single microphone dangling from the ceiling with a tape recorder lying on the kitchen table surrounded by Entenmann's pineapple cheesecake.

Then the musicians showed up. The bassist was Ed Miriam, a new guy in town who was considered quite hip. He didn't say much. The drummer was the famous Noslow Pillip, a really big guy with muscular arms.

The session was held up by Dizzy Jones, who was still a no-show after an hour, then two hours, then three. Fatso started pressing Hank, asking him what he wanted to do. Hank was jittery. He kept calling Jones' house but there was no answer. "I know Jones is cool. He wouldn't hang me up," Hank told everyone.

"We should call another trumpet player," Noslow said. "How about Lulu Aaard?"

Hank didn't care much for Lulu. Also, he smelled politics in the air. Noslow and Jones were at odds. Jones had replaced Noslow as drummer in his own group because he had only showed up for half the gigs.

Aaard, on the other hand, was his soulmate. They already had 12 duet albums out on Mucus Jazz, seven of them released in the last year. They called Aaard. He was apparently in the middle of something but said he'd be on his way. They waited. Fatso made frequent visits to the pineapple cake. The buzzer rang. It was Dizzy Jones. He had spent the last three hours trying to get a cab to pick him up.

"This is a racist country," was the first thing he said. "They wouldn't pick me up because I'm black."

Fatso and Farro took Hank aside. "What the hell are we going to do?" they asked him. "We can't pay two trumpet players." Hank nodded. He tried calling Aaard, but he had already left.

Fatso took out a checkbook, grabbed Hank's hand, and said, "Okay, Hank. Do you really want it? Do you want the two trumpet players?" Chatterbox noticed the recording mogul had managed to smear some of the pineapple goo on High's hand. The tenor player was nodding his head.

"Do you really, really want it?" Fatso repeated. When Hank said yes, that was it. Now it was just a matter of waiting for Aaard to show up.

Hank went over to Chatterbox and said excitedly, "I'm gonna have two trumpet players on my session! Like Mingus!"

Tape was finally rolling about four hours after the scheduled start time. Dan Farro followed each revolution of the tape spool with his eyes.

Chatterbox fled before the whole album was cut. As much fun as it was to be on the recording session scene, he was overwhelmed with his jealousy. Every time either of the trumpet players did anything, he thought about how could have done it better.

But High hadn't given up on Chatterbox. Now he had the go-ahead from Vibramantra for a big band album, perhaps the ultimate dream of every jazz player. The group included many big names. There was trombonist Jimmy Stogie, who put his charts upside down on the music stand at the rehearsal but

told everyone not to worry. "I'll get them right side up when we hit!" And there was Noslow, who kept approaching other bandmembers, handing them money, and sending them out to do little errands for him, while High explained his charts and concepts to the group. Ed Miriam was on bass 50 percent of the time, but he had another gig the same night, so his replacement attended the rehearsals and promised to explain the bass charts to Miriam over the telephone. Blooey Jimson, one of the trumpeters on John Coltrane's epic *Dissension* album, was supposed to be in the brass section, and he even made it to the rehearsals. This was special for Chatterbox, because now he was going to play with someone who had played with Coltrane. But Jimson didn't hit it off with Farro or Fatso. When they came to set up their

> [T]he taping guy got a girlfriend and was no longer available. That was the end of our record company, and there are apparently many record labels that fold for this very reason.

recording machine on the day of the gig, Jimson stood around blasting blurpy sounding notes on his trumpet and demanding that the engineers and "so-called experts" identify what dimension or grade of harmonic he was playing.

"We don't know that stuff," Farro said. "We're fans." They really didn't care about Blooey; word was he slept in an alley.

"I am using the same language the professionals use, and if you can't identify what it is, then you really shouldn't be dealing with it," Jimson's lectured and marched out with his trumpet case under his arm.

"It's cool," High said.

The concert had moments of greatness and would have made a good record. But the owner of the loft where the show was held decided to yack intensely on the telephone through both sets, standing only a few feet away from Vibramantra's trusty microphone. Farro and Fatso shared a fear of women, so neither one would tell her to be quiet. "So, we have a tape of a woman talking, with jazz in the background," Fatso told Farro after listening to it all the way through.

"So much for the big band album," Farro said.

Actually the tape became valuable a few years later when the loft owner got divorced. She'd been carrying on an affair, and something particularly intense was going on the day of the concert that she just had to talk about on the phone. The husband's lawyers came by and bought the reels from Vibramantra for a decent price.

LABEL: FEAR OF TORNADO

NUMBER SOLD: 10

Fear of Tornado accomplished something no other small label ever has or ever will. Before a single record had been released, it was a household word. This feat was accomplished with cold, hard cash. Ralph Martell, one of the partners behind the label, had come into an inheritance. He bought full-page ads in the trendy *Boiled Instead* pop culture digest for 12 months running. The first six months were just buzz about Fear of Tornado. What was it? Was it really weird? Was it completely unique? And so forth. After about five teaser ads, they started announcing releases, all by a group that no one had ever heard or seen. The ads treated the group like they were major stars.

Only the major labels bought ads like this for top releases. Small labels were more likely to buy 1/64 of a page and have to take out a bank loan to pay for it. Martell's money ran out a little over a year into the campaign, but it had done its trick. A lot of people had heard of the label and some of them could even remember the name of the band.

When songwriter Emmanuelle Bert got a call from Fear of Tornado something like 8 years later, they were still a well-known enterprise and had branched out to include releases by Jacques Error, the eclectic guitarist Trav Watson, and a few others. Still, though, the lion's share of the titles were by that first group.

"Emmanuelle, we are big fans," began Sheila, the Tornado A&R lady.

"And I am a fan of your label, of course," Emmanuelle said, sucking up.

"What would you say if I told you we wanted you to make a single?"

Actually she was disappointed. An album would have been better. A single was a cute little item, but it could lead to an album.

"Of course, we'll do an album later," Sheila said as if reading her mind. "And we'll want to do a video, too."

The money that the company used to throw around was now stuffed in a sock. The deal that devel-oped was a cheapie: $300 for a single. One day there was a call about album budgets, but when Emmanuelle told Sheila she'd gotten $8000 to do her last one, Sheila said, "How cheaply could you make a video? We don't want an MTV production. We want something really raw." Emmanuelle squeezed $500 out of them, but pocketed the whole thing by hooking up with an industrial film producer friend in Atlanta who drafted his wife as second camera. They were going to shoot Emmanuelle's concert, which sold out because the posters said it was for a Fear of Tornado video.

While editing, they noticed that during the second set one of the cameras had nothing on it but the floor, out of focus. The film guy had to admit that it looked like his wife had fallen asleep. "I always knew your music was soothing," he told Emmanuelle.

Between this and a few other film shoots, they had about an hour of good stuff, which is what they needed. Just when they were getting the edited master together, Sheila called and said, "Hold it on the video! What we really need is a three-quarter-inch master tape." She was asking for the professional format used by television stations.

"It will cost more. It isn't what we discussed . . . "

"The cost will be fine, just tell us what it is," Sheila assured her.

She called her friend and he estimated another $300 for the transfer. She rang Sheila back and broke the news.

"No problem, the check is coming." And that was the last time the singer and the record company A&R lady ever spoke. What happened? Emmanuelle never really figured it out.

She started getting odd calls from record stores. "We want your single, but Fear of Tornado won't send it out." The video never came out either, but they didn't ask Emmanuelle for the $500 back. And she was able to sell the footage to another record company.

Performers in this position assume they have offended the record company or that they lost interest because of some career setback. But in this case, there might be another explanation. Gyorgy Darnell, a record collector who goes from state to state attending flea markets, swap meets, and other glorifications of the used record pile, said that Martell is like an art speculator with the printed recordings.

"They have meetings to discuss how many of each pressing will be salted away to be sold as collector's items decades from now," Gyorgy claims. "They have allotments set aside for each new time period. They plan when it will be best for them to announce they have 'found' 60 copies of the rare first Fear of Tornado album by Jacques Errors. Then they sell them for two, three, even four times the list price. As the years go on and the supply dwindles, they can then actually auction off the remaining copies. It is all very deliberate. They are making a fortune!"

But even that doesn't explain the strange incident that occurred the one and only time Emmanuelle visited the label's headquarters. The label's main band had been on tour, something they had a reputation for *not* doing in the old days. They never toured, never took pictures, and so on. Nobody had any idea who they were. Anyway, they were doing their third tour now, and to liven it up a little they faked the kidnapping of one of their members. This was an elaborate ruse and had gotten lots of ink for them.

Emmanuelle stopped by a month or so after the tour. She asked Sheila if they'd ever gotten to the bottom of the kidnapping. Sheila smiled secretively. She whispered for Emmanuelle to follow her downstairs. In the basement was a small man. "He wasn't really kidnapped, he's just hiding down here," Sheila said. "We're doing it for publicity and to improve record sales. It really has done wonders. It led to a European licensing deal for the entire catalog, and I think that's really going to help us. And what helps us helps you so we can get the money to make a whole album of your wonderful music!"

The little man gave a little bow. "Welcome to Fear of Tornado," he said with a smile.

LABEL: FREEDOM ALLIANCE

NUMBER SOLD: 11

If there is an outbreak of a deadly disease, scientists search valiantly to contain and cure it. When there is an outbreak of self-produced albums being distributed by distribution companies, musicians search valiantly for their money. Freedom Alliance was created to help the plight of the musician/record label owner. With a staff of a half dozen, a warehouse, and contacts throughout the music business, Freedom Alliance promised musicians regular statements and sales way above whatever they had been able to do on their own.

Just about everybody putting out records signed. The label was getting boxes by the hour. When a record store that had an inclination for music that was off the beaten path was contacted, it was sure to be impressed by this long catalog packed with interesting titles.

Keeping on top of the bills was a struggle, but things worked for the most part. Every now and then there would be a warning from a dissenting voice, such as Dizzy Jones, who refused to let the company have his homemade records that sounded like they'd been pressed with a waffle iron. He thought the management was crooked and did not trust the husband

and wife team of Dennis and Cindy Yoab. "You seen their house out in the woods? You seen that sports car? You seen that nice camper they got? You know how they got that stuff?" Dizzy would ask. "Your records!"

When he told Eddie Chatterbox, Eddie said he'd been in there last week and gotten a $350 check.

"That's just a taste," Dizzy said.

The taste kept coming on a regular basis, though, until Chatterbox relocated to another state. No longer able to just drop by and ask for a check, he now had to ask for payment by phone. "We have a new system," Dennis Yoab told him during one of these calls. "It's kind of a payment schedule system." They would pick a month, generally one that wasn't coming for another half a year, and that would be your month to get paid.

Chatterbox really thought the Freedom Alliance would become enormous when they announced their international expansion. Now there would be a Freedom Alliance England, a Freedom Alliance Switzerland, a Freedom Alliance France, a Freedom Alliance Germany, and a Freedom Alliance Italy. And some countries had their own record stores tied in with the distribution network. Clients were told to hold their breath: Statements were going to get bigger. The only change, however, was that the wait for the statement got longer. Quicker than you could wave a swastika at the entire arrangement, the overseas deal turned into a replay of World War II. Each country's label broke contact with the others, insisting on becoming separate entities. They did not want to put out each other's releases or carry them in the stores.

In England, the situation was even worse. The Freedom Alliance store freed itself from the Freedom Alliance distribution and announced that it planned to start its own label. It was a nasty fight over who would keep the name Freedom Alliance, or whether the new label would be free to use the word "freedom" at all. "They're claiming they own the word 'freedom,'" the record store guy groused.

Yoab didn't let this get to him. He was busy chatting up wealthy investors and grant organizations, presenting the picture of a vital business enterprise that provided an entire world of outlets and opportunities for the most creative musical minds. It sounded groovy to the Ferd Foundation, who coughed up a $50,000 grant. Yoab decided he would use the money to print a catalog. Some staff people didn't believe there was a catalog that could be printed for this price, short of releasing it on gilded paper.

"We are really doing a massive job with this, making it look totally professional to really impress people and make the market more upwardly mobile." Yoab could go on like this for hours. "We've got to go mainstream!" he would shout, but he had the wrong audience with the bunch of misfit iconoclasts that he was distributing. When they didn't like the idea of shelling out money for mainstream ads, he came up with another version: Start sending the label owner's bills instead of checks!

Labels received long letters explaining why it was essential that Freedom Alliance start collecting a "per title fee" for albums they distributed. With some of the longer-running labels that had dozens of titles, this added up. Some of the labels deserted the operation at this stage, and the ones that didn't wished they had.

Yoab next farmed out the actual distribution operation to some company on Long Island that he said was the biggest record distributor in the world. The staff liked this at first. Now they could concentrate on promotion and PR and stop begging orders out of record store clerks so there'd be a reason to stuff another box. At the end of the first month, Yoab eagerly awaited the first statement and check from the new distributor. It was a good check, but it bothered Yoab that it was drawn from a personal account rather than a company check. Assistants became suspicious. "Come on, Dennis, why would such a big company write a check on some guy's personal account? It's not kosher."

"There's nothing wrong with this check," Yoab said. "I'm sure there's an explanation." This one was great compared to the check that came the next month: That one was rubber. Investigative phone calls were answered by bank examiners and accountants who were already tearing this sunken distribution business to pieces. Nobody ever came up with a total count for all the merchandise and money lost by independent musicians because of this bankruptcy. Mr. I-told-you-so Dizzy Jones liked to say this was because the money lost was "like freedom. Infinite."

LABEL: KOR

NUMBER SOLD: 6

There were only a few reasons why there was never a Freedom Alliance Czechoslovakia, but they're good ones. The totalitarian regime of the time had an all-out ban on certain types of music. Avant-garde, protest, progressive rock, regressive rock, heavy metal, folk rock, performance art, and the "Canterbury school" of rock were just a handful of the banned musical genres.

Just as Hitler had a really tough time with the rebellious spirit of swing jazz, the Czech police state had a tough time with this era's rock. No possible promotion, musical brilliance, or incredible charisma can create public interest more intensely than out-right censorship. In Czechoslovakia, the public, especially the young people, was clamoring for live music. The censorship gave this already anti-establishment music unfathomable power. It's amazing that in a democratic society, most of the public is indifferent toward music, while people in other countries will go to great lengths just to get their hands on a recording or to attend a secret concert publicized only by hand-to-hand contact.

Of course this is just what Belak Karchek was afraid would happen when the old regime toppled. "When Havel moves into the castle, it destroys Czech music scene," he says, the government's intimidating headquarters looming like the Black Knight's fort over his shoulder. This thin fellow who wore white suits and drifted from place to place like a phantom was another reason that there was no Freedom Alliance in pre-Havel Czechoslovakia. Belak was the ultimate music fan. He should have been involved with Freedom Alliance, and he should have been the first one to start his own record label when the ban on private publishing was lifted. When he came of draft age, however, he had two choices: enter the fascist Czech army or get out of it by pretending to be insane.

It wasn't difficult to prove insanity. In the eyes of the regime, anybody like Belak was nuts. This went for the entire generation of long-haired anti-Communist hippies. The consequences of being insane were simple. They locked you away forever in some loony bin that had probably once been the summer retreat for Vlad the Impaler. Or you could go completely underground, disappear. This is what Belak did. It required living on the run, squatting in various apartments, and staying completely clear of any possible encounter with the government. This would have made it pretty hard for him to run a record label.

This secret existence, however, didn't keep Belak from getting his fingerprints on banned musical events that would happen from time to time. There were Czech bands that had legendary reputations among the people for doing wild music, as well as foreign musicians sneaking in as tourists and performing mysterious little private concerts. The regime would sometimes sniff out these happenings, but they would arrive after everything had been packed up. Sometimes they wound up looking for Belak, which meant that for some periods of his life, Belak was more of a fugitive than a missing person.

You'd think, then, that he'd be happy about the change in the society, but he wasn't. "The problem is now that people are allowed all music, all they want to have is the pop music from the West they have heard so much about. Pop music now is not the same as it was in the '60s, in terms of the society. It is about conformity now. It is about the styles, and the personalities of these rich stars. It used to mean something about fighting the state, in the old Czechoslovakia. This is really the worst thing for the music scene. We can try to present a concert, but to attract the public is so difficult.

"We are competing with everything that has started now from the West. There is so much pornography, prostitutes walking the streets, new restau-

> *[I]n my high school . . . Mr. Popularity . . . would have been Krame McMillie, who was always in one band or another and looked like Robert Redford. Last I heard he was in a Las Vegas show band.*

rants and movie theaters. People have so many new places to go, and now music is meaning something different to them. Meaning nothing!"

He released music on his Kor label, but any sales were from outside his own country. "People here are not going to buy the music of the local Czech band, whether they are making experiment or playing pop. They are buying only Michael Jackson, Madonna, Metallica . . . " He sold the Czech music around Europe and the USA; he also dabbled with recording artists from outside, working most with a Canadian "drum 'n' bass" duo, Port Lee.

Port Lee were arrested for driving around Prague with no passports. In their cell, a hippie sleeping off a drunk gave them Belak's number when he found out they were musicians. "The Belak, he is knowing everything with the musicians, he is helping the musicians every time." He bailed them out, but they had to pay back the debt by giving him a master tape to put out. It turned out to be the same tape Port Lee had already sold to Freedom Alliance England (the shop got the name after all). It was a good thing Belak had never opened a Freedom Alliance branch, because the British guy would never have been so cooperative about working out a deal for the tape. Belak still wasn't that crazy about what ended up happening.

The two labels split the production deal by format. The English label got the CD rights, Belak got to

print the vinyl. "We'll trade each other so each one has both formats," the Alliance shop guy said. The project saw the light of day a year later, but in music industry standards it was practically a new century. This was during the time when there was a huge anti-vinyl campaign, and the record companies and manufacturers were making it very difficult for stores to carry vinyl. A misinformation campaign was part of the concept, with lots of planted media stuff about "the end of the album." And there were plenty of know-it-alls adding to the din just out of the goodness of their hearts. Belak was told that all trades were off since there was no market for vinyl anywhere that Freedom Alliance England did business.

He got the same song from European contacts. He was able to sell 11 outright to a small American mail order company, who even paid up front. The rest of the pressing sits in the basement of his apartment building. The ground floor is a movie theater.

Sometimes he stands in front of his window, watching crowds line up for the latest message from Hollywood. He watches the people and think, "I should give them the records." He suggests this to the theater manager a few days later. After all, he could use the storage space that the albums are taking up.

The manager is shocked. "No! I don't want you to show this record to my customers. Please don't ask this, that you can give them away to the movie line!" he shouts. "I don't even want them to know about these records that are sitting above. It would be bad for business."

LABEL: DON'T REMEMBER NAME

NUMBER SOLD: 6

In 1970, my family moved to Canada from Boulder, Colorado, to keep all three sons from getting drafted; although my oldest brother had a medical deferment. (For more details about this period, I recommend you read my book *Draft Dodger*, published by the Ridgeway Press.)

I was known in my high school as a guitarist and singer, but I wouldn't say I was Mr. Popularity. That would have been Krame McMillie, who was always in one band or another and looked like Robert Redford. Last I heard he was in a Las Vegas show band.

It would be no exaggeration at all to say I had eight really loyal fans who loved my songs. "Your songs are just as good as the ones on the radio," they would say. "When there's a really good one, some parts of it just keep ringing in my ears, going through my head when I sleep. And not in a way like you're really sick of it." This concept, known as "the hook" in English but perhaps best described by the German expression "like a worm in your brain," is the essential goal for songwriters. So I guess I had it back then in the mid- to late-teen years.

When I moved to Calgary, I also met kids who really liked my songs. Again, it was a core group of about eight. One kid was from Texas with a family in the oil business, and he played a tiny bit of guitar and took a few lessons. One day he brought over a nifty little piece of equipment from that epoch. It was an 8-track machine with a set of microphones, and it had a recording head. We set up the microphones and taped some of my songs. The sound quality was clean and sharp. The fact that the tracks switched actually turned out to be the best thing about this recorder. We used to scoff at the 8-tracks released by the professional companies. They did lame stuff such as change the order of the tunes, divide them in half, or leave extra long spaces to compensate for this track change, when really all you had to do was keep going! The machine would just record, with a lurching click, all the way through the change and right onto the next track.

When I mentioned the tapes on the phone to one of my old Boulder friends, he asked me to send him one right away. "I gotta have that when I'm driving around," my old dishwasher pal Jones said. "You remember what I used to say? A tape deck makes a car."

The owner of the machine said it was too bad he didn't own a duplicator, so we could run dubs of the first tape. "That way we could fill these orders. The way it is now, we can only make one copy, and you're going to have to do a new performance each time."

This didn't seem bad, though. Most nights I would be sitting around somewhere playing through every song I ever wrote anyway. Doing it with a tape recorder turned on was no big deal.

Once we'd created and sent out just about all of these, the taping guy got a girlfriend and was no longer available. That was the end of our record company. There are apparently many record labels that fold for this very reason.

I got used to being in people's cars and having them put on one of the tapes. A few times people would hear the tape that had been made for someone else and make comments:

"I think mine is better."

"I wouldn't mind having a tape with both versions."

It was also fun going back to Boulder to visit. The tapes were getting played there. Four of us drove to Montana where another old friend had moved and we listened to the various versions on the way. In Great Falls, all anybody ever did was drive up and down the main drag. A good tape deck is really a lifesaver in these situations.

I recall one particular night vividly. It was a gor-geous night, the Big Sky completely clear of clouds. We drove to a place where you could jump off a cliff more than 200 feet high into a bottomless lake. The Boulder kid who had moved up there was an old hand at this. Some of my friends were the gutsy types and went diving wildly off the cliff without a second thought. I was standing there, the big chicken, looking out into the darkness.

"Come on!" they yelled from below. "It's great!"

"Be sure to keep your hand on your balls!" someone warned. "Cup them!"

A local kid who hadn't jumped yet asked if it would make me feel better if he put on one of my 8-tracks in the background and proceeded to blast it from his shiny black pickup truck. I listened to a few seconds of the tape, then jumped. If you've jumped from this kind of height, then you've experienced the particular sensation of falling, the exhilarating, and the all too brief feeling of passing freely through thin air.

I liked that I could hear my music reverberating while this was going on. I had my hands cupped where they needed to be, and I was happy to be a recording artist.

CHAPTER 15

Road Bad? Ask Dr. Chad!

Part of my breakfast ritual at home is to quickly peruse the "Ann Landers" or "Dear Abby" columns to see what people are writing about. With my brain in writing gear, I steal ideas from everything I read, particularly the crossword puzzle. I look for a way to present advice to musicians about some of the most common personal problems they get into when living the life, particularly bad habits that develop on the road or, in some cases, exist only on the road. I call these problems "bad roads," as in the blues lyric, "That's a bad road to go down."

I love and care about all musicians, and I would like to help the ones having trouble. How to present such advice, though, without sounding like a preacher, is a challenge. Giving advice tends to sound preachy, no matter what, but if this advice is cast in the format of a "Dear Dr. Chad" advice column, chances are it might be amusing enough to deflate the holier-and-more-perfect-than-thou syndrome.

Does a preacher ever get up and admit that it might be impossible for him to follow his own advice? I've never heard such an admission, unless it was Jerry Falwell sniveling about getting caught with his pants down. I've also never seen a "Dear Abby" or "Ann Landers" say anything like, "This sounds like you need to get counseling, although I'd probably never get around to it."

The difference in my advice column is that right up front I will admit that staying off the bad roads completely is probably more than any human can do. No matter what kind of music you play, the road map of your life will be full of turns you wished you hadn't made. Be assured that much of the advice that appears in the "Road Bad? Ask Dr. Chad!" column is based on either my own screw-ups or horror stories told to me by others.

Before we get into the column, a few philosophical ground rules. As we've discussed before, nothing is consistent when it comes to the music life. This goes for one's personal life and happiness as well. The dedicated musician must make the creation of brilliant music a top priority, but this aesthetic fascism cannot be carried out at the complete expense of everything else in life or the musician will end up a miserable wreck. At the same time, the musician must always remember that some aspect of the music will always suffer whenever it is sacrificed in favor of some personal situation.

So come one, come all. Next time you are sulking backstage, put paper in hand and write to Dr. Chad. I hope I get lots of letters. I understand that successful advice columnists collect all their clippings from various publications and use this mass of newsprint as a pallet in times of trouble.

Dear Dr. Chad: Back when Sally was married to Stu and they were fighting all the time, her records were incredible. Now she has this wonderful affair going with Larry, and they are really happy and kissy-kissy-lovey-dovey all the time, but can you listen to the music? It's really deteriorated! Do we really have to be unhappy to be creatively interesting?

Signed, On the Verge of Misery

Dear Verge: Players would be begging the airlines to destroy their instruments if things were this simple. Most people would rather be happy and healthy. A musician on the road would like to think of people at home missing them, unless of course, it's too depressing to think about. When you're as unconnected personally at home as you are on the road, and one is as depressing as the other, you know you're in trouble.

But this trouble can be converted into creative ideas and perhaps captured on some kind of medium and sold (door-to-door if necessary) to put money in your pocket. And, just as there are musicians whose music thrives on miserable personal lives like mold on cheese, there are listeners who prefer these troubled sounds to those made by a musician who experiences ordinary, day-to-day happiness surrounded by people who love them.

Dear Dr. Chad: When I see the terrible things happening in the lives of people who don't play music, I can't imagine what they do to make themselves feel better. Should I give up performing and go into the new science of music as therapy for all those lost souls out there?

Signed, Wondering How the Other Half Lives

Dear Wondering: Regular advice columnists suggest counseling or a talk with a priest. There are self-help groups, piles of books, and if all else fails, some know-it-all somewhere who's willing to tell you what you should do. Pay attention to any and all advice and information and dismiss nothing because it is hard out there and you'll need any help you can get.

As for music therapy, it is not such a new science. All the great ancient civilizations regarded music as one of the essential sciences of mankind. However, donuts such as Michael Jackson, Elvis Presley, or Madonna weren't wandering around back then.

Dear Dr. Chad: The world of music and the lifestyle of the road have been described by our local Fundamentalist preacher as connected to some or all of the following vices: adultery, alcoholism, drug addiction, insomnia, perversions too varied to list, and complete corruption. Say it isn't so!

Signed, I Play Guitar and I'm Pretty Good

Dear I: Sorry, your preacher is right on the money, but he's left out the misery of fame-o-phobic obsession and the blight of plain old loneliness.

Go on the road and you will have it all offered to you in a way that would make any film noir cast member perfectly comfortable. I started touring right around the same time I developed an interest in sleazy films, and it never bothered me that the two activities were blending into each other.

It isn't so much the bars, the easy availability of alcohol, or the relaxed and permissive atmosphere that characterizes the world of music, though many never get past that part. It is more the intensity of these touring experiences as they unfold.

ULI ARMBRUSTER

**Watch for our advice columnist to arrive in your town.
His equipment always fits onto one luggage cart.**

Dear Dr. Chad: Focus, focus, focus. Then relax. But don't forget, be somewhat relaxed while you are focused. When you're onstage, that is. The audience will like you better if you appear relaxed. Afterwards, when you really do want to be relaxed, then just establishing the appearance of being relaxed isn't enough. You actually do want to be relaxed, no matter what it might look like to anybody. I don't get it!

Signed, Not Relaxed On or Offstage

Dear Not: Let's take it from the top. The audience relaxes if you look relaxed, except for the ones that prefer people who look nervous. Figuring out who is who will be tough, so be sure to look around at all the

> *"There's only one reason we go to a rest stop: Otherwise the harmonica player would pee in my shoe!"*
> *—Big Al Murph, Hank Dollar Band*

faces for clues. Except of course, if it makes you look visibly nervous to make eye contact with anyone. But don't forget, it might be someone that can't tell the difference between relaxed and nervous. This can make you either more relaxed or more nervous.

Dear Dr. Chad: Concert experiences for the players involved are like the changing seasons. There is an empty place, whether it's a hall or a bar or a theater. Then just a few of the people working there showing up. Then the audience comes. Finally, the really friendly or annoying or drunk ones hang around until they get thrown out by some bouncer or bartender or doorman or manager, and then all these types leave. Maybe you leave with one of them, maybe not. Sometimes you are almost the last one there! Does this letter sound depressed?

Signed, Always Alone at the End

Dear Always: There's a season I have come to call Empty. You can be on tour in fall, summer, spring, and winter, and it won't matter; there will always be the Empty season and you will be staring at it.

People do lots of strange things to themselves when they tour. When you see a musician play and the music seems to be full of some kind of intense rage, it probably is. They are probably totally irritated about something, although what it is and how trivial it is would depend on who's doing the brooding.

One thing I've noticed about bandmembers is that everyone has different times when they want to be alone and when they want to be surrounded by groups of weirdoes. Timing can be a problem. You can be alone and depressed and desiring company at 2 p.m. and four hours later no longer be in the mood for company only to have a million shreeves hanging around. Some people specialize in keeping their Company Desire Clock off-balance with what should be realistically expected. In other words, the whole thing is a mental attitude, and you know what that means: People like me will tell you it can be fixed but we all know better, don't we?

Dear Chad: People lose their minds when they get ten miles out of town, I don't care who it is. My example concerns eating habits. Our bassist is a real fatso. Finally, he got on some kind of really good diet, lost weight, and ate the right stuff. Then at the first gas stop on tour, a total transformation! Out come the Cheetos and Moon Pies and all kinds of terrible crap.

Signed, Moanin' with Munchie

Dear Moanin': It's all part of a subconscious reaction. Being on tour is too strange, too alienating for minds too handle. People slip into strange modes of behavior. They act like they are 12-years-old on a picnic or the star of a porno movie or invincible or just unconscious.

Friends of compulsive eaters have a few choices for help-aids:

1. Superglue their mouths shut.
2. Offer them food all the time but poison these morsels so their appetite dies . . . but they don't. Read books about slow poisonings, reduce the doses, and you should be okay. If not, you'll at least increase the guy's record sales.
   I'M KIDDING!
   In other words: MYOB, dearie!

Dear Dr. Chad: Every band I've ever been in was a nerve-wracking flop, so I'm grateful the good Lord has provided such a nice choice of substances to aid relaxation. However, I'm sick of hearing lame talk about discipline, such as:

"Never before noon!"

"Never before six!"

"Never smoke more joints than the time of day it is!"

And I'm sick of hearing bandmembers moaning about their excesses:

"I must have gained ten stone eating salami, cheese, and bread and drinking wine on the last tour."

"I drink the liquor. It makes me mellow. I smoke the reefer. It makes me high. And then I play."

"So-and-so always plays better if he can find someone to whip him before the show."

Anyway, you get the point! Why don't people just do their thing and shut up?

Signed, Don't Talk to Me About It

Dear Don't: Actually, you've mistaken me for somebody that gets your point. But, hey, thanks for writing!

Dear Dr. Chad: There is a tale told about bluegrass legends Jackson and Helms. For some reason they thought the rest stop signs on the highway were legal commands of some kind. If you believe the story, they would pull over for every single rest stop they saw and felt obliged to buy a candy bar or something just to be polite. Crazy, yes, but it's the road. Only problem is that they got to gigs really late because of all this stopping. Sometimes they didn't show up at all.

I don't know if the story is true, but I have developed a peculiar fascination with rest stops, leading to an unfortunate incident with an undercover surveillance officer following me down the highway!

Signed, On the Road Again—Not!

Dear On: Actually, bluegrass and old-time research specialist Samantha Numnelb says your story is a crock. Quoth Samantha: "Actually Jackson and Helms had the opposite reputation. They would sometimes show up at the crack of dawn, having driven all night for fear of missing the engagement. They had a big van with the largest tank available, carried an extra supply of fuel, and always gassed up before leaving a town. If there was any legend about this duo, it was their superior kidneys: They could drive literally all day without urinating. In other words, they never went to rest stops!"

It reminds me of advice from Big Al Murph, pedal steel player with the Hank Dollar Band: "There's only one reason we go to a rest stop: Otherwise the harmonica player would pee in my shoe!"

Dear Dr. Chad: It is becoming more and more apparent to me that the things that bother me are not the same things that bother the stay-at-homes. They can complain to a pair of sympathetic ears, but people who stay at home are always jealous of the situations I am trying to complain about. How do you get any sympathy? And don't say talk to another musician. They're too arrogant!

Signed, Mouth But No Ears

Dear Mouth: Anybody who goes on the road would say the same thing: You'd have to do it to understand.

If you don't like complaining to other musicians, try other people in other traveling trades. I had a neighbor who was a traveling egg carton salesman. He thought I was from Mars, but he had been touring the South five days a week for 40 years, when his company canned him two months before his pension.

Later I immortalized him in my song "I'm Your Neighbor." I tried changing the lyric from "egg carton salesman" because I was afraid the guy might hear the song on the radio and get upset, but I was told to leave the lyric the way it was because his occupation was what made it so funny.

I've also enjoyed sharing thoughts about traveling work with scientists, foreign correspondents, art dealers, diplomats, and even a marshal who brought a prisoner back from Vienna.

Dear Dr. Chad: I'm not a musician; in fact, I hate music. One thing I really don't like is how phony the friendships are. My husband goes on the road with people he barely knows, sometimes he can't even remember their last names. Then two weeks later, it's as if they had grown up together. Two years later he won't even know how to contact the person anymore. Does he have problems with his social life, or am I missing something?

Signed, Married to the Fickle Fiddle

Dear Married: This word in your signature explains everything. If you were married to an engineer for the city water system, you would probably also think his friendships were suspect. And as for you, how many times have you accused your husband of "not liking" your friends? How many times today, that is?

Friendships develop quickly on tour, which you have perceptively noticed. On a car trip or train ride, a group of total strangers can tell each other their life stories. You might join what had been a casual acquaintance in some kind of musical ensemble and two months later feel as if they were your best friend. Feelings run very strong, rushing under the nightly enthusiasms and letdowns. "It's one for all, and all for one on the road," some people will tell you, usually trying to enlist accomplices in some kind of shady scheme. But you can and will be drawn together through the adventure and intrigue, and you will share exhilarating feelings of accomplishment and communication.

Fans talk about going to hear bands play night after night and hearing the music get more and more exciting and the communication between bandmembers becoming like telepathy. That is because the band is becoming so close and wrapped up in each other. There are many different types of relationships developing all the time. Close friendships between different age groups, nationalities, backgrounds, and sexes. And of course, people falling in love. Which leads to our next letter . . .

Dear Dr. Chad: My first marriage broke up because I'd been touring with this female clarinetist and started having an affair with her. You know how it is, these things are unavoidable. Night after night, getting back late, having a few drinks, being in such a rush about the concert, communicating so intensely onstage, looking into each other's eyes. It just couldn't be helped.

The clarinetist left me for someone else, but I married again, this time a dancer. We have a three-year-old daughter and I am quite happy. I have been recording on an album project for a female percussionist/dance mix specialist and am getting some "come hither" vibes.

Since breaking up the first marriage led to something better, might this be a great opportunity in the making?

Signed, Hot Pants

Dear Hot Pants: You've opened up such a can of worms here that some of them are even taking pen in hand and writing in.

Although there is sympathy for personal situations and a willingness to lend a hand to help out, the ultimate judgment here must be musical, because in "Ask Dr. Chad" we are attempting to speak for what creates the best music. There is only one thing you can do. Drive to a motel, find the ice machine, scoop up some ice, and pour it into Hot Pants.

Romance between bandmembers ruins the music of the band. A satisfactory exception to this theory has yet to surface, although this is an ongoing research project. Musical collaborations are almost always better if the couple in question just plays music together and keeps their hands to themselves.

Logically, one has to regard love as one of those phenomena that don't combine well with the day-to-day functioning of a really great band. Not every marvelous thing in life can be done simultaneously, and this is a perfect example. Romances in bands provide an endless series of distractions for the lovers, as well as everyone else, and nothing balances this out. It may be nice for the parties involved to be in love, but it is not necessary for musicians to get along this well. It is overkill. Or overlove.

Beyond that, it is a question of whether the individuals have other attachments and are really free to pursue a romance. For someone single it might be more important to fall in love than to be part of a combo. If you made a random grab of promo CDs in any record distributor's office, it would be impossible to suggest whether the future of any those bands was one tenth as important as even a tepid love affair.

If you are married or otherwise involved in a relationship back home, your decision is one of the most important ones you will ever make. There is no turning back. And there is only a slight chance that you will be forgiven at home or even have a home to go back to.

"There's a ghost in every band," an old-time jazz player from Kansas City said to me one night. "Those are the guys that when the tour is over, they got nowhere to go." Is any love worth becoming a ghost for?

[For another opinion on the subject, read on.—E.C.]

Dear Dr. Chad: I finally took my six-piece on the road after three years of trying to get it together. Halfway through the tour, with an important New York date coming up, the violin player started making it with the saxophone player. And the sax player was married to the guitar player!

The guitar player had to leave because the two of them were making out right in the van. We dropped him off in Tulsa. That meant I had no guitar. It wrecked the tour.

An overly superstitious type can jinx a road trip! The waitress in this case apologized to the band for this "bad luck" tab.

I Hate the Man Who Runs This Bar!

The sax player played better when she was not having the affair. And guess who got stuck baby-sitting their kids, a five- and a seven-year-old, that came along? You guessed it!

Signed, When I Said Sextet I Didn't Mean It *That* Way!

Dear Dr. Chad: Our band had a good record producer, maybe too good. He was looking through pictures of some of the old lineups and noticed the good-looking violin player we used to have. "Who is this?" He got all excited. We were in Austria, but he insisted on flying her in for some overdubs.

Then she got all excited. Who wouldn't? One minute you are sitting on your can watching TV in El Paso, and the next minute you are on a plane to Austria. The producer started romancing her immediately, and by the second night, they were using the studio as a love nest and not doing anything productive.

Now this producer wants to add her to the band lineup. He says he'll cover her salary. And she wants to bring her kid on the road. When we told her it was too hard to have a kid on the road, she said the producer had offered to pay for her dad to come along to baby-sit.

What next, do we pay for dad's golfing buddy to come along so he won't get lonely?

Signed, Hate the Violinist

Dear Dr. Chad: There's a local chamber trio that I quite liked—until they all fell in love with each other. The oboe player was in love with the violin player, and the cellist was friends with both of them—until he fell in love with the violin player and told her she had to choose between the two of them.

I don't know if this romantic triangle is messing up the music of this group, but I do know for a fact that it is affecting their ability to listen to music! I gave a solo concert the other week and the only people that showed up in the audience were the three members of this band, all of them looking menacingly at each other! It was the worst audience I ever played for.

Signed, Let Them Fall Out of Love

Dear Dr. Chad: I've managed to avoid involvements with musicians of the opposite sex, but I don't agree with your column's philosophy. As for your research project, it doesn't take long to find the exception you are looking for: John Coltrane. He had an affair with the vibraphone player, Alice McLeod. Later he put her in his band, ousting McCoy Tyner. Obviously the guy wanted to have his own wife playing on tour with him, and who wouldn't? [*Would you like an alphabetical list or artists classified by genre?—E.C.*] And it improved

the quality of the music, resulting in Coltrane's best period!

Signed, Alice in Wonderland

Dear Alice: Sorry, I can't touch this one. That switch in pianists you mention is a tea and toast topic with jazz buffs, many of whom think ditching McCoy Tyner was a huge mistake. They would use this as an example of why you shouldn't have affairs. By the way, found anyone out there who thinks Yoko Ono was worth breaking up the Beatles for?

Dear Dr. Chad: My wife suggested I get myself castrated like Ornette Coleman in order to avoid entanglements on the road. I am a big fan of Ornette Coleman and would do anything to play like him, but I broke into a cold sweat at the doctor's office and backed off!

Signed, Harmenomore

Dear Harm: Actually, Ornette Coleman never had himself castrated, he just discussed it with a doctor. By the way, good pun on "harmelodic."

Dear Dr. Chad: About a week ago, I was sitting in my motel room writing you an angry letter about how your stance on band romance is stupid. My example was going to be the husband and wife team I have been playing bass with for about a year. They write wonderful songs together, harmonize beautifully, get along really great, and pay the sidemen nice dough.

But just as I got to the end of the letter, I heard furniture being tossed around in the adjoining room that they were staying in. Ever since this big fight, the stage show has gone from bad to worse. They miss each other's cues on purpose to make each other look bad. Then when she plays rhythm guitar and he is flat-picking, she hits chords that are flat in order to make him sound rotten. The whole thing makes me sick, and the worst part is writing and admitting that maybe you are right.

Signed, Bassline on the Rocks

Dear Dr. Chad: I'm the drummer in an all-girl punk band out of Minneapolis. For years we had this good group going, the four of us. Then the bassist starts having an affair with the bass player from a pretty well-known rock group. At first we were excited it might help us with our own career. Then it starts dawning on us that this guy is taking over her mind with his stuff and now his stuff is taking over our band.

Whatever it is he is into, she is into. And then she comes to the rehearsal and wants to do stuff that two weeks ago she didn't even know about until he played it for her.

It's not like we are against all these influences, but we don't see why he should get to take over the band from afar.

Signed, We Don't Need the Man

Dear We: It isn't like the man always dominates these types of influences, but somebody does. And once they do, it is like being bitten by a vampire—and then it's too late. Start looking for another band and hope nobody in it falls in love with this same influential musical dude.

Dear Dr. Chad: I play piano with a pretty well-known producer. He must do a CD every week, and for the most part, I get called to play on them. In return, I let this guy use my apartment for his affairs, and he's got plenty of those going. There's almost always a female musician on every session and he gets to work on them right away, but he needs a place to go because his wife is pretty suspicious.

I can't believe how successful this shmendrick is with these babes! The problem is that he is using my place more and more, and some nights now I can't even go home after work. I am supposed to call my own place and see if it is okay to come home. I like the work I get through this guy, but am I being taken advantage of?

Signed, Who's Been Sleeping in My Bed?

Dear Who: Are you being taken advantage of? Have you checked the picnic lunch they packed for you? It is several sandwiches short, buddy boy.

Maybe you lack the pride to think you can find a niche in the musical world other than being Johnny Joeboy to the totally immoral little twerp you describe. I think you should play your friend a couple of choruses of "Somebody Done Changed the Lock on the Door."

Dear Dr. Chad: As far as your research project goes, here's some evidence that supports your case.

The old-time music duo of Jones and Jones were married for about 15 years, and they were pretty good. But after their marriage split up, they kept playing together, and I have not run into anyone who doesn't think they're much better now! The only problem with the whole situation is with me: Did Jones really have to run off with my girlfriend?

Signed, No Old Times for Me

Dear Dr. Chad: Our bandleader likes to fool around, which offends me because I am faithful to my wife when I am on the road, but live and let live. However, he has told me I will be fired from the band if I mention any of his actions to my wife! He says this is the Code of the Road and my loose-lipped wife might blab it to someone who might take it back to his wife.

I say I am not working PR for this guy and I don't care if I am crucial to his cover-up.

Signed, Sideman to the Stud

Dear Sideman: Not letting a bandleader be in control of what you say to your wife in privacy is a pretty good policy to follow.

As for the Code of the Road, we know all about it. It is a short message, reputedly originating with a small Chinese band featuring relatives of Confucius. The English translation: "Lie down in wrong place, get run over."

> *You've opened up such a can of worms here that some of them are even taking pen in hand and writing in.*

Dear Dr. Chad: You've probably heard this one before. He has a heroin problem and at any concert in any town there's always somebody hanging around who can help him get the stuff.

It would be better for her not to be around booze, but how is she gonna avoid it singing in nightclubs?

She'd like to quit smoking, too. But with everyone else smoking in the place, what's it matter? She's up there onstage trying to sing, sucking in all that secondhand smoke anyway.

Then the piano player puts on 30 pounds during the two-week stand because the cook kept giving him free cakes every night.

Signed, The Break's the Hardest Part

Dear The Break: We're back to how easy it all is, how accessible. The recurring theme is the development of discipline strong enough to vanquish all evil temptations. It shouldn't be so hard for musicians, who are already steeped in discipline—masters of it, even.

The music is what it is all about. We are serving the music. We have to be ready for it all. Getting together and traveling, getting to know each other and passing the time with conversation and shared feelings is all quite trivial compared to the music.

We may create the music and perform it, but

our body is only a house for it, and our mind is hardly up to the task of sweeping the front steps. However it is the rare musician that really believes this because there's too much insecurity in the air. And too much bad music.

Dear Dr. Chad: I like musicians. And I like drinking. I just don't happen to think they go together very well. I've heard people play well when they were drunk, but I know they could have played better sober.

Recently I began helping out an older musician. He has something of a name from the '60s, but he never had that great of a career on his own. I felt good about helping him out because I wanted to give something back to older musicians. However, he starts drinking about noon each day, and after that first beer he is impossible to communicate with. His brain is like mush. By night he is a basketcase, railing and ranting about the same old things. That's the worst part, hearing the same things over and over again. Don't drunks know how boring they are?

Signed, Boozerupt

Dear Boozerupt: You've done a good thing for your older friend, but if his drinking really is a problem, the thing to do is cut him off. At least, that's the advice you would get from the alcoholism experts. And of course he doesn't know how boring he is because when he gets drunk nothing is boring. That might be why he gets drunk. In the meantime, his career is not happening because, although he might be able to pull off playing music drunk—some can, some can't—nobody can pull off taking care of the fine details of business from day to day drunk.

Okay, they're not dead in an alley and they're working, but from your perch on top of Mount Holy Criticism you can see that minus a few million cans of beer they might have had as successful a career as somebody else if only their mind had been more engaged. The more people who push a character like this away, the better the chance the character might kick the drink and get their mind engaged again.

Dear Dr. Chad: I was shocked to find out the trusty trombonist I had in the band, the one who was always on time, full of energy, and played really nicely at the gigs, was a heroin addict and also had a cocaine problem. I pride myself on knowing "what's happening," but I had this guy in the band for two years and didn't notice anything. What gives?

Signed, Won't Get Fooled Again

Dear Won't: If you could always tell that someone was on drugs by the way they performed their job, they would never have had to invent urine testing.

Music just doesn't go that well with any of the "bad roads," which are all habits I lump together as being destructive to some vital aspect of a person's life. With some of these things it is a slow, night-by-night deterioration, maybe just settling into a permanent fuzz. And you can't always tell what's going on.

Dear Dr. Chad: A decision made in the mad dash on the road can change a person's life for the worse. I'm thinking of people who decide to steal money from each other, cheat financially in some other way, or maybe engage in some other form of losing control that results in an ugly scene, a permanently damaged relationship, and inevitably the end of yet another combo. What's the worst situation you can think of?

Signed, Dreadlocks

Dear Dread: The worst would have to be the exploits of Roberto Jimeniz, who played an eight-string Portuguese man o' war guitar. He reportedly said, "I had a one-man band but we broke up."

Maybe it comes down to people on tour being unable to digest it all, always trying to push toward something else. Maybe it's just a desire so intense some people are willing to destroy everything in their way to use themselves up. These people feel the need to drink every bottle of booze in the bar or have sex with every member of the audience. They don't realize that they'd be happy if they could just grasp that the music they are making is the reason they are there. It's an act of creation, not destruction.

Discography

1975

Solo Acoustic Guitar, Vol 1/Original label: Parachute
Out of print. Original edition: 500.

1976

Solo Acoustic Guitar, Vol. 2/Original label: Parachute
Out of print. Original edition: 1000.
The cut "Rocket" was included on the *Slide Crazy* anthology, released originally in France on Sky Ranch then worldwide on Rykodisc. In 1997, Rastascan plans to reissue original album on CD with bonus mini-CD including extra live and studio material from the period.

1977

Improvised Music for Acoustic Piano and Guitar/Music Gallery Editions
Solos and duets with pianist Casey Sokol.

Volume Three: Guitar Trios/Parachute
With Henry Kaiser, Duck Baker, Randy Hutton, and Owen Maercks.

Ice Death, Henry Kaiser/Parachute
Chadbourne and Kaiser perform "Wind Crystals," a composition by Wadada Leo Smith. In 1997, there are plans to reissue this along with recent performances of Wadada Leo Smith compositions by Chadbourne, Smith, and others. Working title for this release is *Traditions.*

1978

School/Parachute
With John Zorn.
This double album was divided between compositions of Zorn and Chadbourne, featuring Henry Kaiser, Bruce Ackley, Polly Bradfield, Davey Williams, LaDonna Smith, and Mark Abbott. In 1997, Zorn plans a reissue of his pieces entitled *The Parachute Years* for Tzadik. The Chadbourne material is also being considered for re-release by other labels.

Lowe and Behold, Frank Lowe Orchestra/Musicworks
With John Zorn, Polly Bradfield, Billy Bang, Philip Wilson, Joseph Bowie, Peter Kuhn, John Lindberg, and others.

1979

Possibilities of the Color Plastic/Bellows
With Toshinori Kondo.

Don't Punk Out/Emanem
With Frank Lowe.

USA Concerts, Andrea Centazzo/Ictus
Collaborations with various Americans and the Italian percussionist. Chadbourne is featured in duet.

Environment for Sextet, Andrea Centazzo/Ictus
With John Zorn, Polly Bradfield, Toshinori Kondo, and Tom Corra.
Reissued in 1996 on New Tone, including the Zorn duet from *USA Concerts.*

The English Channel/Parachute
Orchestra piece with John Zorn, Tom Corra, Polly Bradfield, Toshinori Kondo, Andrea Centazzo, LaDonna Smith, Davey Williams, plus Fred Frith, Steve Beresford, Mark Kramer, Evan Gallagher, Leslie Dalaba, Jim Katzin, Bob Ostertag, and others.

Guitar Solos IV/Rift
Anthology also includes Henry Kaiser, Davey Williams, Fred Frith, and others.

Musique Mechanique, Carla Bley/Watt
With Charlie Haden and others.

1980

There'll Be No Tears Tonight/Parachute
With John Zorn, Tom Corra, David and Dennis Licht, Scott Manring, and Robbie Link.
Later reissued on Fundamental in both vinyl and CD formats.

Pool, John Zorn/Parachute
Chadbourne plays on the "wet" version of "Hockey" with Bob Ostertag and Wayne Horvitz.

Torture Time/Parachute
With Polly Bradfield.

Archery, John Zorn/Parachute
With Polly Bradfield, Bill Laswell, George Lewis, Robert Dick, Wayne Horvitz, David Moss, and others. Material reissued in 1997 on Tzadik.

1982

The Dawn of Shockabilly/Rough Trade
Original issue was 12-inch 45. This material later included on various Shimmy Disc repackagings, including *Just Beautiful* and *Ghost of Shockabilly.*

Blood on the Cats/Cherry Red
12-inch vinyl. Shockabilly track featured on this compilation.

1983

Earth vs. Shockabilly/Rough Trade
Album later re-issued on Shimmy Disc.

"City of Corruption" b/w "19th Nervous Breakdown"/ Rough Trade
7-inch 45.

The You'll Hate This Record Record/Seidboard
One track on compilation. This track later included on Shimmy Disc reissue of *Earth vs. Shockabilly* where sessions originated.

1984

That's the Way I Feel, Hal Wilner/A&M
Thelonious Monk tribute. Shockabilly plays a Monk tune on the double album that was left off both the CD and cassette version.

Shockabilly Coliseum/Rough Trade
Later re-issued on Shimmy Disc.

Shockabilly Vietnam/Fundamental Save
Later re-issued on Shimmy Disc. Original album included giant tour diary poster blamed for hundreds of cases of eye strain.

1985

The Relative Band '85/Hot
With Jon Rose, David Moss, Jim Denley, and others.

Shockabilly Heaven/Fundamental
Later re-issued on Shimmy Disc.

Country Music From SE Australia/RRR
With David Moss, Rik Rue, and Jon Rose. Some tracks reissued on Blotter LSDC&W. Entire project slated for 1997 re-release on Upheavel label with additional material.

Country Protest/Fundamental
With Red Clay Ramblers, David Licht, Lenny Kaye, and others.
Some tracks reissued on *Chadbourne Barber Shop.*

1986

RRR Amerikka/RRR
Limited edition box set featured the track "Spiro Agnew" in an alternate mix.

Passed Normal/Fot
Shockabilly tracks on this vinyl compilation.

Imminent Three/Imminent
Compilation has different version of "KKKremlin."

They Might Be Giants/Bar None
Chadbourne phones in guitar solo for band's debut album.

Corpses of Foreign War/Fundamental
With Violent Femmes.
Some tracks reissued on *Chadbourne Barber Shop* and *Jesse Helms Busted for Pornography.*

"198666" b/w "America Stands Tall" and "Devil on the Radio"/Ralph
7-inch.

1987

Forward of Short Leg, Jon Rose/Dossier
Rose duets with many partners; Chadbourne plays the electric plunger.

What is Truth, Vol. 1/Panic
Chadbourne track on compilation inspired title for what would be a series. All Scott Marshall productions done in re-painted trash vinyl LPs.

Kill Eugene/Placebo
Also released on vinyl and an accompanying video featuring different versions of some of the same songs; distributed under same title.

Vermin of the Blues/Fundamental
With Evan Johns and the H Bombs.
First released on vinyl, then later on CD. One track issued on the German LP *Psychadelic*.

LSDC&W/Fundamental
Originally issued on double album, then a double CD.

Chuck USA/Upheavel
Rare instance of a Chadbourne-produced album for another artist, this is the duo of Murray Reams and David Nikias. Chadbourne plays plunger on one piece.

Camper Van Chadbourne/Fundamental
Originally on vinyl, then CD. With Camper Van Beethoven, Bruce Ackley, Graham Connah, Joee Conroy, and David Stilley. Enjoys distinction of being best-selling Chadbourne LP ever (more than 15,000 sold.)

Art of Kultural Terrorism/Dossier
With Jon Rose.

20th Anniversary Summer of Love/Shimmy Disc
One Shockabilly track on this compilation, later added to the *Just Beautiful* release.

1988

I've Been Everywhere/Fundamental
With Legendary Stardust Cowboy, Murray Reams, Shep the Hep, the Blitzoids.
One track reissued on *Jesse Helms Busted for Pornography*. Originally on vinyl, then issued on CD.

The Eddie Chatterbox Double Trio Love Album/
Fundamental
With Camper Van Chadbourne, Bruce Ackley, Graham Connah.
One track reissued on *Chadbourne Barber Shop*.

Camper Van Beethoven/Pitch a Tent
Band's third LP featured Chadbourne on banjo and lead guitar on several tracks.

What Is Truth, Vol. 2/Panic
Banjo and porthole solos featured on this compilation.

Violin Music for Restaurants, Jon Rose/ReR
Chadbourne is only heard snoring on this CD, contrary to the claims of some reviewers. But what a snore!

1989

Fundamental Hymnal/Fundamental
Sampler has a Chadbourne and Camper Van Chadbourne track, both previously released.

Studio Animals/Private Studio
One Chadbourne solo track on this premiere effort from the Frank Pahl and the Only a Mother band.

Country Music in the World of Islam/Fundamental
With Elliot Sharp, Sun City Girls, and others.
Released simultaneously on CD, vinyl, and cassette.

Just Beautiful, Shockabilly/Shimmy Disc
Vinyl and CD release, the latter featuring considerable extra material.

Lyrics by Ernest Noyes Brookings, David Greenberger/
Shimmy Disc
Chadbourne does multitracked piece on this collection.

1990

69th Sinfunny/Fundamental
With Camper Van Chadbourne, Bruce Ackley, Graham Connah.
Double LP and single CD.

What Is Truth, Vol. 3/Panic
12-minute track with Chadbourne Baptist Church.

1991

"Oil of Hate" b/w "National Bummer"/Blackjack
With Molly Chadbourne and Son of Shockabilly.
7-inch.

Moving Soundtracks/Les Disques des Crepescules
Compilation of artists playing soundtrack music. Camper Van Chadbourne's version of "The Ballad of Easy Rider," identical to the album/CD release, is featured.

Lake Michigan Soda, Bob Wiseman/Warner Bros.
Chadbourne plays electric rake on a classical music piece. One of his rare major label appearances, doubly curious because he is on the same album as Edie Brickel!

"I Cut the Wrong Man" b/w "They Cut Off Mama's Arm"/Detox
With Chadbourne Baptist Church.
7-inch.

Pyloric Waves/Detox
The Camper Van Chadbourne lineup with Walter Malli plays "Out to Lunch" on this compilation.

Blotter LSDC&W/Delta
With Jon Rose, David Moss, Rik Rue, Only a Mother, the Son of Shockabilly, and others.

Chadbourne Baptist Church/Delta
CD release is missing 18 minutes of actual master tape and was mastered with no separations between the tracks.

Coming Down Fast: Manson/Helter Skelter
Compilation presented in both CD and 10-inch vinyl forms. Chadbourne Baptist Church renditions of "How Can You Kill Me, I'm Already Dead" are stitched together.

Strings/Intakt

Songs/Intakt

Passed Normal 4/Fot
Same Shockabilly tracks as *Passed Normal 1* LP, but this time on CD.

Downtown Does the Beatles/Knitting Factory
Chadbourne plays improperly titled medley on this compilation.

Caged/Uncaged/Cramps
The less commercial of two John Cage compilation tributes done this year. Chadbourne created his track with tapes of Jello Biafra reading from a Cage text.

Komunguitar, Jin Hi Kim/What Next?
Korean komungo virtuoso duets with Chadbourne as well as Derek Bailey, Henry Kaiser, Elliot Sharp, and others.

Terror Has Strange Kinfolk/Alternative Tentacles
With Evan Johns and the H Bombs.

Achey Rakey Heart/Alternative Tentacles
"Checkers of Blood" was the single release in the UK

from this project. A Jello Biafra/Mojo Nixon mini-CD and EP from this period also featured the *Achey Rakey* track. 7-inch.

Eugene Chadbourne/Hello Recording Club
Subscription-only mini-CD presented by They Might Be Giants.

Hot Burrito #2/Extraplatter
With Walter Malli and Werner Dafeldecker.

Malli: Artist in Residence soundtrack, Walter Malli/Allegro
Released in conjunction with the film, which presents scenes from the Hot Burrito recording session among many other items of interest. The track on this soundtrack is identical to the one on the Extraplatter release.

Naked Songs for Contortionists, Only a Mother/Tec Tones
Chadbourne plays banjo.

Locked in a Dutch Coffeeshop/Fundamental
With the Jack and Jim Show (Eugene and Jimmy Carl Black).

Electric Rake Cake/Overtone
With Tony Trischka, Joee Conroy, David Stilley, Shockabilly, and others.
Double CD set came in cake box. Limited edition of 500. Mostly collected from cassette releases and unissued sessions, but a few tracks off other CDs.

Feral Chickens, Only a Mother/Tec Tones
Chadbourne plays banjo.

7" single w/*Thicker* magazine
One side with Jimmy Carl Black, the other with Jello Biafra.

Grunge Whore, TRBNGR/Sympathy
Chadbourne plays banjo and does small comedy routine. 10-inch vinyl.

Violin Music in the Age of Shopping, Jon Rose/Megaphone
Remixes of two Chadbourne country tracks to include Rose.

Pachuco Cadaver/Fireant
With the Jack and Jim Show, plus Leslie Ross, Brian Ritchie, Molly Chadbourne, and others.

Nijmegen Hassen Hunt/Nosehair and Noiseville (split release)
With Han Bennink, Jin Hi Kim, Camper Van Chadbourne, Molly Chadbourne, Jim Denley, David Moss, and others.

Sun Ra Tribute: Wavelength Infinity/Rastascan
Double CD features the Jack and Jim Show with Space is the Place.

Half Japanese's Greatest Hits/Safehouse
Triple album and double CD featured a track from a never released 1990 recording session.

The Romantic Side of Schizophrenia, Frank Pahl/Fot
Chadbourne plays banjo.

"I Got Erection" b/w "Jeg Si Bli Jesus," TRBNGR/Hit Me
Chadbourne plays banjo, electric rake, and sings in Norwegian on one side, making this appearance with the Norwegian hardcore band a triple threat. Also Chadbourne smacked a soldier in the head with his banjo en route to the recording session!

"Denim Demon" b/w "I Fucked Betty Page TRBNGR/Munster
Chadbourne plays lead guitar. 7-inch single.

1996

I Love Me, Tiny Tim/Seeland
Chadbourne featured on "Depression Medley," which the late singer called his "Revolution #9."

Jesse Helms Busted for Pornography/Fireant
With Don Helms, Kenny Malone, Michael Rhodes, Violent Femmes, Lol Coxhill, Jimmy Carl Black, and others.

Chadbourne Barber Shop/Airline 61
With Red Clay Ramblers, Violent Femmes, Sun City Girls, Charles Tyler, Walter Malli, Camper Van Chadbourne, and others.

Boogie With the Hook/Leo
Duets with Han Bennink, Derek Bailey, John Zorn, Charles Tyler, and Volcmar Verkerk.

Memories of Nikki Arane/Incus
With John Zorn.

Year of the Grets, Ut Gret/ZNR
Longtime improvising partnership releases collection of collaborations. David Stilley, Joee Conroy, and others, with Chadbourne on a Charlie Parker tune, plus Henry Kaiser, Davey Williams, and others.

Slide Crazy/Rykodisc
American release of compilation originally on French Sky Ranch label, but because they never sent Chadbourne a promo, we'll list the release here. Features "Rocket" from *Solo Acoustic Guitar, Vol. 2.*

Bubbahey Mudtruck/Fireant
The Crude Gene Mannipulappalachian project with Barry Mitterhof, Bob Jordan, and Charles Rosina featured on two songs.

Silkeartbricht Miniaturen/n.r. Kult
Hannover arts centre collects one minute pieces; Chadbourne's is an Insect and Western excerpt.

The Acquaduct/Rectangle E
Pressed on thick vinyl with overdubbed Eddie Chatterbox Trio, as well as Molly and Lizzie Chadbourne, etc. Nashville sessions, Mexican project. Supposedly a limited edition of 500. Vinyl 12-inch.

1997

Patrizio/Victo
With Paul Lovens.

End to Slavery/Intakt

Psychad/Swamp Room
With Jimmy Carl Black, Ed Cassidy, Camper Van Chadbourne, Evan Johns and the H Bombs, the Sun City Girls, and others.
Chadbourne psychedelic material, some never released before, plus autobiographical text about the '60s.

1997 Projected Releases:
Solo Acoustic Guitar: 1976/Rastascan

Country Music From Southeast Australia/Upheavel

From the Hellingtunes/Intakt
Debut release of Ellington Country with Pat Thomas, Alex Ward, Carrie Shull, Leslie Ross, and Paul Lovens.

From the Hellingtunes/Lucky Garage
Featuring Chadbourne and Ellington Country Band.

Index